JESUS CHRIST, HERMENEUTICS, AND SCRIPTURE

Re-envisioning Reformed Dogmatics

Re-envisioning Reformed Dogmatics is a series that explores afresh the rich and diverse dogmatic heritage of the contemporary Reformed tradition. The series will plumb the depths of the riches of the Reformed tradition by engaging in constructive and interdisciplinary study while also challenging assumptions that are sometimes expressed as the Reformed tradition's contemporary consensus. There are in current discussions, contrary trends at work in Reformed Theology. Some are eager to expand Reformed orthodoxy to include all Protestants while others narrow the definition of what is "Reformed" to what characterizes the teachings of, say, the Dutch Reformed Church or the Church in Scotland. *Re-envisioning Reformed Dogmatics* is a series that will explore the rich and complex plurality of thinking in Reformed tradition. The monographs in this series will invite readers to think in fresh ways about various theological loci while exploring constructive developments within this dynamic tradition. They will include subject matter that has been hitherto neglected or excluded from conversations about Reformed theology in an effort to recover the intellectual treasures that once made up the full dogmatic deposit of the confessional era. In this way, the *Re-envisioning Reformed Dogmatics* series is marked by that self-same spirit that once motivated the Reformer's clarion call: *Ad fontes* ("to the sources"). Now, with five hundred years of theological development since this first call was uttered, the authors in this series renew that clarion call. This time, however, the sources to which the authors in this series turn include those of the Reformers and their theological heirs.

EDITORIAL BOARD:

Gijsbert van den Brink, University Research Chair for Theology
   & Science at the Faculty of Theology (Free University of Amsterdam)

Oliver Crisp, Professor of Analytic Theology and Director
   of the Logos Institute for Analytic and Exegetical Theology
   (University of St. Andrews)

Christina Larsen, Professor of Theology (Grand Canyon University)

Paul Nimmo, King's Chair of Systematic Theology (University of Aberdeen)

Carl Trueman, Professor of Biblical & Religious Studies
   (Grove City College)

Adonis Vidu, Professor of Theology
   (Gordon Conwell Theological Seminary)

Willem van Vlastuin, Professor of Theology and Spirituality
   of Reformed Protestantism (Free University of Amsterdam)

Jesus Christ, Hermeneutics, and Scripture

From Epistemology to Soteriology

HANS BURGER

CASCADE *Books* • Eugene, Oregon

JESUS CHRIST, HERMENEUTICS, AND SCRIPTURE
From Epistemology to Soteriology

Copyright © 2024 Hans Burger. All rights reserved. Except for brief quotations in critical publications or reviews, no part of this book may be reproduced in any manner without prior written permission from the publisher. Write: Permissions, Wipf and Stock Publishers, 199 W. 8th Ave., Suite 3, Eugene, OR 97401.

Cascade Books
An Imprint of Wipf and Stock Publishers
199 W. 8th Ave., Suite 3
Eugene, OR 97401

www.wipfandstock.com

PAPERBACK ISBN: 979-8-3852-0503-5
HARDCOVER ISBN: 979-8-3852-0504-2
EBOOK ISBN: 979-8-3852-0505-9

Cataloguing-in-Publication data:

Names: Burger, Hans [author]

Title: Jesus Christ, hermeneutics, and Scripture : from epistemology to soteriology / Hans Burger.

Description: Eugene, OR: Cascade Books, 2024 | Series: Re-envisioning Reformed Dogmatics | Includes bibliographical references and index.

Identifiers: ISBN 979-8-3852-0503-5 (paperback) | ISBN 979-8-3852-0504-2 (hardcover) | ISBN 979-8-3852-0505-9 (ebook)

Subjects: LCSH: Bible—Hermeneutics. | theological hermeneutics. | Bible—Evidences, authority, etc. | soteriology. | Bible—Criticism, interpretations, etc. | Bible—Theology.

Classification: BS476 B87 2024 (paperback) | BS476 (ebook)

VERSION NUMBER 04/16/24

All Scripture quotations, unless otherwise indicated, are taken from the Holy Bible, New International Version®, NIV®. Copyright ©1973, 1978, 1984, 2011 by Biblica, Inc.® Used by permission of Zondervan. All rights reserved worldwide. www.zondervan.com The "NIV" and "New International Version" are trademarks registered in the United States Patent and Trademark Office by Biblica, Inc.®

Cover illustration: Stichting Grote Kerk Naarden

Contents

List of Tables | vi

Preface | vii

1. Introduction: Christ, Hermeneutics, and Scripture | 1

2. Epistemology and Certainty: The Development of the Doctrine of Scripture | 18

3. Secularization and Sin: Additional Reasons for a Soteriological Approach | 72

4. Trinity and Perspective: The New Perspective Given in the Saving Acts of Father, Son, and Spirit | 108

5. Participation and Scripture: Participation in Christ, the New Perspective, and the Reading of Scripture | 148

6. Sola Scriptura and Solus Christus: The Decisiveness of Jesus Christ as the Word of God for Understanding Scripture | 178

7. Literal and Spiritual: Faith in Jesus Christ and the Reading of Scripture | 227

8. Community and Practice: Reading and Transformation in Ecclesial, Moral, and Spiritual Practices | 272

9. Christ and Scripture: Transformation into the Image of Christ and the Use of Scripture in the Ecological Crisis | 322

Bibliography | 335

Name Index | 359

Scripture Index | 365

List of Tables

Fig. 1 – Sign | 294

Fig. 2 – First hermeneutical relation | 295

Fig. 3 – Second hermeneutical relation | 295

Fig. 4 – A formative relation | 298

Preface

AFTER MORE THAN TEN YEARS of work, I am thankful to God that I could finish this project on hermeneutics. Mostly, it is my prayer that this book will help theologians and others interested in the Christian reading of Scripture to understand better the role of Scripture in the Christian life and develop further a Trinitarian hermeneutics that serves participation in Christ and a life in the Spirit. The project started when the Theological University in Kampen (the Netherlands) gave me a position as a postdoc researcher in systematic theology. I am glad that the project results in this monograph, now I started working as a professor of systematic theology at the same institution (that has moved to Utrecht and is now Theological University Utrecht). I hope that this work is worthy of a successor of Herman Bavinck and Klaas Schilder, who both figure in this book.

I am thankful to my colleagues who joined me during this theological adventure and who discussed papers, articles, and parts of chapters with me: Marcel Sarot and Gijsbert van den Brink as my tutors in my tenure tracks; Arnold Huijgen, Koert van Bekkum, Eric Peels, and other members of the beautiful BEST-research group (Biblical Exegesis and Systematic Theology) from two Dutch Theological Universities in Apeldoorn and Utrecht; Ad de Bruijne, coworker in the field of theological hermeneutics; Jan Martijn Abrahamse, Marinus de Jong, and Gerben van Manen, who have read the entire manuscript; participants of the panel on Scripture and Theology at the annual conference of the European Academy of Religion; others like William den Boer, Hans Boersma, Henk van den Belt, Wolter Huttinga, Bruce Pass, Rik Peels, Hans Schaeffer, Wim van der Schee, Geert Jan Spijker, Oliver O'Donovan, Kevin Vanhoozer, Wim van Vlastuin, Rene van Woudenberg, and Maarten Wisse. And of course my students at the Theological University in Kampen and now in Utrecht, who attended my lectures on hermeneutics. Moreover, I owe much to Jacob Raju, who did a lot of work in the final corrections of my texts. Finally, I want to thank my daughter Christi Burger, who has compiled the indices.

Parts of some chapters in this book were published previously as articles and book chapters. I am grateful to the publishers who permitted to reuse the following texts in this book:

1. "A Soteriological Perspective on our Understanding." In *Correctly Handling the Word of Truth: Reformed Hermeneutics Today*, edited by Melis te Velde and Gerhard H. Visscher, 195–207. Lucerna CRTS Publications. Eugene, OR: Wipf & Stock, 2014.

2. "Bavinck's View of the Relation between Scripture and Tradition." In *Neo-Calvinism and Roman Catholicism*, edited by James Eglinton and George Harinck, 46–64. Studies in Reformed Theology 47. Leiden, The Neth.: Brill, 2023.

3. "Christologisch én pneumatologisch: Herman Bavinck en de relatie tussen Schriftleer en Christologie." In *Weergaloze kennis: Opstellen over Jezus Christus, Openbaring en Schrift, Katholiciteit en Kerk aangeboden aan Prof. dr. Barend Kamphuis*, edited by Ad de Bruijne et al., 126–35. Zoetermeer, The Neth.: Uitgeverij Boekencentrum, 2015.

4. "Discernment in the Light of an Authoritative Revelation? Rethinking the Authority of Scripture." In *Roads to Reconciliation between Groups in Conflict: Theology in a World of Ideologies: Authorization or Critique?*, edited by Zsolt Görözdi et al., 216–28. Beihefte zur Ökumenischen Rundschau 133. Leipzig, Germ.: Evangelische Verlagsanstalt, 2021.

5. "Foundation or Perspective? On the Usefulness of Formation and Epistemology." In *Sola Scriptura: Biblical and Theological Perspectives on Scripture, Authority, and Hermeneutics*, edited by Hans Burger et al., 56–78. Studies in Reformed Theology 32. Leiden, The Neth.: Brill, 2017.

6. "God's Character and the Plot of the Bible." In *Reading and Listening. Meeting One God in Many Texts: Festschrift for Eric Peels on the Occasion of His 25th Jubilee as Professor of Old Testament Studies*, edited by Jacob Dekker and Gert Kwakkel, 239–48. Amsterdamse cahiers voor exegese van de Bijbel en zijn tradities. Supplement Series, 16. Bergambacht, The Neth.: Uitgeverij 2VM, 2018.

7. "God's Mercy and Practices of Mercy." In *Mercy: Theories, Concepts, Practices: Proceedings from the International Congress, TU Apeldoorn/*

Kampen, NL June 2014, edited by J. H. F. Schaeffer et al., 99–114. Ethik Im Theologischen Diskurs 25. Zürich, Switz: Lit, 2018.

8. "Hermeneutisch relevante triniteitsleer: De bijdrage van Ingolf U. Dalferth aan de trinitarische renaissance." *Nederlands Theologisch Tijdschrift* 67 (2013) 101–16.

9. "Hoe moeten we vanuit evolutionair perspectief denken over cognitieve gevolgen van zonde en genade?" In *En God zag dat het goed was: Christelijk geloof en evolutie in 25 cruciale vragen*, edited by William den Boer et al., 305–18. Kampen, The Neth.: Summum Academic Publications, 2019.

10. "Kuyper's Anti-Revolutionary Doctrine of Scripture." In *Neo-Calvinism and the French Revolution*, edited by James Eglinton and George Harinck, 127–43. T. & T. Clark Theology. London: Bloomsbury T. & T. Clark, 2014.

11. "Quadriga without Platonism: In Search for the Usefulness of the Fourfold Sense of Scripture in Dialogue with Hans Boersma." In *Scripture and Theology: Historical and Systematic Perspectives*, edited by Tomas Bokedal et al., 377–99. Theologische Bibliothek Töpelmann. Berlin: de Gruyter, 2023.

12. "Receiving the Mind of Christ: Epistemological and Hermeneutical Implications of Participation in Christ according to Oliver O'Donovan." *Journal of Reformed Theology* 10 (2016) 52–71.

13. "Transformatie door de vernieuwing van het denken." In *Verhalen om te delen. Bij het afscheid van Peter van de Kamp*, edited by Hans Schaeffer en Geranne Tamminga-Van Dijk, 95–101. TU Bezinningsreeks 21. Amsterdam: Buijten en Schipperheijn, 2018.

14. "Why Do You Believe That Scripture Is the Word of God? Owen's Doctrine of Scripture Reconsidered." In *John Owen between Orthodoxy and Modernity*, edited by Willem van Vlastuin and Kelly M. Kapic, 127–47. Studies in Reformed Theology 39. Leiden, The Neth.: Brill, 2019.

15. "Zelfverstaan en wereldverstaan tussen geslotenheid en openheid." In *Open voor God: Charles Taylor en christen-zijn in een seculiere tijd*, edited by Hans Burger and Geert Jan Spijker, 23–38. TU-Bezinningsreeks 14. Barneveld, The Neth.: De Vuurbaak, 2014.

Hans Burger

1.

Introduction
Christ, Hermeneutics, and Scripture

1.1 HERMENEUTICS AND SCRIPTURE, NOT SCRIPTURE AND HERMENEUTICS

This is a book about hermeneutics and Scripture. I have chosen this order deliberately, as an alternative to a theological treatment of Scripture and hermeneutics in the light of modern epistemological interests. Scripture should not be isolated from what the triune God does to reconcile us with him and to save us in Christ. He gives us faith in Jesus as Christ and makes us participate in Christ, which includes that we will share in the mind of Christ. Accordingly, my theological starting point in this book is what the triune God does to renew our understanding, baptizing us with the Holy Spirit, opening for us the perspective of the resurrection of Christ, and giving us the community of the church where we together participate in Christ, to give us the mind of Christ. In an unstable and divided world full of crises, we need people with this renewed mind. Because the triune God is using the Holy Scripture to renew our minds, Scripture itself comes into view. The theological pathway this book takes goes from Trinitarian soteriology to hermeneutics, and from hermeneutics to the doctrine of Scripture. Thus, my proposal intends to give a comprehensive overview of hermeneutics and Scripture, embedded in the saving acts of God, who is present in the life of the church and its members.[1]

---

1. Cf. the role of theology in biblical interpretation as described by Darren Sarisky (Sarisky, *Reading the Bible Theologically*, 44–56), or what Kelsey describes as the "imaginative act . . . to catch up . . . the full complexities of God's presence, in, through

In this chapter, I will only give an introduction to this book, and a first impression of its questions, themes, and arguments. In the other chapters, the claims made in this chapter will be fleshed out more with analyses from sources, dialogue with other voices, and more elaborate arguments. It may be clear, however, that the order of hermeneutics and Scripture, as I follow in this book, differs from what has been customary in orthodox Protestant theology, from its Lutheran and Reformed beginnings to their Evangelical and Pentecostal heirs. I will argue in chapter 2 that Protestantism was formed at the time that modernity was formed as well and that Protestant theology and modern thinking have influenced each other over the centuries. The modern quest for epistemic certainty is mirrored in the order of many works of Reformed dogmatics that have the doctrine of Scripture in the prolegomena at its beginning. The entrance to the doctrine of Scripture was epistemological questions. Answering the question of where we can find reliable and certain knowledge of God, theologians dealt with the revelation of God, the inspiration of Scripture, and the illumination by the Holy Spirit. The quest for epistemic certainty in theology easily results in an ambivalent relationship with hermeneutics, for hermeneutics confronts us with uncertainties.[2] The interest in epistemic certainty leads to a focus on revelation, inspiration, and illumination. This interest conflicts with what happens when God speaks, and finite and fallible interpreters try to understand his word. Thus, these hermeneutical uncertainties are easily minimized or even neglected.

This move from epistemology to theology was common in a modern context. This move, however, had a larger plausibility as long as Europe was a Christian continent. The majority of people shared a Christian background and the Christian faith was the default option. Although Christian Europe in (pre-)modern times was divided into different confessional traditions, the Christian faith and the Christian Scripture were common heritage. Within such a context, the theological importance of the common Christian background easily remains unnoticed. The starting points of many dogmatic works were epistemological questions. However, these theological writers presupposed Christian faith, community, and practice. In their epistemologies, soteriological and ecclesiological notions were implied or presupposed.

Theology, however, is "subjected to frustration," together with the entire creation (Rom 8:20). Theological solutions from the past do not always

---

and over-against the activities comprising the church's common life" (Kelsey, *Proving Doctrine*, 163).

2. Thiselton, *Hermeneutics*, 3.

work, and sometimes create new problems, in the present. As the crisis of modernity and secularization is also a crisis of Western Christianity and theology, the path from epistemology (Scripture) to theology has to be reconsidered, for several reasons:

1. The modern view of epistemology has become problematic. The modern quest for absolute epistemic certainty has failed. It is widely acknowledged that the ideal of a detached and disembodied theoretical rationality of an individual subject is problematic, for it denies important aspects of our human existence. Think of the work of Martin Heidegger and the late Ludwig Wittgenstein who both show the importance of the practice of being in the world (Heidegger) and of our language games (Wittgenstein); the phenomenology of Maurice Merleau-Ponty who stresses the embodied nature of human perception; or the hermeneutical philosophy of Hans Georg Gadamer with his emphasis on tradition and prejudgment; or Paul Ricoeur who shows that our self-understanding is narrative, depending on what we learned to tell about ourselves. Rational thinking is an activity of finite embodied persons, whose thinking is shaped by a particular tradition with particular narratives, communities, and practices, as we can learn from Alisdair MacIntyre. Epistemology is no longer seen as a foundational activity, nor the rational subject as absolute and autonomous. Instead, the primacy of practice and ordinary life is emphasized, together with the embedded and embodied nature of theoretical thinking.[3] This means that Christian theology has to face the reality of the "cultural-linguistic turn."[4] Theology does not start with providing a cognitive foundation but with the reality of the Christian life, where we become Christian believers and live as such. Scholarly critical reflection has, therefore, a secondary character. The practice of faith as first order precedes the second-order activity of theoretic thinking in theology; but also, theology precedes epistemology as a "reflexive . . . intellectual operation."[5]

2. It is no longer possible to ignore that the real starting point of theology is the Christian community and practice, that exists as an answer to the saving practice of the triune God. The theological story that starts with epistemology presupposes a Christian context and a Christian community. This implied reality has to be made explicit, now the context of Western theology has changed. Theology in the West no longer stands against a common Christian background, due to the secularization of the European public sphere and the decline of European churches in terms of membership

---

3. Cf. Westphal, "Hermeneutics as Epistemology," 415–17.
4. Vanhoozer, *Drama of Doctrine*, 3–16.
5. O'Donovan, *Resurrection and Moral Order*, 76.

and significance. Christian faith and Christian Scripture have lost much of their plausibility within Western societies. A Christian way of life, Christian formation, and a Christian understanding of God, the world, and the self are under pressure and have become just one option among many alternatives. Now, we discover the theological importance of what was implied in the shared Christian world of the Constantine era in Europe, and was not discussed explicitly. Theologies of the past presupposed this Christian world in their prolegomena. In the context of twenty-first-century Europe, what has been presupposed in the past, or could remain implicit, has to be made the object of explicit theological reflection. A theological epistemology is embedded in a Christian community with shared practices, a Christian perspective, and a Christian theology. It presupposes soteriological notions like revelation, illumination, participation in Christ, the presence of the Holy Spirit, regeneration, and the renewal of the mind. Starting with epistemology is not the best option anymore.

3. The movement from Christ to Scripture is primary to the movement from Scripture to Christ. The story of orthodox Protestant dogmatics normally started with revelation and Scripture and moved to Christology. This can lead to the impression that Scripture brings us to Christ and faith in him and that the Protestant *sola scriptura* precedes the *solus Christus*. Within the (late-)modern European context, however, critical questioning of Scripture as the certain foundation of knowledge with the attitude of a detached observer easily results in the loss of faith in Jesus Christ. The relationship between Christ and Scripture is far more complicated. Theologically, the *solus Christus* precedes the *sola Scriptura* as will be argued in this book. The Christian practice of reading Scripture is part of the Christian life and presupposes the shared commitment of the church to Jesus Christ, as an answer to its encounter with God in the face of Christ through his Spirit.

4. The emphasis on epistemology and certainty easily leads to an ambivalent attitude toward hermeneutics and a lack of honesty in dealing with hermeneutical problems. The more the possibility of theology depends on an absolutely certain epistemic foundation, the more hermeneutical uncertainties seem to endanger theology and faith. A dogmatic narrative that starts with epistemological foundations thereby runs the risk of failing to take into account honestly the actual event of interpreting Scripture. We are limited and fallible people, embedded in the lived perspective of a community and a tradition. In a secularized, post-Christian, pluralist context, however, the particular perspective of the Christian community cannot be ignored. Moreover, in a divided and unstable world, no perspective at all is stable in itself. As the Christian community is under pressure, theology

should serve the church by raising a solid self-awareness that is rooted in the work and presence of the triune God.

To conclude, in the late- or postmodern, post-Christian, pluralist, unstable context of twenty-first-century Europe, epistemology is not the best place to start theology, nor the best way to get access to the doctrine of Scripture.

Theologians order the themes in their works and tell a theological story. The narrative order of theological works is theologically significant. The theological story of Scripture and hermeneutics needs to be retold in the light of soteriology and faith in Jesus Christ. In this book, I chose deliberately to reverse the order of Scripture and hermeneutics, moving in my dogmatic narrative from a Trinitarian soteriology to hermeneutics firstly and secondly to Scripture.

Here, an additional remark has to be made regarding the more general implications of this shift. After the failure of the project of modernity with its quest for absolute certainty of knowledge, theological thinking should not start with epistemology. A theological epistemology needs to be embedded in a Trinitarian soteriology: God the Father reveals and saves in Word and Spirit, Jesus Christ as the incarnate Word embodies the fullness of God's revelation and the new life of salvation, the Holy Spirit gives life, allowing us to share in God's truth and love. Still, I follow in this book the Reformation in their view of the order of Scripture and church.[6] In the story of systematic theology, the narrative order should be something like 1. Jesus Christ and Holy Spirit; 2. Scripture; 3. Church. The practice of the triune God precedes Scripture, Scripture precedes the church as *creatura verbi*. Accordingly, the implication of the order of this book, moving from hermeneutics to Scripture, is not that the doctrine of Scripture becomes part of ecclesiology. The primacy of Scripture signals the *extra nos* of salvation and the *solus Christus*. Here, I would prefer the order of the Nicene Creed, which makes a double mention of Scripture, both times before referring to the church: first, in the second article about Jesus Christ ("On the third day he rose again in accordance with the Scriptures") and, second, in the third article about the Holy Spirit ("He has spoken through the Prophets"). The creed connects the doctrine of Scripture to Christology and pneumatology, not to ecclesiology.[7]

---

6. Cf. Bayer, *Martin Luthers Theologie*, 232–34; Webster, *Holy Scripture*, 44–52.

7. Here I differ from A. van de Beek, who deals with Scripture in his ecclesiology, that is part of his pneumatology. See Van de Beek, *Lichaam en Geest van Christus*, 275–338; Burger, "Christologisch én pneumatologisch." According to David Kelsey, Scripture should be part of doctrines concerning "the shaping of Christian existence," and thus of the doctrine of sanctification or ecclesiology. I would prefer a position between on the one hand Christology and pneumatology, and on the other hand ecclesiology

1.2 A REFORMED CONTRIBUTION: CHRIST, HERMENEUTICS, SCRIPTURE

It should be said that I am not the first one who tries to retell the systematic theological narrative of Scripture and hermeneutics. The amount of literature in the field of theological hermeneutics is large. The contribution of this book is determined by my own theological perspective.

> 1. This book gives a critical evaluation of the Neo-Calvinist views of Scripture and hermeneutics. It is a proposal to correct some of its problematic features, while at the same time building upon this theological tradition. I am a Reformed theologian from a Dutch background, raised in a church standing in the Neo-Calvinist tradition of Abraham Kuyper, Herman Bavinck, and Klaas Schilder. This tradition is clearly influenced by modernity, as we will see in chapter 2. In an attempt to update the Calvinist tradition at the end of the nineteenth and the beginning of the twentieth century, a version of Reformed theology was formulated that mirrors the interests of modern foundationalism. I have written this book because I see that an alternative is necessary, as the foundationalist tendency leads to an unfruitful Cartesian dilemma: certainty without hermeneutical honesty or hermeneutical relativism without strong beliefs. Accordingly, I will engage critically with the Reformed tradition. I do this with a catholic and ecumenical intention, engaging with theologians from other traditions, like the German-Swiss theologian and philosopher Ingolf U. Dalferth (chapter 4) and the British theologian and ethicist Oliver O'Donovan (chapter 5). At the same time, I will continue to build on its characteristic emphasis on the (narrative of) salvation history.
>
> 2. The color of this book will be Reformed with a central emphasis on what the Reformed tradition has called *unio mystica cum Christo*, or in a more contemporary rendering "union with and participation in Christ."[8] As the title *Jesus Christ, Hermeneutics, and Scripture* demonstrates, the Trinitarian soteriology of this book is Christocentric. This emphasis cannot be isolated from the Triune God and the activity of the Father and the Spirit. Concerning the Holy Spirit, I have learned a lot from Pentecostalism and the movement of Charismatic renewal. I see the necessity of ecclesial and sacramental mediation of salvation,

---

and the remainder of soteriology; cf. Kelsey, *Proving Doctrine*, 208–9.

8. For comparable Reformed approaches, see Vanhoozer, *First Theology*, 159–206; Billings, *Word of God*. On union with and participation in Christ, see Burger, *Being in Christ*.

as well as for hermeneutic transformation and the understanding of Scripture. Consequently, I try to write with a catholic, ecumenical intention to serve the entire church. Still, my view of the relationship between Jesus Christ, participation in Christ, and Scripture (in a Reformed way understood as *tota scriptura*) will be Reformed, and this book will be a Reformed contribution to the theological debates on hermeneutics and Scripture.

3. This book will not offer an isolated view of hermeneutics (critical reflection on processes of understanding), nor a separate treatment of the doctrine of Scripture (with her attributes like clarity and authority), but a narrative that brings both fields together. I aim to get beyond the unfruitful division separating the doctrine of Scripture from hermeneutics, either by a doctrine of Scripture that is not hermeneutically sensitive or a theological hermeneutics that does not deal with the doctrine of Scripture.[9]

4. Theological hermeneutics will be presented as part of soteriology. A new perspective is opened when Jesus is presented as Christ, when we are baptized with the Holy Spirit, when Christ is found, and when faith in Christ is awakened. Scripture is read and heard to let us be and remain in Christ, to be filled with his Spirit through the inspired word, and to make us grow in Christlikeness. In hermeneutical terms, this means to share in Christ's mind (or to say it in a Pauline way, his *nous*; 1 Cor 2:16) and his perspective. It is both a matter of mystagogy, leading to the mystery of union with Christ, and of hermeneutics that offers orientation in life in the presence of the triune God.

5. The course this book takes goes from hermeneutics to Scripture, with a special interest in the relationship between Christ and Scripture. I will focus especially on three issues:

> a. Baptized by the Spirit of Pentecost, in the light of the resurrection, and in the community of the church, we receive a new perspective and a new understanding. As a consequence, we no longer know Christ or read Scripture according to the flesh (cf. 2 Cor 5:16). Knowing Jesus as Christ and Lord, reading Scripture as his disciples, we see everything else in this light: God as loving Father, our fellow believers as a new creation, our world as God's creation where God's kingdom is coming.

---

9. Francis Watson has explained why hermeneutics and the doctrine of Scripture need each other, see Watson, "Hermeneutics and the Doctrine of Scripture."

b. This new understanding has Christlikeness as its purpose: an embodied life, guided by the Holy Spirit, in the mind of Christ, formed by Scripture, lived in the body of Christ, to bring hope in our world. The downside of this new understanding is the awareness that transformation in Christ as well as our human sinful nature have noetic consequences.

c. This new understanding includes a new perspective on Scripture as well. A Christian view of Scripture is determined by who Jesus Christ is for us. I will propose to see Christ as the climax and fulfillment of the Scripture of Israel, as the embodiment of what God has to say to Israel and to all gentile peoples, as the representative of Israel and of humanity in whom the realization of God's promise and law can be found, as God's Messiah who reigns in God's coming kingdom, and as the incarnation of the eternal Word of God who is present in the entire Scripture of Old and New Testament.

1.3 HERMENEUTICS

From the sixteenth to the twentieth centuries, hermeneutics has developed from the methodology of the interpretation of biblical or juridical texts to hermeneutical philosophy that takes understanding as a basic feature of human existence. This development has influenced theological thinking on hermeneutics. In the theological departments, a variety of questions nowadays are called hermeneutical questions. In Christian ethics, they are concerned with the interpretation of Scripture and moral phenomena and search for an answer to moral questions in the light of Scripture. In practical theology, they concern the understanding of lived religion or the translation of scriptural texts to the contemporary context. Biblical studies focus on the interpretation of Scripture as part of its historical context and as the word of God for today. Systematic theology interprets Christian doctrine and its history, to understand its meaning in the context of the twenty-first century. The same is the task of missiology, which has also a special interest in the transformation of cultures.[10]

Understanding indeed is a basic feature of human existence, and accordingly of Christian existence. That does not mean that to live and to understand are synonyms: when we live and act, we follow customs and rules but we do not always need to understand what we are doing, although our acts imply a certain understanding of who and where we are and what we

---

10. Cf. De Bruijne and Burger, *Gereformeerde hermeneutiek vandaag*.

do. We start to search for a conscious understanding when we are no longer able to continue our lives without an answer to questions of understanding that arise. Then we start to interpret consciously to make our understanding explicit, using signs and language: someone understands something as something. Often, this can be formulated more specifically: someone understands something influenced by someone in the light of some specific interests.[11]

Accordingly, questions concerning understanding and interpretation are manifold for all humans, also for Christians.[12] They might try to understand Scripture, their neighbors and their situation, their history and their hope for the future, their faith and their doctrine. In this systematic theological work, I have a specific focus. I am especially interested in how Christians understand Scripture in the light of Easter (the resurrection of Jesus as his vindication as Christ and Lord), and in the Spirit of Pentecost (when the bearer of the Spirit baptizes with the Spirit).[13] Moreover, I am interested in how Scripture, read in the light of Easter, and in the Spirit of Pentecost, influences our views and images of God, of our neighbors and ourselves, and of our world. The new perspective of Easter, Pentecost, and Scripture marks a difference from the old perspective of created and sinful humans. This old perspective is important for this book as well. Finally, I am interested in the transformation of the believer from old to new, by participation in Christ and the work of the Holy Spirit that leads to a new perspective on everything.

These developments in the discipline of hermeneutics and these considerations concerning our being human have several consequences for my concept of hermeneutics.

> 1. Hermeneutics regards more than the rules for the interpretation of texts. We understand texts, but we also understand God, our neighbors and ourselves, our communities, and our world in the light of texts. Furthermore, the art of understanding is not just a matter of method and rules. Understanding is a matter of wisdom, imagination, and empathy. Understanding is no purely rational activity, for the process of understanding is partly a subconscious process, and it is influenced by our desires, our moods, our interests, and power

---

11. Cf. Dalferth, *Kunst des Verstehens*, 1–134.

12. For an overview of the variety of hermeneutical questions and the resulting variety of hermeneutical approaches, see Dalferth, *Kunst des Verstehens*, 135–65.

13. Here, I have learned from Pentecostal contributions like Keener, *Spirit Hermeneutics*.

mechanisms. Finally, a part of hermeneutical formation is the formation of hermeneutical virtues.

2. The development of hermeneutics also corrects a too-limited view of epistemology. Hermeneutics reminds us of the necessity of a holistic approach to knowing and understanding. Human subjects live an embodied existence. Their reason is historically, culturally, and linguistically embedded in a tradition and a community. Thus, Merold Westphal concludes that hermeneutics did not bring the end of epistemology, but a richer approach to epistemology than the Enlightenment could offer. "Hermeneutics is epistemology."[14]

3. Hermeneutics gives more than epistemology. Rene van Woudenberg has written a book on the epistemology of reading and interpretation. In his approach, he focuses on reading and interpretation as a source of knowledge.[15] Consequently, he is interested in the text, but not in the world in front of the text, or the discernment of our world in the light of the text. This should not surprise us, for significance in the world in front of the text differs from knowledge. Our views of God, the world, the self, and the neighbor involve more than only epistemically justified beliefs (imagination, significance, etc.).

If this is epistemology, hermeneutics reaches beyond epistemology and gives more than epistemology does. If epistemology is interested in texts as a source of knowledge, theological hermeneutics has a broader scope, for it reflects also on the discernment of our world in the light of Scripture. Epistemology is interested in true propositions and in what is the case. Hermeneutics also has an interest in the significance of something for someone. The formation of the mind of Christ in us is not only important for knowledge, but also for significance, discernment, deliberation, and our acts.

4. Theological hermeneutics cannot be separated from soteriology. Philosophical hermeneutics might observe processes of understanding, a plurality of perspectives, or existential significance. Theological hermeneutics as developed in this book sees and understands everything *coram deo*, as existing in relation to God. Furthermore, Christian theological hermeneutics knows of the difference between an old perspective (fallen in sin) and a new perspective (renewed in Christ and the Spirit). This hermeneutics needs soteriology to explain this difference. This difference transcends methods, rules, and even

---

14. Westphal, "Hermeneutics as Epistemology," 416.
15. Van Woudenberg, *Epistemology of Reading and Interpretation*.

conscious, intended human acts. The renewal and transformation of understanding is part of salvation, a gracious gift of the triune God; human beings are involved as well, but images like "regeneration" or "dying and rising with Christ" indicate that the creation of a new perspective transcends human possibilities. Thus, it is not possible to separate theological hermeneutics from soteriology.

5. Not everything is hermeneutics, for several reasons. First, understanding differs from hermeneutics. I define hermeneutics as "critical reflection on processes of understanding and interpretation." Accordingly, hermeneutics is a reflective, second-order activity. Understanding is a first-order activity, and we do not need hermeneutics to understand. Often, we understand something as something, and no further reflection is necessary. Critical reflection only starts when it is triggered by misunderstanding or conscious interpretation. Second, it is important to see the difference between understanding (someone understands something as something) and deliberation (given discernment of a situation, someone deliberates how to act). Third, hermeneutics cannot replace theological reflection. John Webster has signaled that the incorporation of hermeneutical philosophy in modern hermeneutical theology can lead to a loss of theological content and a decline of theology.[16] Consequently, salvation is more than receiving a new understanding. Hermeneutics is no substitute for good theological thinking. Hermeneutics does not determine what is the case, what should be said, or what should be done. Hermeneutics only helps to understand and interpret what is the case, what is said, and what could be done.

Although I see understanding broadly as a basic feature of human existence, my approach will be thoroughly theological, as human existence *coram deo* is an existence either in the flesh or in Christ. The same will be true where my interest concerns special hermeneutics. This book aims to contribute to the broader field of theological hermeneutics, stimulating the awareness that we live, listen, read, understand, and interpret *coram deo*.[17]

---

16. Webster, *Word and Church*, 49-51.
17. For a similar emphasis, see Bartholomew, *Introducing Biblical Hermeneutics*, 3-16.

1.4 SCRIPTURE

Listening to and reading the Bible *coram deo* means for a Christian hearing it as the canonical Scripture, inseparably connected with the acts of the triune God, and read in the liturgy of the church. This is a statement that is part of the doctrine of Scripture, which describes and reflects on the character of Scripture and how this particular book relates to what the triune God did in the past (which resulted in us receiving Holy Scripture) and to what God does in the present and will do in the future (in which he works through Holy Scripture, with as its result that we will be conformed to Jesus Christ, the incarnate Word of God). Insofar as this book concerns the doctrine of Scripture, a Trinitarian soteriology determines its focus.

Thus, it fits within a broader theological trend to correct modern secularized or deistic approaches to Scripture, emphasizing that Scripture needs to be embedded in the acts of the triune God as his identity is confessed in the creed, that the liturgy of the church where the gospel of Jesus Christ is preached is the primary locus of the reading of Scripture, and that these books have to be read together as canon. Many theologians who emphasize the importance of canon, church, and creed for the understanding of Scripture are part of the so-called movement of "Theological Interpretation of Scripture." As such, the movement is diverse or ecumenical, for theologians from different confessional backgrounds with different theological accents.[18]

My contribution will be colored by my Reformed background, with an emphasis on the primacy of Scripture, an interest in the entire Scripture (of the Old and New Testaments), a salvation-historical approach (although in a canonical and narrative version), with an open eye to the realities of the covenants and God's creation.[19] However, I will engage with theologians from outside the Reformed tradition and also from outside the debate on "Theological Interpretation of Scripture" to enrich my proposal: Ingolf Dalferth and Oliver O'Donovan. How I will locate Scripture within the economy of the triune God will be influenced by my interest in "being in Christ." Furthermore, I will use the creed to identify the three "dramatis personae" of Scripture,[20] but to reconstruct the plotline of Scripture more is

---

18. On the theological interpretation of Scripture, see Billings, *Word of God*; Bowald, "Character of Theological Interpretation"; Burger et al., "Introduction," 4–7; Fowl, *Theological Interpretation of Scripture*; Porter, "What Exactly Is Theological Interpretation?"; Sarisky, "What Is Theological Interpretation?"; Treier, *Introducing Theological Interpretation of Scripture*; Treier, "What Is Theological Interpretation?"

19. Cf. Huijgen et al., "Biblical Exegesis and Systematic Theology," 189–92.

20. Jenson, *Canon and Creed*, 45. See further Jenson, *Systematic Theology*, 75.

needed than in the creed. Here, biblical theology has to fulfill an important role as a supplement to the creed.[21] As far as the canon is concerned, it is important to read the Scriptures as a canon and as a unity. Still, this does not make historical-critical exegesis and a thorough historical reading of Scripture superfluous.[22] Finally, the role of the church is important as an interpretative community and for the sake of its liturgical practice as the primary locus of reading Scripture, but still, the church as *creatura verbi* remains for her existence dependent on the Word of God, and her understanding of Scripture of the Holy Spirit.[23]

1.5 JESUS CHRIST

Since the relationship between Jesus Christ and Scripture is a central theme of this book, I will make some remarks on Christology. My christological perspective is determined both by the resurrection (Easter) and by the Holy Spirit (Pentecost).

In the twentieth century, many theologians emphasized the importance of the resurrection for Christology. Here, Jesus is vindicated and appointed as the Son of God and Lord (Rom 1:4). Now, we no longer have to know him according to the flesh for the new creation has come in his resurrection (2 Cor 5:16–17). This is important for hermeneutics as well: if Jesus Christ determines the new perspective, his resurrection is the decisive moment for the emergence of this new perspective. The resurrection determines the new perspective on Jesus as Christ, and in Jesus Christ, we receive a new perspective. Jesus is the risen Lord.[24]

Coming from a Pentecostal background, Frank Macchia has criticized such an emphasis on the resurrection as it can be found in the work of Wolfhart Pannenberg. Without debating the centrality of the resurrection as the decisive moment of the vindication of Christ's identity, Macchia states that Easter needs Pentecost. Pentecost is the climax of Jesus's mission, where he as the Messiah, baptized with the Spirit, and himself the bearer of the Spirit

---

21. Carson, "Theological Interpretation of Scripture," 192–96, 206; Jenson, *Canon and Creed*, 2010, 14–18, 43–50; Porter, "What Exactly Is Theological Interpretation," 251–53; Wright, *How God Became King*, 10–20.

22. Cf. Carson, "Theological Interpretation of Scripture," 189–92; Porter, "What Exactly Is Theological Interpretation," 247–50.

23. Porter, "What Exactly Is Theological Interpretation," 253–59.

24. See, e.g., Van de Beek, *Kring om de Messias*, 19–23, 38–46; Van de Beek, *Lichaam en Geest van Christus*, 305–9; Dalferth, *Auferweckte Gekreuzigte*, 54–61; O'Donovan, *Resurrection and Moral Order*, 13–15, 157–60.

now has the right to baptize in the Spirit.[25] According to Oliver O'Donovan, Pentecost is not "a fifth in the series, Advent, Passion, Restoration, Exaltation." Pentecost was not done "once for all," but "authorises the church by uniting it with the authorization of Christ." Consequently, the gift of the Spirit belongs to Christ's exaltation.[26] The climax of Jesus's narrative, however, is not his authorization as king, but the incorporating gift of the Spirit of God as the realization of the new covenant. Consequently, Pentecost as the moment of the baptism with the Spirit (and the believers can participate in this act of giving as well, see John 7:38) deserves separate attention. Pentecost is hermeneutically important as well because the mind of Christ that we receive is at the same time the mind of the Spirit (1 Cor 2:10–16).[27]

Looking back from Pentecost, Jesus is the Spirit baptizer who is himself baptized with the Spirit. For hermeneutics, it is important that before the body of the new humanity was formed in the community of Jesus's disciples, Jesus himself lived a human life guided by the Holy Spirit. Our human subjectivity—knowing, interpreting, and understanding—is restored first objectively in Jesus Christ through the Holy Spirit.[28] As Word and Spirit are the two hands of God, we need both a Word-Christology and a Spirit-Christology to understand Jesus Christ in his significance for our human subjectivity.[29]

In the light of Easter and the Spirit of Pentecost, Jesus's entire life is important: from what we use to call his "incarnation" in the Spirit and his birth, his baptism with the Spirit, his preaching of the good news of the kingdom of God, his performance of miracles as signs of the kingdom, the community that he started, until his suffering, death, resurrection, and exaltation. His life was an identification with his people Israel, in his role as representative Messiah of Israel also an identification with humanity, an identification that made him more and more our substitute and representative that lived and acted on our behalf. Doing this, he was also the embodiment, fulfillment, and realization of what God says and promises to Israel and in Israel to the gentile peoples. Also, this dynamic process in which God

---

25. Macchia, *Jesus the Spirit Baptizer*, ix–x, 1–5, 19–29, 289–96.

26. O'Donovan, *Desire of the Nations*, 161. For his own later reflection on the neo-orthodox Christocentrism, see O'Donovan, *Self, World, and Time*, 91–97.

27. Cf. Keener, *Mind of the Spirit*.

28. O'Donovan, *Resurrection and Moral Order*, 24, 85, 149–50.

29. For examples of a combination of both, see Owen, *Works*, pt. 3; Kärkkäinen, *Christ and Reconciliation*, 196–209; Macchia, *Jesus the Spirit Baptizer*; Van der Kooi, *This Incredibly Benevolent Force*, 22–70; Veenhof, *Kracht die hemel en aarde verbindt*, 25–32, 49–65.

does what he says in Jesus Christ is the incarnation of the Word of God: the embodiment of what God has said, is saying, and has to say.[30]

As the embodiment of the word of God, he is at the same time the eternal and preexistent Word of God. His presence with us did not start with his birth. He was and is present, as the living Word and in Scripture—the Torah, the Prophets, and the Psalms. This christological view is important for how we read the Old Testament: it does matter that one believes that Christ is present in the *Tanakh* as well as in the apostolic writings.[31] Moreover, when reading the New Testament this christological view is crucial, for because of our faith in Jesus Christ we read Scripture, and in our relationship with Christ the writings of his apostles are indispensable.

Furthermore, the presence of Christ as the fulfillment and realization of what God says is central to the soteriological approach that I develop in this book. Christ is the Savior who makes the believers share in who he is, which includes participation in his mind and Spirit. Christ is present in his Spirit, in Scripture, and in the church, to be with us and to transform us into Christlikeness. This Christlikeness is a result of reading Scripture, but at the same time makes us more attuned to understanding Scripture as God's word. I will further investigate and explore the relationship between Christ and Scripture in all its richness in this book.

1.6 THE ARGUMENT OF THIS BOOK

The first step of my proposal is an overview of the development of the epistemological approach of Scripture in the history of Western theology, from medieval Scholasticism to Neo-Calvinism in the modern period (chapter 2). Dealing especially with texts by the British Puritan John Owen and the Dutch Neo-Calvinist Abraham Kuyper, I will argue that the medieval epistemological approach of Scripture developed via the conflict of authority in the Reformation and the longing for absolute epistemic certainty in modernity. I will argue that this approach is no longer effective in the present Western context.

In the second step (chapter 3), I give additional reasons to develop a soteriological approach as an alternative to an epistemological one. According to Charles Taylor, the tendency to live without an openness to transcendence is strong, but not necessary. His analysis of secularization and the trajectory to a purely immanent understanding of human existence makes

---

30. Cf. Jenson, *Systematic Theology*, 78–80, 166–67.

31. For this emphasis on the presence of Christ in the Old Testament, see Boersma, *Scripture as Real Presence*.

clear that apart from rational arguments our moral judgments, affections, narratives, and social imaginaries influence us. Our human existence is narrative, social, embodied, and affective. In a secularized but also pluralistic world, an epistemological approach does not suffice to convince people that God exists and that we need to obey Scripture. This is even more the case when it is true that sin has its noetic effects. When sin is a reality, sinners have an interest in denying, misinterpreting, or neglecting what God says to them. The overview of the noetic consequences of sin makes clear that we need salvation to become obedient hearers and interpreters of God's word. We need the renewal of our mind to develop an understanding of God, the world, the neighbor, and the self that is not closed to transcendence. As a consequence, it is necessary no longer to follow an epistemological approach, but to develop a soteriological alternative that is not just rational.

Searching for such an alternative, I investigate the hermeneutical theology of Ingolf U. Dalferth (chapter 4). According to Dalferth, the triune God identifies himself in Christ to someone in the Spirit, so that a new perspective is opened. In this light he also understands Scripture: in the church, we read Scripture to hear the gospel of Jesus Christ, so that in the Holy Spirit God's loving presence is disclosed to us. However, the embodiment of newness in Jesus Christ, the church, and the believers deserve more elaboration than Dalferth offers. Furthermore, his view of Scripture evokes questions concerning God's activity in the history of Israel, the criteriological role of Scripture in theology, and the nature of the Scripture that makes Scripture with its human words so special that God can use Scripture in our lives for the soteriological purposes of participation in Christ.

To answer these questions, I turn to two other theologians, Oliver O'Donovan and Herman Bavinck. O'Donovan helps to better understand the role of Scripture in the transformation of our mind so that we participate in Christ and receive the mind of Christ. His reconstruction of the practical reason, active in reflection and deliberation helps to see how Scripture functions in the Christian practice (chapter 5).

The next step concerns a reading of Herman Bavinck to further develop a Reformed doctrine of Scripture (chapter 6). On the one hand, I give a critical analysis of Bavinck's epistemological approach to Scripture. On the other hand, his organic understanding of the history of revelation with Christ as its climax remains helpful. I will use it to clarify the nature and role of Scripture, by analyzing how Bavinck's view of Scripture depends on the *solus Christus*.

If Christ is the climax of the history of salvation, he is important as well for a Christian reading of Scripture. When Christian believers read Scripture following the teaching of Jesus in Luke 24, they will have regulative beliefs that guide them in their interpretation of the Scripture. After a short investigation of the reading of Scripture by the Dutch theologian Klaas Schilder in his *Christ in his suffering*, I explain what it means to read Scripture as one story. I start in Luke 24, trying to make explicit the impact of Jesus's messianic and missional perspective on the Scriptures of Israel. Furthermore, I discuss what this perspective means for the *quadriga* (the fourfold sense of Scripture), analyzing the views of Hans Boersma (chapter 7).

The following chapter delves deeper into the practice of reading and the process of the renewal of the mind. I give an overview of empirical research on the practice of reading in the life of Christian believers and the church. Moreover, I try to clarify the mystagogical process of the renewal of the mind and the interaction between reading Scripture and participating in (Christian) practices of mercy. Finally, I give an analysis of a text by John Owen about how we grow in understanding the mind of Christ as revealed in the word of God. The renewal of the mind is an aspect of our participation in Christ, mediated in the church, as a gift of the Holy Spirit.

Chapter 9 is the concluding chapter. Here I will bring the lines of this book together. I use the ecological crisis as a case to demonstrate what the proposal of this book implies. Confronted with this crisis, we can see the complexities of reading Scripture, the impact of our life practices, and the necessity of a soteriological approach to theological hermeneutics. Our secular and unstable world needs people who live with faith, love God's world, and have a clear hope for the future. Without God as our Savior we will not understand Scripture well, nor will we develop the mind of Christ that we need to do desperately.

2.

Epistemology and Certainty
The Development of the Doctrine of Scripture

2.1 INTRODUCTION

To rethink the relationships between Christ, hermeneutics, and Scripture, it is important to understand first where we are now and how we have arrived at this place at this moment. How did the Reformed doctrine of Scripture develop historically, with its epistemological interest and its emphasis on certainty? These developments with their strengths and weaknesses have to be clarified first before I will start to develop my own proposal.

In my answer to this question, it will become clear that the developments of Reformed theology and modernity are closely interwoven. Both give primacy to epistemological questions and share the quest for certainty. The combination of the two has led to a common ideal of absolute certainty in knowledge. For many centuries, Protestant reflection on Scripture has interfered with modernity in this respect. Christian believers in the West, the Protestants in their confessional variety as well as the Roman Catholics, are like sisters who have grown up together in one house with their other sisters, humanism, and modernity. Living together, they enjoyed life together, learned, and quarreled, with attraction and repulsion. Together, they are part of one cultural development over the centuries, facing the same questions and finding their answers in interaction with each other.

Theological positions have unforeseen and unintended effects, although weaknesses of a theological tradition often become apparent only much later during new situations of crisis.[1] This is also the case with de-

---

1. McGrath, *Christianity's Dangerous Idea*, 473.

velopments in the doctrine of Scripture. Furthermore, the current crisis of West-European Christianity, characterized by secularization and post-Christendom, is closely interwoven with the crisis of her sister, modernity.[2] To understand the present crisis of West-European Christendom and modernity, it is important to look back in our traditions—from the present to Romanticism and Enlightenment, Reformation and Renaissance, and their shared roots in the second half of the medieval period.[3]

In this chapter, I will focus on developments in the theological tradition which I am part of: the tradition of Neo-Calvinism, which is part of the Reformed tradition and that builds on the medieval church of western Europe. I will divide this history into two parts. In the first part, I will sketch the development from the medieval period until the era of high Reformed orthodoxy. This period starts with a new interest in epistemological questions in the prolegomena of medieval scholastic theology (2.3). As a result, revelation and Scripture come into view. At the end of the Middle Ages, a conflict on authority becomes central. This conflict escalated in the Reformation and the resulting breakup of the West-European church. Especially, the *Reason of Faith* (1677) written by the Puritan theologian John Owen (1616–83) will have my attention in this first part (2.4). This part of the chapter closes with some conclusions concerning this first phase (2.5).

The Enlightenment and the rise of historical-critical biblical studies mark a second phase. Now, it has become a question of whether Scripture can be trusted as a historical and theological source and whether God exists. This creates new theological questions concerning the knowledge of God and Scripture as a source of this knowledge (2.6). The rectorial address *The Biblical Criticism of the Present Day* (1881) by Abraham Kuyper (1837–1920) will be the lens through which I look at this period (2.7). In 2.8 I will look back and argue why I favor a soteriological approach.

But first I want to make some preliminary remarks on modernity and foundationalism, to clarify my interests in drawing the lines of these theological developments (2.2). The reason for doing so is that Reformed and Neo-Calvinist theology share this interest in epistemology and certainty with modernity. Over the centuries, they influenced each other. Regarding

2. On secularization and post–Christendom, see, e.g., Paas, "Post-Christian, Post-Christendom."

3. The development of modernity and its problems is a long and multilayered process in which wrong theological decisions played a role but in which also theological solutions were detached from their theological roots and developed into a secularized, atheist direction. See for inspiring reconstructions of the genesis of modernity and its problems, Boersma, *Heavenly Participation*, 52–94; Gunton, *One, the Three, and the Many*; Milbank, *Theology and Social Theory*; O'Donovan, *Desire of the Nations*, 193–288; Taylor, *Sources of the Self*; Taylor, *Secular Age*.

this shared interest it can be seen that modernity at least partly has Christian roots. More importantly, the crisis of modernity demonstrates why this focus on epistemology and certainty has become so problematic and is not a fruitful approach anymore.

2.2 MODERNITY AND FOUNDATIONALISM

This special modern interest in epistemology and certainty has to be seen together with the emergence of the modern self. The genesis of the modern self was provoked by epistemological and affective skepticism. Out of epistemological skepticism, modern philosophers searched for certain knowledge based on solid foundations. They did so in a disengaged way, detached from body and world. This led to the formation of the modern self and modern reason: an individual subject with high expectations of rationality, and an attitude of objectification and disengagement. Out of affective skepticism, this attitude was turned toward the inner life as well. This new view of the reflective self is related to an understanding of the will of the subject, aware of moral obligations but affectively independent. As a consequence, self-consciousness lost its discursive content, and practical reason more and more lost its deliberative function. Consequently, theoretical thinking constituted by disengaged, instrumental, objectified rationality was favored over practical rationality.[4]

As a consequence, theoretical thinking became more and more important in understanding certainty. This is not self-evident, because the ultimate foundations of certainty ("Letztbegründungen") can only be found in practical contexts, not in theoretical contexts. In a theoretical context, it is always possible to come up with new questions. A theoretical search for ultimate foundations leads to the "Münchhausen Trilemma" of three unsatisfying options: "an infinite regress, a logical circle or the termination of thinking at a certain point."[5] In practice, however, we need to act and we know how to do things. Of course, we do have beliefs that we never will give up, beliefs that are related to our acts, our choices, our identity, and our life forms. Modern thinking, however, tried to legitimize practical or existential certainties by translating them into certainties of theoretical thinking, thus confusing a theoretical concept of absolute certainty with a practical concept of deep-rooted convictions.[6]

---

4. See O'Donovan, *Ways of Judgment*, 297–303; Taylor, *Sources of the Self*, 143–76; Taylor, *Secular Age*, 131–42.

5. Dalferth, *Wirklichkeit des Möglichen*, 360.

6. Cf. Dalferth, *Gedeutete Gegenwart*, 137–38, 154–55; and Ludwig Wittgenstein's

Modernity's quest for absolute certain knowledge has become known as foundationalism. According to a foundationalist epistemology, "a person's noetic structure or the totality of his convictions should be construed according to the analogy of a building," composed of a foundation of basic beliefs, and the non-basic beliefs justified by those foundational beliefs.[7] Modern foundationalism strived for a peaceful coexistence of humanity that is based on an agreement about knowledge, morality, religion, and culture and is achieved according to rational standards. To reach this goal, it prioritized epistemology. The ideal of modern, "classical" foundationalism was a self-evident foundation of indubitable basic beliefs. To rationally attain absolute certain knowledge, two components are required: a universally shared rationality, and a universally shared agreement about "which beliefs are to be admitted as properly basic and thus as part of the foundation."[8] When theology followed the strategy of foundationalism in the period of Modernity, it had the choice of taking the Scriptures, religious experience, or an infallible pope, as its epistemological foundation.[9]

The quest of modern foundationalism failed. It proved to be impossible to reach an agreement about which beliefs could be considered properly basic. Moreover, no one succeeded in formulating a rule that described what could be considered an indubitable justification of a proposition or a theory on the premise of the foundation. Furthermore, rationality itself proved to be embedded in traditions and communities. More fundamentally, the attempt to give an *a priori* epistemological foundation is problematic itself. As a result, non-foundationalism was proposed. The problem with non-foundationalism, however, is its suggestion that epistemological questions seem to be unnecessary or can be answered in a fideistic way. Ingolf Dalferth warns against tribalism: when God is God and truth is truth, we

---

reflections on certainty in Wittgenstein, *On Certainty*.

7. Van den Toren, *Christian Apologetics*, 38. See further Van den Brink, *Almighty God*, 11–13; Sarot, "Christian Fundamentalism," 259–61; Wolterstorff, *Reason within the Bounds of Religion*, 28–30; Van den Toren, *Breuk en brug*, 56–59.

8. Van den Toren, *Christian Apologetics*, 38.

9. For the discussion of modern foundationalism, its problems, and theology, see Beilby, "Contemporary Religious Epistemology," 809–13; De Bruijne, "Geworteld en dan opgebouwd wordend"; Dalferth, *Wirkendes Wort*, 29–40; Echeverria, "Divine Revelation and Foundationalism"; Erickson et al., *Reclaiming the Center*; Frame, *Doctrine of the Knowledge of God*, 128–29, 368–87; Gunton, *One, the Three, and the Many*, 129–35; Hoogland, "Orthodoxie, moderniteit en postmoderniteit," 134–36; Murphy, *Beyond Liberalism and Fundamentalism*; Peckham, *Canonical Theology*, 81–91, 104–8, 136–39; Phillips, *Faith after Foundationalism*; Rauser, *Theology in Search of Foundations*; Smith, "Non-Foundational Epistemologies"; Sarot, "Christian Fundamentalism"; Wolterstorff, *Reason within the Bounds of Religion*; Wolterstorff, "Herman Bavinck," 133–38.

as a group do not determine what is true, and what is truly said about God concerns everyone and has to be justified in public.[10] De Bruijne claims that "Reformed theology will not survive without a foundation-model," although it has to be supplemented by a hermeneutical approach.[11] Comparably, Colin Gunton warns against intellectual sectarianism, and suggests the option of "non-foundationalist foundations . . . in a reasoned approach to truth."[12] More modest forms of foundationalism were developed, for example by Alvin Plantinga.

Although I am doubting whether the foundation-metaphor is most apt to clarify the epistemological relationship between a belief and its justification, it is not my contention that epistemology is useless. Within the New Testament, the foundation-metaphor is primarily a soteriological and ecclesiological metaphor. Christ is the church's foundation or its cornerstone. Primarily, the metaphor concerns life, salvation, and community.[13] Within this soteriological and ecclesiological framework, epistemological questions are implied as well—but less important than a modern framework suggests. Moreover, I prefer a style of thinking that starts with the divine and human practices as a fruitful alternative to a theology that starts with epistemology. Nevertheless, I do not at all intend to say that epistemology is obsolete nor to delve into the technical details concerning foundationalism. Epistemology is necessary and non-foundationalism is no option, if we want to communicate the truth of our beliefs.

Still, with the modern primacy of epistemology and the emphasis on absolute certainty, we are facing problematic ideas, as can be seen in the daily life of Christian believers and the work of Neo-Calvinist theologians from the second half of the twentieth century. G. C. Berkouwer started his volume on Holy Scripture with a chapter on the certainty of faith and writes that the choice of this theme in the first chapter "will probably surprise no one."[14] His choice confirms the centrality of the question of certainty and shows that in Berkouwer's context (1966) this certainty had become a problem. The Dutch theologian Harry Kuitert exemplifies that as long as an ideal of modern rationality is affirmed, the domino effect will be there: when the first stone falls, the other stones will fall as well. Kuitert's rational quest for certain knowledge started with a criticism of metaphysics and an

10. Dalferth, *Gedeutete Gegenwart*, 19–21, 277.

11. De Bruijne, "Geworteld en dan opgebouwd wordend," 157.

12. Gunton, *One, the Three, and the Many*, 134.

13. *Themelios* (foundation) we find in Rom 15:20; 1 Cor 3:10–12 (see further Luke 12:32–33; 1 Tim 6:19; 2 Tim 2:19); Eph 2:20. *Akrogoonaios* (cornerstone): Eph 2:20; 1 Pet 2:6. *Hedraiooma* (foundation): 1 Tim 3:15.

14. Berkouwer, *Holy Scripture*, 9.

investigation of the empirical reality of human religiosity. In the end, he lost the Reformed heritage in which he grew up.[15] The reverse side of the modern quest for certainty is the so-called "Cartesian anxiety" that sees only two alternatives: we find an objective and solid foundation for our knowledge, or the danger of relativism and subjectivism looms.[16] This Cartesian anxiety can be tasted in statements of ordinary believers. Significantly, the quest for absolute certain knowledge does not go well with hermeneutical honesty. In practice, the ideal of absolute certainty leads to fear of hermeneutics. And when the quest for absolute certainty is given up as unrealizable for fallible minds, the result is often skepticism about knowledge and relativism about truth. And so people lose their faith. It all started with a wrong ideal of absolutely certain knowledge, a knowledge that is not available for human theoretical thinking because it would demand a God's eye point of view and implies a denial of human finitude and fallibility.

In this chapter, I am not interested in the question to which extent Reformed theologians have to be identified as foundationalists.[17] I will limit myself to these two topics: the primacy of epistemological questions and the quest for certainty. I am interested in how these two topics influence the doctrine of Scripture, in the position that Jesus Christ received in Reformed doctrines of Scripture, and the attitude toward hermeneutics generated by it. Furthermore, I will search for unforeseen and unintended effects of the Reformed approach to Scripture, and for the questions that this approach does not sufficiently answer. This will help me to formulate my own proposal more sharply. My theological agenda is influenced by two problems in the practice of believers: the reaction of relativism or unbelief out of disappointment with the ideal of absolute certainty, and the suspicion of hermeneutics and the related lack of honesty about what actually happens when we read and understand Scripture.

---

15. Van de Beek, *Van Kant tot Kuitert*, 225–38; Van den Brom, "Kuitert"; Geertsema, *Om de humaniteit*, 13–43.

16. On "Cartesian anxiety," see Bernstein, *Beyond Objectivism*, 16–20.

17. "Foundationalism has been so roundly condemned in recent years, and the term itself so indiscriminately tossed about, that the term has by now lost almost all determinate meaning. What remains is little more than pejorative connotations." Wolterstorff, "Herman Bavinck," 134.

2.3 PROLEGOMENA AND AUTHORITY CONFLICT

2.3.1 Middle Ages, Reformation, and Early Modernity

In the first part of the history that I will sketch, these two themes have become important: first, the primacy of epistemology, and later the quest for certainty. Different elements have added to complex development. First, the development of theology as a *scientia* in medieval scholasticism led to the development of prolegomena and a new interest in Scripture from an epistemological viewpoint. Second, the medieval church developed into a powerful institute with its own canon law. This development evoked questions concerning the authority of Scripture and tradition. Abuse of ecclesiastical power, the papal chaos of the great schism (1378–1417), and other destabilizing factors in the late medieval period made these questions only sharper. The breakup of one church into many confessional churches in the Reformation period and the related religious wars further sharpened these questions. Third, the movement of Christian humanism prompted a renewed interest in original sources and thus in the Hebrew and Greek texts of Scripture. The Vulgate was no longer the unquestioned translation; instead, not only was Scripture studied in its original languages, but also new translations were made. Moreover, fourth, the invention of book printing led to a media revolution and a book culture that resulted in greater availability of the Bible. The Bible became part of a book culture, and this influenced its role and use. Fifth, a central modern theme more and more crystallized, when the sense of individuality became stronger and stronger. And finally, in many developments that caused uncertainty, certainty became an important theme. I will explore these various developments in turn.

From the mid-twelfth century, theology as a discipline with formal theological prolegomena started to develop. In the thirteenth century, the Aristotelian model became influential, and theology as a *scientia* had to rest upon certain *principia*. Among these *principia*, Scripture was discussed as well. The development of a separate doctrine of Scripture received a first stimulus. Thomas Aquinas was the first to explicitly argue that Scripture contains the revealed divine self-knowledge and thus "by its very nature is the ground or foundation of necessary argument in theology."[18] The doctrine of Scripture was used to give an epistemological foundation to theological knowledge as knowledge of faith between *scientia* and *opinio*. The church fathers read Scripture as a book about Christ and the church and were interested in the transformation of its readers—a soteriological

---

18. Muller, *Post-Reformation Reformed Dogmatics*, 2:39. And further 1:92.

perspective.[19] In medieval scholasticism, Scripture comes into view from another interest, from an epistemological perspective. From the beginning of the scholastic tradition, the doctrine of Scripture and epistemological questions are closely related.[20]

The second development concerns the church as an institute with earthly power, its own canon law, and discussions concerning its authority. More and more, relationships between worldly and churchly authorities, between religious orders and the hierarchy, and between pope and pope gave rise to a juridical formalization of the ecclesial institute in its canon law. Malfunctioning of the church authority, abuse of power by the papacy, and the great schism of the fourteenth century led to a decline of western Christianity. The disasters of the fourteenth century—wars, famines, and the black death—contributed to a climate of anxiety that continued in the next centuries and evoked an existential quest for certainty. These developments were important causes of a crisis of authority and evoked movements of reform.[21]

Authority crises and reform movements touched also the authority of Scripture. Oberman has coined the two options to see the relationship between Scripture and tradition as Tradition I (Holy Scripture contains all truths of faith) and Tradition II (Scripture is not the sole norm of doctrine; the church also needs the oral tradition of the apostles and councils as a source of truth). Until the high Middle Ages, the authority of Scripture, the tradition, and the magisterium were not seen in contrast. Most theologians saw Scripture as theology's normative foundation. Canon lawyers, however, emphasized the authority of the tradition and argued that canon law has two sources, Scripture and tradition. In the late medieval period, the relationship between Scripture, tradition, and magisterium became the subject of debate. John Wycliff and Jan Hus argued from Scripture against the church, whereas other late medieval thinkers taught the "metaphysical priority of the authority of the church over that of Scripture."[22] This conflict

---

19. Boersma, *Scripture as Real Presence*, 18–25. Of course, questions concerning the possibility of knowledge of God, authority and historical reliability were not new; yet, a new interest is now being attached to them. See on the church fathers further Hill, "Truth above All Demonstration."

20. See Muller, *Post-Reformation Reformed Dogmatics*, 1:88–96. And Muller, *Post-Reformation Reformed Dogmatics*, 2:24–26, 37–51.

21. Boersma, *Heavenly Participation*, 54–57, 61–64; Milbank, *Theology and Social Theory*, 12–17; Pannenberg, *Systematische Theologie*, 557; Pannenberg, *Systematic Theology*, 516; Taylor, *Secular Age*, 88–89.

22. Muller, *Post-Reformation Reformed Dogmatics*, 2:53–54.

of authority continued in the Reformation, and it became a matter of debate whether Scripture was sufficient or not.[23]

The Reformers unanimously affirmed the authority of Scripture over the authority of the ecclesiastical tradition and magisterium.[24] Martin Luther did so, using the Aristotelian language of principles of theology. Luther was the first who said that Holy Scripture is the only *principium* of theology. As a principle, it is self-evident and the starting point for the development of theology; that is, it is *sui ipsius interpres*. Thus, in the conflict of authority, Luther uses an epistemological concept to formulate his solution.[25] Scripture is "the ultimate source and criterion for faith and proclamation . . . master and judge."[26]

In the *Institutes of the Christian Religion* of John Calvin, we also find traces of this conflict on authority. According to Calvin in Book 1.6.1, we have a twofold knowledge of God, a knowledge of God as creator, and a deeper knowledge of God in the person of the mediator. For both, we need Scripture as a source. Central to Calvin's doctrine of Scripture in Book 1 of the *Institutes* are two discussions; one with Rome concerning the problem of whether the authority of Scripture rests on the authority of the church (Book 1.7), and one with the "fanatics" who place their trust in new revelations of the Holy Spirit, bypassing Scripture (Book 1.9).[27] Both discussions concern the question of the authority of Scripture as the source of our knowledge of God. Important motifs in these chapters are authority, the role of the church and the Holy Spirit, and the *autopistia* of Scripture. Calvin writes that Scripture is the foundation of the church. He substantiates the self-evidence of the authority of Scripture with two new elements, the *autopistia*, and the *testimonium spiritus sancti internum*. The *testimonium* is used to argue for certainty. It is further noteworthy that just as *principium* is, *autopistia* is also an epistemological concept, even if it is used metaphorically by Calvin, with an existential interest in the certainty of faith.[28]

---

23. Boersma, *Heavenly Participation*, 61–64; Muller, *Post-Reformation Reformed Dogmatics*, 2:45–62; Oberman, *Harvest of Medieval Theology*, 361–411; Oberman, *Herbst der mittelalterlichen Theologie*, 335–82; Ryrie, *Unbelievers*, 52–53, 56–68.

24. I will leave open whether the position of the Reformers is the same as Oberman's Tradition I, or differs from this position because the Reformers no longer saw the interpretative tradition as normative but only as an instrument to understand Scripture. See Peckham, *Canonical Theology*, 7–11, 75–77.

25. Lauster, *Prinzip und Methode*, 12–13.

26. Kolb, "Bible in Reformation and Protestant Orthodoxy," 93.

27. Calvin, *Institutes of the Christian Religion*, 69–71, 74–81, 93–96.

28. On Calvin and *autopistia*, see Van den Belt, *Authority of Scripture*, 49–70, 93–115. Van den Belt mentions that, according to Calvin, on the one hand the doctrine of Scripture is part of soteriology; on the other hand, he deals with Scripture at the

Luther, Calvin, and the other Reformers were contributing to a discussion of sources of knowledge during an ongoing authority conflict. What is the decisive authority in the church: Scripture, the tradition, the magisterium, or the individual believer hearing the voice of the Spirit? From the beginnings of medieval scholasticism, this is a question belonging to the prolegomena, which implies that questions of authority and epistemology have become interwoven. Unlike medieval theologians, "the Reformers were in a position to press radically the point of how that scriptural rule functioned in the context of other claims of authority."[29] Of course, the Reformers had their soteriological and existential interests. Nevertheless, epistemology played an important role for them. Significantly, Luther's formulation of Scripture as *principium* and Calvin's use of the concept of *autopistia* were new steps made with the help of epistemological concepts. The authority conflict led to an emphasis on Scripture as opposed to the church authorities and the tradition, and in these developments concerning theological reflection on Scripture epistemological concepts played an important role.

Third, this emphasis on Scripture was reinforced by the movement of Christian humanism. This movement partly emerged from late medieval scholasticism and resulted in renewed efforts to study the biblical sources in their original languages with all available literary and philological means. It resulted in "the establishment of a far more accurate text of the Bible, . . . a considerably greater degree of freedom for the individual exegete, . . . an increased linguistic capability . . . but also a strong anti-scholastic sentiment."[30] This all contributed to the already existing conflict of authority, for the Greek and Hebrew texts were now opposed to the Vulgate, just as the philologist to the theologians; thus, it also contributed to the growing quest for certainty.[31]

Fourth, what should not be forgotten is the media revolution caused by technical development, the invention of the printing press in the fifteenth century. Dalferth has emphasized the theological significance of this media

---

beginning of the Institutes, a choice that might have influenced later developments of the doctrine of Scripture as part of the prolegomena. See Van den Belt, *Authority of Scripture*, 175. Further on Calvin, the testimony and *autopistia* Dalferth, *Wirkendes Wort*, 138–39; Lauster, *Prinzip und Methode*, 15.

29. Muller, *Post-Reformation Reformed Dogmatics*, 2:64. See further Kolb, "Bible in Reformation and Protestant Orthodoxy," 90–111; Muller, *Post-Reformation Reformed Dogmatics*, 2:63–94.

30. Muller, *Post-Reformation Reformed Dogmatics*, 2:60.

31. Kolb, "Bible in Reformation and Protestant Orthodoxy," 91; Lauster, *Prinzip und Methode*, 12; Muller, *Post-Reformation Reformed Dogmatics*, 2:59–62.

revolution. The mass production of books made the Bible available in a way that was previously unthinkable. In the book culture that grew, the text as a readable source for all believers made the book of the Bible much more important to the daily life of many Protestant Christians. This is mirrored in the emphasis on the Bible in Protestant theology.[32] Book printing in itself does not make epistemology more important. However, the increased availability of the Bible as a book and thus as a separate entity in ordinary life, reinforced ongoing tendencies.

In this debate on epistemic sources and authority, the individual and her quest for certainty were and became important issues as well.

The process of the formation of the modern individual already started in the medieval period. Still, the Reformation added to it. In 1520, Luther emphasized the priesthood of all believers over against the institute of priestly power that Rome's church had become. According to Alister McGrath, the priesthood of all believers is directly related to the "dangerous idea" of the Reformation: every individual has the right to interpret Scripture; a dangerous idea that has had unintended effects. The magisterial Reformation struggled with it: although Luther tried to modify this dangerous idea after the Peasants' War in 1525, and the idea of the priesthood of all believers of the early Luther was nuanced and balanced by other Reformers as well, now the idea existed that each individual believer had the right to interpret the Bible. Reformed theology tried to find its way between the Catholic emphasis on the church and the emphasis on the individual found in the radicals and enthusiasts. But the rise of modern individualism and the Reformation cannot be separated; both are part of the same cultural movement.[33]

The Reformed tradition contributed to this development but also was critical of it. This proved to be the case also in a later phase of its history. The controversy with the Remonstrants in combination with the growing anthropological optimism led Reformed theologians to a renewed emphasis on the consequences of sin. Due to sin, humans are blinded and unable to believe. Consequently, the acts of God and especially the Holy Spirit in illumination, regeneration, and sanctification received much attention in Reformed theology. Epistemic certainty is not available apart from the work of the Holy Spirit. Moreover, at a deeper level, the epistemic quest for certainty

---

32. Dalferth, *Wirkendes Wort*, 90, 101–6, 115–16, 245.

33. On the "dangerous idea," see McGrath, *Christianity's Dangerous Idea*, 1–150. See further, e.g., Van den Belt, *"Kan een mens wel zeker zijn?,"* 7–8, 31; Dülmen, *Entdeckung des Ich*, 11–242; Taylor, *Secular Age*, 61–145.

is an existential quest as well. What is at stake are questions of authority and knowledge, but also the question concerning the certainty of salvation.

Furthermore, according to Susan Schreiner, from the fourteenth to the sixteenth century, nominalism, schisms, controversies, and religious wars evoked fear and made (existential and epistemic) certainty a theme of growing importance. The seventeenth century sought for (rationalist) answers. Here also, the Reformation, the formation of Protestant doctrines of Scripture, and early modern developments are intertwined. Each tradition sought a different source for authority and polemicized with the other traditions: Roman Catholicism listened to the Church, the magisterial Reformation aimed to ground their doctrine in Scripture, while the radical Reformation looked to the internal light, and finally, reason served as the foundation for emerging rationalism. All claimed certainty for their authoritative foundation. During the seventeenth century, the quest for certainty became even more pressing. New pressures included the "enthusiasm" with its inner light, the emerging atheism, the upcoming ideal of mathematical certainty, as well as the ongoing disputes between Catholics and Protestants concerning *sola scriptura* and the role of the church with its tradition.[34]

As happened more often in the emergence of modernity, a "*melius*" is followed by a "*peius*" that is only "shaped in imitation and replication of the redemptive good," and might become a "parodic and corrupt development" of a Christian good.[35] The schism within the church and the subsequent religious wars led to renewed quests for "new ground of stability."[36] In response to the rumors of religious battles, Hugo Grotius sought a new foundation of justice and developed a new version of natural law; in response to the uncertainties of the age, Descartes undertook his quest for a new foundation of indubitable certain knowledge. The modern foundationalism of Descartes (and, later, Kant) sought certain, unbiased, and unprejudiced knowledge, apart from the Christian faith. They retained the old ideal of truth with universal implications but changed their concept of rationality into a universal and certain quasi-divine reason. John Perry and Marcel Sarot suggest a shifting view of authority in the background. During the Middle Ages

34. See, e.g., Van den Belt, *"Kan een mens wel zeker zijn?,"* 6–8; Leslie, *Light of Grace*, 42–49; Pannenberg, *Systematische Theologie*, 557; Schreiner, *Are You Alone Wise?*; Ryrie, *Unbelievers*, 5–7, 181–82.

35. O'Donovan, *Desire of the Nations*, 251–52, 275. O'Donovan applies this thought to Christian social and political thought; analogously, his idea can be applied to developments in the field of epistemology. Cf. De Bruijne, "Geworteld en dan opgebouwd wordend," 156–57.

36. Rauser, *Theology in Search of Foundations*, 24. Cf. Pannenberg, *Systematische Theologie*, 557–58; Pannenberg, *Systematic Theology*, 516–17.

auctoritates were trustworthy persons or texts established by God that could differ from and contradict each other. Creative interpretations did not undermine their authority. In the rise of Modernity, the credibility of traditional *auctoritates* was undermined and was replaced by alleged indubitable foundations.[37] The focus of foundationalists narrowed to an isolated treatment of epistemological questions in the light of an ideal of objective absolute knowledge.[38] In conclusion, a climate of epistemic uncertainty surfaced, and it is out of this context that both modern foundationalism and the Reformed doctrine of Scripture developed.

2.3.2 The Reformed Doctrine of Scripture

After the Reformers, a time came of confessional solidification and the building of a new Protestant academic culture. Amidst confessional diversity and polemics with doctrinal opponents, the next generations of Protestant theologians built their theological systems. The landscape of orthodox-Protestant scholastic theology was diverse, with confessional and national differences. At the same time, the shared background in medieval scholastic theology, international exchange of books, teachers, and students led to many similarities within all this variety. The academic culture of scholastic theology was a shared European culture.[39]

For all Reformers and their academic followers, Scripture as the authoritative and infallible word of God was the norm, *principium,* and *fundamentum* for theology. Given this communality, Luther more than all Reformers personified the Word and gave attention to the dynamic, existential encounter with Christ in his reflections on Scripture. This was in contrast to a more textual, cognitive, doctrinal approach to Scripture. From a soteriological perspective, it is important how especially Luther connects Scripture and God's saving acts. For Luther, Scripture as the word of God is an agent of God actually delivering God's justifying power. This emphasis was lost in Lutheran orthodoxy, but for the Reformed tradition, it is important to note that it never was part of the theology of Swiss Reformers like Bullinger and Calvin as it was in Luther's theology. Despite

37. Perry, "Dissolving the Inerrancy Debate"; Sarot, "Christian Fundamentalism," 255–59.

38. The question as to what extent Christianity itself is partly accountable for this development is interesting. Gunton sees the influence of a monolithic (non-Trinitarian) conception of God and truth working in the ideals of objectivity and universality. See Gunton, *One, the Three, and the Many,* 129.

39. On early Reformed orthodoxy, see Muller, *Post-Reformation Reformed Dogmatics,* 1:27–28, 31–34, 49–73, 96–117.

these different emphases, all Protestant scholastic theologians shared the Scripture principle.[40]

A new development in these systems of orthodox Protestant scholasticism, was the formulation of a separate formal doctrine of Scripture, after the prolegomena and before the doctrine of God. From the medieval beginnings of scholastic theology, epistemological questions about Scripture had been raised and answered in the prolegomena. Following Luther, Scripture was now identified as the one and only *principium cognoscendi theologiae*. The council of Trent, however, rejected the *sola scriptura*; Anabaptists questioned it from a subjectivist angle. Building theological systems at the academy within confessional diversity, between the Roman Catholic claims concerning the authority of the tradition and the magisterium of the church, and the Anabaptist claims about the authority of the individual believer, Protestant theologians needed to justify the *sola scriptura* and give Protestant theology a solid foundation as *scientia*. Concepts like *autopistia*, now are clearly used together with the word *principium* in an epistemological context. "In the academic setting, the *autopistia* gained the status of a logical necessity for the *principium* of the theological science."[41] Just as the reflections on Scripture in the prolegomena of medieval scholasticism, this new step in the development of the doctrine of Scripture into a separate *locus de sacra scriptura* was prompted by epistemological interests.[42]

Remarkably, the Reformed doctrine of Scripture was influenced by two works by Lutheran theologians. First of them was Mattias Flacius Illyricus's *Clavis Scripturae Sacrae* (1567), in which the importance of the grammatical, literal meaning of Scripture is stressed and the idea of a multiplicity of meaning is rejected, against the medieval model of the fourfold sense of Scripture. The second book was the critical *Examination of the Council of Trent* by Martin Chemnitz (1565-73). This book was important for the Protestant answer to the statements of Trent about the authority of church, tradition, and Scripture.[43] Consequently, it does not surprise that Lutheran

---

40. Kolb, "Bible in Reformation and Protestant Orthodoxy," 95, 103-4, 111; Lauster, *Prinzip und Methode*, 13-15; Muller, *Post-Reformation Reformed Dogmatics*, 2:64-80. For a recent German view on Luther and Lutheran orthodoxy, see Dalferth, *Wirkendes Wort*, 125-75, 334-76.

41. Van den Belt, *Authority of Scripture*, 175.

42. On the early development of the Reformed doctrine of Scripture, see Muller, *Post-Reformation Reformed Dogmatics*, 2:71-78, 94-96, 104-5. Further Lauster, *Prinzip und Methode*, 15-17. On the development of the use of the concept of *autopistia* in Reformed Orthodoxy after Calvin, see Van den Belt, *Authority of Scripture*, 117-77.

43. Muller, *Post-Reformation Reformed Dogmatics*, 105-7.

and Reformed theologians who also shared their Aristotelian academic context had so much in common in their work on the doctrine of Scripture.

Against this polemic and academic background, a doctrine of Scripture was formed in which—in the diversity of theologians—the following elements were present:

> a) Scripture is identified as the *principium cognoscendi theologiae* and thus the norm and source for theology. The epistemological interest evidently is present.
>
> b) The authority of Scripture is explained and defended. To justify this authority as certain, concepts are used like *autopistia* and the *testimonium spiritus sanciti*. Here the second topic of this chapter returns: the quest for certainty.
>
> c) Scripture is identified with the Word of God, and thus perfect. Although Protestant scholastic theologians knew that the Word of God is also the second person of the Trinity and were aware that the Word of God is more than Scripture, still a tension emerged between the confession that Jesus Christ is the Word of God and the identification of the Word of God with a text and with a book.
>
> d) Scripture is a divine book, containing the revealed doctrine. God has the archetypal knowledge, in Scripture the revealed theology can be found. To substantiate this divine character of Scripture, the doctrine of inspiration is used (already present in medieval reflections on Scripture).
>
> e) These elements are explained further in properties like the necessity, the authority, the sufficiency, and the clarity of Scripture. In the development of these properties, the polemics with other confessions color their elaboration.

It is important to note that Reformed theology is more than the doctrine of Scripture. As has been signaled already, epistemic certainty is not available apart from the work of the Holy Spirit. But in this chapter, I am especially interested in the doctrine of Scripture.

2.4 JOHN OWEN: *THE REASON OF FAITH* (1677)

To investigate more in detail how the primacy of epistemological questions and the quest for certainty work out in the work of Reformed theologians in the period of Reformed orthodoxy, I will now focus on a work by the English Puritan theologian John Owen (1616–83), namely his treatise *The*

Reason of Faith.⁴⁴ Owen is an important representative of the Puritan form of seventeenth-century scholastic orthodoxy. How does he contribute to the doctrine of Scripture, seen against the background of the development and the problems as sketched above?

John Owen's *Reason of Faith*, written in 1677, is a diptych together with his *Sunesis Pneumatikè: The Causes, Ways and Means of Understanding the Mind of God* (1678; see 8.4),⁴⁵ and has become part of Owen's *Pneumatologia*. His aim is "to declare the work of the Holy Spirit in the illumination of the minds of man."⁴⁶ The *Reason of Faith* focuses on, as its subtitle indicates, "the grounds whereon the Scripture is believed to be the word of God with faith divine and supernatural."⁴⁷ *Sunesis Pneumatikè* deals with understanding the mind of God when we read and interpret Scripture.⁴⁸ Owen's questions are practical and pastoral and concern the renewal of our understanding. The primacy of epistemic certainty seems far away.

This is emphasized by Andrew Leslie in his historical study of *The Reason of Faith*, where he shows the strong connection between Owen's doctrine of Scripture and his teachings on communion with Christ.⁴⁹ In Scripture, we discover the glory of God in the face of Christ, which transforms us into his image, which is the image of God, as Paul writes in 2 Cor 3:18. Leslie claims that "the authority of scripture in Owen's thought cannot be properly viewed apart from the mediatorial authority of Christ."⁵⁰ Faith in Jesus Christ and the experience that Scripture is important are the starting point; the doctrine of Scripture and themes like authority and origin only have an

---

44. Owen, *Works*, 4:4–117 (*The Reason of Faith; An Answer unto that Inquiry wherefore we Believe the Scripture to be the Word of God*). On John Owen, see, e.g., Kapic, *Ashgate Research Companion*; Trueman, *Claims of Truth*; Vlastuin and Kapic, *John Owen between Orthodoxy and Modernity*. For Owen's views on Scripture, see Howson, "Puritan Hermeneutics of John Owen"; Leslie, *Light of Grace*; McKim, "John Owen's Doctrine of Scripture"; Rogers, *Authority and Interpretation of the Bible*, 218–23; Trueman, *Claims of Truth*, 47–101; Zimmermann, *Recovering Theological Hermeneutics*, 78–119.

45. Owen, *Works*, 4:118–235 (*Sunesis Pneumatikè: The Causes, Ways and Means of Understanding the Mind of God*).

46. Owen, *Works*, 4:7.

47. Owen, *Works*, 4:7.

48. Owen, *Works*, 4:7.

49. On communion with Christ in Owen's theology, see Burger, *Being in Christ*, 30–86; Kapic, *Communion with God*; Klaassen, *Christus rechtvaardig*, 243–323; De Vries, *Die mij heeft liefgehad*.

50. Leslie, *Light of Grace*, 33, 172. Zimmermann characterizes Owen's epistemology as "relational," see Zimmermann, *Recovering Theological Hermeneutics*, 87–89.

a posteriori character.[51] Comparably, Trueman stresses the relational nature of Owen's theology and the connection between his doctrine of Scripture and other theological themes.[52]

The primacy of faith in Jesus Christ not only becomes clear in Owen's reflections on the work of the Spirit in the introduction but also later in the treatise. Two times Owen begins with faith in Jesus Christ when he shows the importance of the question of how we know that Scripture is the word of God.[53] We believe that Jesus Christ is the Son of God. But why? Because God testifies so about Jesus. Where does God reveal this? In Scripture. How do we know that Scripture is the word of God? Here, in this question, we see the relationship between faith in Jesus Christ and the central question of *The Reason of Faith*: to believe in Jesus Christ, we need to know that Scripture is the word of God. This shows clearly that the central question of the treatise concerning our belief that Scripture is the word of God is closely related to Owen's emphasis on the renewal of the mind of the Christian believer, and on the believer's relationship with Christ, in whom believers find the transforming revelation of God's glory. Nevertheless, Leslie also writes that some of these connections to the relationship with Christ "are not immediately obvious in *Reason of Faith* due to its quite specific, and even somewhat polemical focus."[54] It will become clear that this creates some problems in Owen's argument.

2.4.1 Sin and Illumination

To enable a sinful human being to believe that Scripture is the word of God, the problem of the darkness of the mind due to sin has to be solved. Our minds "are by nature depraved, corrupt, carnal, and enmity against God." We are unable to understand and believe "spiritual things in a spiritual manner."[55] We all need "an internal, effective work of the Holy Spirit, in the illumination of our minds, so enabling us to believe."[56] The effect of this illumination of the mind "is a supernatural light, whereby the mind is

---

51. Leslie, *Light of Grace*, 181.
52. Trueman, *Claims of Truth*, 49, 59, 68, 78, 100–101.
53. Owen, *Works*, 4:19–20, 50–51.
54. Leslie, *Light of Grace*, 33.
55. Owen, *Works*, 4:55.
56. Owen, *Works*, 4:53.

renewed."[57] Only this illumination of our mind makes it possible for us to believe Scripture as the word of God in the right manner.[58]

Leslie has shown that Owen's idea of illumination stands in a long Christian cognitive tradition, which can be traced from Protestant scholasticism through the medieval scholastics and Augustine back to Plato. In this idea of illumination, the source of light is an internal supernatural light, given to enable the mind to know God (Illumination I).[59] Leslie, however, does not note the tension between this Platonic concept of illumination and the biblical use of the metaphor of light. In Scripture, the light is identified as Jesus Christ, as God's revelation, God's salvation, and as the church.[60] This requires a concept of illumination that relates illumination to an external light: Christ, salvation, and Christ's body (Illumination II). In pneumatological terms, this implies that the Spirit illuminates us with the light of Christ, that he takes away our blindness and opens our eyes to this external light.

Owen discusses illumination, accordingly, referring to 2 Cor 4:6 where Paul writes about "the light of the knowledge of God's glory displayed in the face of Christ."[61] The scholastic concept of illumination however refers to an internal light, and its relationship to Christ is not always clear. Owen uses both concepts of illumination. The result is a twofold illumination with two sources of light: illumination oriented to an external, objective, christological light (Illumination II); and illumination by a light that is internal and subjective, in which pneumatology is easily disconnected from Christology (Illumination I). As long as the illumination of the mind is not related to Christ as the external light, Christ does not play a role in the illumination of the mind by the Spirit. This makes it possible to discuss Scripture and the illumination apart from Jesus Christ as the source of light. Where Owen writes about illumination as Illumination I, he fosters an understanding of the authority of Scripture apart from Jesus Christ; and thus, a formal, and not a material understanding of its authority.

---

57. Owen, *Works*, 4:57.

58. Owen, *Works*, 4:60.

59. See Leslie, *Light of Grace*, 71–77. More broadly on illumination, the natural light, and the gift of the new habit, see Leslie, *Light of Grace*, 67–133. In *The Reason of Faith*, however, Owen does not use the concept of habit.

60. In the New Testament, we find three exceptions to this idea of light and illumination: Matt 6:22–23 and Luke 11:34–36 ("The eye is the lamp of the body"); Eph 1:18 ("I pray that the eyes of your heart may be enlightened").

61. Owen, *Works*, 4:57–59.

2.4.2 Important Concepts and Distinctions

Illumination is presupposed in Owen's argument. At its core, some other concepts and distinctions play a central role.

First, Owen distinguishes between "the material object of our faith,—namely, the things which we do believe"; and "the formal object of it, or the cause and reason why we do believe them."[62] This implies that the things which we believe themselves do not cause us to believe. This distinction forces Owen to understand the authority of Scripture in a formal and not in a material way.[63]

Second, Owen defines faith as "assent upon testimony."[64] This concept of faith determines Owen's understanding of the *testimonium spiritus sancti*. This testimony refers to the belief that Scripture is the word of God. To believe that in the right way, one must give assent to a real testimony that says, "Scripture is the word of God." And as we will see, the Spirit alone gives this real testimony.[65]

Third, the assent of faith has various degrees of certainty, and faith exists in different kinds, "according as the testimony is which it ariseth from and resteth on; as being human if that be human, and divine if that be so also."[66] In other words, the quality of the formal object of faith determines the quality of faith, for faith "rests on and is resolved into" its ground.[67] In divine faith, this ground "is divine revelation; which, being infallible, renders the faith that rests on it and is resolved into it infallible also."[68] In faith, our minds and consciences are affected by the grounds of our faith. Thus, when we believe in the authority and truth of God, our minds will be changed by it accordingly.[69] Human testimony results in human faith, and divine testimony in divine faith.

Fourth, according to Owen "God requires of us that we believe [the Scripture] to be his word with faith divine, supernatural, and infallible."[70]

---

62. Owen, *Works*, 4:16.
63. Leslie, *Light of Grace*, 51–52.
64. Owen, *Works*, 4:83; and further 53, 63, 90, 91, 102, 105.
65. Owen, *Works*, 4:64. "However, that work of the Spirit which may be called an internal real testimony is to be granted as that which belongs unto the stability and assurance of faith." Cf. Owen, *Works*, 4:65, 68.
66. Owen, *Works*, 4:83.
67. Owen, *Works*, 4:17. In *The Reason of Faith*, Owen often uses this combination of "rest on and is resolved into" and similar combinations.
68. Owen, *Works*, 4:17.
69. Owen, *Works*, 4:19.
70. Owen, *Works*, 4:15.

When the reason for our faith is human and fallible, our faith will be human and fallible, too. And "if we believe not with divine faith, we believe not at all."[71] This has to do not simply with the fact that real faith is a gift of God, but also with Owen's conviction that God requires us only to believe God for the sake of his own authority and veracity. The only reason that God requires us to believe is that he is saying: "I am the Lord."[72] We believe because God said, "Believe me."[73]

2.4.3 Positions Owen Rejects

To clarify further the consequences of these thoughts, I will first describe the positions that are rejected by Owen. The first position only uses external arguments to defend that Scripture is the word of God. Owen admits that many good external arguments can exist for the divine character of Scripture. He deals with them and sees them as helpful. However, even if some people are convinced by purely rational grounds of the divine authority of Scripture, the result will be a human and fallible faith, and the assurance, only a so-called "moral assurance." When the formal reason for faith—rational arguments—is not divine, the resulting faith will be no real faith. Thus, this "is both contrary to the Scripture, destructive of the nature of divine faith, and exclusive of the work of the Holy Ghost in this whole matter."[74] Any position that denies the necessity of the illumination of the Spirit, is problematic.

Furthermore, Owen does not accept the position that gives effectivity to arguments based on external grounds or on the doctrines we find in Scripture, even when the necessity of the "internal, effectual work of the Holy Spirit" is affirmed. Owen argues that faith has to rest on and resolve into the right formal object. This formal object has to be a real divine testimony about the divine character of Scripture. God himself has to convince us that Scripture is the word of God. Faith needs an infallible divine formal ground. External grounds that make the divine authority of Scripture plausible, or material grounds based on what we find in Scripture and what we believe, differ from the necessary infallible divine formal ground for faith. Thus, Owen refutes that any material argument can be decisive.[75]

---

71. Owen, *Works*, 4:48.
72. Owen, *Works*, 4:47–48.
73. Cf. Leslie, *Light of Grace*, 49–56.
74. Owen, *Works*, 4:47, and further 45–47, 50–51, 54–55, 71–72, 87–88.
75. Owen, *Works*, 4:50–54, 72–73, 87–88.

For the same reason, Owen disagrees with the Roman Catholics who claim that our faith in the authority of Scripture has to rest on the testimony of the church, although they admit the necessity of an internal work of the Spirit. The ecclesiastical testimony of Scripture is human and thus unsuitable as the formal object for a divine infallible faith.[76]

Finally, Owen does not agree with those who state that "our faith is resolved into any such private testimony, immediate revelation, or inspiration of the Holy Ghost."[77] Owen gives several reasons for this disagreement: such a subjective experience is not a real testimony; it does not reckon with objective evidence; God has not promised us to give new revelations after the closure of the canon; such experiences differ from person to person; someone who has had no such an experience cannot be summoned to believe Scripture; and it implies the impossibility of the *autopistia* of Scripture.[78]

Owen does not want to base his faith on human arguments, but he declines a subjectivist position that is indifferent to arguments and evidence. He wants to include all motives of credibility, external arguments, the ministry and the testimony of the church, and the internal effectual work of the Spirit. However, he also wants to maintain the *autopistia* of Scripture. Moreover, we have to believe because we have to believe the Triune God if he speaks to us, because of the "Thus says the Lord."[79] This is an identical obligation for all human beings. How does Owen develop this position positively?

2.4.4 Owen's Constructive Proposal

Having considered which positions Owen rejects, we turn our attention to his positive statement in *The Reason of Faith*. Owen understands the testimony of the Spirit as a real internal testimony of the divine authority of Scripture. His aim is only to show that the divine authority and truth of God—God's revelation in Scripture—is and has to be the formal object of infallible faith in Scripture, but he is not "giving arguments to prove unto others the Scripture to be the word of God."[80] In a dense statement, Owen formulates his position as follows:

---

76. Owen, *Works*, 4:30–31, 56, 72, 80–82.
77. Owen, *Works*, 4:62.
78. Owen, *Works*, 4:60–64.
79. Owen, *Works*, 4:47–49, 71–73.
80. Owen, *Works*, 4:73, and further 70.

> These things being supposed, we do affirm, that it is the authority and truth of God, as manifesting themselves in the supernatural revelation made in the Scripture, that our faith ariseth from and is resolved into. And herein consists that testimony which the Spirit gives unto the word of God that it is so; for it is the Spirit that beareth witness, because the Spirit is truth. The Holy Ghost being the immediate author of the whole Scripture, doth therein and thereby give testimony unto the divine truth and original of it, by the characters of divine authority and veracity impressed on it, and evidencing themselves in its power and efficacy.[81]

Thus, the formal reason for infallible faith is the testimony of the Holy Scripture in and by the self-evidencing revelation of God in Scripture. This is the only good reason to believe in the authority of Scripture with divine and supernatural faith, and because it is God speaking, everyone is obliged to listen, to believe, and to be obedient.[82] Our faith does not rest on human, fallible testimony, but only on the infallible divine testimony.[83] Although we have good external and material reasons to believe, the best evidence we give assent to with our faith is this divine revelation.[84] The resulting assurance of faith is higher "than any given by reason in the best of its conclusions."[85] Both the epistemological character of faith and the quality of the evidence give this high degree of certainty to this supernatural assent of faith that is infallible.[86]

Furthermore, Owen states how the Spirit as the author of Scripture gives evidence to this testimony: first, "by the characters of divine authority and veracity impressed on it."[87] Comparable to the works of creation that show God's power and deity, Scripture demonstrates God's excellencies or properties. "There is in itself that evidence of its divine original, from the characters of divine excellencies left upon it by its author, the Holy Ghost, as faith quietly rests in and is resolved into; and this evidence is manifest unto the meanest and most unlearned, no less than unto the wisest philosopher."[88] It is important to note that in this analogy to natural theology, Christ is not mentioned, only the divine excellencies and the Holy Spirit.

---

81. Owen, *Works*, 4:72–73.
82. Owen, *Works*, 4:70, 73, 78.
83. Owen, *Works*, 4:81–82.
84. Owen, *Works*, 4:90.
85. Owen, *Works*, 4:90.
86. Owen, *Works*, 4:90–91.
87. Owen, *Works*, 4:73.
88. Owen, *Works*, 4:92.

Second, the Spirit gives evidence to his testimony, by the power and efficacy of Scripture that believers experience in their minds and consciences. The fact that we are deeply touched by Scripture and our minds and lives are transformed into the likeness of Christ, is for Owen an argument for the divine origin of Scripture. "It is the effect of an utterance upon a hearer that enables the hearer to recognize it as being spoken by God. It does this because the effect is something that only a divine utterance could produce, and the hearer recognizes it as being so."[89] The experience of the divine power, authority, and efficacy of Scripture gives the strong certainty that divine and supernatural faith has.[90]

2.4.5 Evaluation

Owen's *The Reason of Faith* offers a good prevention against simplistic judgments about theology in the past. Reflections on Scripture in the period of Reformed orthodox scholasticism comprise more than a *locus de sacra scriptura* composed out of epistemological interests. At the same time, his treatise has several problematic aspects, typical of an approach focused on certainty and epistemology.

First of all, several positive elements of his approach can be noticed. Leslie emphasizes that for Owen questions concerning the doctrine of Scripture have an *a posteriori* character. On the macro level of Owen's theology, this is true. Owen did not write a doctrine of Scripture as part of the prolegomena of theology. Following Leslie and Trueman, one could say that Owen does not isolate his reflections on revelation and Scripture from other theological themes, like the doctrines of the Trinity, salvation, the church, and the means of grace. Owen's doctrine of Scripture is embedded within his pneumatology. The fact that he refers several times to 2 Cor 3 and 4 indicates that this pneumatology is closely related to his Christology and the theme of union with Christ.[91] In Owen, we find nothing of a secularized or deistic approach to Scripture, no Scripture that has been isolated from the acts of the triune God. Owen's treatise reminds us of much that has been lost in modern theology and can be used to re-embed the doctrine of Scripture within the acts of the triune God.[92] However, Owen's treatises on Scripture

---

89. Lamont, *Divine Faith*, 198.
90. Owen, *Works*, 4:93–94. See also his examples, Owen, *Works*, 4:94–100.
91. Owen, *Works*, 4:57, 97–98.
92. On the necessity to reestablish the relationship between the Trinity and Scripture, see, e.g., Billings, *Word of God*, 195–228; Vanhoozer, *First Theology*, 127–206; Webster, *Holy Scripture*, 5–41.

are all relatively independent works, although Goold gave two of them a place in Owen's *Pneumatologia*.[93] How Owen himself embedded his reflections on Scripture within his reflections on union with Christ and within his pneumatology, should neither be minimized nor overstated.

However, I have several more critical remarks to make as well. The first one concerns Owen's emphasis on certainty. It can be seen in Owen's treatise that the authority conflict of the Reformation has come in the next phase. For Owen, it is no question whether Scripture, tradition, the magisterium or the individual believer hearing the voice of the Spirit has the final authority. Owen substantiates the authority of Scripture by giving a refined justification for this authority by formulating grounds for it. Owen is glad to promise his readers more than human, fallible certainty. Our faith gives assent to infallible evidence and supernatural testimony. As a result, our certainty can be of the highest degree. Owen includes in this certainty the fact that based on a wide variety of evidence, it can be made plausible that Scripture is the word of God. Achieving certainty was important for Owen. However, we cannot ignore that this often complicates asking honest questions concerning the text and the history of the Holy Scripture, as is evidenced by his *Integrity and Purity of the Hebrew Text*.[94] He saw no theological room for critical questions concerning the vowel points of the Hebrew text, as happened in Walton's *Polyglot Bible* (1657). According to Leslie, one should not read Owen as representing "the embryonic stages of a neo-Reformed evidentialist tradition."[95] Leslie and Carl Trueman are correct in emphasizing that we need to understand Owen within his historical context. Still, we need to ask about the abiding theological significance of Owen's unwillingness to face the problems with the Hebrew text of Scripture.[96] His quest for certainty proves to have problematic consequences.

Second, with the emphasis on certainty, epistemological questions come into view as well. In *The Reason of Faith*, Owen deals with the infallible and supernatural faith about the divine authority and origin of Scripture. This evokes the question of how this faith about Scripture that answers epistemological questions relates to saving faith in Jesus Christ. In both

---

93. I have found no information on the history of the relationship of the two treatises in volume 4 of Owen's Works, dating from 1677 and 1678, to the first, larger part of Owen's *Pneumatologia* from 1674.

94. Owen, *Works*, 24:345–421 (*Integrity and Purity of the Hebrew and Greek Text*). See further Van den Belt, *Authority of Scripture*, 158–61; Muller, *Post-Reformation Reformed Dogmatics*, 2:131–34, 415, 417–25.

95. Leslie, *Light of Grace*, 31.

96. Leslie, *Light of Grace*, 212–15; Trueman, *Claims of Truth*, 66–67. See further Rogers, *Authority and Interpretation of the Bible*, 221–23.

cases, faith is supernatural and the result of divine testimony. Furthermore, it has to be noted that *The Reason of Faith* is followed by a treatise on understanding the mind of God: for Owen, epistemology and soteriology are intertwined. The transformation of our minds was an important theme for Owen. However, crucial in Owen's argument is the distinction between the material object of faith and its formal object. The things we believe (the material object) do not provide the reason why we believe (the formal object). In Owen's epistemological argument, Jesus Christ and his gospel hardly play a role, although faith in Christ and union with Christ are presupposed in Owen's *Reason of Faith*. Owen's focus is further narrowed by his epistemological conviction that a divine faith has to rest on a divine testimony about Scripture. The formal object of faith consists only in the divine testimony that "this is the word of God" and its evidence.

A comparison with Heb 2:1-4 for example, makes clear that a more open attitude toward different kinds of arguments is possible. In this passage, different types of evidence support the message of salvation: an announcement of the Lord, confirmation by those who heard the message, and a testimony of God "by signs, wonders, and various miracles, and by gifts of the Holy Spirit distributed according to his will" (Heb 2:4).[97]

For Owen, however, material arguments cannot serve as a ground for supernatural faith in the divine origin of Scripture. Owen is focused on a real testimony about Scripture. As a consequence, when dealing with several biblical passages about grounds for faith, he makes a strange move: he focuses on formal grounds and other formal notions like the word of God and revelation. Other motifs, also present in these passages are minimized or neglected: events in the life of Jesus Christ, his majesty, his signs, the gospel of Jesus Christ, etc.[98] In the New Testament, the reason for faith often lies in the history and gospel of Jesus Christ or the experience of salvation. When Owen uses these passages to argue for the reason of faith in Scripture, he neglects these material grounds.

Owen's evidence for the testimony about Scripture is twofold. The first evidence parallels the revelation of God's divine attributes in nature. Just as God makes himself known by his attributes in creation, so God has left the impression of his divine excellences in Scripture. The second piece of

---

97. In Owen's exposition of Heb 2:1-4, he does not deal with the question why we believe Scripture is the word of God. He reads it as an exhortation to listen, followed by several enforcements. See Owen, *Works*, 20:256-319 (*An Exposition of the Epistle to the Hebrews*).

98. Owen, *Works*, 4:76-80. Here Owen discusses John 20:30-31; 2 Pet 1:16-21; and Rom 16:25-26. Further, he mentions Acts 26:24; 1 Tim 1:15; John 1:14; 1 John 1:1; Eph 2:20; 2 Pet 3:2; Rom 10:17; Luke 24:25-27; and 2 Tim 3:15-17.

evidence concerns the illumination of the Spirit and the impression of God's revelation on human existence. Leslie has shown how Owen's argument follows the tradition of classic epistemology in line with the peripatetic cognitive tradition.[99]

Even though this epistemological framework has an open eye for natural theology as well as for the necessity of illumination, it has a blind spot for the power of the personal encounter with Jesus Christ and of the narrative of the history of salvation. Yet, the encounter with Jesus Christ is what elicits saving faith. And the plot of the narrative of Scripture has its own persuasive force. This narrative tells about God's wonderful acts, doing what he promises and bringing this story to an unexpected climax in the gifts of his Son and Spirit.

In the end, in Owen's argument, it is epistemology that grounds faith in Jesus Christ. We believe that Jesus is the Son of God because God says it. We believe God because God does not lie. We find this in Scripture. And we believe Scripture because God speaks in Scripture. And we believe that God speaks in Scripture because of the testimony of Scripture. In this way, faith in Scripture (epistemology) is abstracted from faith in Jesus Christ (soteriology), and faith in Scripture (epistemology) grounds faith in Jesus Christ (soteriology).

Interestingly, this narrow focus is partly compensated by the experiential nature of Owen's work. According to Owen, one of the pieces of evidence for divine testimony is the experience of the authority and power of Scripture in the mind and conscience of the believer. This element of Owen's theology can be reinforced by a more integrated understanding of material and formal aspects, of the testimony of the gospel and the testimony about Scripture.

Third, Owen makes a step toward the separation of objectivity and subjectivity. The Reformers used the concept of *principium* to substantiate the authority of Scripture, accompanied by the *testimonium spiritus sancti internum* as a source of the subjective side of certainty. To understand certainty in the Reformed tradition, the difference between objectivity (revelation) and subjectivity (pneumatology) more and more becomes a presupposition. The more Scripture and our beliefs about Scripture are abstracted from a personal encounter with Jesus Christ, the more objectivity and subjectivity will become separated and are emptied from christological and soteriological content.

In Owen's argument, we do not find the difference between objectivity and subjectivity as it developed later in modern nineteenth-century

---

99. Leslie, *Light of Grace*, 151–53, 160–74.

Reformed theology. For this reason, Jens Zimmermann emphasizes the relational character of Owen's epistemology.[100] Leslie, however, follows Richard Muller's verdict that "later Reformed writers found it increasingly difficult to integrate the subjective, spiritual work at the foundation of faith with the objective grounds for that work in the authoritative scriptural Word itself."[101] Owen's preference for formal instead of material arguments shows that he is already part of a problematic development. Furthermore, the concept of illumination bears this difference between objectivity and subjectivity in itself, as at times this concept differentiates between objective illumination (Illumination II; external source of light) and subjective illumination (Illumination I; internal source of light). The concept of illumination can be improved by emphasizing what Paul writes in 2 Cor 3–4, an important passage of Scripture for Owen: it is the light of Christ that shines in our hearts. The light with which the Spirit illuminates us has to be understood as the light of God's revelation in Christ. This is illumination. At the same time, the Spirit heals our blindness to make us see. This pneumatological work of the opening of our eyes, ears, heart, and the reordering of the mind can more accurately be referred to as the healing of blindness. Consequently, the relational nature of illumination and the importance of Christ as light can receive more emphasis.

Fourth, a separation of objectivity and subjectivity easily coincides with an individualist tendency. Within the Reformed doctrine of Scripture, it is a risk that the individual reader comes into view when the testimony of the Spirit occurs, but the formation of individuals within the community of the church to become good readers of Scripture tends to be forgotten. Furthermore, it will become a risk that the individual reader is left alone with a book that is believed to be the revelation of God with absolute certainty, or, when doubt comes in, has nothing to say anymore.

Owen's focus is on the work of God in the individual reader. At the same time, in the next treatise, his *Sunesis Pneumatikè: The Causes, Ways and Means of Understanding the Mind of God*, he reflects further on the formation of the reader using the means that God has given.[102] Here, Owen offers a valuable contribution to the enrichment of the doctrine of Scripture with elements that have been lost in modern (Reformed) theology. In this treatise, Owen deals with spiritual illumination, causes of spiritual ignorance, the importance of prayer, obedience, and spiritual worship, but also scientific methods and ecclesial tradition (see 8.4).

---

100. Zimmermann, *Recovering Theological Hermeneutics*, 87–89.
101. Leslie, *Light of Grace*, 31.
102. Apart from *Sunesis Pneumatikè*, see also Owen, *Works*, 4:13–14.

In conclusion, concerning certainty and the individual, Owen's position is ambivalent. On the one hand, Owen has a strong interest in epistemic certainty and gives a formal treatment of epistemological issues. He does not give a central place to material arguments for our belief that Scripture is the word of God, due to his emphasis on the difference between the formal object of faith and its material object. On the other hand, Owen has much to offer when we want to show that the individual reader is never alone and to re-embed hermeneutics and the doctrine of Scripture in a living relationship with the triune God, a relationship with the Father in union with Christ in the Holy Spirit.[103]

2.5 CONFLICT OF AUTHORITY—SOME CONCLUSIONS CONCERNING THE FIRST PHASE

In the first phase of the development of the doctrine of Scripture (from medieval to Reformed scholasticism), an authority conflict leads to the development of a formally independent doctrine of Scripture. The interest in Scripture of the medieval scholastic theologians arose from epistemological questions in the prolegomena of theology and concerned the character of theology as *scientia*. In the conflict on the decisive authority in the church, epistemological concepts remained important. Reformed scholastic theologians developed their doctrine of Scripture against this background: the justification of Scripture as the decisive authority in church and theology. Especially the justification of Scripture as the only *principium* of theology is an epistemological discussion, but the authority of Scripture in the church has epistemological implications as well. Certainty was an important theme in these discussions, as is exemplified in Owen's text *The Reason of Faith*.

To justify this authority especially arguments are used that concern God, God's word, revelation, inspiration, and the divine testimony of the Holy Spirit. Apart from the transforming effect of Scripture, the used arguments have a more formal character. More material arguments for the authority of Scripture, like arguments from the content of the gospel, a personal encounter with Jesus Christ, or signs, miracles, and powers supporting the authority of the word, are not used by Owen. As a result of this neglect of Christ as the integrating center, it becomes more difficult to keep together the objectivity of the divine revelation and the subjectivity of faith given by the Holy Spirit, whereas, at the same time, the objectivity of divine

---

103. To foster "cognitive reverence" for Scripture, the framework that surrounds hermeneutics and the doctrine of Scripture is very important. On "cognitive reverence," see Yarbrough, "Future of Cognitive Reverence."

revelation and the subjective divine activity lose their christological content. When dealing with Scripture, epistemology, and certainty become primary, whereas Jesus Christ moves to the background.

In Owen's doctrine of Scripture, we find on the one hand tendencies analogous to the modern quest for epistemic certainty, and on the other hand material that has been lost in later developments but that is still present in his theology. His central emphasis remains important: thanks to the illumination of the Holy Spirit, we can and have to listen to the word of God, because it is this speaking God who in his Word and through his Spirit unites us with Christ to transform us into his likeness.

It can be seen that the quest for epistemic certainty in Protestant theology and modern philosophy were part of the same cultural developments. They are rooted in the epistemological justification of the *scientiae*, in the crisis of the late medieval church, and the resulting authority conflict, in disappointment about the magisterium and other Christian authorities. They share the quest for reliable authorities and a high-absolute degree of certainty. A rational or epistemological justification becomes an important condition for faith in modern thinking.[104] Ironically, the doctrine of Scripture in the Reformed tradition has taken over traces of this modern foundationalism: the epistemological quest for a priori absolute certainty in combination with a preference for formal instead of material arguments for the authority of Scripture. Whereas in Christian practice Scripture is embedded in the life of the church with its tradition and the relationship with the triune God, due to foundationalist influences Scripture in theory tends to be isolated from this embedding.[105]

2.6 KNOWLEDGE OF GOD AND HISTORICAL CRITICISM

For the scholastic theologians from the thirteenth to the seventeenth century, the existence of God and the authority of Scripture as the inspired word of God were common grounds for their theologies. This began to change in the seventeenth century. Textual criticism and study of the Masoretic pointing of the Hebrew text challenged the views of Scripture that especially emphasized its divine character. At a deeper level, a theocentric

---

104. Rauser, *Theology in Search of Foundations*, 21, 26.

105. For further documentation of the influence of the modern tendencies as mentioned on the understanding of the Scripture principle within the Reformed tradition, see Van den Belt, *Authority of Scripture*; Goudriaan, *Reformed Orthodoxy and Philosophy*; Rogers, *Authority and Interpretation of the Bible*.

worldview was changing into an anthropocentric direction. Christian Stoicists like Justus Lipsius (1547-1606) already manifested high expectations of the human capacities to accomplish societal change and the civilization of all citizens. In Roman Catholic theology, the growing separation of the natural and the supernatural led to an emphasis on the autonomy of the natural realm. Rene Descartes (1596-1650) emancipated reason and made reason the new source of certainty. Baruch de Spinoza (1632-77) separated the domains of theology and philosophy. For him as well, reason became the judge to determine what is true. Moreover, he argued for a historical approach to Scripture. Deism changed the experience of time and history into a neutral, empty succession of moments on a linear, horizontal line. The result was what Mark A. Bowald has called an "eclipse of God's agency."[106] More and more a worldview took shape that seemed to exclude the existence of a transcendent God who is active in this world. Views of history and Scripture changed due to these developments in philosophy and led to a secularization of the interpretation of Scripture. The context for theology was changing radically, developing historical criticism of Scripture, and questioning the existence of God.[107]

The philosophy of Immanuel Kant (1724-1804) is a watershed that marks these changes. Typical of his thinking are a strong moral interest in humanity, a high trust in human rationality, a view of knowledge as a human construction, a critical attitude toward tradition, and a separation between *theoretical reason* that is unable to know God and *practical reason* that needs God as its postulate.[108] The human subject with its moral, religious, or speculative capacities has become the starting point of theological thinking as well. Accordingly, at the beginning of the nineteenth century, three different theological strategies were developed: finding God in human morality, human religiosity, or human speculative thought. Kant and his followers took the first path, and Friedrich Schleiermacher (1768-1834) followed the second option.[109] In *Der christliche Glaube*, the pious self-consciousness is the finding place of the relationship between God and the world as well as of

---

106. Bowald, *Rendering the Word*, 14.

107. Bartholomew, *Introducing Biblical Hermeneutics*, 206-28; Boersma, *Heavenly Participation*, 64-67; Muller, *Post-Reformation Reformed Dogmatics*, 2:118-48; Woodbridge, "German Pietism and Scriptural Authority"; Zwiep, *Tussen tekst en lezer*, 1:334-64; Taylor, *Secular Age*, 29-41, 54-61, 112-30.

108. Van der Kooi, *Als in een spiegel*, 208-27.

109. Oswald Bayer distinguishes "Ethisierung" (Kant), "Theoretisierung" (Hegel), and "Existentialisierung" (Schleiermacher et al.). Grenz and Olsen speak about "the immanence of God in moral experience" (Kant), "the immanence of God in speculative reason" (Hegel), and "the immanence of God in religious feeling" (Schleiermacher). See Bayer, *Theologie*, 453-86; Grenz and Olson, *Twentieth-Century Theology*, 24-50.

the opposition of sin and grace. The source of the religious life of Christian believers is the influence of the powerful God-consciousness of Jesus Christ on sinners by the Holy Spirit, the common spirit of the church. Scripture is the first presentation of the Christian faith; not the foundation of the Christian faith, for the acceptance of Scripture presupposes faith. Understanding Scripture means that the reader with intuition and empathy, using all divinatory and comparative capacities, has to get access to the world behind the text of Scripture, the (religious) consciousness of the author, and his context.[110] Hegel's philosophy, finally, closely related the structure of human rational thinking with the dialectic of historical processes. According to Hegel, the divine Spirit comes to self-awareness in the process of history. Relating the Trinity with historical dialectics leads to a pantheistic historicized understanding of God. Hegel's philosophy of history influenced the historical work of biblical scholars, who found in his work a stimulus to study the historical development of truth in its context.[111]

Now, Reformed theology faced new challenges in its doctrine of Scripture. In the first phase of the development of the doctrine of Scripture, a theocentric approach was standard amid all the confessional polemics. God exists and reveals his self-knowledge to us in his inspired word. Now, many new questions have to be answered. Can humans transcend their human religiosity and know God really? And even, does God exist? Where do we find the knowledge of God? Is God acting in history and does he reveal himself to humanity? Is Scripture a trustworthy source of knowledge of God or does Scripture only contain human religious feelings and experiences? Are the knowledge of God and our interpretation of this knowledge always fallible and subject to historical relativity, or is it possible to obtain absolute certainty in the knowledge of God? This new context and these new questions bring the doctrine of Scripture into a new phase.

In Germany, England, North America, and the Netherlands Reformed theologians responded to these developments. Abraham Kuyper (1837–1920) was one of them. They came to emphasize the necessity of God's saving act in the history of salvation. Revelation became the stronghold for Christians to speak meaningfully about God: the God of the Scriptures was opposed to the human religious consciousness, that only expresses its own experiences and continues to develop over time. Furthermore, the turn toward the subject and consequential questions about the possibility of knowing reality out there led orthodox theologians to develop a certain form of

110. Bartholomew, *Introducing Biblical Hermeneutics*, 305–8; Schleiermacher, *Christliche Glaube*; Zwiep, *Tussen tekst en lezer*, 1:398–421.

111. Bartholomew, *Introducing Biblical Hermeneutics*, 212–13, 218–21; Grenz and Olson, *Twentieth-Century Theology*, 31–38.

realism. In this realism, however, the object and the subject were still separated from each other. Again, theological epistemology and the doctrine of Scripture developed together, in interaction with modern foundationalism. In analogy to modern foundationalism, theology searched to show in the prolegomena that theological knowledge is based on a solid and firm foundation.[112] In what follows I will analyze a rectorial address by Abraham Kuyper, where he addresses these problems and presents his responses.

2.7 ABRAHAM KUYPER: THE BIBLICAL CRITICISM OF THE PRESENT DAY (1881)

2.7.1 Against the Revolution in Theology

Abraham Kuyper was both modern and anti-modern. He was a believing Christian and at the same time a modern organizer belonging to Charles Taylor's "age of mobilization," working with Reformed principles and building on a Reformed foundation.[113] This mixture of modernity and anti-modernity is present in his rectorial address "The Biblical Criticism of the Present Day," Abraham Kuyper reacted strongly against what he saw as "the revolution in theology."[114] This revolution is the theological expression of what the French Revolution represented in politics and society. In Kuyper's view, a "philosophical revolution-principle" was at work in theology, especially in the doctrine of Scripture and in biblical criticism.[115] Here, he mentions Friedrich Schleiermacher (1768–1834), Wiliam Robertson Smith (1846–94), Abraham Kuenen (1827–91), and John Colenso (1814–83).

---

112. On the various reactions in Germany (Ernst Wilhelm Hengstenberg, 1802–1869) and in America (Princeton and Westminster Schools), see, e.g., Bartholomew, *Introducing Biblical Hermeneutics*, 228–29; Van den Belt, *Authority of Scripture*, 179–228; Huijgen, *Lezen en laten lezen*, 17–19, 20–51, 116–26, 157–59; Perry, "Dissolving the Inerrancy Debate"; Rogers, *Authority and Interpretation of the Bible*, 323–79; Seeman, "'Old Princetonians'"; Staalduine-Sulman, "Evangelical Movement and the Enlightenment"; Trimp, "Amerikaans fundamentalisme"; Zwiep, *Tussen tekst en lezer*, 2:41–46.

113. Bratt, "Abraham Kuyper"; Bratt, *Abraham Kuyper*, xiv–xvii; Taylor, *Secular Age*, 459.

114. Kuyper, "Biblical Criticism," 415.

115. Kuyper, "Biblical Criticism," 417. On the historical background of this rectoral address, see Augustijn, "Kuypers rede." On its theological importance, see Berkhof, "Neocalvinistische theologie van Kuyper," 32–34; Van Bekkum, "Zekerheid en schriftgezag," 94–96; Veenhof, "Honderd jaar theologie," 50–51. More generally on Kuyper's doctrine of Scripture, see Van Keulen, "Internal Tension"; Van Keulen, *Bijbel en dogmatiek*, 20–67.

The most characteristic of Kuyper's view of the spirit of revolution is that it "has transposed the entire human consciousness in every department of life."[116] For theology, this implies that God's Word spoken from "God's own self-consciousness"[117] is no longer the source of knowledge of God, but the human consciousness of God. Conscious knowledge of God springs "from the unconscious mystery of the soul,"[118] by "impressions on the conscience, or impulses of feeling," or "by the inoculation of a lymph of life."[119]

This transposition has consequences for one's view of the Bible and inspiration. "[T]he Holy Scripture as a book of divine authority"[120] is abolished and a difference no longer exists between inspiration and illumination. Kuyper refers to the German theologian Richard Rothe (1799–1867). According to Rothe, the Holy Spirit may elevate sinful human life as he did with the writers of the Bible, "which made their consciousness of God more clear, and from this brightened consciousness of God they were able to produce rich and new thoughts."[121] But Rothe

> held that there can be no mention of an infallibility of Scripture; that most of the writers, but never the Scripture itself, can be called inspired; that inspiration differs greatly in degree among the writers severally; and that therefore the explanation given by the apostles of the Scripture of the Old Covenant often seems to him incorrect; that their representation of Christian truth cannot be taken to be normative for us per se; and that, which is especially noteworthy, even the image, the picture, given us of the Christ is not of itself possessed of a guarantee of being a faithful reproduction.[122]

As a result of this view of knowledge of God,

> you have no right to value your perceptions as being essentially higher than ours: they do not differ specifically, but at most only in degree of development; in the religious life also there is a Darwinistic process. And thus the wall of separation between the holy and the profane fell away; the chasm between the sacred and the common was filled in; idolatries were not taken as the religions of the nations; and, together with the sacred writings

---

116. Kuyper, "Biblical Criticism," 415.
117. Kuyper, "Biblical Criticism," 416.
118. Kuyper, "Biblical Criticism," 416.
119. Kuyper, "Biblical Criticism," 417.
120. Kuyper, "Biblical Criticism," 433.
121. Kuyper, "Biblical Criticism," 437.
122. Kuyper, "Biblical Criticism," 437.

of other people, the sacred books of Israel were tested by the touchstone of all profane literature.[123]

Theology is changed into the "science of religion" without any clear, absolute, normative knowledge of God. Moreover, the doctrine of Scripture is no longer part of the prolegomena, but "removed from the gable of dogmatics, and be given a place in the transept of the *media gratiae.*"[124]

To summarize, the revolution in theology is a shift from God's consciousness to the human religious consciousness, from the word of God as *principium theologiae* to human religiosity as the source of knowledge of God, from a view of the word of God as inspired by the Holy Spirit to the result of religious impressions of pious humans, and from theology to religious studies.

Kuyper pictures the consequences of this shift in dramatic language. He compares the detailed historical-critical analysis of the Bible to "microscopical analysis" without "holy synthesis,"[125] or to "vivisection," forbidden when the human body is concerned but allowed as biblical criticism.[126] He formulates his speech as one large complaint against the modern and ethical theologians[127] of his age. According to Kuyper, "to be ethical of tendency and clear seem never capable of going hand in hand."[128] They leave the church with a theology that is no longer theology. How can young men who have studied this theology start working as ministers in the church? Kuyper writes,

> You offer her a science which has no connection with her confession, and you send her pastors who, however learned and reverend, if in other ways they are serious, must confess shamefacedly their ignorance of the things of the Spirit, and, instead of feeding the church, must needs be fed and warmed by her. And so it is no wonder, that diseases in the church are on the increase hand over hand, that sects are multiplying, that practice does not follow the teaching, and that "shepherd and flock," distrustful of each other, stand mutually opposed, instead of

---

123. Kuyper, "Biblical Criticism," 418–19.
124. Kuyper, "Biblical Criticism," 415.
125. Kuyper, "Biblical Criticism," 414.
126. Most explicitly Kuyper, "Biblical Criticism," 666–67; and further 413, 420, 677, 685, 686.
127. The so-called "ethical" theologians were Dutch theologians comparable to the German "Vermittlungstheologie."
128. Kuyper, "Biblical Criticism," 434.

> unitedly enjoying the glory of Jesus' name. Even society at large, the country, suffers by it. For a spiritual circle which finds its image in a marsh, instead of in a clear lake, throws out of necessity poisonous vapors, which spoil the national spirit. By robbing the church of her theology, she is robbed also of that wonderful power of thought which made us Calvinists for ages together an invincible stronghold in the midst of the land; and, by presenting wandering ethical ideas in the stead of the nourishing bread of practical theology, discipline and order are undermined, and the moral sense of justice is weakened.[129]

Even nationalist feelings are mobilized to support his argument. Calvinists made Holland a free nation, this revolutionary spirit however demolished the free and strong spirit of Dutch Calvinism. "As a free-born son of a nation which purchased its liberty from Spain,"[130] Kuyper argues, he has to protest against this vivisection of Scripture.

2.7.2 Kuyper's Alternative

In another passage, we start to discover what Kuyper is seeking. He wants to allow a strong Christian life, one born out of a deep conviction, to flourish. He writes,

> For to obtain real peace, an unshakable faith, and a full development of powers, our soul must, in the depth of depths and forsaken of all men, depend on God Almighty alone. To draw one's being immediately from God's own hand, consciously and continuously, this renders one invincible, enables one to become heroic, and makes us surpass ourselves. This was the secret of the power by which Calvinism once astonished the world. That forms character, steels the will with energy, and sets man, the citizen, the confessor of Jesus, truly free.[131]

---

129. Kuyper, "Biblical Criticism," 420–21.

130. Kuyper, "Biblical Criticism," 686. Veenhof mentions that according to Kuyper, the decline of theology in the Netherlands was caused by foreign (German) influences. See Veenhof, "Honderd jaar theologie," 46.

131. Kuyper, "Biblical Criticism," 678. Here we see the experience of faith functioning as one of Kuyper's starting points, although Augustijn denies this is the case. See Augustijn, "Kuypers rede," 119. The same is the case when Kuyper starts his second part and tells how he reads the Bible together with the other members of the congregations, see Augustijn, "Kuypers rede," 422–25.

EPISTEMOLOGY AND CERTAINTY

Here we discover two central motives of Kuyper's own position: dependence on God alone[132] and an unshakable faith.[133] The first motive of dependence on God alone has a clear antimodern direction, against the modern perceived disappearance of God's activity in the world.[134] Kuyper's prayer at the beginning of his address exemplifies this motive:

> And may He, before whose glory I reverently bow and for the welfare of whose church I plead, be in this the inspirer of my word and the judge of my thoughts; while in this sacred task, also, our help is in the name of the Lord Jehovah, the Rock of our strength, and the Strength of our life.[135]

Kuyper not only presents himself as a strong Dutch Calvinist but also as a pious simple "day-laborer" who is addressed personally by the Lord my God when he reads the Bible.[136] He is one "with the simple-minded people of God confessing my ignorance"[137] while feeling the "zeal of God come over me."[138]

The dependence upon God and especially upon God's Spirit returns again and again. It comprises the entire movement from God's conscious self-knowledge (*theologia archetypa*) via revelation, inspiration, regeneration, and illumination to human conscious knowledge of God (*theologia ectypa*) as a result of the reading and interpretation of Scripture. Kuyper writes,

> In anthropology, man is the centrum, and the Almighty is considered only as the interpretation of the religious sense; but in theology, God himself is the centrum, and no mention of man is justified, except in so far as God uses him for his own sake.
>
> Again, in all other sciences man observes and thoughtfully investigates the object, and subjects it to himself, but in theology the object itself is active; it does not stand open, but gives itself to be seen; does not allow itself to be investigated, but reveals

---

132. Cf. Van der Schee, "Kuyper's Archimedes' Point."

133. Van Keulen, "Internal Tension," 129–30; Van Keulen, *Bijbel en dogmatiek*, 31–33, 43–44, 61–62.

134. Cf. Kuyper, *Biblical Criticism*, 673: "The 'wisdom of the world' constantly seeks to reduce the immediate work of God in history to ever smaller dimensions and cannot rest until the factor 'God' has entirely disappeared from the same."

135. Kuyper, "Biblical Criticism," 410.

136. Kuyper, "Biblical Criticism," 422.

137. Kuyper, "Biblical Criticism," 676.

138. Kuyper, "Biblical Criticism," 677.

itself; and employs thinking man as instrument only to cause the knowledge of his Being to radiate.[139]

The Bible as a book, as such, is not especially valuable. Kuyper does not isolate Scripture from its relation with God. Only in relation with God, when the Holy Spirit casts his light of illumination on it, does Scripture become precious.[140] Kuyper compares this to a beautiful diamond seen in its beauty only if the light is shining on it. Furthermore, although he writes that the image is profane, he nevertheless uses the image of a telephone, suggesting that through the book God is speaking as someone speaks from a distance through the telephone.[141] In opposition to the active knowing subject of modernity, Kuyper places God who makes himself known to human beings.[142]

This knowledge of God is the central element in Kuyper's view of an unshakable faith, his second motive. In his emphasis on absolute, determinate, certain knowledge, Kuyper follows modernity's quest by focusing on epistemological questions. In his lecture, Kuyper does not often use foundational imagery: only twice does Kuyper refer to theology as a building.[143] Significant, however, is the foundational twist Kuyper gives to the image of a rock in a passionate passage dealing with human anxiety and thirst for certainty. Whereas in the Bible the image of a rock is used personally referring to God as a rock, Kuyper uses the image of a rock referring to the Scriptures.

> Thus a conflict is waged as of giant forces in his breast, and that oppresses him; he sees no way of escape; he faints beneath its tension, except He who is compassionate takes compassion on him, and sets him up upon the Rock of the Word. Only when he stands on that Word, does the oil of gladness drip in his soul instead of mourning, and the garments of praise begin to shine forth in place of the spirit of heaviness, and the man breaks forth in singing the praises of Him who has set him free from bonds;

---

139. Kuyper, "Biblical Criticism," 411; cf. 669.

140. Elsewhere, Kuyper writes, "To him who does not feel that, at the moment when he opens the Holy Scripture, God comes by and in it and touches his very soul, the Scripture is not yet the Word of God, or has ceased to be this; or it is this in his spiritual moments, but not at other times, as when the veil lies again on his heart, while again it is truly such when the veil is taken away." See Kuyper, *Encyclopedia of Sacred Theology*, 364.

141. Kuyper, "Biblical Criticism," 424. In 1894 Kuyper used the telephone metaphor again but in that instance without mentioning its profanity. See Kuyper, *Encyclopedia of Sacred Theology*, 364.

142. Cf. Veenhof, "Honderd jaar theologie," 49–50.

143. Kuyper, "Biblical Criticism," 411, 669. In his *Encyclopedia*, Kuyper does use this foundational imagery, see Kuyper, *Encyclopedia of Sacred Theology*, 155–56, 161, 164.

also from those oppressing bonds of dependency upon man, who at best is but a creature of dust.[144]

Moreover, the core of his address is his defense of the Scriptures as a firm foundation for absolute, certain knowledge of God. Kuyper makes a comparison between the Scriptures and God's work of creation:

> It is a mystery of love and comfort which can be explained only when each and every writer, whose inestimable grace and honor it was to record a larger or smaller part of that Scripture, was not his own master in the writing, but only rendered service as an instrument of the Holy Ghost, and was so wrought upon and directed by the Holy Ghost, that the page of Scripture, which, after pencil and pen had been laid aside, lay before him, contained and was possessed of equal fixedness, as though it had originated by an immediate, divine creation.[145]

Kuyper does not claim the inerrancy of Scripture. Nevertheless, he writes "it would be presumptuous and disrespectful" to exclude that the autographs were infallible. Kuyper acknowledges the possibility that the autographs were without error. In any case, we cannot exclude that they were faultless.[146]

Further, the rhetorical structure of his argument evidences that absolutely certain knowledge is at the heart of his address. In the first encyclopedic part, Kuyper safeguards that theological knowledge is built on determinate communication of truth from God's self-consciousness by God himself in a form appropriate to our consciousness. The second step of Kuyper's argument consists of an exposition of his doctrine of the inspiration of Scripture. Kuyper aims to defend that God spoke "with indeclinable certainty in the highest form, viz. in that of the Conscious Word."[147] After the explanation of inspiration, Kuyper concludes:

> Hence the result is, that, apart from the question of whether the writers realize it or not, by them as instruments a book or song or epistle was written, which in its original form, i.e., as *autographon*, bare in itself the infallible authority of having been wrought by the Holy Ghost.[148]

---

144. Kuyper, "Biblical Criticism," 678.

145. Kuyper, "Biblical Criticism," 426–27; cf. 425. More generally on Kuyper's doctrine of inspiration, see Van Keulen, *Bijbel en dogmatiek*, 28–36.

146. Kuyper, "Biblical Criticism," 671.

147. Kuyper, "Biblical Criticism," 425.

148. Kuyper, "Biblical Criticism," 432.

According to Kuyper, the central issue is whether "the fact of inspiration remains untouched and its result immovable." Again, we see the centrality of the motive of certain knowledge. He writes,

> The divine fixedness over against the uncertainty of all human ponderings is chiefly that which makes the Holy Scripture "holy," i.e., a bible for the church of God.[149]

The important question in studying the Scripture is

> only and exclusively whether it leaves us in the possession of such an inspiration of the Scripture, whose result offers us for its entire content the unweakened guarantee of divine certainty.[150]

Kuyper continues with a critical discussion of modern and ethical theology. Here again, his focus is on the defense of Scripture as the principle of our knowledge of God. He states very clearly a diametrical antithesis between the spirit of the world and the philosophy of our age on the one hand and the Spirit of God on the other hand. The spirit of this world bends "its energies toward the breaking down of the authority of the Scripture."[151] He concludes his discussion with his diagnosis of the spiritual impulse of his age "to transpose in every way the '*Deushomo*' into the '*Homo-deus*,'" a "humanizing of the Scriptures."[152]

He then finishes his treatment of inspiration with a short discussion of several problems that might threaten this divine certainty. The introduction of this discussion is significant:

> That, after the subtraction of all this, there still remain serious objections at several points to the absoluteness of the inspiration of the Scripture, we neither deny nor hide, even though one readily sees to what small dimensions this mountain of insurmountable obstacles has already fallen away.[153]

What others see as a huge threat to absolute certainty, is minimized to tiny proportions by Kuyper. Then follows the third part, which starts with the most passionate defense of our human need for absolute certainty. "A troubled soul, tossed with tempest and not comforted, is filled with anxiety, and thirsts after certainty."[154] But immediately from God's hand, we receive the

---

149. Kuyper, "Biblical Criticism," 433.
150. Kuyper, "Biblical Criticism," 433.
151. Kuyper, "Biblical Criticism," 668.
152. Kuyper, "Biblical Criticism," 674–75.
153. Kuyper, "Biblical Criticism," 675.
154. Kuyper, "Biblical Criticism," 677–78.

life that "renders one invincible, enables one to become heroic, and makes us surpass ourselves."[155]

Once again, Kuyper discusses the problems that threaten this absolute certainty: the number of books in the canon, the errors in the received text of Scripture, the fact that we usually need a translation, and the problem of interpretation. These four problems constitute a serious threat to the epistemological model. They question the absoluteness of the foundation, our possibility of knowing this foundation, and our capacity to draw absolute and certain conclusions from this foundation. Kuyper solves these serious difficulties by transcending the horizon of the human quest for certainty. Within our human horizon, we only find *fides humana*, no "absolute faith."[156] However, God gives a more than satisfying treatment of these problems. It is the immediate divine witness of the *testimonium spiritus sancti* that guarantees absolute assurance:

> A witness of the Holy Spirit which is born, as Calvin puts it, when that same God the Holy Spirit who spoke centuries ago through the mouth of the apostles and prophets enters into my heart, and by a supranatural witness imparts to me the indisputable assurance: I, God-myself, have inspired this Scripture, this divine Word.[157]

It is the Holy Spirit who provides the necessary assurance.

The result of this transcending move is an unsatisfying theoretical discussion of the four mentioned problems. Here, Kuyper's lecture demonstrates the problematic character of attempts to justify practical or existential certainties by translating them into certainties of theoretical thinking, thus confusing a theoretical concept of absolute certainty with a practical concept of deep-rooted convictions. He does not admit that his discussion of the four problems is unsatisfactory, nor does he acknowledge the resulting epistemic uncertainties. Instead, the internal testimony of the Holy Spirit functions on the theoretical level as a reflection stopper. Further, one might ask whether we feel the Cartesian anxiety in Kuyper's dealing with these problems: is his strategy a symptom of fear? Although it is difficult to answer this psychological question, it is significant that Kuyper himself pictures the absolute certainty in question as an answer to human anxiety.[158]

---

155. Kuyper, "Biblical Criticism," 678.
156. Kuyper, "Biblical Criticism," 682.
157. Kuyper, "Biblical Criticism," 683.
158. Kuyper, "Biblical Criticism," 678. According to Augustijn, Kuyper was afraid of these problems. J. Kamphuis denies this is the case, but he does not confront himself with the unsatisfying theoretical treatment of the problems that pose serious problems

Kuyper's rhetorical strategy demonstrates the influence of the modern quest for epistemic certainty.

In Kuyper's treatment of these problems, we see a combination of the two motives: dependence on God alone for absolute, determinate, certain knowledge. The two motives are intertwined in what might be called a pneumatologically embedded foundationalism. Together, the graphical inspiration of the Scriptures and the internal testimony of the Spirit safeguard absolute certainty.[159] It is clear from the beginning of his address that this is Kuyper's position when he says:

> Hence the confession of God, the Holy Spirit, speaks of him also as ‘ο θεόλογος, *Ecclesiae Doctor*; "the things of God knoweth no man, but the Spirit of God," "for the Spirit searcheth all things. Yea, the deep things of God" (1 Cor. ii. 10); and all real theology is essentially one beautiful building which, in all ages and among all nations, has been reared, according to a fixed plan, by that *Spiritus Architectonicus* whom we, who are called theologians, merely assist as upper servants.[160]

In his *Encyclopedia*, though we find the same foundationalism, Kuyper has further developed the pneumatological embedding. When dealing with science in a fallen world, he uses two types of imagery. First, Kuyper uses organic imagery to distinguish between two kinds of people, due to the *paliggenesia*: the people of the wild vine and the regenerated people of the true vine.[161] This pneumatological emphasis is elaborated christologically. According to Kuyper, humanity has a general subject which is the subject of science. An individual scientist is organically related to this general subject. The general subject of renewed humanity is Christ. In him, the revealed knowledge of God is taken up into the human consciousness.[162] Secondly,

---

to a foundationalist model. Van Bekkum also states that Kuyper was not afraid of modern biblical studies and questions the relevance of such a psychological interpretation. Nevertheless, Van Bekkum also leaves open the possibility that fear played a role and signals the theoretical weaknesses in Kuyper's model. See Augustijn, "Kuypers rede," 120, 142; Van Bekkum, "Zekerheid en schriftgezag," 94, 97, 100, 103, 107–8; Kamphuis, *Signalen uit de kerkgeschiedenis*, 183.

159. Cf. Van Keulen, *Bijbel en dogmatiek*, 33, 42–44.

160. Kuyper, "Biblical Criticism," 411.

161. Kuyper, *Encyclopedia of Sacred Theology*, 150–54.

162. Kuyper, *Encyclopedia of Sacred Theology*, 67, 85, 101, 150, 283–88, 291–92, 296, 584. Hence, Van Bekkum's sketch of a development from a christological view of the Scriptures in 1870 to a pneumatological view in 1880 has to be completed with the development of a christological and pneumatological view in his *Encyclopedia* in 1894. Cf. Van Bekkum, "Zekerheid en schriftgezag," 98–99.

Kuyper uses the image of two different buildings to refer to two kinds of science with two different starting points.¹⁶³ The image of a house with a foundation, referring to science, is combined with the christological-pneumatological image of the new organism of humanity. The same combination of organic and foundational imagery is more frequently found in Kuyper's work, e.g., *Geworteld en gegrond*.¹⁶⁴

2.7.3 Evaluation

What we find in Kuyper is on the one hand an anti-modern defense of God's activity in the world and hence of God's activity in theology. According to Bowald, the eclipse of God's agency is one of the big problems of the epistemology of modernity.¹⁶⁵ He values a hermeneutic that acknowledges the divine activity. Accordingly, we should positively value the opposition to the spirit of a modern revolution in theology, and the emphasis on the work of the triune God, in Kuyper's thought. On the other hand, Kuyper is influenced by modernity's quest for absolute certainty and gives a formal defense of Scripture that fits very well in the conservative type of theological responses to modern theology and historical criticism.¹⁶⁶ In the anti-modern and anti-revolutionary defense of the believer's dependence on God (his first motive) he uses the very modern model of foundationalism to justify the possibility of an unshakable faith (his second motive).

The influence of this modern quest for absolutely certain knowledge can be seen in Kuyper's treatment of Scripture. He shares the focus on epistemological questions and foundationalism's ideal of absolutely certain knowledge. Kuyper tries to give a theoretical justification of the existential assurance of faith; a deep conviction that is always born in relation to our actions in practical contexts but that is now translated into a theoretical concept of absolute theoretical certainty. As we saw above (2.2), such theoretical attempts to establish final foundations lead to the "Münchhausen Trilemma" of three unsatisfying options: an infinite regress, a logical

---

163. Kuyper, *Encyclopedia of Sacred Theology*, 155.

164. Kuyper, *Geworteld en gegrond*. As "Rooted and Grounded" in Kuyper, *On the Church*.

165. Bowald, *Rendering the Word*, 1–23.

166. Cf. Augustijn, "Kuypers rede," 119, 121, 142–44; Van Bekkum, "Zekerheid en schriftgezag," 94–95, 104, 106–8; Van Keulen, *Bijbel en dogmatiek*, 61–64.

Kuyper's conflict with the "ethical" theologian J. H. Gunning, close to Kuyper and different from him, shows that Kuyper had the possibility to choose an alternative; see Augustijn, "Kuypers rede," 112–29; Mietus, *Gunning en Kuyper in 1878*.

circle, or an abrupt termination without good reasons.[167] The third option is found as a reality in Kuyper's rectorial address. Scripture can never give the demanded absolute certainty, due to problems concerning the number of books in the canon and the received text of Scripture, the difference between the original text and its translation, and questions of interpretation. Kuyper knew this but did not really face these problems. We might feel the Cartesian anxiety, where Kuyper explicitly refers to anxiety as well as where he deals with problems that threaten absolute certainty. In any case, his discussion of these problems is not satisfying from a theoretical perspective. Furthermore, a satisfying theoretical justification of the choice for the Bible as an epistemological foundation cannot be given.[168] Kuyper could not solve these problems theoretically but presented the immediate divine witness of the *testimonium spiritus sancti* as its solution (albeit insufficient at a theoretical level).

Significant is furthermore, that in this formal defense of Scripture, the content of the gospel of Jesus Christ itself does not play a role in the argument. This is remarkable given that the young Kuyper longed for a return to the subject matter of the Scriptures, back from the bibliolatry of the Reformed Orthodoxy that reduced the Scriptures to a collection of divine words.[169] This does not change when Kuyper in his *Encyclopedia* refers to the relationship with Christ as the general subject of renewed humanity. This relation makes clear that the believer as a knowing subject participates in Christ. However, it does not change the (formal) argument for the significance of Scripture.

2.8 FROM EPISTEMOLOGY TO SOTERIOLOGY

2.8.1 Retrospect

Reformed theology and modernity are like sisters who lived together for a long time and have much in common. From their common roots in the Middle Ages to the twentieth century, they shared an interest in epistemology and a quest for certainty. Both began in the epistemological debates on the principles of the *scientiae* in the Middle Ages. However, two phases

---

167. Dalferth, *Gedeutete Gegenwart*, 154–55; Dalferth, *Wirklichkeit des Möglichen*, 359–60.

168. Murphy, *Beyond Liberalism and Fundamentalism*, 14, 80; Wolterstorff, *Reason within the Bounds of Religion*, 58–62.

169. Augustijn, "Kuypers rede," 111; Van Bekkum, "Zekerheid en schriftgezag," 98; Veenhof, "Honderd jaar theologie," 52.

have to be distinguished in their theological developments. Both phases contributed to the primacy of epistemology, as the doctrine of Scripture was developed out of epistemological interests. Furthermore, in both phases, a quest for certainty is evidently present.

In the first phase, an authority conflict was the center of the debate: who has the final authority in the church—Scripture, the church fathers, the magisterium, or the individual believer hearing the voice of the Spirit? After the polemics of the Reformation and the breakup of the church, all West-European confessional streams developed their own answer to this question. Outside the church, philosophers formulated their secular answers to a comparable quest for reliable sources of knowledge, referring to reason, natural law or later the human will, emotions, or empirical data. In Reformed theology, this has led to the development of a doctrine of Scripture that justified the final authority of Scripture for church and theology.

In the second phase, after the Enlightenment, the context was changed due to new questions concerning the existence and knowledge of God and the development of historical criticism in biblical studies. Now, Protestant theology further diversified. Accepting the turn to the subject, a theology should adopt as its starting point the human moral sense (Kant), speculative thought (Hegel), or religious capacities (Schleiermacher). This led to the further development of liberal theology in all its variety. At the right wing of the theological spectrum, Lutherans, Reformed, and Evangelicals developed their own answers. Kuyper and the Neo-Calvinists were among them.

The context had changed. Modern philosophy had become a possible dialogue partner. Both modern questions and modern answers influenced these Protestant theologians. As can be seen in Kuyper's work, he wants to demonstrate where knowledge of God can be found, that Scripture is a reliable source of knowledge, and that this knowledge of God is absolutely certain, because of the testimony of the Holy Spirit. New epistemological questions lead to renewed reflections on Scripture, and to an affirmation of the absolute certain character of the knowledge of God that believers receive.

Although the context was different, the position of Kuyper stands in clear continuity with Owen. Kuyperians and Neo-Calvinists are often seen as too modern and too rational by more experiential ("bevindelijke"), Puritan Reformed theologians.[170] Kuyper and Owen, however, share the

---

170. For a caricatural but insightful critique of Neo-Calvinism from a Puritan, Presbyterian perspective Young, "Historic Calvinism and Neo-Calvinism." In the Netherlands, Reformed Christians from an "bevindelijke," experiential background also did not trust Kuyper. However, the estrangement between Kuyper on the one hand and the later members of the Dutch *Christelijke Gereformeerde Kerk* as well as of the

same formal argument for the defense of Scripture in which Jesus Christ and his gospel play no role. They have a common longing for certainty and a common emphasis on divine testimony and infallible certainty. Both do not suffer from the "eclipse of God's agency" but give a pneumatological embedding of their doctrine of Scripture.

A difference does exist between the Reformed and Evangelical theologians who defend the inerrancy of Scripture and those who confess the infallibility of Scripture. Here, Owen's argument for the perfection of the original text and the inspiration of the Masoretic punctuation comes closer to inerrancy than Kuyper's. Owen's argument differs a little from Kuyper's statement that the perfection of the original manuscripts cannot be denied. Owen shared the belief of many Reformed theologians that the original manuscripts were without faults. However, Kuyper did not defend the inerrancy of Scripture, although in the same year 1881, as Kuyper gave his rectorial address, Archibald A. Hodge (1823–86) and Benjamin B. Warfield (1851–1921) published their article on inerrancy.[171] The inerrancy became a controversy among Reformed theologians. Kuyper and Bavinck rejected inerrancy, although they affirmed the infallibility of Scripture.[172] However, both Kuyper and Owen are reluctant to accept epistemic uncertainties, as they see them as a threat to the certainty of faith.

At the same time, we find in Owen and Kuyper elements that remain important and can be used in further developing the doctrine of Scripture. Both resist the eclipse of divine agency. Scripture is embedded in the acts of the Father, Son, and Spirit. John Owen's use of 2 Cor 3 and 4 could provide us with a basic framework for understanding Scripture as part of a Trinitarian soteriology. In Scripture, we see the light of Christ, and the Holy Spirit uses this light to enlighten our minds. The noetic consequences of sin demand the necessity of a soteriological approach. Without the Spirit, we will not see the light of Christ.

Still, as has been shown Owen and Kuyper both are part of the long development of the doctrine of Scripture out of epistemological interests and a quest for certainty. They did not invent both but shared them with

---

Gereformeerde Bond within the *Nederlands Hervormde Kerk* was not caused by issues related to the doctrine of Scripture. See Van der Graaf, "Hoe en waarom," 67–69; Van 't Spijker, "Enkele hoofdlijnen," 23–33; Veenhof, "Openbaring. Geschiedenis. Bijbel," 150–51.

171. Hodge and Warfield, *Inspiration*.

172. On inerrancy (and the difference with infallibility), see Huijgen, *Lezen en laten lezen*, 157–73; McGowan, *Divine Spiration of Scripture*, 84–164; Rogers, *Authority and Interpretation of the Bible*, 323–405; Seeman, "'Old Princetonians'"; Trimp, "Amerikaans fundamentalisme"; Woodbridge, "German Pietism and Scriptural Authority."

many other theologians. The fact that especially from Schleiermacher on, many theologians made other choices, does not prove that they were wrong. Kuyper explicitly rejected the possibility of giving the doctrine of Scripture its place in soteriology and maintained the doctrine of Scripture in the *prolegomena* of theology. Thus, an open question needs to be answered: what is the problem of the traditional Reformed approach of locating the doctrine of Scripture in the *prolegomena*?

2.8.2 Problems

Some of the problems of this approach are connected to the primacy of epistemology, others to the quest for certainty. I will start with the problematic character of the epistemological nature of the doctrine of Scripture.

1. An epistemological starting point is no longer effective because our context has changed. During the Reformation, debates about the doctrine of Scripture were in-house Christian discussions between Roman Catholics, Anabaptists, and Reformed Christians in a conflict on authority. In such a Christian context with many shared background beliefs, a start with epistemology is not problematic. But the Christian faith lost its majority position, the questions have changed, and the interest in theoretical issues has diminished. The modern questioning of the possibility of knowledge of God resulted in a shift in focus: the problem of the knowledge of God became the central question. Pluralization and secularization made these questions more intense. At the same time, as theoretical questions they lost part of their urgency, as in our postmodern cultural climate a shift has been made from theory to practice, and spirituality or practical relevance has moved to the foreground. In a pluralist context, it has become clear what a theological epistemology presupposes. We discover that the house carries its foundation, as Wittgenstein wrote.[173] A theology that begins with the doctrine of Scripture suggests that epistemology is a primary and foundational activity, instead of a secondary and reflective activity, that critically reflects on the process of theological thinking.

2. In this new context, a theology that starts with Scripture evokes many unanswered questions:

> a. Why should we read the Bible as Holy Scripture? We live no longer in a Christian Europe where the Bible is the sacred book of the majority of the population. In a formal defense of the authority of Scripture, the revelation and authority of God are important arguments—*Deus*

---

173. Wittgenstein, *On Certainty*, sec. 248.

dixit. However, this leaves open whether God can reveal himself and speak to us, but also why we should believe that he revealed himself in the books of Israel and Jesus's disciples, rather than in the Qur'an or another book. Finally, we need to confront the question of why we should accept the authority of a sacred book at all. Here the preference for a formal defense of Scripture shows its weaknesses. The saving character of the good news of Jesus Christ and its content should play an important role when these questions are to be answered.

b. Why this old book? For the Reformers who were humanists as well, it was a great joy to return to the original sources. We live after the development of historical consciousness and are aware of the historical distance. Furthermore, to many of us, old knowledge is superseded knowledge. Why should we read such an old book as the Bible? Again, to answer these questions we need material-theological arguments, e.g., about God's eternity, about the universal significance of Jesus Christ as representative of humanity, or about the work of the Holy Spirit who unites the church of all times and places to Jesus Christ, her head.

c. Where is God? For the theologians from the twelfth to the seventeenth century, the existence of God was above all doubt. We, however, live in a pluralist and maybe secular age, and make efforts to realize what Abraham Kuyper expressed as follows:

> To him who does not feel that, at the moment when he opens the Holy Scripture, God comes by and in it and touches his very soul, the Scripture is not yet the Word of God or has ceased to be this.[174]

To understand the authority of Scripture, a Trinitarian embedding is needed: we believe the gospel because it is God the Father who speaks, God the Son who is the Word of God in whose identity and mind we come to share, and God the Spirit who guides us in all truth and makes us understand.

3. Other problems concern the elaboration of the doctrine of Scripture itself.

a. In Reformed dogmatics, from scholasticism until Neo-Calvinism, the doctrine of Scripture has become part of the prolegomena. As a result, reflection on revelation and Scripture is isolated from other

---

[174]. Kuyper, *Encyclopedia of Sacred Theology*, 364.

theological themes, like the doctrines of the Trinity, salvation, church, and means of grace. As a result, Scripture can be easily seen as self-sufficient and the text of Scripture is isolated from God's saving self-presentation. This, however, is misleading because Scripture is not self-sufficient.[175] A theological epistemology needs the doctrine of the Trinitarian God, including soteriology. Due to the noetic consequences of sin, a theological epistemology presupposes salvation.

b. Formal questions concerning the possibility of knowledge of God, authority, and historical reliability come to the fore. They are answered especially in a formal, epistemological way, referring to revelation, inspiration, and divine testimony. Owen denied that a material argument for the authority of Scripture as the Word of God could be decisive.

c. As a consequence, Jesus Christ and his gospel are discussed late in the doctrine of Scripture or completely absent. The belief that Scripture is the word of God is abstracted from faith in Jesus Christ. More and more, the Word of God is identified with the inspired text of Scripture, and the difference between Jesus Christ as the Word of God and the book of Scripture as the word of God is forgotten. The *sola scriptura* is emphasized, but the *solus Christus* is neglected.

d. Easily the impression is raised that Christianity is a religion of a book and not of a person. Van Bruggen warns that Christianity is no "book religion." "Christians do not kiss the book, but kneel for their living Saviour in heaven," says Van Bruggen.[176] McGrath, however, signals that for some Protestants, Fundamentalists, and Evangelicals, the Bible stands at the center, as the Qur'an for Islam.[177]

4. The effect that Scripture became a book on its own evokes problems as well.

a. The Reformed *sola scriptura* easily becomes "the text alone." Luther developed his "Scripture principle" when printing was only recently developed. Scripture was especially heard Scripture (not read Scripture), because it was read aloud, preached aloud.[178] The theological implications of a media revolution should not be

---

175. Webster, *Holy Scripture*, 5–6.
176. Van Bruggen, *Kompas van het christendom*, 9.
177. McGrath, *Christianity's Dangerous Idea*, 474.
178. On the importance of hearing and preaching Scripture for Luther, see Dalferth, *Jenseits von Mythos und Logos*, 247–95; Dalferth, *Wirkendes Wort*, 72–74, 95–102, 109–16. See also Huijgen, *Lezen en laten lezen*, 27–31.

underestimated. For us, who live in a world full of books (and screens), and where positive facts and empirical data are highly valued, *sola scriptura* easily becomes "the text alone."[179] We need to explain that Scripture is more than its printed text.

b. When "the text alone" began to mean "the historical source alone" so that biblical texts were read especially with a historical interest, and when biblical studies were secularized, historical-critical studies of the Bible received a problematic character as well. A deistic worldview reading of the biblical texts with an interest in the historical world behind the text will lead to interesting historical reconstructions of the religious history of Israel and its neighbors. The Bible, however, will no longer be read as the Holy Scripture and the word of God.

c. After postmodern hermeneutics, it has become an open question whether a text on its own has a meaning. For the Reformers, the question was how the *sensus literalis* of Scripture was related to the allegorical, moral, and anagogical sense of Scripture. They never questioned the meaning of Scripture itself. For us, who are faced with the presumed death of God and the author it has become a question whether the text itself has a meaning. To answer that question, it is not enough to focus on the text. Instead, we need to zoom out to rediscover God's agency in using Scripture.[180]

5. In the Reformed doctrine of Scripture, the reader comes into view in a way too limited, in terms of faith in Scripture and illumination. In Reformation times, it was a liberation to return the Bible to the members of the church and to emphasize the priesthood of all believers. For us, living after the development of the modern and/or Protestant individual, there is a danger that the individual reader with his authentic emotions alone uses the Bible to prove whatever he wants. With McGrath, we see the threats of the dangerous idea of the Reformation: every individual has the right to interpret Scripture for himself.[181] Thus, reflection on the reader is crucial. However, the individual reader only comes into view when the testimony of

---

179. How infertile it is to deal with Scripture especially as text, becomes tangible in Wierenga, *Macht van de taal*.

180. See Vanhoozer, *First Theology*, 207–35. And more extensively Vanhoozer, *Is There a Meaning?*; Wolterstorff, *Divine Discourse*, 130–70; Van Woudenberg, *Filosofie van taal en tekst*, 105–42. For a critical discussion of Vanhoozer and "authorial discourse interpretation," see Wisse, *Scripture between Identity and Creativity*, 166–74.

181. McGrath, *Christianity's Dangerous Idea*, 2.

the Spirit is concerned. The formation of individuals within the community of the church to become good readers of Scripture tends to be forgotten.[182]

Apart from these problems related to the primacy of epistemology, the quest for certainty leads to some additional problems.

1. The existential certainty of faith in Jesus Christ is not distinguished clearly enough from the epistemic certainty of doxastic beliefs.[183] The eschatological, saving faith is a gift from the Holy Spirit. Both Owen and Kuyper know this, but they translate this practical faith in Jesus Christ into a theoretical justification of doxastic beliefs about Scripture. Furthermore, they build a theoretical, formal argument to justify beliefs about Scripture, without using material arguments and mentioning Jesus Christ. As a result, they abstract doxastic belief in Scripture as the word of God from existential faith in Jesus Christ. This is problematic for two reasons.

> a. An existential quest for certainty has to be answered but the source of this certainty is not mentioned. This is dangerous because now the question becomes whether Scripture should give what only Jesus Christ can give. In the practice of believers and how they give words to their faith, it happens that, in fact, the Bible and not Jesus Christ is the primary foundation. That means that Scripture instead of Christ has to provide the necessary assurance. We risk that the individual reader is left alone with a book that is believed to be the revelation of God with absolute certainty, or, when doubt comes in, has nothing to say anymore. Within this frame, "Cartesian anxiety" (if no absolute certainty exists, everything is uncertain) easily can become a self-fulfilling prophecy. If the quest for certainty fails, we have nothing, and relativism and subjectivism loom. Here we find indeed the domino effect, as a result of searching in a book what only a person can give.

> b. Epistemic (or hermeneutical) uncertainties now become existential uncertainties. Difficult and unsolved problems will not just undermine the desired theoretical certainty. When doxastic belief and existential faith are not clearly distinguished and Scripture instead of Jesus Christ becomes the foundation of life, epistemic uncertainties receive an urgent, existential character.

>> In an extreme form, doubts about Scripture will lead to the loss of faith. In a less extreme form, uncertainties will be denied or

---

182. On the importance of a theological account of the reader, see Sarisky, *Reading the Bible Theologically*, 44–56.

183. On the difference between eschatological faith and doxastic belief, see Dalferth, "Über Einheit und Vielfalt"; Dalferth, *Transzendenz und säkulare Welt*, 129–77.

smuggled away, for they undermine the supposed need for unquestionable absolutes. This complicates an honest reflection on themes such as how the Scriptures came into existence, the character of biblical historiography, the cultural distance between our world and the world of biblical figures, the development of the canon, textual criticism, as well as exegetical and hermeneutical problems. As a result, the dialogue between "conservative" and historical-critical scholars of the Bible is increasingly difficult.

Moreover, such a doctrine of Scripture with an emphasis on certainty will have problems with hermeneutics. Hermeneutical reflection necessarily confronts us with human finitude, the noetic consequences of sin, difficulties of translation, historical and cultural distance, the influence of power, and human self-interest. Good hermeneutical reflection aims at openness, honesty, self-criticism, the acknowledgment of relativity, and the limitations of our knowledge and understanding. This openness and honesty, however, will be an existential danger if Scripture has to provide us with existential safety instead of Jesus Christ, who is the Savior and Lord. When existential safety is found in Jesus Christ, honesty about problems with Scripture and its interpretation will be less problematic.

2. When Scripture itself has to be the source of certainty, apart from Jesus Christ the crucified Lord, no existential space is found to acknowledge the difficulties of Scripture and its interpretation. Instead, perfections have to be ascribed to the Bible, to safeguard its divine character as the source of certainty. The result is a doctrine of Scripture that is closer to a theology of glory than to a theology of the cross.

3. In understanding certainty, the difference between objectivity (revelation) and subjectivity (pneumatology) becomes a presupposition. It is impossible to find certainty in Scripture alone because the believing subject has to be certain about Scripture. Accordingly, certainty is understood both objectively and subjectively. This subjective understanding of certainty evokes the reproach of subjectivism or fideism.

2.8.3 A Way Forward

The developments in the Reformed doctrine of Scripture have resulted in a doctrine of Scripture that answers epistemological questions for theologians, authority questions for church officials, and questions of certainty without reference to Jesus Christ, the source of eternal safety. Thus, in our post-Christian, pluralist context that suffers from the loss of transcendence, dangers loom: that the doctrine of Scripture is isolated from other theological themes, that Scripture as the text becomes isolated from its context, and that the believer becomes an isolated reader of this text. As a consequence, we risk that Scripture becomes the foundation of existential certainty.

But Scripture cannot serve as a foundation that gives existential certainty, because of the epistemic uncertainties attached to Scripture itself (historical, textual, linguistic). Furthermore, as a consequence of hermeneutical problems, the epistemic justification of our beliefs by Scripture will include uncertainties as well. Most significant: a text can not act, whereas God is the divine actor. It is important to see that the metaphor of a foundation in Scripture primarily is not epistemological but soteriological and it concerns our new life while dead in our sins. It is also an ecclesiological metaphor for the new community that is created and exists in Jesus Christ (see 2.2). Only secondarily does the metaphor have epistemological implications.

The doctrine of Scripture needs to be reconstructed. What I will propose in the next chapters is a Christocentric doctrine of Scripture that presents Scripture as the Word of the good shepherd who proclaims the good news, invites us to faith in him, baptizes us with his Spirit, unites us with himself, transforms us into his likeness, and brings us home in his Father's house. Such a doctrine of Scripture will be part of soteriology instead of epistemology. Jesus Christ comes before Scripture, the *solus Christus* precedes the *sola scriptura*.

Furthermore, I will reconnect the doctrine of Scripture with the doctrine of the Trinity and with ecclesial practice. Karl Barth was the to make this connection explicitly. He discusses the Trinity in his doctrine of the Word of God. Barth wrote:

> God's Word is God Himself in His revelation. For God reveals Himself as the Lord and according to Scripture this signifies for the concept of revelation that God Himself in unimpaired unity yet also in unimpaired distinction is Revealer, Revelation, and Revealedness.[184]

The Trinitarian God is the Revealer (Father), the Revelation (Son, the Word of God), and the Revealedness—the revelation understood by believers in

---

184. "Gottes Wort ist Gott selbst in seiner Offenbarung. Denn Gott offenbart sich als der Herr und das bedeutet nach der Schrift für den Begriff der Offenbarung, daß Gott selbst in unzerstörter Einheit, aber auch in unzerstörter Verschiedenheit der Offenbarer, die Offenbarung und das Offenbarsein ist." Barth, *Kirchliche Dogmatik*, I/1, 311; Barth, *Church Dogmatics*, I/1, 298.

its significance for their existence. Thus, Barth makes the doctrine of the Trinity into a theological framework to understand both hermeneutics and Scripture. It is very well possible to connect this Trinitarian hermeneutic with important elements of the "theological interpretation of Scripture" (see 1.4) that we find in the practice of the church, where the Holy Spirit is active: canon (the unity of Scripture as a normative rule), creed (the perspective for reading Scripture faithfully), liturgy (the ecclesial context of hearing Scripture), and church ministry (church leadership that refers to Christ). In this way, a reconstruction of Scripture should be Trinitarian and ecclesiological as well.[185]

Thus, reasons to read Scripture primarily have no epistemological character. I will argue that Christians read Scripture as followers of Christ who found their salvation and their life in him and as participants in the community of the church and her practices. These soteriological and ecclesiological elements need to be used in explanations of the authority of Scripture. Material arguments have to be included in the answer to the question of why Christians listen to Scripture, for listening to Scripture is part of imitation of Christ and being his disciples.

Because existential certainty is found in Christ, honesty about epistemic uncertainties is well possible. Again, a christological connection is important: the quest for certainty relates to the weakness of the cross of Jesus Christ and to what Herman Bavinck and Gerrit C. Berkouwer have called the "servant form" of Scripture.[186] Just as it is easy to deny the significance of the cross with its weakness and ugliness, one can ignore Holy Scripture. At the same time, the weakness of Scripture and the resulting epistemic uncertainties do not have to undermine the certainty of faith. The central part of the Reformed argument of faith as assent to a divine testimony should be maintained, whereas at the same time, this position can be improved by adding motifs from a theology of the cross, emphasizing the strangeness of Scripture. Precisely because we trust the God of the cross of Jesus Christ, we can live with unanswered questions and fragmentary arguments. We can try to solve epistemological problems, but these solutions do not save us

---

185. Here, I follow Reformed theologians like Todd Billings, Kevin Vanhoozer, and John Webster. The Lutheran theologian Ingolf Dalferth proposes a comparable combination of Schleiermacher's pneumatological doctrine of Scripture with Barth's christological doctrine of Scripture. From a Pentecostal perspective, Veli-Matti Kärkkäinen approaches the trinity starting with the triune revelation. See Billings, *Word of God*; Dalferth, *Wirkendes Wort*, 35–41; Kärkkäinen, *Trinity and Revelation*; Vanhoozer, *First Theology*; Vanhoozer, "Holy Scripture"; Vanhoozer, *Drama of Doctrine*; Webster, *Word and Church*, 9–112; Webster, *Holy Scripture*; Webster, *Domain of the Word*.

186. "Dienstknechtsgestalte"; see Bavinck, *Gereformeerde dogmatiek*, 1:352; Bavinck, *Reformed Dogmatics*, 1:380; Berkouwer, *Holy Scripture*, 195–212.

from sin, devil, and death. Jesus Christ, not Scripture is our foundation. The doctrine of Scripture is part of soteriology.

3.

Secularization and Sin
Additional Reasons for a Soteriological Approach

3.1 INTRODUCTION

Chapter 2 evidences that historical developments in theology and modernity influence how we perceive questions concerning hermeneutics and Scripture. The history of theology shows that it is possible to construct the doctrine of Scripture as part of a theological epistemology and with a special interest in certainty. However, this leads to a problematic relationship with hermeneutics because hermeneutics confronts us with the uncertainties of the human nature of our knowing and understanding. A problematic relationship with hermeneutics implies a problematic relationship with the reality of how we as human beings know and understand.

In this chapter, I will further substantiate the claim that today an epistemological approach is not the best entranceway to theological hermeneutics and the doctrine of Scripture and that theological hermeneutics and the doctrine of Scripture are to be reconstructed as part of soteriology. To do so, I will offer in this chapter an orienting exploration of our human existence. As humans, we are embodied, historical, social, and linguistic creatures, facing certain questions and problems maybe. We are located at a specific place, at a certain time, within a particular community, speaking one or more languages. To exist is primarily to live, and to think theoretically is a secondary activity (and to engage in epistemology as a reflective theoretical activity). Furthermore, our existence is not automatically open to God, our creator. It is easy to live in the Western world as if God does not exist. This chapter aims to clarify why our existence is not by itself open to

God. During this exploration of what it means to live a human existence, the importance of a soteriological approach will become clearer. At the end of the chapter, I will conclude that the findings of this chapter constitute two additional reasons for such a soteriological approach.

Although I will argue for a soteriological approach, this chapter itself will not have an explicit soteriological character. One could argue very well that an existential orientation needs the light of the gospel of Jesus Christ. In the light of his salvation and the new existence in Jesus Christ, our perspective on our being is transformed and we start to see what we do not see without Jesus Christ. My orientation presupposes a soteriological perspective, for it is in Christ and the Holy Spirit we find the existential rest to honestly face the reality of our human life, with the epistemological and hermeneutical questions it evokes, without getting stuck in relativism or skepticism. This chapter, however, only will contain two further arguments for a soteriological approach. As a consequence, it is inescapable on the one hand that the existential orientation will have a limited character, while on the other hand it will already be informed by the soteriological approach toward it is directed.

I will start my exploration of our human existence with Charles Taylor. The primary interest of theological hermeneutics and a theological doctrine of Scripture is to enable listening to Scripture and God and to foster an understanding of God, the world, and the self *coram deo*. My anthropological reflections in this chapter serve a theological purpose. In our Western world, however, faith in God is not self-evident. Whether we call our world post-Christian, pluralistic, or secular, all these adjectives indicate this. For many, not believing in God seems "not only easy but even inescapable."[1] But is it inescapable not to believe in God? Taylor explicitly confronted this question. His analyses in *A Secular Age* show that faith in God is no longer obvious, but has become a voluntary option in the secular West correspondent to the consumerist atmosphere of modern life as a whole. In the first part of this chapter, I will use his philosophical analyses to better understand what makes one's understanding of self and the world open or closed to God (3.2). After all, an important question for theological hermeneutics is what does it take to stimulate our human existence to be open to God? What obstacles are there, what are the external pressures our context places on a life of faith? What is the human reality that theological hermeneutics must face if we are to foster understanding *coram deo*?

Furthermore, I will use the analyses of Taylor and other philosophers to gain better insight into our human existence and its various dimensions.

---

1. Taylor, *Secular Age*, 25.

We are more than rational beings asking critical-reflective questions about our knowing and understanding. An alternative soteriological approach of theological hermeneutics and Scripture should reckon with the full reality of our human existence (3.3)

The third step will be more theological, bringing in notions of creation and sin. To argue that a soteriological approach is needed, especially the notion of sin will be used. Who are humans that their existence can be open or closed to God? And what happened that many or not all of us seem to have a problem living in an open, good, and loving relationship with God? The focus here will be on the noetic consequences of sin—the consequences of sin for our knowing and understanding. If sin has noetic consequences, a theological epistemology that does not explicitly deal with sin and salvation will be impossible. It is even stronger: if sin has noetic consequences, a theological epistemology itself has to be embedded in soteriology.

3.2 CHARLES TAYLOR: A SECULAR AGE?

Our human existence is not in itself open to God. The development of the modern Western world demonstrates this. At the same time, Charles Taylor's *A Secular Age* shows the problematic aspects of modernity. Moreover, he argues that to be part of late modern society does not mean that it is necessary to be agnostic or atheistic. It is possible to make "the 'closed' spin on immanence," but this "anti-religious spin" is not a necessary consequence of the development of modern culture.[2] Many tell the story of modernity as "subtraction stories," stories of liberation from earlier religious illusions. If these stories were true, the emergence of modernity is the history of liberation from the bondage of misguided religious superstition, to the freedom of a life without gods. Taylor, however, argues that modern secularity is the result of "new inventions, newly constructed self-understandings, and related practices, and can't be explained in terms of perennial features of human life."[3] Thus it is a matter of how we understand our existence and whether our lives will be open or closed to transcendence. This evokes an important question: what makes someone's understanding of the self and the world closed toward God, and what creates openness to God? In what follows, I will use Taylor's analysis to answer this question.

His analysis has several aspects. The first two concern our understanding: our self-understanding and our social imaginary (3.2.1). However, more is at stake than a change in theoretical insight. Taylor emphasizes

2. Taylor, *Secular Age*, 579, 580.
3. Taylor, *Secular Age*, 22.

that theoretical and conceptual changes do not suffice to arrive at a factual life form with an immanent understanding of self and world. Knowing is a moral activity, and moral judgments and emotions play a role as well (3.2.2). Although moments of judgment and decision exist, Taylor emphasizes that our understanding is largely formed implicitly. The role of the context with its plurality of options and its implicit narratives should not be neglected. Furthermore, Taylor refers in his analyses to open spaces in our context and to the role of dilemmas we all are facing (3.2.3).

3.2.1 Understanding

The first precondition for a closed understanding of the self and the world is that it must be possible conceptually to think of a self and to imagine a world without a relationship to a transcendent reality: an anthropocentric understanding of the self and an immanent understanding of the order of the world. In passing, Taylor also mentions a significant third precondition, a changed understanding of God. However, Taylor himself does not deal extensively with it.[4]

Taylor refers to the closed understanding of self as the "buffered self." In *Sources of the Self*, Taylor sketches the development of this new understanding in several steps: Descartes's disengaged reason, Locke's punctual self, Kant's pure rational nature with its moral will, and the Romanticist expressive interiority.[5] This new self-understanding could not develop without a new, instrumental, and disengaged understanding of reason. Reason thus understood, posits itself in an "instrumental stance . . . of reconstruction" over against reality and seems to be able to control it.[6]

According to Taylor, this reason has drawn several borders. In the process of disenchantment, a border is drawn between subject and things, but also between mind and world. The border between mind and world (including other spirits) is not conceived as porous and accessible for a spiritual reality outside. This border also is experienced as a border between mind and body, resulting in a disengaged or disembodied self. Due to this clear border between the physical objects outside the mind and the self as an inner space, the porous self has become a buffered self. Moreover, a border was drawn between "the laws of physical science and the meanings things have for us," between the physical and the moral. The buffered self

---

4. Taylor, *Secular Age*, 293–95.
5. Taylor, *Sources of the Self*.
6. Taylor, *Secular Age*, 131; further 130–36.

is formed as a non-relational self: autonomous, apart from others and the living environment.[7]

To make this self-understanding a viable alternative, it had to survive without transcendent moral sources. Taylor describes how this self-understanding was attached to a feeling of power and invulnerability, a sense of self-esteem and self-confidence. This was seen as a source of universal benevolence that could serve as an alternative to the Christian agape. This moral source was localized in the inner self. The impartial observer becomes a benevolent person. Hand in hand with this new self-understanding goes a changed evaluation of emotions. Earlier emotions were seen as passions that had to be controlled by reason, later they were valued more positively as the manifestation of the inner nature that deserves expression. With its own moral sources, this new self-understanding became a viable alternative to a life lived by God's grace.[8]

Gradually, the downside of this self-understanding became clear as well: the individual self is vulnerable and threatened by uncertainty; the self is empty and in need of meaning and inspiration. These malaises of modernity resulted in renewed spiritual and religious quests for deep authentic feelings and experienced significance.[9]

For theological hermeneutics, these developments have many consequences. The "buffered self" sees itself as detached from God's acts and presence, from union with the Son, or the inhabitation of the Holy Spirit. It becomes possible to develop epistemology as the self-reflection of a self-sufficient reason that is in control of the process of knowing. Further, the understanding of the self that emerged can develop in various directions. First, in a rationalist manner with an emphasis on reason. This leads to a critical attitude toward religion, an active attitude of rational control instead of a receptive attitude that is necessary to listen. Second, it might result in an expressivist option, that attaches great importance to the expression of the inner life and its emotions. Third, the ambivalence of the "buffered self" sometimes results in feelings of malaise and emptiness, leading to renewed spiritual quests for immanent or transcendent fulfillment. Sometimes this creates a new openness for the Christian faith, sometimes the Christian tradition is seen as obsolete. Thus, this understanding of the self makes it more complicated to foster an understanding *coram deo*.

Apart from the understanding of the self, the understanding of the world changed. In the genesis of the new world understanding, Taylor

---

7. Taylor, *Secular Age*, 76–91.
8. Taylor, *Secular Age*, 242–59, 300–301.
9. Taylor, *Secular Age*, 299–304, 307–21, 507–9, 544–46, 716–20.

distinguishes two phases: the increasing independence of the created realm from God, and the emergence of a new social imaginary, leading to the Modern Moral Order (MMO).

In the first phase, the created universe full of significance increasingly was seen as an enchanted, neutral cosmos detached from the creator. The instrumental understanding of rationality contributed to this development. Medieval nominalism already understood the cosmos as a result of God who sovereignly imposes his will on reality, thus bringing order without assuming an already existing natural teleology.[10] The more the trust in the human ordering, the stronger the instrumental attitude toward a world more and more disenchanted. At the same time, God's act in the created realm more and more disappeared in the background. Science and technology contributed to this development, but also aversion to superstition, fanaticism, and enthusiasm, associated with divine intervention. Here also were important the new borders between the natural and the supernatural, between laws of nature and significance, and between the inner and outer world. Together with an understanding of the world as an ordered cosmos grew a coherent understanding of time and space. The secular and homogeneous clock time replaced an experience of time as connected with higher times like a Platonic eternity or the liturgical year. The experience of time was disconnected from transcendence, too.[11]

The second phase of the new world understanding is the rise of the Modern Moral Order (MMO). This new social imaginary cohered with the new view of the individual, reason, and the world. Reality was no longer seen as intrinsically ordered, whereas the confidence in the human capacity to order was augmented. This order has a normative character and must be imposed on social reality. The order is formed where free individuals with equal rights come together and submit voluntarily to the rules of this order. The source of agreement is the common good, the promotion of mutual benefit. As this order has a commercial character, trade and economy are a way to peace and harmony. The accompanying ethics is an ethics of freedom, mutual benevolence, and service to mutual benefit.[12]

The MMO is compatible with the "buffered self." The MMO only has immanent ends, trusts human capabilities, and is rationally comprehensible. The rise of the MMO resulted in a reversal in thought. No longer does thinking start with God and proceed to order, but it starts with the order

---

10. Taylor, *Secular Age*, 130–31.
11. Taylor, *Secular Age*, 48, 59, 95–97.
12. Taylor, *Secular Age*, 159–211.

and asks for God's existence.[13] Together, the MMO and the "buffered self" make an understanding of self and world *coram deo*, and in relation to God less obvious. However, an opposition between religion and the MMO does not exist necessarily.[14] The MMO can remain open to transcendence.

3.2.2 Moral Activity

According to Taylor's analyses, the understanding of the self and the world plays a role in whether human existence and understanding are open to God or not. However, knowing and understanding is also a moral activity—the second aspect of Taylor's analysis of the closedness of human existence. Decisive are moral judgments about the moral superiority of the chosen understanding of the self and the world. Often, two factors play a role: the persuasiveness of a life form, but also feelings about Christians and their life form (like anger and annoyance). Thus, the acceptance of a new understanding of the self and the world is not just a matter of theoretical concepts and social imagining. It is furthermore based on a positive moral judgment about their superiority.[15]

The new self-understanding was received primarily positively from the ethics of rational control. The buffered self feels powerful and invulnerable within the MMO. The detached attitude thus gained ethical prestige. The success of science and technology reinforced this prestige of the disengaged subject. More and more, optimism grew about human unaided forces, whereas beliefs about human sin or the necessity of divine salvation lost their plausibility and the significance of the self's transformation by divine grace increasingly was undervalued.[16]

So, according to Taylor, it is not the facts or the arguments that are decisive in favor of this new understanding of the self and the world, but it is carried by a persuasive life form or an ethical judgment concerning the moral superiority of a life attitude.[17]

Often, positive moral judgments about a new view of the self and the world alone are not decisive but merge with negative judgments about the Christian alternative. Within a Christian society, such negative judgments have been an expression of anger and annoyance, based on negative experiences with Christianity. As a reason for this anger, Taylor mentions the

---

13. Taylor, *Secular Age*, 159–201, 221–34, 275–92, 375–76, 388–89.
14. Taylor, *Secular Age*, 544–49.
15. Taylor, *Secular Age*, 171–81, 200–201, 213–14, 282–86, 595–96.
16. Taylor, *Secular Age*, 228–29, 237–39, 242–61.
17. Taylor, *Secular Age*, 85–86, 361–63, 388, 548.

juridical-penal model of Orthodox Christianity (especially Calvin), the coercion that often accompanied pursuits of reform, or superstition and fanaticism.[18] In a post-Christian society, other emotions will play a role like apathy or disinterest.

For an adequate contemporary theological hermeneutic it is important to acknowledge the role of convincing life forms and the moral judgments they evoke. A sustainable Christian understanding of self and the world must be supported by a convincing life form. Thus, theological reflection on understanding should contribute to the development of life forms where the Christian faith is embodied in such a manner that the significance of the faith becomes tangible, leading to positive judgments and emotions.

3.2.3 Context as Background

Furthermore, Taylor emphasizes that our understanding largely is formed implicitly. This is the third aspect of Taylor's analysis of the closedness of human existence. He mentions several contextual factors that influence us in the background.

In the twenty-first century, the formative practices of life are very plural, a spiritual supernova. According to Taylor, there has always been pluralism, but our current context is nevertheless a new situation compared to previous forms of pluralism. In our situation, which is determined by modernity, we share a lot and in terms of our way of life, there is great homogeneity. Faith is distinctive. The self must believe while spirituality easily becomes an isolated reality. At the same time, we face a dizzying amount of religious and spiritual options available. This makes any form of religion or spirituality vulnerable to undermining by dissenters. Taylor argues that the destabilizing effect of plurality on religion in our society is maximal.[19]

Moreover, Taylor points to the influence of master narratives and "unthoughts," which guide our judgments and choices in the background. Also in our society, grand narratives are told about the development of secular modernity and religion. Here, Taylor uses Michel Foucault's term "unthoughts": thoughts present in the background of our thinking, from there directing our judgments and choices. Taylor refers to these narratives and "unthoughts" as Closed World Structures (CWS).

Taylor sketches two attitudes or perspectives, a perspective of transformation that reckons with a transformation or deification of humans by God,

---

18. Taylor, *Secular Age*, 78, 223–24, 239, 261–64, 266, 274, 493. On the role of emotions like anger and fear, see also Ryrie, *Unbelievers*.

19. Taylor, *Secular Age*, 300, 303–4, 374, 435, 437, 531.

and a perspective of immanence that is restricted to the immanent possibilities of humanity. Transcendence experiences can deepen the connection with God and stimulate a spin toward openness.[20] Although according to Taylor there should not be a contradiction between modernity and the MMO on the one hand and religion on the other, people who choose disbelief do see that contradiction. "Unthoughts" and Closed World Structures play an important role in the twist of the immanent framework toward closedness or openness.[21] Unthoughts subtly affect a person's mental framework and thus limit his imagination. Such unthoughts are that religion must decline because religion is untrue, or becomes increasingly irrelevant, or based on authority.[22]

Taylor describes a CWS as "ways of restricting our grasp of things which are not recognized as such."[23] They create "the illusion of the 'rational obviousness' of the closed perspective."[24] These images and aspects of grand narratives shape how reality is experienced and how it is thought of without their role being made aware. Taylor clarifies the functioning of a CWS based on the modern epistemological image: we know the external world through inner representations. We can attribute value and significance to the information thus acquired. Any knowledge of a transcendent reality is at the end of a complicated chain of reasoning. Although this image is controversial from an epistemological point of view, it can still be maintained. The ethics of the disengaged subject, in control and responsible for himself, make the image attractive. Living within such a CWS feels "natural," while other possibilities are not explored.[25]

Typical of the closed world structures that Taylor describes is that they are all stories with a similar structure: we used to live in a world where we believed in God, knew less than we do now, and were belittled. Now that we know more about the world and man, we no longer need God and religion. Human development to human freedom is perfectly possible without God or any other higher authority. The disappearance of God and religion leads to empowerment, equality, and space for real humanity. Important recurring motives are liberation, progress, and coming of age, which makes the disappearance of faith in God a "naturally" sensing process.[26] However, Tay-

---

20. Taylor, *Secular Age*, 430–36, 728–33.
21. Taylor, *Secular Age*, 347, 387, 544–51.
22. Taylor, *Secular Age*, 427–29.
23. Taylor, *Secular Age*, 551.
24. Taylor, *Secular Age*, 556.
25. Taylor, *Secular Age*, 557–60.
26. Taylor, *Secular Age*, 557–92.

lor has shown that another story can be told. Whoever lets go of the closed world structures can stand in the open space where the question of an open or closed worldview is undecided.[27]

Thirdly, in our world spaces have developed where no choice has to be made between worldviews or between faith and unbelief. He thinks especially of poetry and music that do not depict or tell a story, but unlock a world that evokes emotion. Thus arises a sense of mystery and depth that meets the desire for spirituality, without any connection to a transcendent reality. In this way, art is a "free and neutral space, between religious commitment and materialism" with "a kind of undefined spirituality."[28] According to Taylor, nature and tourism can also fulfill such a function because they evoke "a certain admiration, wonder, mixed with some nostalgia."[29] This same space can be kept open by the gracious attitude of cool distant irony. In these open spaces, the pulling force of the various positions can be experienced.[30]

The fourth of the contextual aspects of the movement between closedness and openness is the real existential dilemmas that demand an answer. These questions regard the limitations of the modern instrumental view of reason, moral ideals, or the goal and fullness of human life. Taylor shows that believers are not automatically placed in a more disadvantageous starting position. Everyone has to think about how justice can be done to our bodily existence; what is pursued as human fulfillment and how; whether the transformation of our being is needed and how it can be achieved. The field of cross-pressures, pulling toward a twist to openness or closedness, is at the same time the space where real problems require a solution. The struggle with these problems also plays a role in the choice for or against faith.[31]

Since Taylor wrote his book *A Secular Age* in 2007, the awareness of unanswered existential questions has increased because of many crises that followed the attacks of the 11th of September 2001. We have to face the instability of our world and the urgency of these crises. A financial crisis in 2008, the election of several populist leaders like Donald Trump in the USA (2017) or Jair Bolsonaro in Brazil (2019), the COVID-19 pandemic beginning in 2019, the Russian attack on Ukraine in 2022, and of course the ongoing ecological crisis, all have contributed to this awareness. At many

---

27. Taylor, *Secular Age*, 548–49, 592.
28. Taylor, *Secular Age*, 360.
29. Taylor, *Secular Age*, 360; and further 336–46, 352–61.
30. Taylor, *Secular Age*, 301–2, 478.
31. Taylor, *Secular Age*, 600–605, 613–710.

different levels—national and international, economic, social and political, biological and meteorological—we sense the instability of our (eco)systems. The challenges we are facing are huge, and it is an open question of which faith or worldview can offer real hope and guidance.

Theological hermeneutics cannot suffice with claiming that it is self-evident that the Christian faith does have the answer to all these challenges. These crises also question the Christian tradition, the existence, and the presence of God in our world. At the same time, these open spaces and these existential problems can be seen as places and problems where God's general revelation can be experienced, and where human creatures are facing the beauty and greatness of the creator. If the general revelation is a reality, his presence is a hopeful, active reality in the background of our context.[32]

3.3 HUMAN EXISTENCE

Taylor's analyses constitute the first argument for the necessity of a soteriological approach to hermeneutics and Scripture. Understanding the Bible as Scripture and word of God *coram deo* only is possible when hearers and readers have an existential openness to God. An epistemological approach to hermeneutics and Scripture presupposes a reason that is open to God and able to answer rationally all questions about God, our knowledge of God, and our understanding *coram deo*. Such reason might be a Christian reason, as was the case in medieval theology. After Modernity, however, it is an illusion to suggest that a neutral and independent human reason exists—a reason that is without any resistance open to God's existence, that does not experience (existential) crises that put pressure on the relationship with God, and that can find God in a purely rational quest. Where does human reason find the necessary existential openness to God?

Taylor's analyses show that neither faith and openness to God, nor unbelief and atheism are self-evident. Whether or not his historical narrative is correct, his analysis clarifies, for the present, many aspects of human existence and the complexity of openness or closedness to God. In our world with its immanent ways of thinking, we all live in a field of pressures in opposite directions: an anti-religious spin is possible, but the same is true of openness toward a perspective of transcendence and transformation. These pressures are not just consciously rational. Our religious, and spiritual position depends on our self-understanding, our social imaginary, and our image of God, but whether we have an open or a closed attitude is not fixed. Our attitude toward transcendence and religion is influenced

---

32. See, e.g., Bavinck, *Religieus besef en christelijk geloof.*

by moral judgments, our affections, the narratives with which we live both consciously and subconsciously, and by the world where we live with all the life options, dilemmas, and problems we have to face.

Before moving to a discussion of sin, I will now further analyze human existence in its various dimensions. Human existence has more dimensions than the rational alone, as can be concluded from Taylor. An effective approach to theological hermeneutics and Scripture should reckon with the full reality of our human existence.

To Taylor's analyses an element should be added: the role of desire and the human heart. Taylor already indicates this when he mentions the role of moral judgments and affections. According to Augustinian anthropology, fundamental decisions are decisions of the human heart. "Intellectual arguments against Christianity not infrequently serve to legitimize decisions that have been made in the heart."[33] The decision between openness to God or not is a choice made in the heart. Desires give direction to our life. What matters is whether the desire for God is the leading desire in the human heart or not.[34] Our desires are not static but can be formed and schooled. Here, the role of our thinking, our practices, our social imaginaries, and the "unthoughts" of our society comes in.

This addition only confirms that human existence in her search for meaning, transcendence, and God is too complicated to justify an epistemological approach. The quest for an existence open to God is not a quest to be solved with theoretical thinking solely as a mathematical sum. Necessary is a more holistic approach that does justice to the complexity of human existence, more than a purely rational-reflective epistemology.[35] Human existence is narrative, social, embodied, affective, and at the deepest level determined by our desire.

Our existence is narrative, which cannot be separated from our historicity and the hermeneutical dimension of our existence. To be human is to be historically situated. Our attitude toward the world, our fellow humans, and God is influenced by our self-image, our worldview, and our image of God. Human life has a hermeneutical dimension: it matters how we understand, and how we understand influences our experience, it is not fixed

---

33. Paul, *Slag om het hart*, 41.

34. For a view of secularization beginning in the human heart, see Paul, *Slag om het hart*. On human desire and its formation see further Smith, *Desiring the Kingdom*; Smith, *Imagining the Kingdom*.

35. Cf. Westphal, "Hermeneutics as Epistemology." Because of the noetic consequences of sin (see 3.4), I differ from Westphal that a more holistic approach of epistemology would suffice. Theological hermeneutics and the doctrine of Scripture already include and presuppose a Trinitarian soteriology and ecclesiology.

how we understand, and accordingly, it is not fixed how we experience. Our understanding of the self, fellow humans, the world, and God influences whether our attitude toward ourselves, our fellow humans, our world, and God is receptive or closed.

This hermeneutical dimension of our human existence clearly can be seen in Ricoeur's analysis of the identity of the self as a narrative. The self is not the subject of Descartes's *cogito*, a "pointlike ahistorical identity" but "the narrative identity of a concrete person."[36] Paul Ricoeur distinguishes *idem*-identity (sameness) and *ipse*-identity (selfhood). *Idem*-identity presupposes a third-person perspective. *Idem*-identity can be identified and reidentified. *Ipse*-identity presupposes a second-person and a first-person perspective. As *ipse*-identity, the self is self-conscious and has a relation to itself.[37]

Between *idem*-identity and *ipse*-identity exists a dialectical relationship. The self as *ipse* has a permanency in time, even if in the domain of *idem* we see developments and changes. Narrative enables us to deal with this dialectic. In a narrative, by the connection of events in a plot, the diversity in time can become part of an integral story. The narrative operation of employment can reconcile diversity and identity. According to Ricoeur, "characters . . . are themselves plots."[38] Furthermore, the story can be told in different ways. The story of my life is a "concordant-discordant synthesis,"[39] bringing discordant elements together, but the story of my life is still open. The story constructs someone's identity, but this story can be reconstructed. Reading fiction enables us to experiment in our imagination with different versions of our life stories. Through other narratives, the configuration of our life narrative can be reconfigured.[40]

In Ricoeur's concept of narrative identity, the social and embodied nature of our existence becomes clear as well. The self with a narrative self-understanding has a dialogical nature, and humans are social beings, aiming at relationships in equality and mutuality. We are not completely free to tell and retell our identity, for our bodily condition, living on this earth is not a mere variable.[41] Living as a body, we are embodied as well. Thus, I am not the author of my life story, although according to Ricoeur, I can

36. Ricoeur, *Oneself as Another*, 7.
37. Cf. Dalferth, *Wirklichkeit des Möglichen*, 196–99.
38. Ricoeur, *Oneself as Another*, 143; and further 140–44.
39. Ricoeur, *Oneself as Another*, 147.
40. Ricoeur, *Oneself as Another*, 147–48, 159–61, 164. On narrative identity, see Tromp, "Verleden als uitdaging."
41. Ricoeur, *Oneself as Another*, 151.

"make myself its co-author as to its meaning."[42] Someone's identity implies an understanding of that identity as a story, told as self-understanding by someone herself, or by others. However, the expectation of the other makes me responsible. With thinkers like Levinas, Ricoeur speaks of "the ethical primacy of the other than the self over the self."[43] What attitude we develop toward the other (and the Other) is still open and dependent on our story.

A good theological hermeneutics should do justice to these various dimensions of our human life. Our existence has a narrative (hermeneutical) aspect. The identity of the self is a narrative and we are shaped by the interpretative stories we hear and tell, even the narratives that are present at a subconscious level as "unthoughts." This is important for theological reflections on hermeneutics and Scripture. How we hear Scripture is influenced by the stories that we tell about ourselves, our fellow humans, our world, and God. At the same time, Scripture tells stories that can influence and challenge the stories that we tell and reconfigure them.

But, we with our understanding and stories are living beings. Life is more than understanding and telling stories. Taylor's concept of social imaginaries indicates that we live with more than just stories. Social imaginaries are embodied, lived, dialogical, and social, and have an affective dimension. To be human is to be corporeal and affective, social and living in communities, acting and participating in practices. Our understanding is interwoven with and formed by our social, bodily, and affective existence.

As Heidegger has shown, we live in our world, we use the things that are available ("zuhanden"), and in doing so we show that we understand them as something. In our practices, an understanding of our existence and our world is implied. Furthermore, Heidegger's holistic view of "being in the world" draws attention to the "being with," the importance of practices, our acts in daily life, and the ordinary use of things. This implies an emphasis on bodily participation in practices.[44] Wittgenstein emphasized the social, linguistic, and embodied nature of the language games in which we participate and the life forms these language games are part of.[45] Merleau-Ponty took the human body as his starting point in his analyses of human perception. He demonstrated in all his careful and detailed analyses how our spatial and sensitive body is the place where our experience is constituted.[46]

42. Ricoeur, *Oneself as Another*, 162; cf. 160.
43. Ricoeur, *Oneself as Another*, 168.
44. Heidegger, *Sein und Zeit*, 52–54, 59–62, 66–72, 83–88, 102–13, 142–53.
45. Wittgenstein, *Philosophical Investigations*.
46. Merleau-Ponty, *Phénoménologie de la perception*. The work of Merleau-Ponty has an important place in the liturgical project of James K. A. Smith. Bodily participation now in the liturgy plays an important role in Christian formation; see Smith,

Taylor, finally, makes clear that our perceptions have an affective aspect, and that our perspective on our world is determined by moral judgments.[47] Our reason and our affections do not consist of binary opposition, but the mind has a rational and an affective dimension.[48] Epistemological reflections on processes of knowing and understanding are an abstraction of the dynamics of our human life. Such abstractions can be useful, but they remain abstractions. What these thinkers have emphasized, is the importance of our body for epistemology.[49]

This also is important for theological reflections on knowing (epistemology), understanding (hermeneutics), and Scripture. Listening and hearing, knowing God and thinking about God, understanding ourselves and our world *coram deo*, cannot be isolated from our life in our world with or without God. Without a life with God, we cannot know God; to know God, we have to live with him; and living with God implies learning to understand our lives in the light of God's presence. Finally, at the most fundamental level, our desires give direction to our lives with or without God. It matters whether we are people with conflicting desires and divided hearts, or whether our desires are focused on God. We need a holistic view of human existence to see how knowing God and living with God are inseparably connected.

But in our embodied existence, the human heart never has been automatically undivided and centered on God. Moreover, in the Western context, God's presence is no longer self-evident. It is not possible to solve questions about God's presence and our desire easily, referring to general revelation, natural knowledge of God, or common grace. A holistic understanding of our existence, our understanding, and our knowledge implies that a problem in knowing God will be inseparably connected with a problem in our life with God. Restoration of our knowledge of God is not available without restoration of our life with God and the renewal of our hearts. If God exists and if it is possible to know him, knowing God and living with God are one. This means that if we have a problem with God and if we need salvation, epistemology, and soteriology cannot be separated. If something like sin exists, epistemology cannot do without soteriology.

Desiring the Kingdom, 39–73; Smith, *Imagining the Kingdom*, 29–100, 139–50.

47. See apart from Taylor, *Secular Age*; also see the articles by Taylor and others in Coakley, *Faith, Rationality, and the Passions*, and further Ryrie, *Unbelievers*.

48. Both pre-Enlightenment thinkers and recent developments in neuroscience evidence this. See the volume edited by Sarah Coakley: *Faith, Rationality, and the Passions*.

49. See also the holistic covenant epistemology of Esther Lightcap Meek, using Michael Polanyi in Meek, *Loving to Know*; and comparably Clark, *Divine Revelation and Human Practice*, 171–96.

3.4 NOETIC EFFECTS OF SIN

3.4.1 Preliminary Remarks

To further substantiate the claim that epistemology needs soteriology, I will now move from the problem of secularization to the problem of sin. The central question is: does sin have effects on our knowing and understanding? If this is not the case, an epistemic quest for God and a right understanding of Scripture could still be possible. From a position that is neutral in religious and spiritual respect, we could develop an epistemological argument about the (non-)existence of God. However, if sin does have consequences for our knowing of God and understanding of Scripture, this would prove to be problematic. It would imply that we need salvation from sin to know God and to understand Scripture. Furthermore, it would mean that our knowing and understanding would need some form of salvation, restoration, or transformation. Finally, the noetic effects of sin provide another argument for the thesis that epistemology in some respect needs soteriology.

Evil in its different manifestations (egocentrism, biases, power structures, etc.) has cognitive effects. The Christian tradition understands these effects as a consequence of sin. Christian hymns sing about these noetic consequences of sin, e.g., the Lutheran hymn "Liebster Jesu, wir sind hier," written by Tobias Clausnitzer. These are the first lines of the second verse (in the English translation by Catherine Winkworth): "All our knowledge, sense, and sight lie in deepest darkness shrouded." The best way to develop theological reflections on sin is to do this in the light of the gospel of Jesus Christ, which results in a fuller picture of sin than an approach that confines itself to the law. Salvation as the solution to the problem of sin sheds a revealing light on our problems that Jesus Christ has solved. Consequently, my reflections will presuppose the light of Easter and the Spirit of Pentecost. When he rose from the dead, Jesus Christ demonstrated his victory over sin and its consequences, embodying in his risen and glorified body a transformed human subjectivity. When he baptized his church at Pentecost with the Holy Spirit, he gave his Spirit to unite his followers with himself and to make them participate in who he is, also in his mind and thoughts, to transform them into Christlikeness.[50] In the light of the transformation by and the guidance of the Spirit of the risen Christ, we come to see the reality of sin and its effects more sharply.

When we speak about the effects of sin in an argument that defends a certain approach to hermeneutics, the impression may arise that

---

50. On union with and participation in Christ, see Burger, *Being in Christ*; Burger, *Life in Christ*, 42–63, 96–172, 216–19.

hermeneutics itself is a consequence of sin. However, this would be a false conclusion. Understanding is part of creation. God is a speaking God, who created humans who listen, understand, and answer.[51] God created humans as corporeal, affective, linguistic, temporal, and relational beings, to live an existence that is embodied, affective, narrative, historical, and social. He created a great variety of people, but none of them with a God's-eye point of view. It is good to be created as someone who is living in a human perspective, with a body situated in a certain place at a certain moment. Moreover, God created us to participate in his creation by knowing, understanding, and giving names (Gen 2:19–20). Creation has a certain plasticity and by our linguistic and technical capacities, we constructively enrich his creation. Always, someone (a human person) understands something, influenced by someone, in the light of some specific interests, whereas someone else might understand this something differently, from another perspective. Physicality with the plurality and spatial finitude it implies, historicity and language, the need for cooperation, and community life are no effects of sin, but I regard these to be part of God's good creation. It would be wrong, therefore, to cherish homesickness for a pre-hermeneutic paradise lost. It is exactly characteristic of sin to desire to be like God and to have access to an absolutely unambiguous divine point of view.

Still, it is the question of whether the noetic effects of sin exist indeed. In an article from 2013, Helen de Cruz and Johan de Smedt deny this. They discuss Alvin Plantinga's concept of the *sensus divinitatis*: an innate propensity to form true beliefs about God. As a result of sin, this *sensus divinitatis* no longer works properly, leading to unbelief and false religious convictions. De Cruz and De Smedt focus their argument on the effects of sin on the *sensus divinitatis*. Consequently, they limit themselves to the effects of sin for the natural knowledge of God. But as will be demonstrated below, the effects of sin are far more comprehensive. If God calls people and interacts with them, knowledge of God comprises more than natural knowledge resulting from *sensus divinitatis*. Moreover, the noetic effects of sin do not concern our knowledge of God only. Whether or not human beings have lived in a historical paradise, sin is a reality and so are the noetic consequences of sin. Thus, what can we say about the noetic effects of sin?[52]

I will understand by "noetic effects of sin" the effects of sin in the world of our *noemata*, or of our *nous*, that is, the consequences of sin for our mind,

51. Geertsema, *Het menselijk karakter*, 47–62, 102–49.

52. De Cruz and De Smedt, "Reformed and Evolutionary Epistemology." For a more extensive discussion, see Burger, "Hoe moeten we vanuit"; Van Eyghen et al., "Cognitive Science of Religion." On general revelation, see Bavinck, *Religieus besef en christelijk geloof*.

our knowledge, our thinking; and *nous* both as the personal mind of an individual (organ of thought) and as the corporate mind, which tends toward "mindset."[53]

3.4.2 Biblical Motifs

To give a first impression, I will start with an overview of some relevant biblical motifs.[54]

Guidance and authority play a role in human knowledge. In Gen 2, Adam's process of knowing is guided by God. God stimulates a process of discovery to let Adam make discoveries. Adam participates in this process and gives names, but also discovers by difference what he is missing. The process of knowing has a social character, in which guidance and authoritative testimony is important. Genesis 3 shows what goes wrong when humans listen to the wrong authority and not to God.[55]

Later in the Pentateuch, the role of the prophetic authority returns. Dru Johnson emphasizes this role of authenticated authorities as a "socio-prophetic role" that the knowing subject has to submit to in obedience to come to know reality. Error comes in when someone does not listen to the authenticated authorities or listens to the wrong authority. Moreover, he stresses the diachronic character of the process of knowing. Finally, "knowledge requires the embodiment of instructions given by the authenticated authorities."[56] We have to participate in the way of life that we learn from the prophetic authorities. As a consequence of disobedience and sin, we are fallen and live in a world that bears the consequences of this fall. Just like Israel, humanity needs prophetic guidance to release the bondage of untruth.[57]

Scripture furthermore diagnoses the impact of sin on our human existence. Important in the Old Testament but also the teaching of Jesus (e.g., Mark 7:18-23) is that sinners have evil hearts. As Peels has shown, although the concept of the heart has different aspects, "there clearly is a cognitive

---

53. Cf. Bell, "But We Have the Mind," 180–87; Oldhoff, "Hedendaagse theosis," 266–70; Oldhoff, "Soul Searching with Paul," 221; Vanhoozer, *Drama of Doctrine*, 255–56. See also Keener's overview of Paul's concept of the mind in Keener, *Mind of the Spirit*.

54. For a survey of biblical motifs, see Johnson, *Biblical Knowing*.

55. Cf. Johnson, *Biblical Knowing*, 22–64.

56. Johnson, *Biblical Knowing*, 199.

57. Johnson, *Biblical Knowing*, 7–11, 65–96.

side to the concept of heart."⁵⁸ Consequently, the evil and deceitful character of the heart is important for the analysis of the noetic effects of sin.

According to Johannine theology, the human condition can be characterized as "epistemic darkness." The opposition of light and dark plays an important role in the gospel and letters of John. The *logos* brings light, but he brings this in a situation of darkness, which has epistemic implications. The dark does not understand the light (John 1). The not seeing in the situation of darkness is connected to blindness, another Johannine theme (John 9; 1 John 2:11). This darkness is both a human responsibility and a consequent, fallen situation from which only the light of God can save us.⁵⁹

Also in Paul's theology, a combination of responsibility and resulting impotence can be found. Humans refused to glorify God. Instead, they "suppress the truth by their wickedness" and turn toward images to worship them as gods. However, as a result of these free acts, "their thinking became futile and their foolish hearts were darkened" and "God gave them over in the sinful desires of their hearts" (Rom 1:18–25).⁶⁰ The concept of *nous* (singular) that Paul uses here to refer to their "unfit mind," has a social dimension, and mental processes in the mind are "linked to behavior."⁶¹ The same idea of human foolishness we find in 1 Cor 1 and 2. Without the Holy Spirit, humans, although they even boast of their wisdom, are incapable of grasping the divine wisdom, and prove themselves to be fools.⁶² Ephesians 4:17–19 contains similar ideas. Paul warns of the gentiles and the "futility of their thinking." They are responsible for separating themselves from God and for hardening their hearts. However, now they are "darkened in their understanding," living in "ignorance" and "having lost all sensitivity."⁶³

As a result of salvation in Christ Jesus and the Holy Spirit who makes believers participate in Christ, a new way of perceiving reality has become possible. Consequently, Paul distinguishes between two ways of knowing, an old way of knowing *kata sarka*, "from a worldly point of view" and a new interpretation of reality starting from the new creation in Christ (2 Cor 5:16–17). However, both perspectives still exist.

Having a new perspective, however, we still "live by faith, not by sight" (2 Cor 5:7). We do not see the Lord Jesus Christ, we do not see our own

---

58. Peels, "Effects of Sin," 49; and further 47–50.

59. Cf. Bennema, "Christ, the Spirit and Knowledge of God," 109–14.

60. Cf. Keener, *Mind of the Spirit*, 1–30; Oldhoff, "Soul Searching with Paul," 185–89; Peels, "Sin and Human Cognition of God," 400–406.

61. Oldhoff, "Soul Searching with Paul," 186.

62. On 1 Cor 1–2, see Bell, "But We Have the Mind"; Healy, "Christ, the Spirit and Knowledge of God"; Keener, *Mind of the Spirit*, 173–201.

63. Cf. Peels, "Effects of Sin," 61–63.

glorified body. Salvation still is a matter of hope and of the future. Living in the Spirit, between the ascension and the return of Jesus, we only know in part (1 Cor 13:12). Our present knowledge is imperfect, incomplete, even deficient, and sinful.[64] Paul calls us to transform our lives by the transformation of our thinking. The worldly patterns of thinking still exert their influence (Rom 12:1-2).[65] This process of renewal of our thinking is still ongoing, as Col 3:10 indicates. In 2 Cor 10, Paul compares arguments and beliefs that oppose the knowledge of God with strongholds. He urges his readers to "take captive every thought to make it obedient to Christ" (2 Cor 10:5). The noetic effects of sin still influence the thinking of a regenerate believer.

This first overview of biblical motifs indicates that the noetic effects of sin are a serious problem indeed. Nevertheless, a more systematic analysis is necessary to understand where and how sin exercises its influence in the human mind.

3.4.3 An Analytic Approach

Such a more systematic analysis could follow an approach in line with analytic philosophy and focus on propositional knowledge, i.e., warranted true belief. As a consequence of sin, we have fewer warranted true beliefs than if there were no sin. We have true beliefs without warrant, we have false thoughts with or without warrant, sometimes simply have no beliefs if we stay ignorant, etc.[66] Sin has influenced our cognitive faculties. We can understand a cognitive faculty as "a mental mechanism that has a certain input—beliefs, visual perception, bodily sensation, etc.—and a doxastic output; that is, certain beliefs, disbeliefs, or withholdings of both belief and disbelief."[67] It is difficult to determine to which extent this influence of sin reaches, but as far as we know sin has not taken away cognitive faculties.[68] Normally—if, e.g., we are not blind, deaf, or suffer from dementia—our cognitive faculties as such seem to function well enough.

As an example of such an analytic approach, we find in Alvin Plantinga's treatment of sin and its cognitive consequences in his *Warranted*

---

64. Peels, "Sin and Human Cognition of God," 397-400.

65. On Rom 12:1-2 see Keener, *Mind of the Spirit*, 143-72.

66. Van Woudenberg, "Over de noëtische gevolgen," 239; Peels, "Sin and Human Cognition of God," 400, 406. Cf. Willard, *Renovation of the Heart*, 103, 110.

67. Peels, "Effects of Sin," 46; Peels, "Sin and Human Cognition of God," 395.

68. Peels, "Effects of Sin," 50, 67-68; Peels, "Sin and Human Cognition of God," 408-9; Van Woudenberg, "Over de noëtische gevolgen," 239.

Christian Belief.[69] Plantinga's epistemological treatment of sin is determined by the question of whether the Christian set of beliefs that we find in, e.g., the Nicene Creed is justified, rational, and warranted.[70] According to Plantinga, humanity is created in God's image, i.e., as persons having intellect and will. More specifically, we resembled God, both in our beliefs and understanding, as well as in our affections and intentions. We were created to have "intimate knowledge of God" and "sound affections, including gratitude, for God's goodness."[71] Our fall into sin had big consequences, cognitive as well as affective. "Our original knowledge of God and his marvelous beauty, glory, and loveliness has been severely compromised."[72] According to Plantinga, we can still have knowledge of God, for he assumes that the *sensus divinitatis* did not disappear completely as a consequence of sin.[73] This, however, is no reason for relief. Sin is primarily a problem of the human heart, a problem of affective disorder. Fallen in sin, our love and hate no longer correspond with reality. We aggrandize ourselves pridefully and are prone to hate God and our neighbor.[74] Only when God reveals himself, when we read the Scriptures that are inspired by the Holy Spirit, when the truth of God is revealed to our minds and sealed in our hearts, can we have again true beliefs about God and his gospel.

The approaches of these analytic philosophers substantiate the complexity of the noetic effects of sin. The analytic tools have their strengths because of their clarity and focus on our cognitive faculties. However, the fall and conversion of human existence should receive explicit attention, due to the dynamics of sin, and epistemic transformation and holiness.[75] For a further analysis, more has to be said from a theological perspective about our relationship with God, our position within creation, our own human existence, the place where we live, and about sin.

---

69. Plantinga, *Warranted Christian Belief*.

70. Plantinga, *Warranted Christian Belief*, 202–3.

71. Plantinga, *Warranted Christian Belief*, 204.

72. Plantinga, *Warranted Christian Belief*, 205.

73. Plantinga, *Warranted Christian Belief*, 210; cf. Peels, "Sin and Human Cognition of God."

74. Plantinga, *Warranted Christian Belief*, 205, 208–14, 243, 268–70, 280.

75. Cf. the contributions of Westphal and Coakley to the volume *Analytic Theology*, Westphal, "Hermeneutics and Holiness"; Coakley, "Dark Contemplation and Epistemic Transformation."

3.4.4 Human Existence: Creation and Sin

According to Ricoeur, the self with its narrative self-understanding has a dialogical nature, aiming at relationships in equality and mutuality. From the perspective of Easter and Pentecost, the understanding of this dialogical nature has to be deepened.

a. Relationship with God: The most fundamental relationship of human existence is the relationship with God, as Oliver O'Donovan substantiates. According to O'Donovan, it is the Holy Spirit who gives life to the self; and it is God who calls the self to awake as responsive agents and who invites us to call on Him.[76] This relationship with God is necessary for a healthy relationship both with oneself and with the other. In the love for God, we receive good self-love. Only when we discover ourselves in God, can we discover our neighbor in his relationship with God, love the neighbor, and live together in equality and mutuality. And Christ is "the neighbour par excellence."[77] Apart from God, a different form of self-love comes to exist, "'concupiscence,' which is the attempt to absorb the not-self into the self." A broken relationship with God will make the self unstable, and distort its ability to love truly.

b. Self with a center: This relationship with God determines the center of the self. This idea of the center of the self is developed by Miroslav Volf. According to Volf, the self has a center, and important is the "question of the *kind* of center the self ought to have."[78] Volf hints at psychological processes in which the self produces its own center, struggling and even using violence. He concludes from Paul's letters that as fallen humans we all have a wrongly centered self.[79] Again, we see the influence of a broken relationship with God: it makes the self unstable and even dangerous for others and itself, restlessly in search of a new center where it has lost God as its center.

c. Affections and desire: Our existence has an affective nature, and our life is directed by our desire. Affections and desires play an important role in the processes of thinking and decision-making.[80] Because our existence is embodied as well, our (bodily) practices shape our desires,

---

76. O'Donovan, *Finding and Seeking*, 1–12, 53, 60.
77. O'Donovan, *Finding and Seeking*, 50.
78. Volf, *Exclusion and Embrace*, 69.
79. Volf, *Exclusion and Embrace*, 69.
80. Clore, "Psychology and the Rationality of Emotion."

as Coakley, Smith, and Paul emphasize. As our relationship with God is the most fundamental relationship, and as our whole being longs for God (Ps 63:2), this formation should direct our desire to God by worship and contemplation. Sin has influenced our affective life, and we need affective transformation.[81] A desire that is wrongly directed by idolatry, will mislead the mind and result in a deformed focus of our attention.

d. The other as part of the self: God's interaction with humanity in Christ and the Spirit, the reciprocal identification of Christ and the believers, and the mutual indwelling of Christ and the believers, has a revealing nature. For Volf, what is true of Christ for the believer shows what is true of the self and the other: the other is part of the self. The self has reconfigured itself to make space for the other and let the other inhabit the self so that the other is co-constitutive for the identity of the self. This makes the self vulnerable. If the other is not what I want her to be, or if the other wants to make me what I do not want to be, the step toward exclusion is easily made.[82]

Thus, the self has a social and communal dimension. Martine Oldhoff has shown that according to Paul's use of *nous*, the mind also has a communal aspect. If it is important to exhort humans to be one in mind as Paul does, it is problematic if we are not one in mind.[83] The renewal of humanity will lead to unity of mind by participation in the mind of Christ. Sin instead breaks the unity of humanity and leads to fragmentation and problematic pluralism.

e. *Dominium*: Humanity received a special position within the order of creation, that can be characterized as "*dominium*" (Gen 1:26–30; Ps 8:6–9).[84] This concept defines humanity's position toward God as acknowledging God as the creator to be worshipped and obeyed and toward the further creation as authority over creation and the freedom to respond to reality that is itself ordered and meaningful. Shortly, human beings are created to reign on behalf of God and under God.

---

81. Coakley, "Dark Contemplation and Epistemic Transformation"; Coakley, *God, Sexuality, and the Self*; Paul, *Slag om het hart*; Smith, *Desiring the Kingdom*; Smith, *Imagining the Kingdom*; Stewart, "Evagrius Pontus."

82. Volf, *Exclusion and Embrace*, 90–91.

83. Oldhoff, "Soul Searching with Paul," 209, 221, 225.

84. Moo and Moo, *Creation Care*, 74–86; Nullens, *Leven volgens Gaia's normen?*, 207–316.

This concept should be distinguished sharply from domination or manipulation. In *dominium*, "authority over nature and salvific concern for the true being of nature go together inseparably."[85] O'Donovan extends this to human knowledge. True knowledge is characterized by love that apprehends reality and it is attentive to what reality is. "Knowledge is the characteristically human way of participating in the cosmic order."[86] Essential for that knowing is that we are present listening, and live in the reality with which we are connected. As long as humans are obedient to God, love for reality and worship for God go hand in hand. Lovingly, humans know God and his creation.

Humans participate in creation as knowing beings by using language. Genesis tells us that Adam gave names to all the livestock (Gen 2:19-20). This implies that humans observe, select, interpret, and communicate. We observe phenomena together with other phenomena, and by focusing on something we select, leaving out others. We understand this something as something, disclosing this phenomenon semiotically and reconstructing it symbolically. This enables us to communicate about phenomena. Now we can identify something as something to someone else, maybe influenced by someone else and in the light of some specific interests. Adam saw the animals coming, one by one he observed them and selected them as a certain kind, he used signs and words to invent names, and using language he now could describe a certain animal according to its characteristics. Now he could tell Eve "This large feline animal is a lion" (and he missed her dearly). We can use many signs and words to disclose reality, and we can do this in a good or bad way, true or false, as becomes clear when sin enters the world.[87]

f. Safe environment: Fundamental for human flourishing is a safe environment, living in God's presence. In traditional theological anthropology, the emphasis is on human nature, whereas the place where humans live mostly is neglected. However, the land as the place where humanity receives a place to live in peace is as important as human nature.[88] It is significant that "being in Christ" implies that believers receive a new safe place to live.

85. O'Donovan, *Resurrection and Moral Order*, 26.
86. O'Donovan, *Resurrection and Moral Order*, 81.
87. Dalferth, *Kombinatorische Theologie*, 87-90; Dalferth, *Gedeutete Gegenwart*, 122-27; Dalferth, *Wirklichkeit des Möglichen*, 19-21, 31, 127-32; Dalferth, *Radikale Theologie*, 246-50; Dalferth, *Kunst des Verstehens*, 27-34, 48-59.
88. Gestrich, *Christentum und Stellvertretung*, 12-13, 21-33, 125-28, 240-44,

It is important to see what God did according to the narrative of Gen 1 and 2: He placed Adam and Eve in a safe environment with a high calling. The world was unsafe outside the garden, but peace was in the garden because people were allowed to live there in God's presence in a God-ordered setting. The creation narrative nowhere denies that humans are flesh, small, fragile, and mortal, living in an unsafe world. But life is no struggle in the garden of God's presence, and eating the fruits of the tree of life makes possible immortality.[89]

This safe environment has epistemic importance. Human beings can open up to their environment and walk upright, which has a mental and spiritual significance: Man is invited to live open-mindedly—open to God and his world. Thus, empathy and love can gain the upper hand. Those who are free inside and who live upright get an open eye not only for God, the neighbor, and God's world but also for themselves. In that safe setting, people were called to expand that safe garden and let the world outside share in that presence of God who takes care of everything very well. God placed humanity in his presence, in a safe environment, without the threat of death, in an open epistemic relationship with each other and creation, and with a calling vital to the future of that creation.[90]

Whether we believe that a first human sin has been a historical reality or not, does not matter here. Looking in the mirror of the narrative of Gen 1–3, we discover that we live as mortal beings in an environment that is no longer safe, where immortality is no longer a possibility within reach.[91]

If this is true, it will not be hard to see that sin has far-reaching effects. Sin begins with not listening to God, disobedience, and refusing the possibilities that God gives. When God is no longer worshiped and obeyed, he will be replaced by other gods and authorities. Idolatry enters human existence and humans start to reconstruct their world accordingly (a). The self and its desire are no longer centered on God. Another center of desire

---

333–38; Leder, "Presence, Then the Covenants (Part One)"; Moo and Moo, *Creation Care*, 88–98; Wright, *Mission of God*, 27–28, 393–96.

89. Ten Brinke, *Erfzonde?*, 134–35, 143–50; Van Veluw, *Waar komt het kwaad vandaan?*, 369–75.

90. Peels, Van Eyghen, and Van den Brink apply this especially to the *sensus divinitatis*. They emphasise that a cognitive mechanism to function in a trustworthy manner needs the "environment for which it was meant." See Van Eyghen et al., "Cognitive Science of Religion," 210, 212.

91. Van den Brink, *Reformed Theology and Evolutionary Theory*, 174–99.

will change the (epistemic) interests of the self (b, c). Other human selves are no longer perceived as part of the self but as a potential threat. As a consequence, sin changes the nature of communities into groups that are either exclusive to others or oppressive to members. The (epistemic) interests of some will be absolutized, whereas the (epistemic) interests of others will be ignored (d). Together disobedient, humans do not perform their role of dominium faithfully (e). This results in expulsion from that safe environment, to the unsafe world outside the garden, far from the glorious presence of God (cf. Rom 3:23), and far from the tree of life that gave immortality. The unstable self now has to live in an unsafe environment (f). Thus, it would be wrong to understand sin primarily as moral, as nothing more than doing morally wrong things. It is important to see that sin is both the act for which one is responsible as well as a condition in which we have imprisoned ourselves. Our existence is damaged, and so is our act of knowing and understanding.[92]

The relationship with God no longer is a source of peaceful communion, but becomes infected with guilt and shame. This makes human beings unstable, living between arrogance and anxiety and focused on themselves. Now we are guided by a quest for stability, idols, self-justification, a will to dominate, or cowardice. The broken relationship with God has changed our heart, the center of our existence, into a foolish and darkened heart, a source of evil within.[93]

According to theological tradition, sinful humans became curved into themselves, *homo incurvatus in seipsum*. This expressive image shows the impact of sin on all our relationships. People become hedgehogs that curl up, put up their spines, and especially have an eye for their own interests. Or as Gen 3 tells, Adam and Eve made coverings for themselves and hid from God among the trees.[94]

Eberhard Jüngel has powerfully described this. Our existence depends on God's creating and saving "yes." Evil begins when we deny God's creating Word and speak our lies. God creates; sin can only imitate and has no substance. Instead, it disturbs reality including human existence, and imprisons us in lies. Trust and love are overtaken by a spiral of greed and distrust. In all relationships, sin has its destructive effects. Those who want to be God

---

92. Peels, "Effects of Sin," 44; Peels, "Sin and Human Cognition of God," 393. See further Jüngel, *Evangelium von der Rechtfertigung*, 78, 97, 100.

93. Cf. Kuyper, *Encyclopedia of Sacred Theology*, 110–13; Peels, "Sin and Human Cognition of God," 402–3, 406, 408; Westphal, "Taking St. Paul Seriously," 200–202; Van Woudenberg, "Over de noëtische gevolgen," 231–33, 240; Van Woudenberg, "Greijdanus' kentheologie," 170.

94. On *homo incurvatus in seipsum*, see Jenson, *Gravity of Sin*.

themselves can no longer be together with God. Humans, who learned to distinguish good and evil, now have to identify themselves as evil. Because self-knowledge has become deadly, we start to identify others as sinners and judge them. Our perception becomes selective, guided by shame, guilt, and self-interest. Greed and pride result in stupidity, due to intelligence without relationships.[95]

O'Donovan adds that this damages our subjectivity. Living in harmony with God, our reason and our will, our hearing and our doing are at one. Moreover, the mind "loves as it understands and understands as it loves."[96] But when we act in disobedience, hearing and doing go apart, which creates a tension between reason and will. We know without the appropriate love, or love without justification based on knowledge. Our will embraces a world without God's order, where our reason finds no rest. Afterward, sin brings along its own self-hatred and vain regrets. Moreover, our reason tries to rationalize our wrong decisions by creating new orders, centered around wrong orientations, in an imitation of the true reality. Hence, disobedience and sin result in a loss of harmony between the rational and the voluntative self. The alienation of sin effects our subjectivity. And when our will chooses a wrong orientation and forces reality to follow, we cut ourselves off from our cognitive access to reality.[97]

The communities of this *homo incurvatus in seipsum* also change. Communities have common objects of love and what we share forms our community. As a consequence of sin, God is no longer the common object of love, but he is replaced by other objects, turned in fact into idols. The communication about the identity of the community no longer respects diversity. False social representation becomes leading when communities are no longer constituted by representations of God. A false sense of unity is created, which limits the epistemological possibilities of the community members.[98] Sin has damaged our existence and this has noetic effects.

3.4.5 Noetic Consequences

God is no longer worshiped, humans no longer obey God and do not perform their role of *dominium* faithfully. God has hidden his presence from us. Our hearts have become deceitful (Jer 17:9), willing to survive without God and the God-given possibilities. Our cognitive mechanisms might be

---

95. Jüngel, *Evangelium von der Rechtfertigung*, 89–97, 108–9, 117–25.
96. O'Donovan, *Resurrection and Moral Order*, 110.
97. O'Donovan, *Resurrection and Moral Order*, 110–14.
98. Cf. O'Donovan, *Common Objects of Love*.

influenced by sin, we use them wrongly, and partly they receive the wrong input. Still, the memory of lost safety in God's presence causes a gnawing restlessness. As a result, human knowledge of God and created reality are compromised.

We reject our knowledge of the creator and of our ordered world. Our knowing is no longer the intended communion with things as God created them. Confusion has entered our views of the world. We continue to think and know, but our knowledge is mixed up with "misknowledge," as O'Donovan phrases it;[99] with deception, ignorance, and mistakes. Disobedience results in our perceptions taking strange and wrong shapes, following our prideful self-interest. People come up with alternative facts so that our problems become more bearable. We come up with excuses, we justify ourselves, we look for something to hold on to, and we ignore others around us. Our desire to survive with all inner and outer unrest and insecurity disfigures us.

Insightful is the typology of sin O'Donovan gives, distinguishing sin against the self, against the world, and against time.[100] Sin against the self is the denial of God's call. The result is an imaginary self, that refuses the real self and creates its own world, self-enclosed but ambitious. However, we are not able to deal with the shame caused by the painful discovery of failure and the collapse of a self-ideal. As a result, we can become cowardly, morally detached, or have a negative view of life.[101] Sin against the world blinds us to reality.[102]

Exactly our position of dominion, having an overview of creation but created to be obedient to God, makes it possible to construe wrong and at times terrifying worldviews. With our language and our thinking, we can worship idols and create our own pseudo-universes and pseudo-communities. Consequently, our knowledge becomes fragmentary, misunderstood, and interpreted within a misleading framework. God's creation is no longer understood as God's creation, and God is exchanged for idols.[103]

99. O'Donovan, *Resurrection and Moral Order*, 82, 88–90.

100. O'Donovan, *Finding and Seeking*, 18–19. These three types consists in the refusal of our own agency, of the created goods, and of our destiny. All of these three include four three sub-types.

101. For sins against the self, see O'Donovan, *Finding and Seeking*, 19–23 (the refusal of God's call), 43–46 (doubt of purpose), 65–69 (sin of disparagement and of moral detachment).

102. For sins against the world, see O'Donovan, *Finding and Seeking*, 84–88 (inconsiderateness; the folly of opinion that pretends to be wiser than it actually is), 95–99 (prejudice), 108–14 (ideology).

103. O'Donovan, *Resurrection and Moral Order*, 19, 55, 80–82, 86–89, 122, 126–27, 142.

After this sketchy impression of the impact of sin on our knowledge, I will give a more detailed analysis of the noetic effects.

1. Problem with authority: Sin influences our attitude toward authority. In his *Epistemology of Error*, Dru Johnson emphasizes the role of prophetic guidance in the process of knowing. In the present situation in Western Europe, the focus is often on the individual, knowing subject in its relationships. The activity of knowing seems to be an individual activity. Johnson wants to make clear that knowing is a social process, of listening to authorities to know what we see, learning to participate in practices, and giving guidance to help others understand what they see.[104] Sin may have consequences at different moments of the process: we can listen to the wrong authorities, refuse to listen, refuse (to learn) to participate in practices that are developed to come to know, and refuse to give guidance to others. This will all lead to forms of error.

2. Distance toward reality: Sin changes our attitude toward the reality that surrounds us. Esther Lightcap Meek has developed a "covenant epistemology." Inspired especially by the epistemology of Michael Polanyi, she proposes to see the relation of knowing as a covenant: a transforming relationship, with a normative dimension, and a perichoretic character for the knower has to indwell the known reality. Consequently, the knower has to develop a humble, loving, and inviting attitude. This covenant epistemology makes her very sensitive to dualities that have become problematic dichotomies in the modern West, due to wrong epistemologies. Many of these dichotomies show that sin creates distance and has disturbed many of our relationships: knowledge and belief, fact and value, reason and faith, reason and affection, objective and subjective, theory and practice, mind and body, etc. These and other dichotomies show the impact of sin on our mind and our relationship with our world, the known.[105]

3. Language: Sin changes how we articulate our knowledge of our world, using signs and language. With signs and language, we identify something as something to someone. This indicates the importance of the words, images, and symbols we use. In the nineteenth century, Abraham Kuyper mentioned this influence of language. "All kinds of untruth have entered into our everyday speech, and names and words we use unconsciously mold our self-consciousness. The proverbs and

---

104. Johnson, *Biblical Knowing*.
105. Meek, *Loving to Know*.

common sayings ... affect us no less strongly."[106] Similarly, O'Donovan stresses the importance of good concepts and descriptions. According to O'Donovan, "large moral disagreements all turn on competing descriptions." "The world-shaping, cultural sins have to do with bad descriptions."[107] From a mystagogical point of view, Annemiek De Jong-Van Campen notes that we need the language of faith and a faithful view of reality to understand and have spiritual experiences. We need words and symbols referring to God, to perceive God, to understand our experience of God, and to mediate them to others.[108] Comparably, Peels mentions the problem of the ignorance of sinners of their sins and sinful nature. Even if we recognize moral evil, "of most sins we would not have known that they are sins and we would not consider ourselves as sinful because we would not be inclined to relate our acts, words, deeds and being to God, our creator, and redeemer."[109] Disclosing phenomena semiotically and reconstructing them symbolically requires fitting language and the ability to use this language properly—and on this level also sin is active.

4. Corporate effects: As language already implies, sin is working on a corporate level. Stephen Moroney, writing about the noetic effects of sin, signals that theological treatments of the noetic effects of sin, often neglect this corporate level. Kuyper does mention the influence of education, language, social-cultural context, and worldview. Here, he has the corporate dimension in mind, for "no one exists atomistically in his consciousness."[110] This is emphasized by Moroney as well: our thinking is influenced by historical communities and traditions. Consequently, "sinful elements in human traditions have distorting noetic effects on the thinking of people within those traditions."[111] When we experience sexism, racism, or other forms of injustice, we see that sin becomes part of our societal structures. These forms of injustice all have a cognitive aspect, influencing how we perceive and value the other. Traditions and communities have a formative effect, positive and negative. Sin as well as sanctification has a corporate dimension.[112]

---

106. Kuyper, *Encyclopedia of Sacred Theology*, 108.
107. O'Donovan, *Desire of the Nations*, 14.
108. De Jong-Van Campen, *Mystagogie in werking*, 84–86.
109. Peels, "Effects of Sin," 67; and further 63–67.
110. Kuyper, *Encyclopedia of Sacred Theology*, 109; and further 108.
111. Moroney, *Noetic Effects of Sin*, 39.
112. Moroney, *Noetic Effects of Sin*, 38–39. On the corporate dimension of

5. Logic: Westphal suggests that logic also is influenced by sin. This might seem counterintuitive, but this changes once the moral dimension of logic is unveiled. Westphal writes, "It is not hard to see that logic, as the theory of what inferences we are entitled to make and with what level of confidence, is but a subdivision of epistemological ethics, specifying an important subset of epistemic rights and duties."[113] Westphal concludes that sin has influenced our logic as well.

6. Mechanisms of cognitive selection: It is important to realize what it is to have or live a perspective. In a perspective, we observe, select, interpret, orientate, and communicate. We observe phenomena together with other phenomena, and by focusing on something we select, leaving out others. We understand this something as something, and we do this within a cognitive frame, placing phenomena within larger wholes. Doing so, we have the standpoint that we locate somewhere which implies that we orientate ourselves. Furthermore, during these processes of observing, selecting, interpreting, and orientating we meet other perspectives and communicate with them.[114]

Sin influences our motives when we select and interpret. Kuyper classifies this as the working of sin "upon our consciousness through an endless variety of moral motives." He sees the influence of various "moral differences, which are governed by self-interests."[115] Other authors mention wrong and sinful longings and intentions, egoist or dominating motives, and personal interests both on a personal and corporate level. The work of the "masters of suspicion," Nietzsche, Marx, and Freud, confirm the influence of sin on our (unconscious) motives and desires for power and domination.[116] This influences the processes of selecting, interpreting, orientating, and communicating.

In these processes, we can discover what Westphal refers to as the "Law of Inverse Rationality": "The ability of human thought to be undistorted by sinful desire is inversely proportional to the existential import of the subject matter."[117] Likewise, according to Moroney "the noetic effects of sin generally are expected to be most evident

---

understanding, see Dalferth, *Kunst des Verstehens*, 23–25.

113. Westphal, "Taking St. Paul Seriously," 200–201.

114. See Dalferth, *Kombinatorische Theologie*, 87–90; Dalferth, *Becoming Present*, 26; Dalferth, *Radikale Theologie*, 246–50; Dalferth, *Kunst des Verstehens*, 20–21, 72.

115. Kuyper, *Encyclopedia of Sacred Theology*, 110.

116. Moroney, *Noetic Effects of Sin*, 37–41, 89–98; Westphal, "Taking St. Paul Seriously," 218–19; Zwiep, *Tussen tekst en lezer*, 2:50–62.

117. Westphal, "Hermeneutics and Holiness," 205.

in the knowledge of God, less evident in the knowledge of human beings, and least evident in the knowledge of impersonal aspects of creation."[118] Consequently, one might expect that in the field of theology, the effects of sin on our knowing and understanding will be most far-reaching.

Of course, this has an emotional aspect as well. Cognition and emotion are closely intertwined, for "emotions are cognitive-shaped affective reactions." Moreover, "anticipated affect" is "an important criterion for decision and action."[119] As sin influences our cognitions and our affections, misconceptions, and misguided affections will influence us in a way that shows the interwovenness of both. Furthermore, enhanced existential importance will lead to a greater intensity of emotions and a greater motivational influence. As Clore observes, "The power and impact of emotions depend on the magnitude of their objects."[120]

7. Social relations: In social relationships, we see the impact of sin specifically in injustice and its noetic consequences. As Miroslav Volf shows, the relationship between the self and the other is vulnerable; exclusion is a recurrent evil. Miroslav Volf defines exclusion as "the sinful activity of reconfiguring the creation."[121] Again, language plays a role. Practices of exclusion always are preceded by symbolic exclusion, the use of language and cognitions that support excluding acts. This is not so much a matter of ignorance, but "a willful misconstruction": "We refuse to know what is manifest and choose to know what serves our interests."[122] This is only a radicalization of the fact that our knowledge is shaped by our interests and filtered through our cultures, paradigms, and traditions. The postmodern idea of "regimes of truth" reveals that often we produce truth and knowledge to exercise power over the other.[123] Acts of exclusion, and our cognitions and interpretation, the linguistic activities of our mind, are inseparably related.

---

118. Moroney, *Noetic Effects of Sin*, 37. Moroney refers to Brunner as his source, see Moroney, 31–33.

119. Clore, "Psychology and the Rationality of Emotion," 220.

120. Clore, "Psychology and the Rationality of Emotion," 221.

121. Volf, *Exclusion and Embrace*, 66–67.

122. Volf, *Exclusion and Embrace*, 76. According to Volf, evil is able to create an illusion of well-being. This illusion appears to us as the truth. Living with such lies, they shape our selves. As long as evil is not recognized, we can feel free and comfortable, living with these illusions. See Volf, *Exclusion and Embrace*, 89–90.

123. Volf, *Exclusion and Embrace*, 67, 75–76, 243–49.

Because our will plays a crucial role in our knowledge, we have to be interested in the truth and want to use our power in the right way, before we can discover the truth. As Volf phrases it, "Both the 'clenched fist' and the 'open arms' are *epistemological stances*: they are *moral conditions of moral perception*."[124]

8. Large bodies of knowledge: As knowing subjects, we construct larger bodies of knowledge or place information within these larger cognitive frames and narratives. But often we understand, the true knowledge we have, within a wrong perspective and cognitive frame, according to Van Woudenberg. This can be the result of metaphysically untrue ideas, or—as Abraham Kuyper phrases it—wrong "life- and worldviews." Van Woudenberg refers to the Dutch philosopher Herman Dooyeweerd, who had a sharp eye for our tendency to absolutize ideas or motifs that are not wrong in themselves but become distorted being absolutized.[125] Because cognitive frames use semiotic means, this level is closely intertwined with the level of language. This becomes clear when the destructive influence of wrong interpretations, powerful images, and one-sided narratives is concerned, which has been emphasized from different sides. Different forms of cognitive therapy, narrative concepts of identity, and Feminist analyses of sexist language all agree in this respect: interpretations, images, and narratives are not innocent.[126] Dallas Willard, writing on spiritual formation, also emphasizes the importance of ideas like "very general models or assumptions about reality" as well as "images that occupy our minds."[127] Also here the influence of sin is working.

This overview shows that sin is working at many different levels of our human existence and of processes of knowing and understanding. The reality of sin and its consequences is messy, as the reality of evil always is. Although sin can be removed by salvation, this does not mean that the restoration of our existence, of our acts of knowing and understanding is a quick fix. The process of the renewal of our existence and the mind by

---

124. Volf, *Exclusion and Embrace*, 216; and further 249, 254, 270. On epistemology and injustice, see Fricker, *Epistemic Injustice*.

125. Van Woudenberg, "Over de noëtische gevolgen," 240; Van Woudenberg, "Filosofie en de verduistering." Kuyper diagnoses this problem as a consequence of a wrong used or over exited imagination, subjecting the mind to the dominion of imperfect images. See Kuyper, *Encyclopedia of Sacred Theology*, 108–9.

126. See, e.g., Keyes, *Beyond Identity*, 1–72; Verkerk, *Sekse als antwoord*, 89–115, 138–40, 143–46.

127. Willard, *Renovation of the Heart*, 96, 99; and further 96–101.

participation in Christ is complicated, too complicated to give a clear-cut overview of it.

In Abraham Kuyper's view on the sciences as he develops this in his *Encyclopedia of Sacred Theology*, it seems that although the noetic consequences of sin are many, the regeneration (*paliggenesis*) of humanity in Christ results in a restoration of the human mind. Kuyper distinguished two kinds of people, and accordingly two kinds of science. The different starting points will result in two unfinished buildings of sciences, the building of the sciences with *paliggenesis* as the foundation, and the building of sciences without *paliggenesis*. The renewal of the mind by faith, by the union with the organic head of the renewed humanity, by the Holy Spirit seems to bear fruit in a Christian building of science where the noetic consequences of sin are more or less removed.[128]

If this were the case, the noetic consequences only were a problem to unregenerate, nonbelievers. Regenerate Christian believers, however, were free from these noetic consequences. This is too optimistic a view—it would be a kind of noetic perfectionism. Although noetic sanctification is a reality as well and the renewal of the mind by participation in the mind of Christ is the reality in the life of Christians, this does not imply that the noetic consequences of sin are completely removed at once.[129]

3.5 SECULARIZATION AND SIN: THE NECESSITY OF SOTERIOLOGY

A theological hermeneutic aimed at understanding *coram deo* is not self-evident. The Western world is plural and has largely distanced itself from the Christian faith. There are multiple ways to read the Bible—Jewish, different Christian ways of reading, from a non-believing perspective—and there are different ways to understand God, the self, and the world. Charles Taylor's analysis of the Western "secular" world shows that this plurality is destabilizing for everyone and that no option is the most obvious one. The crises we are facing are huge, and it is an open question for many whether the Christian faith will have good answers to these crises. Often, human desires are attached to different objects, and human hearts are divided. It is possible to be a Christian, to be an atheist, to adhere to another religion. Which position we have depends on our self-understanding, our social imaginary, and our image of God; but also on our affections, the stories we

---

128. Kuyper, *Encyclopedia of Sacred Theology*, 150–76, 275–92.
129. Cf. Vanhoozer, *Drama of Doctrine*, 302–5.

live with, the desires of our heart, and the way we deal with the challenges of our lives.

A characteristic of human beings is that we understand. We live with a self-image, a worldview, and an image of God. These images are not purely rational and intellectual but are related to the practices in which we participate, to our physical actions, and to our passions and affections. Our existence is an embodied existence, in which what we experience in that bodily embodied existence has a formative effect on our desires, our understanding, and our faith.

Theologically, however, there is another layer: sin plays an important role in our embodied existence. Fundamental to human existence is the relationship with God and the desire of the human heart. A break in this relationship with God affects all of existence: where the center of one's existence is, what one's desires are centered on, how one takes one's place in the order of creation, and how secure one's environment is. To miss God means to live in a fundamentally disrupted existence. This has noetic consequences, which become more pronounced when ideological, spiritual, and religious interests are at stake. So whether a person's life is open to God or not has everything to do with sin. Sin is both a matter of responsibility and guilt as well as an enslaving power. The noetic consequences of sin show the complexity of sin.

Given our pluralistic and "secular" context, the nature of our human existence, and the noetic consequences of sin, it is not obvious to start theology with epistemology. First, a neutral starting point for such an epistemology does not exist, because God himself and faith in God are controversial. The plurality of our context puts pressure on our beliefs so that to live a Christian life more is needed than a discussion of the epistemic reliability of our faith. Second, an epistemological starting point wrongly suggests that we are primarily rational beings asking critical-reflective questions about true knowledge. As humans, we are being formed in the entirety of our embodied lives, and the knowledge we have is part of the life form in which we participate. Our knowing is inseparably connected to the narratives in which we live, our communities, our practices, our actions, and our feelings. Ordinary life has the primacy of reflective activities such as epistemology. And finally, before we can know God well, we have to deal with the problem of the noetic effects of sin. Or better, God himself has to restore us so that we can know, trust, and love him. Thus, thinking about hermeneutics and Scripture cannot start as epistemology. From the beginning, reflection on knowing and understanding has to be embedded in a Trinitarian soteriology and ecclesiology, and in the (first order) reality of Christian life and practice that precedes our (second order) theological reflections.

To live with God in our Western world requires conversion and spiritual formation. This formation can not only be rational but must extend throughout the embodied life. This formation should primarily have the character of redemption, life within a Christian community, rebirth, and sanctification. Our existence needs transformation to understand *coram deo*. Consequently, theological reflection on the Bible, our understanding, and our knowledge should be embedded in soteriology.

4.

Trinity and Perspective

The New Perspective Given in the Saving Acts of Father, Son, and Spirit

4.1 INTRODUCTION

In theology, we need a soteriological perspective on hermeneutics and Scripture, as an alternative to an epistemological approach of Scripture and hermeneutics. Such an epistemological approach with its emphasis on certainty is not the best entranceway to Scripture and theological hermeneutics in our pluralistic, secularized context. It is not only that our culture made a pragmatic turn and has a raised awareness of the embodied character of human existence, but more importantly, we see more clearly than in a Christian culture that the epistemological quest for knowledge is not the primary human quest. First comes the soteriological quest for the restoration of our relationship with God and our life *coram deo*.

This sets an agenda for this and the next chapters. In an alternative soteriological approach, it is important not to isolate the doctrine of Scripture from other theological themes, just as Scripture should not be abstracted from the relationship with the Triune God. Theology should clarify how Scripture is located within the relationship with the Triune God, and how human listening to Scripture is embedded in the saving acts of the Triune God. In the Christian life, the existential certainty of faith in Jesus Christ has priority on the epistemic certainty of beliefs about Scripture. Consequently, it is necessary to rethink the relationship between Christ and Scripture. Moreover, it is important not to forget the formation of the hearer of the Word and the reader of Scripture. This should receive explicit theological attention, especially now our Western context is no longer Christian, and this formation is no longer naturally folded into Christian education followed by all. Reflection on the understanding of Scripture has to be closely intertwined with the reflection on the transformation of the human perspective. Conversion has a hermeneutical aspect. Theology further should take seriously that hearing, reading, and understanding Scripture is closely connected with Christian practices, with liturgy, and with a life of faith.

The best way to start these reflections is with the doctrine of the Trinity. For revelation, soteriology, hermeneutics, and Scripture, the importance of the Trinity cannot be underestimated. As Herman Bavinck knew, "The dogma of the Trinity . . . tells us that God *can* reveal himself in an absolute sense to the Son and the Spirit, and hence, in a relative sense also to the world." And he wrote, "Now in Christ, God himself comes out to us, and in the Holy Spirit he communicates himself to us. The work of recreation is Trinitarian through and through."[1]

In the "Trinitarian renaissance" of the twentieth century, the practical relevance of the doctrine of the Trinity has been rediscovered. Unfortunately, this practical relevance has been understood in the Anglo-Saxon theological world especially as social. Accordingly, critics of the Trinitarian renaissance focus on the social doctrines of the Trinity. However, the practical relevance of the doctrine of the Trinity encompasses more than its social relevance and also concerns the hermeneutical relevance of the doctrine of the Trinity.[2]

Eberhard Jüngel has drawn attention to this hermeneutical relevance. In the theological Germany of 1960, Karl Barth's doctrine of the Word of God and Rudolf Bultmann's hermeneutics seemed to be diametrically opposed. Jüngel was driven by the desire to bring together the "anthropocentric" hermeneutical school of Bultmann and the "theological" school of Barth, emphasizing the importance of the Word of God.[3] First of all, Jüngel states that Barth's decision to place the doctrine of the Trinity at the beginning of his treatment of his dogmatics, in the doctrine of revelation,

---

1. Bavinck, *Reformed Dogmatics*, 2:333-34; Bavinck, *Gereformeerde dogmatiek*, 2:300-301. See further Paddison, "Authority of Scripture"; Webster, *Holy Scripture*, 11-16.

2. On the Trinitarian renaissance, its critics, and on the practical relevance of the doctrine of the Trinity, see Van den Brink, "Social Trinitarianism"; Burger, "Hart en wezen"; Burger, "Hermeneutisch relevante triniteitsleer"; Fermer, "Limits of Trinitarian Theology"; Holmes, "Three versus One?"; Kärkkäinen, "Trajectories of the Contemporary 'Trinitarian Renaissance'"; McDougall, "Lässt Sich die praktische Bedeutung?"; Venter, "Taking Stock of the Trinitarian Renaissance."

3. On Jüngel's development, see Dvorak, *Gott ist Liebe*, 198-274.

is "a hermeneutical decision of the greatest relevance."[4] Barth's decision evidences the structuring function of the doctrine of the Trinity for the entire systematic theology.

But the Trinitarian formulation Barth chooses to refer to God in his revelation shows that the hermeneutical relevance goes further, including our understanding of God. Barth argues that God himself "in unimpaired unity yet also in unimpaired distinction is Revealer, Revelation, and Revealedness"[5] Barth finds the roots of the doctrine of the Trinity in God's revelation, where God's Word is identical with God himself, where God himself ensures that his revelation is understood, and he himself is known as the Triune. Jüngel characterizes Barth's doctrine of the Trinity as "the interpretation of revelation and thus the interpretation of the being of God which is made possible by revelation as God's self-interpretation"[6] The Triune God is the Lord of his own revelation and remains the subject of his revelation. This function of the doctrine of the Trinity, to prevent any objectification of God in speaking about God, corresponds to the function of Bultmann's program of demythologizing.[7]

However, more is at stake than just our understanding of God. Jüngel argues that Barth in his theological statements does not abstract from the anthropological relationship given by revelation.[8] Because God reveals himself in Jesus Christ, we are confronted with the hermeneutic problem in a twofold way, according to Jüngel. After all, in Jesus Christ, we have to do with the elect God and the chosen man. Thus, in God's revelation, we face the question of our understanding of God, but also of our understanding of ourselves and our world.[9] When God is revealed, our existence is brought into a relationship with God's existence. God's "Gegenständlichkeit" ("being-as-object") evokes our love and fear of God, although we can also deny that love and fear of God in sin. Given this relationship between God's existence and our existence, Jüngel can speak of "God's being-as-object as

---

4. "Eine hermeneutische Entscheidung von äußerster Relevanz." Jüngel, *Gottes Sein ist im Werden*, 15; Jüngel, *God's Being Is in Becoming*, 16.

5. "In unzerstörter Einheit, aber auch in unzerstörter Verschiedenheit der Offenbarer, die Offenbarung und das Offenbar–sein ist." Barth, *Kirchliche Dogmatik*, I/1, 311; Barth, *Church Dogmatics*, I/1, 298.

6. "Die durch die Offenbarung als Selbstinterpretation Gottes ermöglichte Interpretation der Offenbarung und damit des Seins Gottes." Jüngel, *Gottes Sein ist im Werden*, 27; Jüngel, *God's Being Is in Becoming*, 27.

7. Jüngel, *Gottes Sein ist im Werden*, 33–34; Jüngel, *God's Being Is in Becoming*, 33–34.

8. Jüngel, *Gottes Sein ist im Werden*, 72; Jüngel, *God's Being Is in Becoming*, 71–72.

9. Jüngel, *Gottes Sein ist im Werden*, 10–11; Jüngel, *God's Being Is in Becoming*, 10–11.

anthropological existentiale."[10] God's revelation in Jesus Christ and through the Holy Spirit therefore also has significance for our understanding of ourselves and our world.

The importance of the bridge that has been built by Jüngel between the Word of God theology and hermeneutical theology cannot be overestimated. As long as hermeneutics is seen as having a liberal tendency, more orthodox theologians will cling to a Word of God theology, fearing hermeneutics and contextuality. However, when it is emphasized that the Triune God reveals himself and speaks to us in Christ and the Spirit, this can change. First, it can be shown that in Christ and the Spirit God enables us to understand his Word. Second, in Christ and the Spirit, understanding the Word leads to a renewal of our understanding of God, of our neighbor and our self, and of our world and our context. In Christ we receive clarity, in the Spirit we receive insight, standing in the plurality of all our contexts. Crucial for contemporary understanding of God's Word in Christ is not our hermeneutical activity, but the gracious and saving act of God who makes us understand.

Nevertheless, an important question concerning such a soteriological hermeneutics should be kept in mind. Jüngel has made a synthesis between the theologies of Bultmann and Barth, who were both students of Johann Wilhelm Herrmann (1846-1922). Herrmann's Christocentric theology is characterized by the duality of a secularized world and the inner life of Jesus (and the transcendental subjectivity of religious humans). Bultmann takes human existence as the center of his work and shares with Herrmann the duality of Kant's two worlds. He developed a "hermeneutics of self-explanation."[11] Barth's Christocentric theology is critical of natural theology and metaphysics, as was Herrmann's. According to Berkhof, Barth's starting point of the transcendental subjectivity of God did not result in a better entranceway to human history than Herrmann's theology.[12] Herrmann, Bultmann, and Barth share the problem that the immanent world is seen as neutral and their theological perspectives have difficulties in getting access to creation and human history.[13] Does hermeneutical theology after Jüngel solve this problem?

Ingolf Dalferth signals that hermeneutical theology until Jüngel and Ebeling did not succeed in giving a "coherent interpretation of our reality

10. "Gottes Gegenständlich-Sein als anthropologisches Existential." Jüngel, *Gottes Sein ist im Werden*, 69, and further 70-71; Jüngel, *God's Being Is in Becoming*, 69, and further 70-71.

11. Dalferth, *Radikale Theologie*, 81.

12. Berkhof, *200 Jahre Theologie*, 200.

13. Berkhof, *200 Jahre Theologie*, 149-50, 165-67, 172-73, 197-200.

of life and experience."[14] Hermeneutical theology did give a systematic explication of faith, starting from the Word event. The interpretation of our life and experience in the light of faith, however, remained fragmentary, making only a first exploratory step. Hermeneutical theology evokes two questions: the *ontological* question concerning how our worldly experience relates to the Word of God that has created it; and the *epistemological* question concerning the relationship between the human word, the world of experience, and the Word of God. Again, Dalferth signals a deficiency: a good creation-theological answer to the ontological question has not been given, nor has a good pneumatological answer to the epistemological question.[15] Thus, it is an important question whether a Christocentric, soteriological starting point for theological hermeneutics succeeds in giving access to our world. Does such a theological hermeneutic help to understand our world God's creation where he is present and active, and accordingly to the created world, to human history, and to human experience?[16]

In this chapter, Ingolf U. Dalferth (1948) will be my primary dialogue partner.[17] Although Dalferth has studied in Cambridge and knows the Anglo-Saxon analytical tradition well, first of all, he is a German theologian educated by Eberhard Jüngel. From 1995 to 2013, he was the professor of systematic theology and philosophy of religion at the university of Zürich (Switzerland); from 1998 to 2012, he was also the director of the Institute of Hermeneutics and Philosophy of Religion of that university. Moreover, he held the Danforth Chair in Philosophy of Religion at Claremont Graduate University (United States of America) from 2007 to 2020. In his recent publications, he has profiled himself as a hermeneutical thinker who wants to continue the German tradition of hermeneutical theology and philosophy.[18]

In line with Jüngel, Dalferth understands the revelation of the Triune God as a saving event in which God identifies himself to someone. This is an event with many consequences: one is relocated *coram deo* and enabled to understand everything in the light of God's loving presence. Thus, God's Trinitarian self-revelation renews and changes one's understanding of God,

---

14. Dalferth, *Radikale Theologie*, 92–93.

15. Dalferth, *Radikale Theologie*, 110–11.

16. In Fickert's study of Dalferth's work, it is a recurrent question whether Dalferth in his theology bridges the gap between the conditions of general experiential reality and of revelation in the Word event. See Fickert, *Erfahrung und Offenbarung*.

17. See on Dalferth's work Burger, *Being in Christ*, 399–452; Burger, "Hermeneutisch relevante triniteitsleer"; Fickert, *Erfahrung und Offenbarung*; Laube, *Im Bann der Sprache*; Rieger, *Theologie als Funktion der Kirche*.

18. Dalferth, *Wirklichkeit des Möglichen*; Dalferth, *Malum*; Dalferth, *Radikale Theologie*; Dalferth, *Kunst des Verstehens*; Dalferth, *Wirkendes Wort*.

the self, and the world. In search of an alternative soteriological approach to hermeneutics and Scripture, I will in this chapter examine Dalferth's hermeneutical theology.

To do this, I will sketch the development of Dalferth's hermeneutical theology in 4.2. In the next step, I will analyze in detail the central theological concepts of his thinking (4.3). In 4.4, I will give a short evaluation to see to which extend his hermeneutical theology helps in my own project to construct a soteriological approach to hermeneutics.

4.2 DALFERTH'S DEVELOPMENT

4.2.1 Phase 1: Self-Identification, Location, Orientation

To give a first impression of Dalferth's position, I start with a sketch of his theological development. In the first phase, Dalferth develops the basic structure of his soteriological hermeneutics, in three works: his PhD thesis *Religiöse Rede von Gott* (1981), his habilitation *Existenz Gottes und christlicher Glaube* (1984), and the English publication *Theology and Philosophy* (1988).[19] In this phase, questions concerning the existence and the doctrine of God are his starting point. The end of this phase is marked by a volume with essays with the title *Gott* (1992).

Religiöse Rede von Gott offers a theological treatment of the Anglo-Saxon analytical philosophy of language and religion from a German perspective. It is a quest for an understanding of religious (Christian) God-talk. Dalferth understands the basic structure of Christian religious discourse as the answer to the experience of being addressed by God.[20] According to Dalferth, to experience something means that something is observed and identified, and this observed something is experienced as something by someone.[21] Accordingly, the Christian experience of being addressed by God is an experience of Jesus by someone as an address—an address of God.[22] The paradigmatic situation of the Christian religious experience is the experience of Pentecost: the historical events of the life and death of Jesus are experienced as an address of God, which leads to the confession:

---

19. Fickert divides Dalferth's development in three phases: 1. Die Verständlichkeit religiöser Rede von Gott (*Religiöse Rede von Gott*); 2 Dalferths Konzeption einer eschatologischen Ontologie (*Existenz Gottes und christlicher Glaube*); 3. Die Radikalität hermeneutischer Theologie Heute. See Fickert, *Erfahrung und Offenbarung*.

20. Dalferth, *Religiöse Rede von Gott*, 373–91.

21. Dalferth, *Religiöse Rede von Gott*, 460–61.

22. Dalferth, *Religiöse Rede von Gott*, 396–97.

Jesus is the Christ.[23] The basic Christian experience implies that someone experiences Jesus as God's address and hence God as the subject of this address.[24]

This basic Christian experience makes it possible to identify God christologically. We cannot specify who God is by description or *deixis*, but only thanks to God's Trinitarian individuation, which enables us to experience Jesus as God's address. This address is Trinitarian, for God is the subject

"– whose address is experienced in Jesus
– who makes it possible to experience Jesus as address
– who brings himself in Jesus to experience as address."[25]

After he discusses the problem of the identification of God, in the next step, Dalferth analyses the problem of predication. Propositions referring to God have the form of "God is *p*." This predication of *p* to God, is characterized by Dalferth as parabolic predication, which implies its perspectival character and narrative structure.[26] Its perspectival character means that this predication is self-involving and includes an implied attitude toward God. To state "God is Father" implies that it is appropriate for us to have the feelings, thoughts, and attitudes toward God as toward a father.[27] Due to its narrative structure, predications are always short versions of the story of Jesus in which God is experienced by the experience of Jesus as God's address. Thus, Christian God-talk is bound to the particular story of Jesus Christ. This story bears in itself a tension between the certitude asserted by faith ("Gewissheit"), and the eschatological security hoped for ("Sicherheit").[28] As a result of this self-identification, God is always viewed as speaking and saving. He makes his saving presence knowable and accessible, a presence that creates, restores, and helps.[29]

Existenz Gottes und christlicher Glaube builds on the idea of God's self-identifying address in Christ and through the Spirit. The book is an attempt to sketch an eschatological ontology "*sub specie fidei*," as the ontological implications of the Christian faith.[30] In this exposition of the new understanding of God, the self, and the world, Dalferth unfolds the new

---

23. Dalferth, *Religiöse Rede von Gott*, 469–70. In his later work, Dalferth does not refer to Pentecost but to Easter; see, e.g., Dalferth, *Auferweckte Gekreuzigte*, 38–84; Dalferth, *Crucified and Resurrected*, 39–82.

24. Dalferth, *Religiöse Rede von Gott*, 473.

25. Dalferth, *Religiöse Rede von Gott*, 604, and further 598–606.

26. Dalferth, *Religiöse Rede von Gott*, 647–48, 666.

27. Dalferth, *Religiöse Rede von Gott*, 648–52.

28. Dalferth, *Religiöse Rede von Gott*, 652–68.

29. Dalferth, *Religiöse Rede von Gott*, 678.

30. Dalferth, *Existenz Gottes und christlicher Glaube*, 76.

perspective that results from God's self-identification. Doing so, he develops a new element that will prove to be an important building block of his hermeneutical framework: location.

Language is important in this ontology. In language, we refer to entities, with designators, in propositional acts. An entity is a semiotic construction that we construct in a semiotic process as an object to which we refer as an entity. Dalferth carefully differentiates between *semantic constructions*, which do not refer to an existing entity, and *semantic reconstructions* which represent something that exists independently of its symbolic representation. Moreover, he also makes a distinction between our model of reality and reality itself. It is an important hermeneutical principle to differentiate critically between reality and our model of reality.[31] Although this implies (critical) realism, it also implies the relativity of all ontological reflection. Our models of reality are hypothetical and always open to revision. Moreover, ontological reflection depends on a certain view of reality, in this case, the Christian faith. Dalferth concludes: "to be is to be related to our story."[32]

Consequently, Dalferth comes to an understanding of existence as a relational location. By stating "*a* exists," a person says something about himself, locating "*a*" in relation to himself. Utterances of the form "*a* exists" are locating, relational and self-involving. In the case of an existing object, this relation is a real relation.[33] This ontological concept of relational location will turn out to be a crucial element in Dalferth's theological hermeneutic framework.

Although human beings live in time and space, existence is not necessarily spatio-temporal. Consequently, Dalferth differentiates between spatio-temporality (ontic relations) and existence (ontological relations).[34] To claim that God exists and that a real ontological relation exists between a person and God (a relationship between a spatio-temporal person and God who is not spatio-temporal), it has to be possible for that person to identify God. Apart from the difference between the creator and his creatures, the problem of sin appears. The separation of sinful human beings and a righteous God perverts this difference between the creator and creatures, and results in the epistemic blindness of humanity.[35] Human sinners have absolutized their spatio-temporality, assuming that their spatio-temporal reality

---

31. Dalferth, *Existenz Gottes und christlicher Glaube*, 32–36.
32. Dalferth, *Existenz Gottes und christlicher Glaube*, 73; and further 55–57, 65–66.
33. Dalferth, *Existenz Gottes und christlicher Glaube*, 121–22, 126–28. Already in Dalferth, *Religiöse Rede von Gott*, 590–91. See further Dalferth, *Gott*, 23–50.
34. Dalferth, *Existenz Gottes und christlicher Glaube*, 144–50.
35. Dalferth, *Existenz Gottes und christlicher Glaube*, 172–73.

is the only reality, and ignoring both the creator and our own creatureliness. As a result, God's reality in his glory and our spatio-temporal world have become total alternatives, and as sinners, we can no longer identify God. As sinners, humans have no shared identification system with God.[36]

However, God is able to let sinners experience his existence under the conditions of time and space. When God addresses someone in Jesus as Christ, God identifies himself to someone and locates that person within God's identification system. As a result, two identification systems are juxtaposed. From that point on, this person and also his world can be identified within two different identification systems: the ontic one influenced by sin, and the identification system of God, living in his glory. Hence, God's self-identification results in an identification system shared by God and this person, and a location within God's identification system. This makes the communal existence of God and humans possible, and the unambiguous identification and location of existing entities in their relation to God and to Christ as the center of God's identification system. This not only leads to a new experience of all known reality in the light of God's presence but also to the experience of new realities and possibilities given by God's loving presence. To conclude, the self-identification of God, including humans in God's identification system, results in a new location in God's presence and consequently in a new human perspective.

In *Theology and Philosophy*, Dalferth develops these ideas of a new location and a new perspective toward the concept of orientational knowledge. Dealing with the rationality of theology and the relation between a theological and a philosophical perspective, Martin Luther's thinking is an important source. Luther does not divide knowledge according to a formal or methodological scheme, but he distinguishes between human knowledge *extra Christum* and *in Christo*. As a result, the distinction between philosophy and theology is reframed theologically. Philosophy and theology "are different kinds of knowledge of the same things, placed in different perspectives and frames of reference: viz. the *coram mundo* perspective and its relations to things in the world and the *coram deo* perspective of its relations to God."[37] Both the perspective of worldly relations (*coram mundo*) and the perspective of relations to God (*coram deo*) are necessary, but these two discourses should not be mixed. God does not exist as an empirical phenomenon *coram mundo*, but he is the ground of everything that exists and is invisibly present in natural phenomena. Reason *coram mundo* is unable to

---

36. Dalferth, *Existenz Gottes und christlicher Glaube*, 179–83. In *Existenz Gottes*, Dalferth refers to this identification system as a "Gegenständlichkeit." In an article, summarizing his habilitation, he uses "Identifikationssystem," see Dalferth, *Gott*, 47.

37. Dalferth, *Theology and Philosophy*, 77.

know that God exists, that he created the world, or that he brings the world to its eschatological end. Because reason cannot identify God, reason cannot understand things in their relation to God. Only to faith is God identified. Consequently, only faith knows that God exists as the creative origin and the eschatological end of the world and that God qualifies all existence as existence *coram deo*. God "is not a relation in the world, but the relation which defines the world."[38] Predicates like "is created" or "is a sinner" do not describe, but locate before God and imply God's self-identification and our identification of God, both in Jesus Christ.

It must be noticed yet, that these different predicates indicate the internal differentiation of the *coram deo*-perspective: God relates to the world in a twofold way, according to the Law and according to the Gospel, and all entities can be characterized with a Law-description, and a Gospel-description, e.g., as a sinner (Law) and saved sinner (Gospel).[39] Using Luther, Dalferth refers to the perspective of absolutized spatio-temporality as *coram mundo*-perspective, and the perspective opened by God's self-identification as *coram deo*-perspective.

The concept of location returns in relation to the concept of orientational knowledge and the problem of the relativity of self-knowledge. God's self-identification in his revelation to someone has a locating impact: we are located before God and God is located relative to us. Location makes orientation possible. Orientational knowledge is practical knowledge, with two functions: to locate and to organize. Locating knowledge always implies personal self-knowledge, which emerges only in linguistic interaction between persons who communicate. The intersubjective character of self-knowledge, however, does not remove its relative, contingent, and to some extent inconsistent character of our self-knowledge. Consequently, location and orientation retain a relative character. This would change if someone knows me absolutely if I can share in this absolute knowledge of myself, and if I can apply this absolute knowledge to my own identification and knowledge of myself. That God exists and knows me totally, that he reveals his knowledge of me in the gospel of Jesus Christ in personal communication to me, and that I know myself according to God's knowledge in the internal perspective of faith, results in absolutely locating self-knowledge. The organization of our world begins with God's self-disclosure in Christ as saving and creating love. Now we can restructure our world according to

---

38. Dalferth, *Theology and Philosophy*, 78.

39. Dalferth, *Existenz Gottes und christlicher Glaube*, 254, 339–40; Dalferth, *Theology and Philosophy*, 77–80, 85–87.

this pattern of love and reorganize our world according to the will of God.[40] To summarize, the self-identification of God and the resulting location in God's identification system are in *Theology and Philosophy* understood as absolute location, which enables orientation.

At the end of the first phase, Dalferth coined his three central concepts: Triune self-identification, location, and orientation. They constitute the backbone of his hermeneutical framework.

Of course, language, signs, and communication are important to Dalferth. We understand our world using language. Basic to his thinking is the idea that "someone understands something as something." The concept of the Triune self-identification concretizes what this idea implies for understanding God. Through the Spirit, Jesus is experienced by someone as Christ and hence as the address of God the Father.

God's presence has a saving character, which has hermeneutical implications as we shall see. Once God's presence is disclosed to someone, a process starts of renewal of one's understanding of God, the world, and the self. Here we find *in nuce* the soteriological character of his hermeneutics. This soteriological character is closely connected to the self-involving character of Christian God-talk. If I am addressed by God and if I understand that address, this divine self-communication has consequences for my attitudes, primarily but not only toward God. God's Trinitarian self-identification will change my understanding and my life.[41]

In this self-identification, we are absolutely located *coram deo*. Where we used to live as sinners *coram mundo*, now a new perspective *coram mundo* opens up. Due to this new location and this new perspective, we can orient ourselves in a new way. God's self-revelation to someone leads to orientational knowledge that is always practical and self-involving. We are enabled to orient ourselves in our world and organize our world in a way following God's self-disclosure as loving nearness.

God's self-disclosure changes our perspective on all phenomena. Because God is not a phenomenon under the phenomena, but gives us a new perspective on all phenomena *coram deo*, theology itself cannot be phenomenology. Still, Dalferth has a realist attitude, in this sense that he emphasizes that God's presence is a reality. Otherwise, "it becomes virtually impossible

---

40. Dalferth, *Theology and Philosophy*, 158–62, 190, 194, 204–13, 219, 212.

41. According to Dalferth, this self-involving character of Christian God-talk and the implied renewal of our orientation, is neglected in the work of recent theistic philosophers like Richard Swinburne and Alvin Plantinga. As a result, their work has little to say to the daily life of Christians. See, e.g., Dalferth, *Becoming Present*, 135; Dalferth, *Wirklichkeit des Möglichen*, 217–18, 300–303, 451–52.

meaningfully to distinguish between God and our views and imaginative constructions of God."[42]

4.2.2 Phases 2 and 3: Further Development of a Hermeneutical Theology

In the second phase of his development, Dalferth expanded this position in studies that clarify his view of the method and content of systematic theology.[43] Hermeneutically, central to Dalferth's reflection is the tension between plurality and particularity, on the one hand, and the reality and universal presence of God's love on the other. This can be seen clearly in the volume with articles on hermeneutical themes that mark the transition to the third stage of development: *Gedeutete Gegenwart* (1997). As human beings, we use signs and language. Again, Dalferth emphasizes the epistemic structure of our human experience: someone experiences something as something. That means that human experience is plural and particular.[44] The same is true of the experience of faith. Still, Dalferth opposes tribalism, as if one can determine, by oneself, what God is. If God is God, he is a reality even if we can live with that reality only as participants. According to Dalferth, God's love is an active reality that is universal, although this reality is disclosed in Jesus Christ. For that reason, theology has to be a public activity. The rational discourse of the university is a way to discuss the truth and reality of the claims of the Christian faith in an open and public accessible manner.[45]

The third phase was a very productive one, that started with his appointment as professor of systematic theology and philosophy of religion in Zürich (1995). The first important publication in this third phase is *Die Wirklichkeit des Möglichen* (2003), his proposal of a hermeneutical philosophy of religion. According to Dalferth, the philosophy of religion helps to orient in thinking about religious orientations in life. For the philosophy

---

42. Dalferth, *Becoming Present*, 33. Further Dalferth, *Gedeutete Gegenwart*, 29–35, 113–21, 129–32, 190–92.

43. Because theology should be transformed christologically, is does not surprise that Dalferth writes a monograph on Christology: *Der Auferweckte Gekreuzigte* (1994). In 2015, the English translation has been published (Dalferth, *Crucified and Resurrected*). On the christological transformation of theology, see Dalferth, *Jenseits von Mythos und Logos*.

44. Strange in the critical discussion of Dalferth's position by Valerie Fickert, is that she presupposes a reality of "general experience," and ignores that the structure of Dalferth's concept of experience (someone experiences something as something) implies that experience is never "general." See Fickert, *Erfahrung und Offenbarung*.

45. Dalferth, *Gedeutete Gegenwart*.

of religion, God is a possibility, a possibility that helps humans to orient. Theology speaks in an "eschatological indicative": grammatically, theology uses the indicative to speak about eschatological realities. To philosophers of religion, this eschatological indicative sounds like a conjunctive or an *irrealis*. For theology, here we are dealing with eschatological truth *coram deo*. *Coram deo*, we are located absolutely, so that absolute orientation becomes possible. He interprets "God" as index words like "here," "now," and "I." Dalferth is critical of rational religion that tries to give a rational foundation for faith. He gives a critical discussion of philosophical theology, be it as philosophical theism or as an attempt to find a foundation for religion in human subjectivity. For Dalferth, the emphasis is on orientation, given as a possibility by the reality of God.[46]

It is in accordance with this idea of God as "Wirklichkeit des Möglichen" (reality of the possible) that Dalferth's larger works never begin with God. Already in his PhD thesis and later works, he starts with language, with phenomena, continues with religion, and ends with a theological perspective. Although he stands in the tradition of Luther, Barth, and Jüngel, the theological perspective is a possibility that is never mentioned in the beginning. Still, as a Barthian, he is thinking from the end. Sooner or later, the perspective of faith, resulting from God's Trinitarian self-revelation appears to be a possibility and a reality. In light of this theological perspective, we receive a new sight of all phenomena.

In *Die Wirklichkeit des Möglichen*, Dalferth clarifies his understanding of signs. He does not propose a dyadic sign concept that distinguishes only between a signifier (the visible or audible bearer or carrier of the sign) and the signified (the mental concept to which the sign refers).[47] Dalferth follows C. S. Peirce with a triadic sign concept: the sign is a triadic relation of a sign or "representamen," over the object to which the sign refers, with the interpretant determined by its relation to both (its meaning: an idea, an interpretation).[48] This triadic concept fits better with Dalferth's realist and pragmatic attitude than a dyadic one. We use signs to refer to reality and we act by speaking.[49] Accordingly, signs have four dimensions: the material dimension (relations between sign and material sign bearer; in *Kunst des*

---

46. Dalferth, *Wirklichkeit des Möglichen*. God is not only a possibility that is a reality, he is also *"poet of the possible,"* not *"cause of the actual."* See Dalferth, *Becoming Present*, 162.

47. On structuralism and its dyadic concept, see Dalferth, *Kunst des Verstehens*, 176–83.

48. Dalferth, *Wirklichkeit des Möglichen*, 6–7. Also Dalferth, *Kunst des Verstehens*, 28.

49. Cf. Dalferth, *Radikale Theologie*, 89; Dalferth, *Kunst des Verstehens*, 184, 224–25.

Verstehens "medial dimension"), the semantic dimension (relations between sign and the signified), the syntactic dimension (relations between different signs) and the pragmatic dimension (relations between signs and sign users).[50] Language is not a world in itself, but we use language in our human interaction with each other and with our world.

Where according to Dalferth hermeneutical theology did not succeed in giving a "coherent interpretation of our reality of life and experience,"[51] he tried to accomplish this in some other publications. An important publication, again a hermeneutical approach focusing on orientation, deals with evil: *Malum: Theologische Hermeneutik des Bösen* (2008). In other works also, he tries to interpret our reality of life and experience.[52]

Moreover, Dalferth has published a book in which he explicitly discusses the tradition of hermeneutical theology and chooses his own position within this tradition: *Radikale Theologie* (2010). In line with what he already wrote in *Theology and Philosophy*, Dalferth argues that a phenomenological theology is impossible. God and God's acts are no phenomena, and "Those who speak of God's action see phenomena differently, but they do not see other phenomena."[53]

At the same time, the central concept of "Wortgeschehen" (Word event) of hermeneutical theology is problematic, according to Dalferth. First, hermeneutical theology sees the same Word-event in the interpretation of Scripture and the interpretation of our experience. However, both have a different hermeneutical, internal structure. Both cannot be seen as completely parallel.[54]

Second, hermeneutical theology presupposes that God understands and explains himself, our world, and ourselves; but we also understand God, our world, and ourselves. Hermeneutical theology is not able to

---

50. Dalferth, *Wirklichkeit des Möglichen*, 19. Also Dalferth, *Kombinatorische Theologie*, 114–15; Dalferth, *Radikale Theologie*, 247–48; Dalferth, *Kunst des Verstehens*, 33, 184.

51. Dalferth, *Radikale Theologie*, 92–93.

52. See, e.g., Dalferth, *Malum*; Dalferth, *Umsonst* (in English: Dalferth, *Creatures of Possibility*); Dalferth, *Transzendenz und säkulare Welt*; Dalferth, *Kunst des Verstehens*, 326–76.

In her criticism of Dalferth, Fickert does not take into account that in these works Dalferth at least has tried to give an interpretation of our world.

53. Dalferth, *Radikale Theologie*, 210; and further 206–17, 242. Cf. Dalferth, *Kunst des Verstehens*, 69–71. Fickert (Fickert, *Erfahrung und Offenbarung*, 223) wonders whether it is possible to think phenomenologically within the framework of Dalferth's hermeneutical theology. The beginning of both *Malum* and *Kunst des Verstehens* evidence that this is possible.

54. Dalferth, *Radikale Theologie*, 95–97.

make clear how the divine Word-event and the creational word-event can be distinguished. Moreover, hermeneutical theology has not succeeded in formulating criteria to distinguish between significance given by God and significance created by us, between God's self-explanation and our misinterpretations and misleading explanations, and between what is true and what is not.[55]

Third, hermeneutical theology uses an incoherent combination of various hermeneutical approaches. Hermeneutical theology starts with historical criticism, searching for the intention of the original author. It continues with a non-intentionalist approach, using methods of literary criticism to find the theological meaning of scriptural texts. Next, focusing on theological use, it uses non-intentionalist methods of reception analysis. Finally, in the dogmatic reconstruction of the theological "Sache," its approach follows an intentionalist model of conversational hermeneutics. The result is a mixture of a personal, intentionalist paradigm and a non-intentionalist paradigm of a Word event. Moreover, hermeneutical theology finds in all steps the divine Word-event of law and gospel. The intention of the author in the first step is replaced by the divine Word-event; the structure of the text in the second step is identified as the divine Word-event; the structure of the reception of the text follows the same Word event; and this Word-event is traced back to a divine intention. According to Dalferth, this leads to various problems: why should the intention of a human author be replaced by a divine Word event? Is it reasonable to find the same Word-event of law and gospel in all scriptural texts? Moreover, the difference between the logic of the divine Word-event and the literary structure of texts is neglected. And finally, a non-intentionalist model of a Word-event is interpreted in intentionalist terms.[56]

It is noteworthy that Dalferth is more critical of Gerhard Ebeling than of his teacher Eberhard Jüngel. Ebeling interpreted the word-Word-event as a personal communication from subject to subject. He understood God as a supra-person and missed a Trinitarian understanding of the word-Word-event. In Ebeling's approach, Dalferth signals a tension between the communication of co-present persons and the interpretation of God's word as the interpretation of the work of an absent author. Jüngel has understood the word-event more consistently as a Trinitarian-event.[57] Following Jüngel, Dalferth favours a view of God as "sich selbst auslegendes Grundgeschehen,

---

55. Dalferth, *Radikale Theologie*, 123–24, 129, 132–37.

56. Dalferth, *Radikale Theologie*, 141–55. On the place of the authorial intention in the interpretation of texts, see Dalferth, *Kunst des Verstehens*, 293–98, 301–4.

57. On Ebeling and Jüngel, see Dalferth, *Radikale Theologie*, 90–97, 151–55, 157–71; Dalferth, "Hermeneutische Theologie—heute?," 27–37.

das eine Welt hervorbringt, mit deren Mittel es sichselbst durch anderes für andere als Gott verständlich machen kann" (self-interpreting fundamental event which brings forth a world by means of which it can make itself understandable to others as God).[58] The starting point for hermeneutics is neither phenomenology nor human self-understanding, but the Triune event of the divine self-explanation. Because this event leads to a radical change of perspective, Dalferth proposes a radical theology.[59]

This radical theology is an event hermeneutics ("Ereignishermeneutik"). It follows in its reflection the structure of faith that is both anaphoric (referring retrospectively, looking back to its origin) and kataphoric (referring prospectively, looking toward its destination). It is an explorative and imaginative hermeneutics of the Trinitarian self-presentation ("Selbstvergegenwärtigung"). It does not focus on the history of salvation, but on the event of salvation that enlightens human existence.[60] Central to this hermeneutics is the difference between old and new, unbelief and faith, and disorientation and new orientation.[61] It is the already well-known idea of the Trinitarian self-identification to someone, resulting in a radical change in one's existence: the disclosure of a radical new perspective that gives a new view of all phenomena *coram deo* and that makes a new orientation *coram deo* possible. Now, Dalferth uses a phrase used by Ebeling and Jüngel to characterize this renewal: an "experience with experience," that deepens and renews our experience; not a new phenomenon, but a new perspective on all phenomena.[62]

In 2018, Dalferth has published *Die Kunst des Verstehens* In this book, he gives a thorough overview of the field of hermeneutics, in four steps: philosophical hermeneutics ("Verstehen des Verstehens"), textual hermeneutics ("understanding meaning in communication through texts"), hermeneutics of human existence ("Daseinshermeneutik"; "understanding as a fundamental mode of human orientation") and hermeneutics of the Christian faith (a "theological hermeneutics").[63]

The final chapter of the book is a systematic sketch of a theological hermeneutic, that wants to understand the understanding of faith, only present in ambivalent form, but still attempting to understand from a certain point

58. Dalferth, "Hermeneutische Theologie—heute?," 37. See further Dalferth, *Radikale Theologie*, 167–68, 170–71.

59. Dalferth, *Radikale Theologie*, 190–91.

60. Dalferth, *Radikale Theologie*, 229, 235.

61. Dalferth, *Radikale Theologie*, 242–82.

62. Dalferth, *Radikale Theologie*, 159, 166, 189, 235. Also earlier in Dalferth, *Auferweckte Gekreuzigte*, 186; Dalferth, *Crucified and Resurrected*, 183.

63. Dalferth, *Kunst des Verstehens*, vi.

of view (*sub specie aeternate*), within a certain horizon (*coram deo*), and in the light of the difference of God as creator and the world as creation.[64] In his Word, God discloses his creating presence through the work of the Spirit so that unbelievers come to understand in faith how God understands himself and them, what he does, and how they can live accordingly. God's creative presence now is the decisive point of orientation, and the difference between faith and unbelief is fundamental in this orientation.[65]

Dalferth mentions five hermeneutical task fields: act-hermeneutics of Scripture (on the use of canonical texts in the Christian and ecclesial life); text-hermeneutics of the Bible (philological, exegetical, and historical work on the texts of the Bible); event-hermeneutics of the Word of God (on God's self-communication and the resulting transformation of human existence); practice-hermeneutics of the Christian life (on the Christian life, personal and ecclesial); and culture-hermeneutics of the Christian tradition (on the effects of the Christian life, thought, and acts on history and culture).[66] The challenge of theological hermeneutics in all these fields is to discern critically to enable orientation in life in God's presence.

Dalferth closes the book with the well-known theme of orientation. New, however, is that he elaborates on how the new understanding relates to the old one. An existing process of meaning becomes a means for a new process of meaning. A given understanding is understood differently from a new perspective. First and second understanding now are co-present and the tension between them results in further understanding. Accordingly, the Word of God opens a new understanding and a discontinuity in the understanding of self, world, and God. Here, we are fundamentally passive. But this combination makes it possible to understand the old within the horizon of the new, in a new way. Now, it is necessary and possible to distinguish and to learn more and more to discern. God's revelation is a reason to make distinctions (e.g., creator—creature; unbelief—faith; *coram mundo—coram deo*) that believers learn to use in their discernment. More and more, they learn to understand themselves in line with how God understands them. Accordingly, they understand more and more that the world is richer than expected.[67]

---

64. Dalferth, *Kunst des Verstehens*, 426–27.

65. Dalferth, *Kunst des Verstehens*, 432.

66. Dalferth, *Kunst des Verstehens*, 445–48.

67. In the final chapter, Dalferth gives an answer to a problem signaled by Fickert, although he does not mention her book: does it matter who we are in the moment of conversion? Is our new understanding a renewal of something that already exists? Is seems that the "experience with experience" is not a transformation of experience, but a radical different experience. She signals a Flacian tendency in Dalferth: we are

Besides *Die Kunst des Verstehens* a book on hermeneutics, Dalferth wrote a book on Scripture: *Wirkendes Wort* (also 2018). He elaborates his ideas on the Triune self-identification and theological hermeneutics for the doctrine of Scripture. He is critical of the doctrine of Scripture as it was developed in Protestant orthodox theology. Originally, the Reformation was a rediscovery of the gospel and a movement of preaching. However, Protestantism fell into the trap of Gutenberg and turned into a movement of a printed book. Instead of listening to the preaching of the gospel (a situation of communication in co-presence of speaker and hearer) attention now shifted to the reading of a book (where the reader is alone with his book). This "book theology" led to many aporetic theological proposals, which all made the same mistake: they tried to interpret a book as the Word of God.[68] Dalferth signals that Protestantism does with the Bible as a book what Roman Catholicism does with the sacraments: they identify God's activity with created elements that God uses in his acts.[69] As we experience in our culture the crisis of the book culture that was the context of the theology of orthodox Protestantism, it is a challenge to make clear again how Scripture can be used in the formation and interpretation of our lives.[70]

Formulating an alternative, Dalferth uses Luther to navigate between Schleiermacher who focuses on the pneumatological use of Scripture in the church, and Barth who concentrated on the christological event of the Word of God.[71] Theology and church should be interested in the gospel, in which the Holy Spirit through Jesus Christ discloses to us the loving presence of God the Father. This implies that we only understand Scripture when we understand how God is present in our lives, how we can reorient our lives in the light of his presence, and how his presence transforms our lives. This understanding is not produced by us but is a gracious result of the divine self-communication of God in Christ and the Holy Spirit. Thus, this new understanding is the result of a situation of co-presence: in the communication of the gospel in the community of the church, we refer to God's co-presence in Christ. Interestingly, Dalferth refers in this book to the emphasis of the Pentecostal movement on the freedom of the Holy Spirit. *Wirkendes Wort* makes clear what Dalferth's Trinitarian hermeneutics implies for his view of

---

completely passive, without any personal responsibility or created worth. See Fickert, *Erfahrung und Offenbarung*, 197–98, 220–23.

68. Dalferth, *Wirkendes Wort*, 19–35, 101–5, 108–9, 134–75, 369–75, 404–11.
69. Dalferth, *Wirkendes Wort*, 331.
70. Dalferth, *Wirkendes Wort*, 105–7, 427–47.
71. Dalferth, *Wirkendes Wort*, 35–40.

Scripture: he is primarily interested in the communication of the gospel that discloses God's loving presence to us through the history of Jesus Christ.[72]

4.3 ELEMENTS OF DALFERTH'S SOTERIOLOGICAL HERMENEUTICS

Having sketched this basic structure of self-identification, location, and orientation as it was developed by Dalferth in the first phase of his development, and its further development into a hermeneutical approach of theology that is characterized as "radical theology," I now will investigate further some elements attached especially to the soteriological character of Dalferth's hermeneutics. I will successively deal with God's Trinitarian activity to disclose his presence to us and make us share in his perspective (4.3.1); the importance of faith and the change of perspective in conversion (4.3.2); the eschatological character of this perspective and the resulting relation to other forms of knowledge (4.3.3); and finally the relation between Dalferth's hermeneutical perspective and the Bible (4.3.4).

4.3.1 Trinity

When communicating using signs, we use media. According to Dalferth, God in his self-communication makes himself to be the medium in his Word and his Spirit. The Trinity is the "event ontology of God's self-revelation."[73] God's Trinitarian activity has two important hermeneutical results: first that God identifies himself and his loving presence to someone, and second that God makes us share in his divine perspective: in how he understands himself, humanity, and our world.

Dalferth has analyzed the Trinitarian self-identification of God more precisely in *Der Auferweckte Gekreuzigte*. Its horizon is Israel's faith, which Jesus lived and eschatologically concretized. Jesus proclaimed that God's kingdom dawns and that God's love is near. He both proclaimed this nearness as the messenger and embodied it personally as the agent. He presented and represented God's presence, and God's coming reign is linked with himself. Moreover, he identified God who is present and near as a loving Father. Then Jesus died on the cross, but his disciples still experienced his active

---

72. Dalferth, *Wirkendes Wort*, 40–76, 326, 357. On the importance of Pentecostal theology, see Dalferth, *Wirkendes Wort*, xxii, 326, 357.

73. "Ereignisontologie der Selbstoffenbahrung Gottes," Dalferth, *Kunst des Verstehens*, 162; and further 120–123.

presence. Both these experiences were interpreted in the light of Jesus's proclamation of God and God's loving nearness. At the same time, Jesus's proclamation was colored by the experience of Jesus's death and resurrection. God's presence was near to him, even in death, as the God who saves from death. Furthermore, this understanding of the cross and the resurrection leads to a new understanding of God. Jesus's identification of God as Father is understood in the light of the cross and the resurrection. God proved himself to be a loving Father, who does not want to be God without Jesus and everything else that is separated from him. Even death cannot separate us from God. As a result, God confirmed Jesus's identification of him as a loving Father. By raising Jesus from the dead, God proved himself as Father, that Jesus is his Son, who is loved eternally, and who distinguished himself from God to serve God's love and to make us share in God's loving nearness. In death and resurrection, God's identity is determined in an eschatological new way as "unconditional, inexhaustible, and unfettered love."[74] Finally, Christians know that only when God makes himself known in his Spirit, can they know him as a loving Father, and Jesus as Christ and Son of God.[75] To summarize, the combination of Jesus's public appearance, cross, resurrection, and the gift of the Spirit results in a self-identification of God as love and as Father, Son, and Spirit.

Within these hermeneutical processes, Father, Son, and Spirit represent different types of action. Dalferth characterizes the Father as "the center of creativity and reality." He is the origin who constitutes the "process of the self-actualization of God's love,"[76] but also the creator of reality. The Son is the "center of intelligibility and truth." The particular determination of God and God's presence becomes accessible in the Son. Finally, Dalferth gives the Spirit the characteristics of "newness and assurance."[77] It is the Spirit who opens our eyes to God's presence, makes us believe in God as our Father, and gives us the certainty of the truth disclosed in Christ.[78]

---

74. Dalferth, *Crucified and Resurrected*, 160. "Unbedingte, unerschöpfliche und uneingeschränkte Liebe," Dalferth, *Auferweckte Gekreuzigte*, 162.

75. Dalferth, *Auferweckte Gekreuzigte*, 93–111, 123–24, 160–67, 206–7, 279–80; Dalferth, *Crucified and Resurrected*, 91–108, 118–20, 157–64, 203–4, 277–79; Dalferth, *Existenz Gottes und christlicher Glaube*, 218–19, 228–30; Dalferth, *Theology and Philosophy*, 193; Dalferth, *Becoming Present*, 50–52, 108, 148–51, 154; Dalferth, *Wirkendes Wort*, 50–56.

76. Dalferth, *Crucified and Resurrected*, 228. "Prozess der Selbstkonkretion göttlicher Liebe," Dalferth, *Auferweckte Gekreuzigte*, 231.

77. Dalferth, *Crucified and Resurrected*, 202. "Zentrum der Kreativität und wirklichkeit," "Zentrum der Wahrnehmbarkeit und Wahrheit," "Zentrum der Neuheit und Gewissheit," Dalferth, *Auferweckte Gekreuzigte*, 205.

78. Dalferth, *Theology and Philosophy*, 220; Dalferth, *Kombinatorische Theologie*,

We have seen that this divine self-identification opens God's identification system for sinners. We receive a new perspective *coram deo* and become able to identify everything according to its relation to God. This implies that believers share in God's absolute knowledge of ourselves. According to Dalferth, it is not only relating to our self-knowledge that we share in God's perspective, but also concerning God and all other entities. Regarding God, Dalferth stresses that to know God means to share in God's self-knowledge.[79] This does not mean that Dalferth identifies the thinking and understanding of believers with the thinking and understanding of God. To orient one's thinking and understanding in the light of God's thinking and understanding means to differentiate critically between human (autobiographical) judgments and God's judgments. Still, it is possible to know the divine ideal and to learn to follow that ideal more and more in the process of life.[80] How is that possible?

The answer to this question has pneumatological and christological aspects. First, let us take a look at the pneumatological answer. God knows himself in his Spirit. In the process of Trinitarian self-differentiation, the Spirit integrates the different divine perspectives into a comprehensive self-transparency. Further, the Spirit has absolute certainty concerning the truth of God's reality. God knows the truth of his being as overflowing love. Thanks to this divine epistemic self-transparency, the Spirit can clarify God to others than God. More emphatically, because God knows himself in the Spirit, only the Spirit can make God known. The Spirit makes us participate in God's self-transparency so that we become part of this divine self-transparency. He opens our eyes and makes us free to discern unexpected realities. Further, he takes away the ambiguity of all our worldly experiences as far as the self-disclosure of God is concerned. In this way, we can know God as he knows himself. According to Dalferth, this is a basic precondition of real knowledge of God: we can only claim to have certain knowledge of God if the ground and conditions of being known are all determined by God himself.[81]

132, 134; Dalferth, *Auferweckte Gekreuzigte*, 33, 81, 137, 164–65, 182, 202–3, 205, 216, 231; Dalferth, *Crucified and Resurrected*, 33, 80–81, 133, 161–63, 179–80, 199–200, 202, 213, 226; Dalferth, *Radikale Theologie*, 80, 125–26; Dalferth, *Kunst des Verstehens*, 120–23; Dalferth, *Wirkendes Wort*, 66–69.

79. See, e.g., Dalferth, *Radikale Theologie*, 59–62; Dalferth, *Kunst des Verstehens*, 435–37.

80. Dalferth, *Kunst des Verstehens*, 506–15.

81. Dalferth, *Theology and Philosophy*, 190, 220; Dalferth, *Kombinatorische Theologie*, 132–38, 140, 143–44, 150; Dalferth, *Auferweckte Gekreuzigte*, 134, 164–70, 179–84, 186–87, 206, 216, 230; Dalferth, *Crucified and Resurrected*, 133, 161–67, 176–84, 203, 213, 226–27.

Further, the love of Father and Son is realized in the Spirit. The Spirit is the principle of the openness and unity of this love. He unites Father and Son in their love but opens also their loving communion to others. The loving acts of God as acts of the Holy Spirit are intended to make others participate in this love of Father and Son.[82] The same can be said of the life of God: the Trinitarian differentiated life of God is a life in the Spirit. Dalferth characterizes this life of God as a field, and the Spirit as "Vollzugsform des Gott-Feldes" (execution form of the God-field).[83] God's Spirit is God's "fundamental life process."[84] As Spirit, God can be present to all of us, disclose himself, and make us share in his perichoretic, loving fellowship, to enable us to live a life in accordance with his loving presence.[85] Consequently, the Spirit can make us share in God's self-knowledge, because he opens God's life of love to others and because he knows God as he knows himself.

Moreover, the Spirit makes us participate in God's perspective on Jesus. Now, we no longer know Jesus just according to the flesh, but also according to the Spirit. This brings us to the christological answer. The proclamation and the history of Jesus make, in their particularity, the presence of God perceptible, as we saw. But this is not the entire answer. The history of Jesus Christ is open and inclusive. The process of death, resurrection, and the emergence of faith in Jesus as Christ incorporates us so that we can live in Christ. He has identified himself with us in his life and death and incorporates us in himself. In Christ, God has found us at the low point of human existence, in our death. Due to this identification, we are integrated into his story and come to share in his identity. In the resurrection, God identifies himself with Jesus, so that we are incorporated in God's glory and God's identification system. This is being in Christ and being in God's glory, according to Dalferth.[86]

It is important to be cautious here: participation in Christ does not imply that we participate in the human perspective of Jesus or his human subjectivity (e.g., his mind). Rather, we participate in the perspective on

---

82. Dalferth, *Kombinatorische Theologie*, 134–36; Dalferth, *Auferweckte Gekreuzigte*, 162–67, 225–32; Dalferth, *Crucified and Resurrected*, 159–64, 221–29.

83. Dalferth, *Kombinatorische Theologie*, 134.

84. Dalferth, *Crucified and Resurrected*, 162. "Der fundamentale Lebensprozess Gottes," Dalferth, *Auferweckte Gekreuzigte*, 165.

85. Dalferth, *Kombinatorische Theologie*, 131–37; Dalferth, *Auferweckte Gekreuzigte*, 166, 184, 216, 230, 235–36; Dalferth, *Crucified and Resurrected*, 163–64, 181, 213, 226–27, 232–33.

86. Dalferth, *Existenz Gottes und christlicher Glaube*, 228–33, 280–81, 306–10; Dalferth, *Kombinatorische Theologie*, 148–51, 156; Dalferth, *Auferweckte Gekreuzigte*, 70, 81, 206, 276–80, 303–5; Dalferth, *Crucified and Resurrected*, 70, 80–81, 203, 274–79, 302–4. And further Burger, *Being in Christ*, 407–8, 415–18, 421–22.

God's nearness disclosed in Christ. Not Jesus as such is important, but "that he is the place of God's revelation."[87] As a result of this Trinitarian self-identification of God, we can participate in his perspective and live in the presence of God who is loving, creative, renewing, and saving.[88]

4.3.2 Faith and Conversion

Triune self-identification has radical consequences. We cannot truly identify God and go on living as if nothing has changed. Dalferth writes, "We cannot discern God without discerning the difference God makes to us and everything else in our lives."[89] When God is truly identified to someone, one understands that this has soteriological and practical consequences; everything changes. For this reason, Dalferth identified his approach to hermeneutical theology as "radical."[90]

If God identifies himself to someone, that person is located *coram deo* and included in God's identification system: a radically new perspective opens. This "is a change not in our life but of our life"[91] concerning the mode of our existence: not "a change within our view of life," but "a change of our view of life."[92] The difference between faith and unbelief is an orientating difference. It is not a distinction between two ways of life that we can classify and describe phenomenologically. Dalferth explains, "Rather, it formulates the theological guiding distinction that allows every human life to be judged from the point of view of its relationship to the presence of God."[93] Unbelief and faith are two modes of existence, from a self-centered to a God-centered life.[94] Faith is an eschatological occur-

---

87. "Dass er der Ort von Gottes Offenbarung ist." Dalferth, "Gott für uns," 64; and further 63–65, 72–74; Dalferth, *Auferweckte Gekreuzigte*, 252–53, 277; Dalferth, *Crucified and Resurrected*, 250–51, 275.

88. Dalferth, *Gedeutete Gegenwart*, 282–85.

89. Dalferth, *Becoming Present*, 135.

90. Dalferth, *Auferweckte Gekreuzigte*; Dalferth, *Crucified and Resurrected*, 79–80; Dalferth, *Becoming Present*, 30; Dalferth, *Radikale Theologie*, 15, 184, 189, 191.

91. Dalferth, *Becoming Present*, 36.

92. Dalferth, *Becoming Present*, 47.

93. "Vielmehr formuliert sie die theologische Leitunterscheidung, die jedes menschliche Leben unter dem Gesichtspunkt seines Verhältnisses zur Gegenwart Gottes zu beurteilen erlaubt." Dalferth, *Kunst des Verstehens*, 431. See also Dalferth, *Kunst des Verstehens*, 330, 441.

94. Dalferth writes about a "Moduswechsel von einen selbstzentrieren zu einem gottoffenen Leben." Dalferth, *Kunst des Verstehens*, 434.

rence, that constitutes a person as truly human, "menschlicher Mensch."[95] Becoming a believer is a paradoxical experience: we live a life of choosing and deciding and we cannot become a believer without living this life; however, our choices and decisions do not make us a believer: we cannot locate ourselves *coram deo*, only God can by his self-identification. Once we are convinced of God's loving presence because we have undergone God's self-identification, we can decide freely to live in faith. Faith is the gift of the Holy Spirit, the pneumatological reverse side of God's address in Jesus Christ.[96] Consequently, God's self-identification, absolute location *coram deo*, the genesis of faith, and the shift from a *coram mundo* perspective to a *coram deo* perspective belong together inseparably.

Because Dalferth understands faith in the light of God's gift and God's judgment in Christ, he emphasizes the unambiguous character of faith against the manifold human experience and ambivalences of human trust, belief, and hope.[97] The reality of faith introduces an ideal in human life. Normative ideals help us to orientate and to distinguish practically in life. Faith receives various embodied forms of faith life in different traditions, times, and contexts. Moreover, faith is individualized personally in an experiential context. Because of this diversity, we need paradigmatic and normative practices and formulations (liturgy, confession, canon, catechism, church order, etc.). They help in the formation of faith lives to develop and improve the Christian life and to distinguish between successful and unsuccessful forms.[98]

The radical change of perspective involves *delocation*, a new orientation as a result of the new and absolute location *coram deo*, and conversion. In this new perspective everything is seen in the light of God and of its

---

95. Dalferth, *Existenz Gottes und christlicher Glaube*, 245. Cf. Dalferth, *Auferweckte Gekreuzigte*, 156; Dalferth, *Crucified and Resurrected*, 151–52.

96. Dalferth, *Existenz Gottes und christlicher Glaube*, 242–55; Dalferth, *Kombinatorische Theologie*, 138; Dalferth, *Wirklichkeit des Möglichen*, 123–25; Dalferth, *Evangelische Theologie als Interpretationspraxis*, 82–89; Dalferth, *Becoming Present*, 29–31, 36–43, 108–11, 199, 235–42, 253; Dalferth, *Radikale Theologie*, 15–17, 61–66, 73–77, 191, 201, 221–23, 243, 254–55, 261, 267, 274–79; Dalferth, *Kunst des Verstehens*, 330, 426–28, 430–33, 438–41.

97. Dalferth, "Über Einheit und Vielfalt," 99–101, 108–13, 128–37; Dalferth, *Gedeutete Gegenwart*, 91–98.

98. Dalferth, *Kunst des Verstehens*, 426–31, 433–35. Fickert (2016) is critical of Dalferth's lack of attention to historical processes and to ecclesial practices and documents in which faith is given concrete form; Fickert, *Erfahrung und Offenbarung*, 114, 154–56, 162–65, 198–99, 205. In *Kunst des Verstehens* (2018), Dalferth does write about these themes related to the historical diversity of faith life in churches and individual lives, where in earlier works he focused on the ideal of faith.

relations to God, and accordingly in the light of two guiding differences: between creator and creature, and between faith and unbelief. That does not mean that this change is realized completely at once. No, this means that due to this newness, our understanding is irreducibly plural and characterized by an insoluble fracture. At least we can understand according to our personal experience ("erleben"; *coram seipso*), according to the experience of others, our shared worldly experience ("erfahren"; *coram mundo*), and according to God's eschatological judgment ("eschatologisch Urteil"; *coram deo*). Consequently, a difference is introduced between the new as it is eschatologically qualified in the resurrection of Christ, and the old world of the known historical processes, a world of sin and death. It becomes necessary to reorient ourselves: God's existence implies a new understanding of God, of Jesus Christ, of ourselves, and our world. All our beliefs, practices, knowledge, etc., and all our understanding of ourselves, our world, and God have to be evaluated in the light of this new orientational perspective. During this process, the eschatological victory of the new life over the old life not only has a pneumatological dimension but also enables us to know more and more according to the Spirit. As a result of our integration in the God-field that the Spirit is, we learn to distinguish between new and old, between salutary and non-salutary knowledge.[99]

As we saw already, the *coram deo* perspective itself is a soteriologically differentiated perspective, that enables us to learn to differentiate and discern between the old, self-centered life and the new, eschatological, God-centered life. God appears as the creator and the justifying God, relating to the world in the twofold way of law and gospel, as we saw. Faith or unbelief defines everyone's relation to God. We discover ourselves as creatures and sinners, but also as justified sinners; and our world as old and new creation. In the process of our life, we learn to perceive and experience ourselves in the light of God's judgment that makes us into who we are according to his eschatological truth. We learn to distinguish between the old life, alienated from God and his creation, from ways of life that damage or are themselves damaged; and the new life in a communality of love and service. We come to see that life is richer than we can grasp.[100]

---

99. Dalferth, *Existenz Gottes und christlicher Glaube*, 336–38; Dalferth, *Kombinatorische Theologie*, 139–40, 142–44, 155; Dalferth, *Auferweckte Gekreuzigte*, 78–83, 201–2, 208–9; Dalferth, *Crucified and Resurrected*, 77–82, 198–200, 205–6; Dalferth, *Wirklichkeit des Möglichen*, 126–27, 132–33, 198; Dalferth, *Evangelische Theologie als Interpretationspraxis*, 134–36; Dalferth, *Radikale Theologie*, 17–22, 60–61, 230, 254–58, 276, 279–80; Dalferth, *Kunst des Verstehens*, 427–28, 438–39, 494–95, 504–7, 511–16.

100. Dalferth, *Existenz Gottes und christlicher Glaube*, 226–28, 234–35, 300; Dalferth, *Theology and Philosophy*, 86–87; Dalferth, *Gedeutete Gegenwart*, 91–98; Dalferth,

As this process is set in motion, the question must be asked to what extent someone can live according to his eschatological identity *extra se*, to be who he really is. As a result of this re-orientation and conversion, a new life should emerge, fitting God's loving and creative nearness. Although believers still live in the old ontic world and share in the *coram mundo* perspective, they are more and more able to live a new life under the conditions of the old world. By incorporation in Christ, we are more and more transformed so that it is possible to live, according to this new understanding, a life in conformity to God's love.[101]

4.3.3 Eschatological Perspective

God's self-identification in Christ and through the Holy Spirit results in a radical change to a new, eschatological perspective. This might seem to imply some form of fideism as if the new perspective were purely private and arbitrary. However, Dalferth opposes all kinds of religious individualism or tribalism, as I already indicated. He maintains a balanced position of a combination of a participant's perspective as the sole possible access to God's presence disclosed to faith in Christ and the Spirit, and a realist emphasis on the presence of God that evidences its reality in God's self-disclosure. God's active presence effects a change of perspective, from unbelief to faith.[102]

On the one hand, Dalferth emphasizes the necessity of a particular perspective. We are humans and see the world from where we are. We need to concentrate our attention, guided by specific interests. To be human is to live with a plurality of perspectives, characterized by "Standpunkte, Bezugsbereiche, Selektionsgesichtspunkte" (viewpoints, areas of reference, points of view guiding the selection).[103] From a perspective, we perform cognitive selection (we select under certain guiding aspects), and symbolization (we disclose our world semiotically and reconstruct it symbolically).[104] The same is the case when God reveals himself. When God makes himself understandable to someone as God, he does so using specific signs.

Auferweckte Gekreuzigte, 83, 302–3, 309–11; Dalferth, *Crucified and Resurrected*, 82, 301–2, 307–10; Dalferth, *Becoming Present*, 141–45; Dalferth, *Radikale Theologie*, 236, 256; Dalferth, *Kunst des Verstehens*, 431, 433–34, 439–40, 517–18.

101. Dalferth, *Existenz Gottes und christlicher Glaube*, 279–81, 283–86, 330; Dalferth, *Theology and Philosophy*, 223; Dalferth, *Kunst des Verstehens*, 436, 439–40.

102. Dalferth, *Gedeutete Gegenwart*, 10–17, 118–21. Dalferth's eschatological ontology *Existenz Gottes* is an attempt to keep perspectivity and realism together, developing an ontology *sub specie fidei*.

103. Dalferth, *Kombinatorische Theologie*, 88.

104. Dalferth, *Kombinatorische Theologie*, 89.

Consequently, God's self-identification cannot be separated from the particularity of the communicative practice in which God communicates his presence. Moreover, because no one is born a believer since all human beings, as sinners, ignore God, God has to identify himself to a specific person in a Trinitarian way to open a new perspective on his presence and everything else in the light of his presence. This change from sinner to believer, from sinful creature to justified believer, cannot be made collectively, but only personally. The effect of this change is that the believer starts knowing himself as part of God's eschatological identification system and as located in God's presence.[105]

On the other hand, if God exists and is really God, then no one can live without God, even if many live without religion and faith in God. Hence, according to Dalferth, it has to be made clear, that we do not just speak of a Christian God, but of the one and true God. The Christian view of reality is not an arbitrary one, but a disclosure of reality. Consequently, we always need to distinguish between our understanding of God and God's reality, although we can make this difference only within our language. Moreover, in faith, we do not perceive new phenomena. God's presence cannot be distinguished as a phenomenon among other phenomena. Instead, once God's presence is disclosed to us, we begin to see all phenomena in the light of God's presence. Thanks to God's presence, we receive a new perspective with a new horizon in which we see all phenomena differently, but no new phenomena. Accordingly, this knowledge is orientational, as we saw. However, what may be considered trustworthy orientational knowledge is not determined by orientational knowledge itself. Instead, true knowledge decides what may be suitable as orientational knowledge.[106]

This balanced relation between a particular perspective and a realist attitude leads Dalferth to concepts like eschatological ontology, eschatological truth, eschatological indicative, and eschatological sense. In a process of gradually growing participation in the self-transparency of the Spirit, we learn to see things in the light of God's presence, so that we see more than

---

105. Dalferth, *Kombinatorische Theologie*, 87–90; Dalferth, *Gedeutete Gegenwart*, 24–29, 118–19, 122–27, 179–82; Dalferth, *Auferweckte Gekreuzigte*, 180–86, 215, 309; Dalferth, *Crucified and Resurrected*, 176–84, 212, 307–8; Dalferth, *Becoming Present*, 25–28, 127–29, 182, 226; Dalferth, *Radikale Theologie*, 20, 68–70, 72, 171, 276–79; Dalferth, *Kunst des Verstehens*, 452–53, 488–89, 494–95. See further Burger, "Belang van een deelnemersperspectief," 331–34.

106. Dalferth, *Kombinatorische Theologie*, 157–58; Dalferth, *Gedeutete Gegenwart*, 129–32, 181–90; Dalferth, *Jenseits von Mythos und Logos*, 310; Dalferth, *Auferweckte Gekreuzigte*, 168–69, 179, 196–97, 211–12, 217; Dalferth, *Crucified and Resurrected*, 165–66, 176, 193–95; Dalferth, *Becoming Present*, 33–36, 137–40; Dalferth, *Radikale Theologie*, 210–11, 217, 221, 230–35.

is just the case phenomenologically. Theologically, we can describe phenomena in their relation to God and hence according to the eschatological possibilities he gives.[107]

4.3.4 Gospel, Scripture, and Bible

Central to Dalferth's theology is a Christian understanding of God as Trinity, according to which God has identified himself in Christ through the Spirit to a believer. This self-identification is inseparably linked to the specific communicative practice of the communication of the gospel. Through human communication of the gospel in word and sacrament, God can make himself understandable, using the human words of the gospel, to disclose his divine presence to someone. This communication of the gospel in word and sacrament is another central element of Dalferth's hermeneutical theology.

The concept of the gospel guides Dalferth in developing his view of the Holy Scripture and Bible, which is embedded in his Trinitarian view of God. The gospel is proclaimed in the church, using the Bible, which is read in the ecclesial liturgy as Holy Scripture, to hear the Word of God by hearing about Jesus who revealed and embodied God's presence. We hear the gospel and the Word of God when God himself by his Spirit opens our eyes to his loving and saving presence. This happens through the action of God himself as Word (*verbum externum*) and Spirit (*verbum internum*). When we hear and understand the Word of God, this has an existential impact, because it changes our lives and gives them a new direction and orientation.[108]

Accordingly, theology has to distinguish between (a) the Word of God (an act of the Triune God in which he discloses his loving presence to someone), (b) the Scripture (the practice of liturgical reading of scriptural texts as to use these canonical texts for the communication of the gospel), and (c) the Bible (the library of all the texts in one printed book). We can hear the Word of God as "gospel" and as "law." "Gospel" and "law" are no textual categories, for "one and the same text can be read and understood as law and as gospel."[109] They are "Vollzugsweisen des Wortes Gottes" (ways of carrying out the Word of God) that expose sin (law) and overcome sin

---

107. Dalferth, *Kombinatorische Theologie*, 143–44; Dalferth, *Wirklichkeit des Möglichen*, 132–33; Dalferth, *Radikale Theologie*, 265, 269; Dalferth, *Kunst des Verstehens*, 504, 512.

108. Dalferth, *Kombinatorische Theologie*, 26; Dalferth, *Evangelische Theologie als Interpretationspraxis*, 87, 99–103; Dalferth, *Kunst des Verstehens*, 489–96; Dalferth, *Wirkendes Wort*, 42–76, 327–29.

109. Dalferth, *Wirkendes Wort*, 130.

(gospel).[110] For Dalferth, the emphasis is on the gospel, not on law, because God comes to us as his gospel. In God's Word, God helps us to discern our situation in his loving and creative presence. "Word of God" is inseparably linked with the action of God himself. "Holy Scripture" refers to an activity of the church of reading the Bible in the liturgy, trusting that God will speak his Word in, with, and under ecclesial communication. "Bible" refers to a text.[111]

The textual hermeneutics of the Bible occupies itself with the exegesis of biblical texts; this is a secular and profane discipline, abstracting from the ecclesial use of the scriptural text. The act-hermeneutics of Scripture ("Handlungshermeneutik der Schrift") is a systematic theological activity, interpreting Scripture, gospel, and contemporary experience, in the light of each other. This activity serves the churchly proclamation of the gospel. The event hermeneutics of the Word of God ("Ereignishermeneutik des Wortes Gottes") is interested in this divine self-communication. The event of hearing and understanding the Word of God is a "Widerfahrnis" (passive experience) that enables us to understand in a new way. Accordingly, Dalferth also uses the phrase "Widerfahrnis-Hermeneutik des Evangeliums" (Experience hermeneutics of the gospel).[112]

The Word of God and the Spirit of God are the media of God's self-communication. In his Word, God "makes himself the medium through which he communicates himself understandably to man."[113] Dalferth presents a differentiated understanding of the Word of God: as the eternal Word of God (*verbum aeternum*), as the personal Word of God in the history of Jesus Christ (*verbum personale*), as the external Word of the proclamation of the gospel (*verbum externum*), and as the Word that is appropriated personally (*verbum internum*).[114] "Word of God" is the expression of the experience and insight "that Jews and Gentiles (people of all origins) are included in the history of Jesus Christ and thus in the history of God's salvation through faith worked by the Spirit and participate in salvation through God's working of the Spirit."[115] In the communication of the gospel, Holy Scripture can become the Word of God if it discloses God's presence and leads to faith.

110. Dalferth, *Wirkendes Wort*, 130.

111. Dalferth, *Wirkendes Wort*, xix-xx, 75-76, 95-102, 115-24, 134, 187-89, 245-47.

112. Dalferth, *Kunst des Verstehens*, 445-47; Dalferth, *Wirkendes Wort*, 85-89, 120-21, 124, 376-81, 421-26.

113. Gott macht "sich selbst zum Medium, durch dass er sich den Menschen verstehbar vermittelt," Dalferth, *Kunst des Verstehens*, 122.

114. Dalferth, *Wirkendes Wort*, 72, 288.

115. Dalferth, *Wirkendes Wort*, 289.

This divine self-communication is the foundation of the church as *creatura verbi*, a creature of the Word. The texts of Scripture testify to this divine activity. For this reason, the ground of the canonicity of Scripture is not the decision of the church. Scripture became canonized because of the experience that these texts have authority.[116]

In his Spirit, God "makes himself the medium through which he overcomes the refusal of men to communicate himself in his Word, making himself a witness to the truth of his self-testimony among men."[117] Due to the Spirit, the Word of God can be communicated in a situation of co-presence with God. In this situation of co-presence, the Spirit takes away ambiguity and gives clarity to the Word.[118] This situation of co-presence should not be understood as the communication between two human persons, as Ebeling does. Only the Trinity as "event ontology of God's self-revelation" makes it possible that the Word-event occurs in a situation of co-presence: the Triune God can use the communication of the gospel in the church as the Word-event in which the Word of God is spoken and heard. It is part of a communicative situation of co-presence that the Word is heard, not read. Not the reading of a written text (communication with an absent author), but the hearing of a spoken word is the manner of communication of the gospel.[119]

Consequently, Dalferth regrets that the rediscovery of the gospel by the Reformation degraded into a movement of a printed book, due to the inventing of the printing press. He rejects the orthodox Protestant identification of God's Word with the text of Scripture. This approach was foundationalist, seeing the Word of God as a source of information and as the epistemological principle of theology. Protestant theology made the mistake of attributing the perfections of the Word of God (its authority, clarity, sufficiency, and efficacy) to a text. As mentioned already, Dalferth rejects an identification of God's acts with the creaturely elements that God uses. These four characteristics are no textual properties, but characterize the work of the Triune God in Word and Spirit, using Scripture to communicate the

---

116. Dalferth, *Kombinatorische Theologie*, 26, 148–51; Dalferth, *Wirkendes Wort*, 66–72, 163, 218, 219.

117. "Gott macht sich selbst zum Medium, durch dass er die Verweigerung der Menschen gegenüber seiner Selbstvermittlung in seinem Wort überwindet, indem er sich selbst zum Zeugen der Wahrheit seines Selbstzeugnisses bei den Menschen macht." Dalferth, *Kunst des Verstehens*, 122.

118. Dalferth, *Kombinatorische Theologie*, 144–48; Dalferth, *Wirkendes Wort*, 72.

119. Dalferth, *Jenseits von Mythos und Logos*, 247–57; Dalferth, *Wirkendes Wort*, 55, 107–17, 345.

gospel. God's Word is not a printed book.[120] According to Dalferth, orthodox Protestantism failed to clarify the relationship between the prophetic and apostolic word, the Word of God, and the Holy Scripture.[121] How does Dalferth understand these relationships?

For Dalferth, it is clear that the Word of God discloses "a new understanding of the self, the world and God, in which they understand themselves as they are in truth, that is *coram deo*."[122] The Word of God does what God did in the resurrection of Jesus Christ: manifest its creative power in eschatological clarity, working something good and new, and bringing sinners to faith, so that believers can live and act in the consciousness of this divine presence.[123] But how does this Word of God relate to the words of the prophets and apostles?

As far as the prophets are concerned, Dalferth has not written much about the Old Testament. The exception is *Malum*, where he writes extensively about God and evil in the Old Testament. He makes clear that in the Old Testament, experiences of God have led to important discoveries of the righteousness of God and the love of God.[124] Still, Dalferth does not reflect on the question of how God was active in the history of Israel so that these important discoveries were made.

Jesus was resurrected from the dead as Christ, and the Word of God was born as a Jew within the history of Israel. His resurrection was according to the Scriptures, and these Scriptures were the "primary horizon of understanding and interpretation of that, what people experienced with, in and by Jesus, and experienced in the work of the Spirit in the community."[125] They "documented Israel's history of promises, to which Jesus himself belonged, as the history of the elected people of the God, whom Jesus called his Father and whose dawning reign he proclaimed."[126] The story of Jesus is interpreted within the horizon of Israel's history and Jesus is presented as the fulfillment of that history of salvation. In the Christian writings of the New Testament, the church wrote down how they understood the gospel of Jesus Christ, their own situation in its light, and how they interpreted the writings of Israel's tradition.[127]

---

120. Dalferth, *Wirkendes Wort*, 29–35, 134–75.
121. Dalferth, *Wirkendes Wort*, 30.
122. Dalferth, *Radikale Theologie*, 163.
123. Dalferth, *Kunst des Verstehens*, 463, 475.
124. Dalferth, *Malum*, 400–518.
125. Dalferth, *Wirkendes Wort*, 119.
126. Dalferth, *Wirkendes Wort*, 120.
127. Dalferth, *Wirkendes Wort*, 120–21, 179–87.

The resulting collection of biblical texts is diverse and not a unity in itself. Scripture gives words to the gospel, but in many different ways, and not always adequately.[128] For that reason, Dalferth is critical of canonical criticism. Canonical criticism focusses on the text and follows the reformed *tota scriptura* instead of the *sola scriptura* of the Reformation.[129] Canonical criticism itself offers no principle of interpretation, in which light we can read and understand.[130] In reading the Old Testament, Christ is decisive. "Not the Old Testament texts as such are Holy Scripture of the Church, but these texts insofar as they point to Christ, in whom God's universal will for salvation is manifested in eschatological finality," Dalferth writes.[131] The same is true of all Scripture: the Christian interpretation of Scripture searches not the sense of the texts on themselves, but the pragmatic meaning they receive in their use for the proclamation of the gospel.[132] "Scripture," according to Dalferth, is a threefold concept: (a) certain texts, not all biblical passages, that (b) are used liturgically to testify God's loving presence as disclosed in Jesus Christ for all people; (c) so that God's presence becomes understandable here and now for the hearers.[133] The Bible is a plurality of texts, the gospel however, which is the Word of God, is unambiguous, telling about God's saving presence and calling to convert to a life in God's loving nearness. Not the reading of the Bible, but the hearing of the gospel of Jesus Christ, preached in the church, is the paradigmatic situation for understanding the Word of God.

An important and connected idea of Dalferth's view of Scripture is that Christ is the external center of Scripture. We do not find the center of the Scriptures inside the Bible: Jesus Christ, the center of the Scripture, is outside the Bible. This is because, in God's Word, God discloses, in his Spirit, his loving presence. What matters is what God is doing here and now. Christ is the center of Scripture because he is the center of human life, the center

---

128. Dalferth, *Radikale Theologie*, 132; Dalferth, *Wirkendes Wort*, 303–6, 312.

129. According to Dalferth, the Reformation affirmed the *sola scriptura*: Scripture with Christ as its centre discloses God's presence. The Reformed tradition made the entire Bible normative and did not see the difference between Scripture and the entire Bible. In Dalferth's view, they followed the *tota biblia* or *tota scriptura* and neglected the difference between Scripture and books of the Bible. See Dalferth, *Wirkendes Wort*, 117, 312–13.

130. Dalferth, *Wirkendes Wort*, 234–39.

131. "Nicht die alttestamentlichen Texte als solche sind Heilige Schrift der Kirche, sondern diese Texte, sofern sie auf Christus hintreiben, in dem Gottes universaler Heilswille in eschatologischer Endgültigkeit manifest ist." Dalferth, *Wirkendes Wort*, 182.

132. Dalferth, *Wirkendes Wort*, 204–7, 226–28, 237–39.

133. Dalferth, *Wirkendes Wort*, 243.

of the world, and the center of God as well. He is the point of departure for the interpretation of Scripture because he is the center of the Christian orientation and the Christian understanding of God, the world, and the self. The Protestant *sola scriptura* is another way to formulate that we find life in communion with God only in Christ, *solus Christus*.[134]

The *solus Christus* posits a reality: Christ as the external center of Scripture, as he remains outside the text of Scripture. Accordingly, he is the center of an event and not the intended, thematic, center of meaning of a coherent body of texts. Dalferth rejects the Reformed idea of *tota scriptura*: the Bible is a plurality of voices and the Scriptures as a whole do not disclose God's presence but rather obscure it. *Sola scriptura* does not mean *sola biblia* but is closely connected to the *solus Christus*. The *solus Christus* is necessary to determine which voices in the Scriptures will receive great weight and which will receive less. Of course, the New Testament testifies to Christ. We need canonical texts to discern the gospel. At the same time, Jesus Christ as the center is the critical principle in whose light the Scriptures are used in the Christian community. The criterion is whether in Christ and by the Holy Spirit, God's loving presence is disclosed.[135]

4.4 EVALUATION

Having described Dalferth's position, I will now analyze the strengths and weaknesses of his hermeneutical framework to see what he contributes to the project of this book, the development of a soteriological perspective on hermeneutics and Scripture. What are valuable elements in his hermeneutical theology? What are the important questions that he asks? What are the problems in his approach that need to be solved?

Dalferth's hermeneutical theology is an impressive attempt to analyze the internal, hermeneutical, relations of the Christian perspective: from the faith of Israel to the proclamation of Jesus, to the resurrection as the decisive moment for the genesis of the perspective of the Christian faith, to a process of renewal of our understanding of everything—of Jesus as the Christ, of God as Triune, of God's revelation as Triune act, of ourselves as sinners but justified and saved in Christ, and of our world as a creation to become a new creation. Christian doctrine is not a theoretical matter but concerns our understanding for it is self-involving, practical, and orientational.

---

134. Dalferth, *Wirkendes Wort*, 301–2.

135. Dalferth, *Wirkendes Wort*, 122, 221–24, 243, 307, 310, 312–13, 317. See further Dalferth, "Von der Vieldeutbarkeit der Schrift"; Dalferth, "Die Mitte ist Aussen."

Moreover, his emphasis on the hermeneutical necessity of re-orientation and conversion for our understanding is important. Believing the gospel of Jesus Christ, we have to learn to see everything in the light of this good news. Finally, the soteriological character of his hermeneutics is valuable. Dalferth shows that the renewal of our perception of everything is included in salvation. In the light of the gospel of Jesus Christ, hermeneutics is a soteriological activity.

The basic structure of his hermeneutical theology is important and here I will follow Dalferth. Christian believers will discover that we need, and receive, a radical renewal of our understanding. It all starts with faith in Jesus as Christ. In the light of Easter and the Spirit of Pentecost, we hear in Jesus the Word of God, and this changes everything. This change is the result of the activity of God in Christ and the Spirit. Faith in Jesus Christ evokes Trinitarian doctrine. As a result of faith in Jesus Christ as the Word of God, all our understanding will be transformed: our understanding of God, of ourselves, and our world. A new perspective on everything has opened. Scripture plays an important role when we want to further access that perspective.

Dalferth is right when he strives for a consistent hermeneutical approach. He criticizes the hermeneutical theologies of Jüngel and especially Ebeling for their incoherent combination of approaches as has been mentioned. Ebeling partly uses personal intentionalist and partly non-intentionalist methods (related to the Word-event). Dalferth's alternative is coherent: the Trinitarian disclosure of God's loving presence to someone, in the proclamation of the gospel, by means of usable passages of Scripture, leading to a radically new perspective. Although I have several serious questions about this approach, still it is important to construct a hermeneutical approach that is coherent. For my project, this demand for coherence will be a quality criterion for good theological hermeneutics. However, I will do things differently, because Dalferth's position evokes questions.

4.4.1 God's Trinitarian Self-Revelation and Human Reality

A very important question to answer concerns the relationship between God's Trinitarian self-revelation and human reality. Dalferth wants to do more than Ebeling and Jüngel did: he wants to give a systematic explication of faith, starting from God's Trinitarian self-identification (as they did as well), and to develop (more than they did) a coherent interpretation of our reality of life and experience.

From the beginning of his writings, Dalferth's larger books do not start with God, but their theological end does influence the beginning implicitly. *Religiöse Rede von Gott* starts with language, *Die Wirklichkeit des Möglichen* with thinking that seeks orientation, *Malum* with an overview of the problem of evil, our experience of it, and how we deal with it, and *Die kunst des verstehens* with a chapter on understanding, and philosophical hermeneutics. In all these works, God's presence will be shown sooner or later as "the reality of the possible." God is a possible option that shows itself to be a reality—the reality that gives new possibilities, the reality that we thank for making the possible real. This means that in the context of discovery, Dalferth's thought is theological (in the sense that he observes everything "*sub specie fidei*") and thus starts his thinking with God. In the context of justification, however, he does not begin with God but with the phenomena that are disclosed to us.

Dalferth intends to give orientation to our life and experience, and he does so from a perspective that is deliberately theological, particular, and realist. For Dalferth, God and our view of reality belong together. The orientational knowledge he offers in his hermeneutical theology is an orientation in the light of God's Triune self-identification, and hence *coram deo*. Moreover, this perspective *sub specie fidei* is not shared by all, but it is a particular point of view. God's self-identification opens up a new perspective, demands conversion and faith, and gives a radically new view of everything in the light of God's loving presence. At the same time, Dalferth's attitude is *realist* for God's presence is a reality. Accordingly, he does not use a dyadic but a triadic sign concept. In our speaking, the speaking subject, the signs that are used, and the reality within which we interact, are related.

Consequently, more than his predecessors in hermeneutical theology, Dalferth succeeds in giving an interpretation of life and experience in the light of the Word of God. Thus, Fickert is too negative in her judgment that Dalferth starts with the Word-event and is unable to do justice to the phenomena of our common human experience.[136] She seems to presuppose the possibility of a phenomenological perspective that is neutral. According to Dalferth, such a phenomenological perspective has no access to God's acts and presence, and in the light of God's acts and presence, all phenomena look different. Thus, somewhere a phenomenological approach will encounter the irreducible difference between *coram mundo* (sin) and *coram deo* (salvation).

However, Fickert does indicate some problematic aspects of Dalferth's approach. Dalferth views our world in an eschatological light, in the

---

136. Fickert, *Erfahrung und Offenbarung*, 30–32, 35, 199.

perspective of God's love coming from the end and giving new possibilities. Dalferth's approach is eschatological, and he is less interested in protological questions of origin, creation, and the emergence of evil in our world. Fickert signals the danger of a dualism involving a radical revelation theology and a this-worldly immanentism that is blind and deaf to God.[137] The relationship between God's new eschatological world and the created but fallen old world remains unclear, and God's action appears only as eschatological, saving and renewing, not as protological, creating and sustaining.

To conclude, Dalferth's hermeneutical theology, more than the work of his predecessors, is able to provide orientation in the world of daily human experience. At the same time, he faces the same problem as other theologians who followed the lines of Herrmann: an immanent view of the world and a soteriological view of God in Christ that are difficult to connect because of a defective doctrine of creation. Thus, my project in this book has to face the risk that a soteriological approach accepts a tendency toward deism or atheism and leaves our world behind as a reality where God does not act nor is present as creator and sustainer. The challenge is to develop mystagogical pointers that evoke curiosity for the mystery of God's presence. After all, our world still is God's world, even after the entrance of sin and evil, where God is still present and active.

4.4.2 Scripture

A second issue to discuss is Scripture. It is important that Dalferth alerts to the impact of the invention of book printing on the doctrine of Scripture. He is right in emphasizing the importance of listening with the ear. Thus, he stresses the verbal communication of the gospel that discloses to us God's loving presence through the history of Jesus Christ. Dalferth's focus is on divine self-communication, and our practice of preaching and proclaiming the gospel of God's loving presence should serve and follow God's praxis. In this light, it is valuable to distinguish with Dalferth the event hermeneutics of the Word of God ("Ereignishermeneutik des Wortes Gottes") and the act-hermeneutics of Scripture ("Handlungshermeneutik der Schrift").

Still, Dalferth's view of Scripture knows some problems and provides points of attention for my own project. John Webster has warned of the danger that in modern theology the relation between God's revelation and the Bible can become "almost arbitrary: the text is considered a complete and purely natural entity taken up into the self-communication of God.

---

137. Fickert, *Erfahrung und Offenbarung*, 56, 105, 135, 188, 199.

The result is a curious textual equivalent of adoptionism."[138] For Dalferth, there has been no history of salvation in which God works toward a climax: his final revelation in his Son Jesus Christ.[139] Thus, it becomes difficult to see Jesus Christ, with the New Testament authors, as the fulfillment of the *Tanakh*. Dalferth relates Jesus to the faith of Israel but does not reflect on the question of how God was active in the history of Israel, as has been indicated. Here, the influence can be seen of an immanent worldview in historical-critical studies of the Bible, that does not reckon with the activity of God in Israel's history. The question for what follows is, whether a stronger view of the history of salvation will lead to another view of Scripture and a more positive attitude toward the Reformed *tota scriptura*, which Dalferth rejects.

Dalferth criticizes the attribution of the perfections of the Word of God (authority, clarity, sufficiency, and efficacy) to the text of the Bible. In the case of authority, clarity, and efficacy this might seem convincing. However, in the case of sufficiency problems arise. The sufficiency of Scripture is closely related to the canon, in opposition to what can be said by the pope, church, tradition, or prophet. Somehow, the canon always had a criteriological role in church and theology. The refusal to attribute perfections to the text of Scripture leads to a question concerning theological criteria.

As we saw, Dalferth signals as problematic that hermeneutical theology did not succeed in formulating a criterion to distinguish what is true (significance given by God's self-explanation) and what is not true (significance created by our misinterpretations and misleading explanations). According to Fickert, Dalferth has seen the problem but does not give a solution.[140] Dalferth does formulate a criterion, based on the efficacy of God's Word: God's Word results in providing certainty for the hearers of the Word, so that they "understand their own life-situation in the light of God's reality-changing presence, and accordingly act, live, and die in awareness of this God-presence."[141] So the end result gives the criterion: whether in Christ and by the Holy Spirit, God's loving presence is disclosed.

If this is a criterion indeed, what does it mean to use this criterion? When is it possible for a preacher to conclude, "I have written a good sermon," or for a pastor "This pastoral advice was good," or for a theologian

---

138. Webster, *Holy Scripture*, 24.

139. Fickert, *Erfahrung und Offenbarung*, 90–91, 136.

140. Fickert, *Erfahrung und Offenbarung*, 210.

141. "Ihre eigene Lebenssituation im Licht der wirklichkeitverändernden Gegenwart Gottes verstehen und dementsprechend im Bewusstsein dieser Gottesgegenwart handeln, leben und sterben können." Dalferth, *Kunst des Verstehens*, 475. Cf. Dalferth, *Radikale Theologie*, 163.

"This was a good theological article"? In practice, it will often, if not always, be difficult or even impossible to know the fruits of our interpreting, translating, and communicating activities. Moreover, this criterion seems to favor the gospel over the law. What does this imply for the Word of God as law? If Dalferth intends this result-oriented criterion to be a real criterion, this lack of usefulness in the practice of church and theology is problematic. Fickert thinks that we need a more positive appreciation of ecclesial consensus and norms.[142] I will take these questions as a point of attention in what follows and as a reason to reconsider the Reformed doctrine of Scripture.

4.4.3 Participation in Christ and Embodiment

Fickert's emphasis on churchly consensus and norms signals a broader problem. For Dalferth, it is difficult to do justice to the bodily embodiment of newness in Christ and the new life of the church and the believers.[143] How does the newness of the life in Christ receive continuity and embodiment in church and believers? For hermeneutics, this touches on the Pauline notion of the renewal of the mind of the believer.

Dalferth relates the renewal of our understanding especially to the Holy Spirit, acknowledging the importance of Pentecost. According to Dalferth, the Holy Spirit makes us share in God's self-knowledge, integrating us in the self-transparency of God living as God-field.[144] According to his first letter to the Corinthians, Paul would agree with Dalferth, that the Spirit knows God and reveals God to us; by the Spirit we understand. But he adds: "We have the mind of Christ" (1 Cor 2:9–16). This element of the mind of Christ (cf. Phil 2:15) is lacking in Dalferth's theological hermeneutics. As we saw, participation in Christ does not imply for Dalferth that we participate in the *human* perspective of Jesus. This is not inadvertent, but characteristic of Dalferth's thinking. All emphasis is on the acts of God and the revealed nearness of God. Jesus Christ is not a person who acts to save us (apart from identifying God as a loving Father), but only the *place* where God acts for our salvation. If the God-man Jesus Christ does not add something

---

142. Fickert, *Erfahrung und Offenbarung*, 198.

143. As far as Fickert is concerned, see Fickert, *Erfahrung und Offenbarung*, 105, 114, 154–56, 198.

144. This leads Dalferth to the problematic position that our knowledge of God is not subjective, because we know God as he knows himself (Dalferth, *Auferweckte Gekreuzigte*, 179–87). But how do we know that we now as God knows himself? Cf. Schaafsma et al., "Vervreemding en vertrouwen," 21.

substantial to salvation, the renewal of our mind cannot be understood as participation in Christ.[145]

One can distinguish in Dalferth's work a universalizing tendency, abstracting from the concreteness of the story of Jesus Christ. According to Dalferth, the gospel has no semantic identity. It is the pragmatic identity of the gospel that matters: changing a life toward openness for God's good presence. The specific content of the gospel fades into the background.[146]

Moreover, Dalferth's reconstruction of the hermeneutical processes behind the New Testament and the Christian faith, from the Trinitarian self-identification of God toward a *coram deo* perspective and a life in gratitude for his loving presence, does not correct this abstracting tendency. Further, his choice for a clear-cut description of the gospel in favor of the polyphonic Scriptures leads to a self-affirming system of theological thinking. How can Scripture still contradict the theologian?

However, if Christ is the key to what God is doing as Kathryn Tanner suggests, and if Christ's humanity is a "vicarious humanity" (Christian Kettler / Thomas F. Torrance), or if Jesus Christ is humanity's representative in whom we participate (Oliver O'Donovan), then more has to be said.[147] It is crucial to point out that in the process of incarnation and identification, the Word of God truly becomes flesh, bears my life, makes that he is my life (Col 3:4), and lives in me (Gal 2:20). By his incarnation, the divine *logos* communicates, in his vicarious humanity, this divine life with believers.[148] Through the cross, incarnation and identification result in participation and transformation. Tanner writes, "One with Christ, incomprehensible in his divinity, we take on the very incomprehensibility of the divine rather than simply running after it, working to reproduce it in human terms."[149] This has epistemological and hermeneutical implications. In the words of Kettler, "It is through the humanity of Christ that God actually works upon our

---

145. In *Existenz Gottes*, Dalferth does refer to Jesus Christ as "wahrer Mensch," Dalferth, *Existenz Gottes und christlicher Glaube*, 185, 223, 225, 274, 313, 316, 344. In his later work, Dalferth does not develop this theme. Instead, it seems to disappear. This influences Dalferth's doctrine of the Trinity, where in his work after *Existenz Gottes* the Son receives too little hypostatical weight. See further Burger, *Being in Christ*, 412–25, 432–35, 448–52; Burger, "Hermeneutisch relevante triniteitsleer," 113–14. For a comparable criticism of Karl Barth, see Clark, *Divine Revelation and Human Practice*.

146. Dalferth, *Evangelische Theologie als Interpretationspraxis*, 100; Rieger, *Theologie als Funktion der Kirche*, 375.

147. Tanner, *Christ the Key*; Kettler, *Vicarious Humanity of Christ*, 6, 121–54; O'Donovan, *Resurrection and Moral Order*.

148. Cf. Kettler, *Vicarious Humanity of Christ*, 128.

149. Tanner, *Christ the Key*, 56.

thinking and speaking."[150] This changes our thinking, concerning God as well as humanity. Through the life and mind of Christ in which we participate, the divine mind becomes accessible (cf. Col 2:9–10).[151] The Holy Spirit makes us share in a divine perspective, mediated by the mind of Christ. Moreover, the Holy Spirit uses Scripture to make us participate in the mind of Christ. To further develop the hermeneutical significance of participation in Christ, I now turn to Oliver O'Donovan.

---

150. Kettler, *Vicarious Humanity of Christ*, 129.
151. Kettler, *Vicarious Humanity of Christ*, 132, 137–38, 160, 176, 181–86.

5.

Participation and Scripture
Participation in Christ, the New Perspective, and the Reading of Scripture

5.1 INTRODUCTION

Searching for a soteriological perspective on hermeneutics and Scripture, I started with the doctrine of the Trinity and with Ingolf Dalferth's hermeneutical theology. Dalferth's work enabled us to reflect on hermeneutics and Scripture within the activity of the triune God and to relate it to soteriological notions like conversion, a new perspective *coram deo*, and the resulting new understanding of God, the world, and the self. God's triune self-identification opens our eyes to the loving and saving presence of God.

Whereas Dalferth has a clear focus on the acts of the triune God, topics such as the embodiment of newness in Jesus Christ, the church, and a believer's life deserve more elaboration than Dalferth offers. As we saw in chapter 3, we live in a secular society and face the noetic consequences of sin. For the believing subject, living with the pressures of secularity and sin, it is important to live a life that is solidly rooted. In this book entitled *Jesus Christ, Hermeneutics, and Scripture*, I, first of all, look to Christ in my search for such a rooted life, following the call of Col 2:7–8, to "continue to live your lives in him, rooted and built up in him," that is, in Christ. Thus, in this chapter I will continue the quest for a theological hermeneutic by paying attention to participation in Christ and the "mind of Christ" (1 Cor 2:16).

Because we never have the mind of Christ by default, theology has to reflect on the formation and nourishment of "the mind of Christ." In this chapter, I will explore the work of Oliver O'Donovan to see to what extent his work helps understand the formation of the mind of Christ. The idea of the "mind of Christ" brings us to the other notion, "participation in Christ," which is a central motif of O'Donovan's moral theology.[1] I will interpret O'Donovan's moral theology as a theological contribution to the development of the mind of Christ by participation in Christ. By doing so, we will soon discover that it is impossible to reflect on the mind of Christ, and participation in him, without mentioning the Holy Spirit and his work. In O'Donovan's more recent trilogy *Ethics as Theology*, the work of the Holy Spirit is the focus of attention more than in earlier works.

I will start this chapter with a short overview of O'Donovan's theological development. It will turn out that he takes the gospel of Jesus Christ as the starting point for theology. In that sense, he is an epistemological nonfoundationalist (5.2). Second, I will describe his view on the relationship between knowledge, order, dominion, and participation in Christ (5.3). Third, we move from the more objective viewpoint of resurrection and Christology to the more subjective side of Pentecost and practical reasoning (reflection and deliberation) (5.4). Fourth, I answer the question of how the Scriptures are related to knowledge in Christ and how they function in the renewal of the mind. I will deal with his view of true moral concepts and their relationship to Scripture (5.5). Finally, I assess whether his theology is helpful for understanding (the formation of) the mind of Christ (5.6).

5.2 FROM RESURRECTION AND MORAL ORDER TO PENTECOST AND MORAL AGENCY

In the publications of O'Donovan after his first book on Augustine,[2] three main phases can be distinguished. In the first phase, O'Donovan starts writing about "Christian moral concepts" in *Resurrection and Moral Order*,[3] with a clear focus on the resurrection and on the objectivity of what Jesus Christ has achieved in it. O'Donovan uses the notion of moral order, restored and transformed in the resurrection, to counter the voluntarist tendency of modern morality. Order and value are no creation of the human will; neither is reality itself inert and meaningless. God has created the world in which we act.[4]

---

1. On the hermeneutical implications of O'Donovan's work, see, e.g., Baker, "Transformation of Persons"; Bartholomew, *Royal Priesthood?*

2. O'Donovan, *Problem of Self-Love in St. Augustine*.

3. O'Donovan, *Resurrection and Moral Order*, vii.

4. O'Donovan, "Natural Ethic"; O'Donovan, "Evangelicalism and the Foundations," 99; O'Donovan, *Resurrection and Moral Order*, x–xv, 16, 18, 20, 25, 32, 49, 52, 58,

In his second phase, he turns to political theology and writes two important works in this field. The first book *The Desire of the Nations* approaches political authority reflectively, starting from the biblical proclamation of the kingdom of God; the second book *The Ways of Judgment* again writes about the correspondence of "theological and political concepts . . . but it approaches the correspondence more from the political side."[5] By this point, the interest is more guided by practical deliberation. In O'Donovan's view, moral thinking has to be both reflective and deliberative. *The Desire of the Nation* and *The Ways of Judgment* both present political theology and reflect on the reality of political authority. Together, the two books are "two phases in a single extended train of thought; the first starting more from theological reflection, the second more from political deliberation."[6]

In the third phase of his work, O'Donovan returns to elementary reflection on Christian ethics and Christian moral concepts. In his trilogy *Ethics as Theology* (published between 2013 and 2017), he presents all the moral wisdom he has gained over the years. Looking back on *Resurrection and Moral Order*, he writes that this book "looked principally towards the objective order of created goods and the restoration of human agency by the resurrection of Christ." *Ethics as Theology* presents "a necessary complement to it," now shifting its focus toward "the subjective renewal of agency and its opening to the forward calling of God."[7] From *Resurrection and Moral Order* to "Pentecost and Moral Agency," he writes in the preface to *Self, World, and Time*.[8] The French philosopher Jean-Yves Lacoste, who also translated *Resurrection and Moral Order* into French, contributed to this shift. The influence of his theological phenomenology can be traced in the footnotes of *Ethics as Theology*.

The first part of the trilogy, *Self, World, and Time*, focuses on the awakening of moral thought itself and its place in the world, time, and the life of faith. Volume 2, *Finding and Seeking*, deals with the path of moral reason, from the self (in faith) to the world (in love), acting in time (in hope). The final book *Entering into Rest* deals with the object of moral reasoning, the responsibilities, and the goals of moral reasoning.

60, 67, 127, 220. The same can be found in *Ethics as Theology*, see O'Donovan, *Self, World, and Time*, 21–23, 93, 116–17, 125–26; O'Donovan, *Entering into Rest*, 37, 108–9, 163–65, 170.

O'Donovan shares this unease with voluntarism with Alasdair MacIntyre. For a comparison of O'Donovan and MacIntyre, see Bretherton, *Hospitality as Holiness*.

5. O'Donovan, *Ways of Judgment*, x.
6. O'Donovan, *Ways of Judgment*, x.
7. O'Donovan, *Self, World, and Time*, 93–94.
8. O'Donovan, *Self, World, and Time*, xii.

What remains constant in this development, is that the gospel of Jesus Christ provides the theological starting point for O'Donovan's work. Christian ethics should be evangelical: "Its concepts must express the inner logic of the gospel."[9] The gospel of Jesus Christ qualifies the path for Christian ethics: it makes the heart rejoice and gives "light to the eyes because it springs from God's gift to mankind in Jesus Christ."[10] This gospel is the primary source of the Christian life and the starting point for theology. Our world is not self-explanatory but has to be seen in the light of the gospel. Christocentrism should imply that we put Christ at the center of our world. As we will see, this Christocentrism remains important for the later O'Donovan, even if he sees that the Christocentrism of Barthian theology needs to be qualified.[11]

In epistemological respect, O'Donovan is a non-foundationalist. The gospel of Jesus Christ is not a universally shared starting point for living and thinking, and O'Donovan is well aware that nowhere do we find such a starting point. We always start with "complex readings of the world," "as such arguably from the beginning."[12] Accordingly, epistemology is a secondary, reflective activity that presupposes an existing practice of life. He regards it as a mistake of Protestantism to treat biblical studies as foundational to theology.[13] Not Scripture, but the gospel is the starting point of his non-foundationalism.

The gospel tells us about Jesus Christ and the triumph of God's kingdom. Although all moments of the Christ-event shape the Christian life, his resurrection is especially significant in this regard. Furthermore, because the Holy Spirit connects us with Christ, Pentecost is important as well. We find this combination of Easter and Pentecost throughout his work. The careful reader will find a lot of "Pentecost and Moral Agency" already in O'Donovan's *Resurrection and Moral Order*.[14]

According to O'Donovan, Easter has a twofold significance: God's vindicating his creation as an ordered totality, and also his transforming

9. Bartholomew, "Introduction," 21. And further O'Donovan, *Resurrection and Moral Order*, xii–xv; O'Donovan, "Evangelicalism and the Foundations," 96–97; O'Donovan, *Finding and Seeking*, ix.

10. O'Donovan, *Resurrection and Moral Order*, 12. And further O'Donovan, ix, 11, 13–15, 22, 36; O'Donovan, "Evangelicalism and the Foundations," 96–97; O'Donovan, *Desire of the Nations*, 3, 19; O'Donovan, *Self, World, and Time*, 91.

11. O'Donovan, *Self, World, and Time*, 96.

12. O'Donovan, *Self, World, and Time*, 30.

13. O'Donovan, *Resurrection and Moral Order*, vii, 76–77, 86–87; O'Donovan, "Response to Walter Moberly," 66; De Bruijne, *Levend in Leviatan*, 74.

14. O'Donovan, *Resurrection and Moral Order*, 22–26, 101–20.

creation by bringing it to its eschatological *telos*. Pentecost concerns our personal participation in what is achieved in Christ. Both Easter and Pentecost are related to our human perspective. In the risen Christ, human subjectivity is restored objectively (objective restoration of our agency); and in the Spirit, believers participate in what has been achieved in Christ (subjective renewal of our agency). Pentecost presupposes that the resurrection gives us access to the created reality, epistemologically as well as ontologically. It does so epistemologically, insofar as God's judgment of Jesus Christ in his resurrection provides a perspective that sheds its light on our world. Furthermore, it does so ontologically, in that the resurrection does not solely open up a new perspective, leaving that which existed unchanged. As indicated, resurrection implies the eschatological fulfillment of the intelligible order together with its restoration.[15]

Accordingly, both Easter and Pentecost have significance for our knowledge and interpretation, for epistemology and hermeneutics. Taking Easter as his starting point, O'Donovan combines a thoroughly theological non-foundationalism with universal notions like creation, order, and humanity. The gospel of Jesus Christ implies the creation and restoration of an ordered world. Because order implies intelligibility, epistemology and order are twins. Moreover, participation in Christ implies the renewal of our minds (5.3). Starting in pneumatology at Pentecost leads O'Donovan to compatible reflections, more influenced by phenomenology, about the renewal of the subject, the perspective of the believer in world and time, and the trajectory of moral thinking (5.4).

5.3 ORDER, DOMINION, AND PARTICIPATION IN CHRIST

Central to O'Donovan's understanding of the mind of Christ according to the Easter perspective is a conceptual framework constituted by the moral order, the human position within creation as dominion, sin, and salvation by participation in Christ.

To be human is to be created within the moral order in a position of "*dominium*." To participate in this order humanly is foremost to live in freedom. Freedom is characteristic of a person truly participating in knowing and acting. It is our responsible answer to God's call to serve him. Second,

---

15. O'Donovan, *Resurrection and Moral Order*, ix, xv, xvii–xviii, 13–15, 17, 19, 22, 24, 26, 31–32, 36, 55–58, 85, 87–88, 101–103; O'Donovan, "Evangelicalism and the Foundations," 96–97; O'Donovan, *Desire of the Nations*, 19, 161–162, 181; O'Donovan, *Self, World, and Time*, xii, 92–95.

the human mode of participating is through knowledge, discernment, and comprehension of reality. The presence of mind and reason make possible knowledge of a universe that is not inert but rather ordered and meaningful. The act of knowing is coordinated with obedience and is religiously and morally qualified. As O'Donovan states, "his knowing will stand or fall with his worship of God and his obedience to the moral law."[16] To be truly perceptive is to understand reality with love. Third, this love is the overall shape of a life in harmony with reality's moral order. As ordered love, love is "shaped in accordance with the order that it discovers in its object."[17] Hence, the theme of love transcends the sphere of choice and will, and it comprises perception, motivation, and action. To exercise the dominium to which Adam was called, humanity has to act and know lovingly.[18]

Humanity, however, refused to exercise *dominium* in the right way, and thus it has voluntarily deprived itself of its cognitive access to the reality of created order, giving away this freedom. Sin, understood as idolatry and rebellion, injures our existence. Our mind is corrupted and disordered, and the unity of reason and will is broken. O'Donovan finds this disintegration of the powers of our mind in the rational and voluntative self of modern voluntarism. This modern self is detached from God's love and grace, from others, and the world, thus risking despair. Idolatry and rebellion distort our view of the whole, due to misconstruction of the moral order, false conceptions, and wrong worldviews.[19] Discussing the modern concept of conscience, O'Donovan has shown that a broken relationship with the redemptive goodness of the triune God results in affective independence and indifference.[20]

At the heart of O'Donovan's theology stands Jesus Christ. The salvation of human agency is given by participation in Christ—in his position, and his subjectivity. According to O'Donovan, Jesus Christ represents

16. O'Donovan, *Resurrection and Moral Order*, 81. And further O'Donovan, "Natural Ethic," 28.

17. O'Donovan, *Resurrection and Moral Order*, 25–26.

18. O'Donovan, "Natural Ethic," 28; O'Donovan, *Resurrection and Moral Order*, 24–26, 35, 52, 55, 76, 81–82, 87–88, 107, 127, 181, 243; O'Donovan, *Ways of Judgment*, 79; O'Donovan, *Common Objects of Love*, 11, 23; O'Donovan, *Self, World, and Time*, 37–38, 111–15; O'Donovan, *Church in Crisis*, 113–40; O'Donovan, *Finding and Seeking*, 77–78.

19. O'Donovan, *Resurrection and Moral Order*, 19, 81–83, 87–89, 110–14, 119, 127, 151; O'Donovan, "Evangelicalism and the Foundations," 98–99; O'Donovan, *Ways of Judgment*, 77, 79, 279–312; O'Donovan, *Self, World, and Time*, 4, 10, 13, 22–24; O'Donovan, *Finding and Seeking*, 19–23, 81–87, 173–79.

20. See his discussion of modernity and conscience in O'Donovan, *Ways of Judgment*, 297–312.

Israel and humanity. In his glorification, Jesus Christ receives the position of *dominium* and takes the proper place of humanity within the order of reality. Salvation had to include the restoration of humanity to its position of dominion because humanity is an integral and crucial part of creation. Furthermore, human subjectivity had to be restored. This healing of human subjectivity is given objectively in the realization of freedom, knowledge, love, and obedience in the subjectivity of Christ.[21]

Moreover, in his glorification, Christ is brought to the fulfillment and destiny of humanity. In their representative, both humanity and creation are transformed eschatologically and brought to their eschatological *telos*. Consequently, the order of creation itself has a history, which causes each specific subject area in ethics to have its own salvation history, as we shall see below.[22]

The renewal of the universe has to touch a person "at the point where I am a moral agent, where I act and choose and experience myself as 'I.'"[23] Eschatological participation in Christ is made possible by the gift of the Holy Spirit. The Holy Spirit makes the reality of Christ actual so that we can be "in Christ." Through participation in Christ, humanity is re-enabled to exercise dominion within the restored and transformed moral order. However, to be able to live in this position, we need the renewal of our capacity to know, understand, and rejoice, which we receive by participation in the subjectivity and freedom of Christ. "Christian knowledge" is grounded, then, "in Christ's human being."[24] In Christ, our access to reality is restored: true knowledge is "knowledge 'in Christ.'"[25]

O'Donovan uses the concept of authority to explain this participation. The Spirit makes the reality of redemption authoritative to us. As a result, our participation in this reality is renewed, as we respond to its authority freely. We are thus authorized to take our place of *dominium* (*Resurrection*

---

21. O'Donovan, *Resurrection and Moral Order*, 24, 85, 149–50. Cf. O'Donovan, *Self, World, and Time*, 75, 92–97. For more on O'Donovan's view of salvation by participation in Christ as our representative, see Burger, *Being in Christ*, 457–94.

22. O'Donovan, "Natural Ethic," 26; O'Donovan, *Resurrection and Moral Order*, xvii, 55–57, 60–62, 64–65; O'Donovan, *Desire of the Nations*, 19, 143; O'Donovan, *Self, World, and Time*, 94–97.

23. O'Donovan, *Resurrection and Moral Order*, 23.

24. O'Donovan, *Resurrection and Moral Order*, 87.

25. O'Donovan, *Resurrection and Moral Order*, 85, 107; further 22–24, 85, 97, 101, 150; O'Donovan, *Desire of the Nations*, 161, 181; O'Donovan, *Ways of Judgment*, 75, 82, 85, 185, 298; O'Donovan, *Self, World, and Time*, 5, 7, 42, 92, 94–97, 109–10. O'Donovan's existential interest is influenced by Kierkegaard, who, as De Bruijne has shown, long-served as one of O'Donovan's dialogue partners. De Bruijne, *Levend in Leviatan*, 163–68.

and Moral Order) and authorized as the communion of the church (*The Desire of the Nations*). Finally, the Spirit evokes our free and joyful response to salvation in Christ. We receive the freedom and love for a responsive participation in the reality of which we are part. We will be freed from the bondage of our will and the inability to obey. Furthermore, the dividedness of our reason and will, as well as reason and will themselves, are to be healed. In short, God's judgment in Christ lays its dual claim on us: a "critical opposition to the falsely structured reality in which we live," and a calling into existence of "a new and truer structure for existence."[26]

Participation in Christ implies conversion and self-denial, a moment of being "crucified with Christ." As we saw, idolatry has led to misknowledge and false conceptions of the world. If the Spirit convicts us of sin and unbelief, however, we discover the necessity of conversion and repentance. We need to evaluate our moral intuitions critically since we must return from our freely chosen alienation from reality. This conversion from the imagined order, our will has created, involves a radical reorientation of will and reason.[27]

According to O'Donovan, conversion has two sides, each with epistemic implications: a decisive formative moment in which our view of the whole shape of things is changed, comparable to justification, and an ongoing process in which we internalize what we already know in outline, comparable to sanctification. In his study of O'Donovan, Baker states that the first decisive formative moment of conversion implies the gift of a new capacity to discern revealed knowledge. Hence he sees two opposing ontologies at work here in O'Donovan's theology: a static one, presuming the gift of a new epistemic capacity, and a dynamic one with an ongoing participation in a moral reality. Using Dalferth's concept of a *coram deo* perspective, the first formative moment can be interpreted differently. According to Dalferth, a new perspective *coram deo* is opened when God identifies himself to someone in Christ by the Holy Spirit. This perspective sheds new light on God and gives a new view of the world and the self before this newly identified God. However, it does not presuppose the gift of a new epistemic capacity or a static cosmology.[28]

---

26. O'Donovan, *Resurrection and Moral Order*, 104; further 22-26, 85, 101-8, 110-11, 121, 141, 163-64; O'Donovan, *Desire of the Nations*, 158-61, 174; O'Donovan, *Self, World, and Time*, 41-42.

27. O'Donovan, *Resurrection and Moral Order*, 92-93, 97, 104-5, 109-13, 116, 227; O'Donovan, *Church in Crisis*, 13; O'Donovan, *Self, World, and Time*, 8, 88.

28. O'Donovan, *Resurrection and Moral Order*, 91-92, 256-58; Baker, "Transformation of Persons," 153-59; Dalferth, *Theology and Philosophy*, 85-88, 158-61, 212, 219-23; Dalferth, *Becoming Present*, 36-43.

The renewal of our agency by faith, love, and hope, however, does have epistemic implications. Receiving a new point of view in Christ, we enjoy the restoration of the "possibilities of recognizing and rejoicing in the objective reality of the good."[29] This restoration has an aspect of wisdom and attentiveness (recognizing), but also more affectively, of joy and delight (rejoicing). We will receive the new integrity of the "attentiveness of faith," which according to O'Donovan contains "the whole of our response to God, from hearing, understanding and assenting, to willing and acting."[30] In addition, it includes joy about, love for, and delight in reality. Our joy is first and foremost an exuberant worship of the God of the resurrected Jesus Christ. Second, joy is the appropriate answer to God's goodness in creation and as such is a moral attitude. Joy keeps the moral life from pathology and destructive attitudes. Our gratitude for God's created order lets us participate in this order and makes it complete. In our present participation in the resurrection of Christ, joy, therefore, plays a key role.[31]

Moreover, the renewal of our agency and the gift of the "attentiveness of faith" have hermeneutical implications. Faith is necessary in order to understand the Scriptures. Faith is, first, *trust* in the saving work of God. Secondly, faith is *belief* that Scripture is the testimony of God. It implies the willingness to understand Scripture in obedience. This obedience to God is an important concept in O'Donovan's reflections on hermeneutics. However, as O'Donovan emphasizes, obedience has to be freely performed, which requires understanding. Hence, true obedience is not blind but thoughtful. O'Donovan, therefore, stresses both: obedience needs hermeneutics, and hermeneutics only makes sense if we are resolved to be obedient.[32]

His hermeneutics of obedience makes O'Donovan critical of most hermeneutical thinking. We should not treat the Bible with our constructions or presuppositions but try to read it on its own conditions. If we are not willing to learn something new, any attempt to understand is useless. If we find ourselves facing difficult judgments in a text and practice hermeneutics, "to handle this recalcitrant material," this hermeneutical approach does not

---

29. O'Donovan, *Resurrection and Moral Order*, 109.

30. O'Donovan, *Resurrection and Moral Order*, 110.

31. O'Donovan, *Resurrection and Moral Order*, 26, 109–13; O'Donovan, "Evangelicalism and the Foundations," 96–98, 106; O'Donovan, *Desire of the Nations*, 181–86; O'Donovan, *Self, World, and Time*, 102–3, 106. See on the order of love, O'Donovan, *Resurrection and Moral Order*, ch. 11; O'Donovan, *Problem of Self-Love in St. Augustine*.

32. O'Donovan, *Resurrection and Moral Order*, 142; O'Donovan, *Desire of the Nations*, 12–13; O'Donovan, *Ways of Judgment*, 130–42; O'Donovan, "Scripture and Christian Ethics," 124; O'Donovan, "Moral Authority of Scripture," 165, 168–69, 175; O'Donovan, *Church in Crisis*, 69–71, 77; O'Donovan, *Self, World, and Time*, 77–80.

promise "an interpretation of these judgments," but "only a refusal of them."[33] A more appropriate hermeneutic approach seeks a still unknown answer to a real unsolved question. Of course, we have and need our hermeneutical pre-understandings. However, the imagery of a "fusing of horizons" and a "hermeneutic circle" leaves out the possibility of a real discovery and the presence of a reality outside our pre-understandings. The moment of obedience is at the same time a moment of transcendence. Trying to understand the text deeper and more accurately, we wait upon God. O'Donovan eagerly wants to maintain a real openness to God's word to protect our freedom. He states, "If only we understood what freedom really meant, and how difficult freedom is to accomplish, we would surely ask that text to give us rivers of living water!"[34]

Another reason for this openness is that our participation in Christ is still incomplete. We hope for the redemption of creation, but the hope of our resurrection with Christ refers to a still unknown future, as our life is hidden in Christ (cf. Col 3:3–4). We wait for the public disclosure of that life when Christ appears at the *parousia*. Our lives retain an ambiguous character as long as our participation in Christ is incomplete. This unsatisfying incompleteness combined with the tension between old and new leads to many external ambiguities. Until our own resurrection, conformity to Jesus Christ as the perfect model of participation in the restored order of creation remains partial; we do not even know what such participation is comprised of. Our act of knowing (including our knowledge of ourselves) also remains incomplete and ambiguities linger because the act of knowing is itself part of this still-hidden life.[35] Hence, it is important to participate in Jesus Christ, "this narrow point in the human race," the only place where the vocation to human knowledge as well as the vocation to human being are fulfilled. As we already saw, "knowledge is grounded in being, human knowledge specifically in human being, and Christian knowledge in Christ's human being."[36]

Participation in Christ, as the source of the Christian perspective, implies a narrative about God and a related conceptual framework, about

---

33. O'Donovan, *Church in Crisis*, 61.

34. O'Donovan, *Church in Crisis*, 68. Further O'Donovan, *Resurrection and Moral Order*, 162; O'Donovan, *Desire of the Nations*, 13, 27–29; O'Donovan, "Response to Walter Moberly," 68; O'Donovan, "Scripture and Christian Ethics," 214; O'Donovan, "Moral Authority of Scripture," 168; O'Donovan, *Church in Crisis*, 59–68, 80.

35. O'Donovan, *Resurrection and Moral Order*, 14, 83, 85, 246–47, 249, 253–54, 256–58, 261–62; O'Donovan, *Self, World, and Time*, 94–95, 123; McIlroy, *Trinitarian Theology of Law*, 96.

36. O'Donovan, *Resurrection and Moral Order*, 87; cf. 85.

creation and humanity, and their redemption in Jesus Christ. Moreover, participation in Christ implies that the individual subject needs to recover the proper relation of the believer to the church. This conviction is the result of O'Donovan's growing awareness of the role church and narrative play in the process of moral formation. We need a community like the church with its liturgy that constitutes its life form.[37] Although O'Donovan sees the importance of a community and its life forms, this is not the main emphasis of his work. In chapter 8, I will discuss the role of community and practices.

5.4 SELF IN THE WORLD AND TIME: REFLECTION AND DELIBERATION

Objectively, according to O'Donovan, human subjectivity is restored in the resurrection of Jesus Christ. But as we saw, the Holy Spirit has to make us participate subjectively in this renewal. Christian moral agency thus presupposes the presence and activity of the Holy Spirit who makes us share in Jesus Christ. In the trilogy *Ethics as Theology*, O'Donovan explores with more phenomenological sensitivity the renewal of our moral agency in the Spirit. We are given a life in the Spirit and led by the Spirit that is opposed to a life according to the flesh. Living in between the resurrection of Jesus Christ and the resurrection of our flesh, the future does not remain abstract, but as the firstfruits of God's future, we receive the Holy Spirit to strive for what we do not know yet.[38]

O'Donovan uses the metaphor of waking to indicate what the Spirit does with our moral awareness. First, "to be awake is to be aware of the truth of a world."[39] This world precedes my existence, has its own objectivity, and lays moral demands on me. Thus, moral thinking demands an attentive moral description of the world as an intelligible world.[40] We have our "imaginative representations" of the world, but knowing and loving reality

---

37. O'Donovan, *Resurrection and Moral Order*, xviii–xx; O'Donovan, "Response to Walter Moberly," 2, 92; O'Donovan, *Self, World, and Time*, 43–46, 65; Burger, *Being in Christ*, 482; De Bruijne, *Levend in Leviatan*, 74; Baker, "Transformation of Persons," 134–35. Hauerwas played a role in this development. On the relationship between Hauerwas's narrative ethics and O'Donovan's Christian moral realism, see Black, *Christian Moral Realism*.

38. O'Donovan, *Self, World, and Time*, 1–9; O'Donovan, *Finding and Seeking*, 12, 6–10.

39. O'Donovan, *Self, World, and Time*, 10.

40. O'Donovan, *Self, World, and Time*, 10–12. On love as the "affective cognition of reality," see O'Donovan, *Finding and Seeking*, 124–26.

means that our representations continuously have to be corrected by the world.[41]

Second, this awareness of the world is *our* awareness of the world. Accordingly, "it means bringing ourselves into view together with the world."[42] Our (active) presence in the world precedes our awareness of this presence and our awareness of ourselves as an "I." But becoming aware of the world will lead to awareness of our presence in the world at a certain place, as a (possible) "point of view," and as "distinct agents" active also in self-reflection. To be called to wake up implies responsibility and confronts ambivalence. We are living between the saving and the losing of our souls. We are "centers of initiative" who are capable of the "moral failure to attend to oneself," but also of pride and humility.[43] Consequently, it does not surprise that O'Donovan writes a lot about sin—sin against the self, sin against the world, sin against time—in *Ethics as Theology*, doubt of meaning and doubt of purpose in *Finding and Seeking*, and sin against the community in *Entering into Rest*.[44]

Third, we discover that we live in time. O'Donovan argues, "World and self are co-present only in the moment of time which is open to us for action."[45] Following Jean-Yves Lacoste, O'Donovan characterizes the present as "the native element of feeling, prior to any thinking or acting, . . . a privileged moment within time, . . . looking back and forth across it."[46] In reflection, we can look back on what has been done, and in deliberation, we focus on "the available future, the possibility that lies open to our action."[47] Further, it is in time that we pay attention to the world, hear the call of wisdom, and make progress in knowing the world.[48]

These three, self, world, and time, constitute the basic framework of O'Donovan's trilogy *Ethics as Theology*. Not because other themes do not matter (like God, the laws of logic, mathematics, or metaphysics), but

---

41. O'Donovan, *Finding and Seeking*, 108.

42. O'Donovan, *Self, World, and Time*, 12. In knowing the world, "objectivity and subjectivity are necessarily co-present," O'Donovan, *Finding and Seeking*, 102.

43. O'Donovan, *Self, World, and Time*, 13–14. On perspective, prejudice (and Gadamer) see further O'Donovan, *Finding and Seeking*, 95–99.

44. O'Donovan, *Finding and Seeking*, 19–23, 43–46, 65–69, 81–88, 173–78; O'Donovan, *Entering into Rest*, 65–71.

45. O'Donovan, *Self, World, and Time*, 15.

46. O'Donovan, *Self, World, and Time*, 15.

47. O'Donovan, *Self, World, and Time*, 17.

48. O'Donovan, *Finding and Seeking*, 101–3. On the historical character of our knowledge, see also O'Donovan, 114–19.

because, as an ethicist, he is interested in "the roots of *practical reason*."[49] To our consciousness self, world, and time are "co-eventual," and our moral thinking orders them discursively "as the rational expression of our existence-towards-action," corresponding to the "journey . . . which leads in a certain direction towards a certain end."[50]

According to many, we should act reasonably. This leads O'Donovan to an exploration of moral thinking. Moral thinking is a "communicative inquiry with a social basis."[51] He explores how we communicate, give moral advice, acknowledge persons with moral authority, and receive moral teaching. The social nature of responsibility prevents us from misleading ourselves.[52] Primarily, however, the "content of our responsibility" is "God's call to us to serve him."[53] For this reason, O'Donovan emphasizes that "self-conscious moral thinking begins and ends by calling on God."[54] The form of our prayers matters, for "the rightly formed petition is at the same time the rightly formed train of moral thought."[55] Just as it does matter that the Lord's prayer begins with God, the prayer for forgiveness is important because in it "we ask for discontinuity, for the inauguration of a new justice."[56] This newness includes our own agency: we pray for "a new possibility of initiative which restores and renews the relation to the past as well as to the future."[57] Thus, "at the heart of moral thinking is a prayer for the coming of God to reshape our freedom from within."[58]

Clearly, this newness does not imply perfection. "Perfectionist expectations" will "produce frustration and incomprehension."[59] Following Augustine, O'Donovan writes that in our age, the time characterized by the eschatological tension of the "yet" and "not yet," our righteousness "is no more than forgiven sin."[60] As I have already mentioned, sin is an important theme in the trilogy at various moments "tracing the ways sin fans out into

---

49. O'Donovan, *Self, World, and Time*, 18.

50. O'Donovan, *Self, World, and Time*, 19.

51. O'Donovan, *Self, World, and Time*, 44.

52. O'Donovan, *Self, World, and Time*, 43. See further chapter 3 of *Self, World, and Time*.

53. O'Donovan, *Self, World, and Time*, 38.

54. O'Donovan, *Self, World, and Time*, 38. See further O'Donovan, "Prayer and Morality."

55. O'Donovan, *Self, World, and Time*, 39.

56. O'Donovan, *Self, World, and Time*, 41.

57. O'Donovan, *Self, World, and Time*, 42.

58. O'Donovan, *Self, World, and Time*, 42.

59. O'Donovan, *Self, World, and Time*, 91.

60. O'Donovan, *Self, World, and Time*, 91.

the variety of forms is assumes in the world."[61] The same is the case with sanctification and renewal. Here, O'Donovan clearly wants to maintain the Christocentrism of Barthian theology and his own earlier phase of "resurrection and moral order." Resurrection and ascension indeed imply that the new life is "full of the unknown and the inarticulatable."[62] Therefore, participation in Christ and the work of the Spirit in the light of "Pentecost and moral agency," need a qualified Christocentrism as it can be found in Bonhoeffer's idea of "ethics as formation." We will be conformed to Christ who is incarnate, crucified, and risen. According to O'Donovan, Bonhoeffer's polemics are directed against bad philosophy and bad theology, not against moral thinking as such. We need our "own styles of creaturely and redeemed thinking-to-act; being conformed to Christ and not to the world is . . . the renewal of the mind."[63]

The themes of participation in Christ and renewal by the Spirit thus return. When O'Donovan writes about how we hear God's "testimony to the meaning of world and time," he writes about Jesus as the representative, Christ who embodies God's history of salvation: "We discover in him the representative moment in history that gathers the intelligibility of world and time into itself, and sets other happenings, however unintelligible and misunderstandable, in relation to it."[64] His history is our history, he fulfills the righteousness of God to restore Israel and realize God's purposes for all humanity. God's testimony in Christ is communicated in the Spirit with us, and we receive and share it in the Spirit-filled community of the church. In this divine testimony and communication, the reading of the canonical texts of Scripture plays a central role.[65] Reading Scripture is part of the process of the renewal of the mind.

As far as O'Donovan is concerned, this renewal of the mind is urgently needed in moral thinking, given the modern problem with moral deliberation and the voluntarist attitude of modernity. Firstly, he regards

61. O'Donovan, *Self, World, and Time*, 84. According to O'Donovan, sin can be explored in two ways, in relation to "protological definitions" and to "broad phenomenological surveys"; O'Donovan, *Self, World, and Time*, 84.

62. O'Donovan, *Self, World, and Time*, 94.

63. O'Donovan, *Self, World, and Time*, 97. O'Donovan already hints at such a qualified christocentrism in line with Bonhoeffer's "ethics as formation" in the prologue to the second edition of *Resurrection and Moral Order*; see O'Donovan, *Resurrection and Moral Order*, xvi–xvii. Furthermore, this conformation to the incarnate, suffering, risen (and ascended Christ) is developed extensively in O'Donovan, *Desire of the Nations*, 133–46, 175–92. On sanctification, see O'Donovan, *Entering into Rest*, 72–101. On the renewal of the mind, see O'Donovan, *Entering into Rest*, 21–22.

64. O'Donovan, *Finding and Seeking*, 126–27.

65. O'Donovan, *Finding and Seeking*, 126–36.

the distinction between theoretical reason ("*x* is the case") and practical reason ("*y* has to be done") as problematic. Instead, he favors the Augustinian unity of knowing and loving. In classic moral thought, *what is the case* and *what has to be done* were clearly related. Still, according to Thomas Aquinas theoretical and practical reason both had their own principles and axioms. Consequently, the distinction could lead to the idea that both are separate reasons, following their own disconnected trains of thought and leading to a separation of fact and value. Instead, O'Donovan proposes that moral thinking is one train of thought, which has to do justice to two poles of reason: goodness ("an aspect of what *is*"), and rightness ("what *is to be done*").[66] Phrased in terms of ways of thinking, they are *reflection*, looking backward to the description of realities, and *deliberation*, looking forward to a decision and an act.[67]

Another layer of the same problem is caused by one of what he perceives as the roots of modernity: affective skepticism. This skepticism was no longer convinced of "the moral coherence" of the "affective impulses of the soul," and resulted from "the sixteenth century's radical perspectives of the sinfulness of the heart."[68] To prevent the most negative position, "viewing human motivation as reducible to an interest in self-preservation,"[69] new moral certainty was necessary. Such a new moral foundation had to be affectively independent. Francis de Sales found this in a "state of immediate responsiveness to God's will, free of self-orientation or calculation such as inevitably characterized interactions among human beings."[70] Accordingly, humans have to love God necessarily because of his essence, "quite independent of his actual love for us."[71] As a result, our love for God was a pure love, without hope, and without self-commitment. He clearly prefigures Kantian ideas: a "positive and formal will ... the principle of all disinterested desires which the written law commands."[72]

The modern idea of conscience had developed analogously. The conscience was "drained of Christ-centered formation and cut off from the

---

66. O'Donovan, *Self, World, and Time*, 28.

67. O'Donovan, "Christian Moral Reasoning," 122; O'Donovan, *Common Objects of Love*, 2–23; O'Donovan, *Self, World, and Time*, 21–32.

68. O'Donovan, *Ways of Judgment*, 298. Cf. on the problematic early-modern doctrine of original sin ("separating anthropological dogma from behavioral realities," "it had reduced the thesis of universal sin to incomprehensibility") O'Donovan, *Self, World, and Time*, 83.

69. O'Donovan, *Ways of Judgment*, 299.

70. O'Donovan, *Ways of Judgment*, 300.

71. O'Donovan, *Ways of Judgment*, 301.

72. O'Donovan, *Ways of Judgment*, 301.

discursive content of practical reason" and transformed into "an immediate and peremptory awareness of obligation."[73] The conscience no longer is a "discursive self-consciousness, a roomy mental space for reflection and deliberation," leading to "cutting short deliberation and negotiation."[74] Instead, the "conscientious individual is stripped even of the knowledge of God himself, leaving only the bare imperative countering him in abstraction."[75] The moral voice in the conscience has turned into a "tyrant," a "voice that came from nowhere and could be mediated by no rational argument."[76] This is the result: "Modern man is distinguished by sudden eruptions of raw moral certainty, moments of moralistic and ideological judgment which permit no reflective or deliberative interrogation."[77] Reflection, moral reflection, and self-reflection, no longer is "formed by hopeful attention to the inner dialogue with God, but by the incessant and disappointing struggle to get to the core of things, to occupy a position of strategic command."[78] The modern subject no longer longs "to be conformed to the image of a self-communicating God, and so become similarly self-communicative."[79] God is reduced to an "absolute will," and the modern self is "unsituated," and constantly has to create itself.[80]

If moral thinking has become so detached from the actual love of God, Christ-like formation, and discursive content, it is not a surprise that modern theologians have problematic views of moral deliberation. For Schleiermacher, theological ethics was a description of the peaceful Christian life of a modern liberal church. Deliberation only was necessary to eliminate "conflicts of duty," resulting from "contradictory ideas" or "complications of circumstance."[81] For Schleiermacher, moral thinking only has the task of "smoothing the ruffled surface of moral experience."[82] This association of deliberation with dilemma "is too easily assumed." According to O'Donovan, "A dilemma is an affective experience . . . ; deliberation is a train of thought."[83] Barth emphasized the theological character of ethics

---

73. O'Donovan, *Ways of Judgment*, 301–2.
74. O'Donovan, *Ways of Judgment*, 302.
75. O'Donovan, *Ways of Judgment*, 301–2.
76. O'Donovan, *Ways of Judgment*, 302.
77. O'Donovan, *Ways of Judgment*, 308.
78. O'Donovan, *Ways of Judgment*, 309.
79. O'Donovan, *Ways of Judgment*, 310.
80. O'Donovan, *Ways of Judgment*, 310.
81. O'Donovan, *Finding and Seeking*, 191–92.
82. O'Donovan, *Finding and Seeking*, 192.
83. O'Donovan, *Finding and Seeking*, 192. See further O'Donovan, *Self, World, and*

and had a "persistent nervousness of general moral principles which would be applied to actual cases discursively.... The result was a collapse of the discursive character of moral reason."[84] As a result, moral decisions are "left isolated and absolute, answerable only to the immediacy of the divine, unapproachable by thought, and refusing every attempt to give form."[85] Other theologians have emphasized the "quantum leap from idea to act without intermediate thought"[86] or made moral thinking difficult by separating ethics from dogmatics.[87] For ethicists who have a high view of Scripture, it is important that O'Donovan also warns against the danger that "in the name of obedience to scriptural authority" deliberation and moral thinking will be "effectively abolished." Obedience implies deliberation, and Scripture does not completely determine what we do.[88]

Interesting and insightful is further his evaluation of Dutch Neo-Calvinism. Although the idea of a Christian worldview is valuable, the Neo-Calvinist "preoccupation with the organization of sciences allowed too little place in their worldview for the love of the good. Operationally, this vacuum of moral direction left room for the return of civil conformity in the form of a political pluralism with which the sovereignty of Christ had little to do."[89]

For O'Donovan, the restoration of moral agency means that a new self is awakened, a self who is loved by God, shares in Christ, is led by the Spirit, is formed by the Scriptures (as we will see in 5.5), and so experiences a renewal in the mind. This renewal of the mind will lead to a renewal of moral thinking. According to O'Donovan, this moral thinking is one train of thought, a combination of reflection and deliberation. The path of moral thinking follows the way from the self (rooted in faith), directed to the world (living in love), toward action in time (acting in hope). *Finding and Seeking*, the second part of the trilogy, offers an elaborate overview of the trajectory of moral thinking within this framework of self, world, and time, connected with the theological virtues of faith, love, and hope. It ends in deliberation and discernment. We should learn to think from the gospel in faith, to discern reality in the light of the gospel in love, and to act in the power of the gospel in hope.

Time, 85–86.

84. O'Donovan, *Self, World, and Time*, 101.

85. O'Donovan, *Finding and Seeking*, 188. See on Barth further O'Donovan, "Christian Moral Reasoning," 122; O'Donovan, *Self, World, and Time*, 100–102; O'Donovan, *Finding and Seeking*, 188–90.

86. O'Donovan, *Finding and Seeking*, 190.

87. O'Donovan, *Self, World, and Time*, 87–88.

88. O'Donovan, *Self, World, and Time*, 77.

89. O'Donovan, *Finding and Seeking*, 112–13.

5.5 SCRIPTURE AND THE RENEWING OF OUR THINKING

In the renewal of the mind, and also in the discernment of our world, Scripture plays an important role. This role of Scripture has to be clarified. Why is the Scripture important and how is Scripture related to knowing in Christ?

According to O'Donovan, we can only understand the authority of Scripture in light of the authority of Christ. Christ's authority liberates and gives us true freedom. His authority authorizes the church and within the church the apostles and prophets. Moreover, Scripture is authoritative because of what it contains, namely, salvation and everlasting life in Christ Jesus.[90]

Christ is the climax of the history of God's people Israel, which makes it possible to read the Old and the New Testament as a coherent narrative. This is, however, not self-evident. Without Jesus Christ, the Bible does not contain a single harmonious story, but rather different stories with moral incompatibilities. Additionally, these stories tell the drama of exile and the cross. However, the manifestation of God's kingdom and the vindication of creation in the resurrection of Christ as the fulfillment of Israel turn these fragments into a story with a coherent plot. The future of Israel, realized in the resurrection of Jesus Christ, offers a perspective on the future of the world. This christological perspective makes the story of Israel relevant to humanity. Christ has conquered death and all other powers of evil, which are Israel's real enemies. In Christ, the story of Jewish election is a story with universal authority, relevant to all people.[91]

Accordingly, Christian moral thinking must follow the history of salvation. O'Donovan uses the history of Jesus Christ as the entrance into salvation history. He sums up the history of Jesus Christ in four moments: advent, suffering, resurrection, and glorification.[92] O'Donovan claims that

90. O'Donovan, *On the Thirty-Nine Articles*, 51; O'Donovan, "Scripture and Christian Ethics," 122, 124–25; O'Donovan, *Church in Crisis*, 54–55, 75; O'Donovan, "Moral Authority of Scripture," 166–67, 173–74.

91. O'Donovan, "Natural Ethic," 30; O'Donovan, *Resurrection and Moral Order*, xv, 14–15, 43, 55, 157–60; O'Donovan, *On the Thirty-Nine Articles*, 56–64; O'Donovan, *Desire of the Nations*, 23, 27, 130; O'Donovan, "Deliberation, History and Reading," 140–41; O'Donovan, "Scripture and Christian Ethics," 123–24; O'Donovan, *Church in Crisis*, 61–62; O'Donovan, *Finding and Seeking*, 135. Further Burger, *Being in Christ*, 457–63; McIlroy, *Trinitarian Theology of Law*, 97, 107. For several critical reflections on O'Donovan's view of the history of salvation, see Furnish, "How Firm a Foundation?"; Schweiker, "Freedom and Authority," 116–19; Moberly, "Use of Scripture."

92. Jonathan Chaplin prefers another summary of salvation history (e.g., creation-fall-redemption/salvation), but misses the fact that O'Donovan deliberately chooses four notions that summarize the story of the representative of Israel and humanity; see

each area of moral interest "has to be given . . . a salvation-history of its own."[93] It is to be viewed, therefore, in light of the whole historical account of God's dealings with this area.[94]

Consequently, an important feature of O'Donovan's hermeneutic is that he reads the Scriptures in their entirety. He declines a selective use of Scripture where one focuses only on certain texts that fit well to analogies from our world or texts that we like and seem useful. If God's commands are isolated from their context in the narrative of God's history with his world, their meaning becomes less intelligible. Since moral deliberation is not our project, our moral thinking "should be shaped in any significant way by the Scriptures."[95] We should search for a comprehensive moral viewpoint, connecting our views with the whole of salvation history by a "unifying conceptual structure," an "architectonic hermeneutic" that does justice to the entire narrative of Scripture.[96] *The Desire of the Nations* exemplifies such a reading of the Bible, focusing on the moral area of politics.[97]

O'Donovan refuses to understand the role of the biblical narrative in terms of an incomplete drama (a "theodrama") that needs to be completed by the believers by means of dramatic improvisation, as it has been proposed, e.g., by N. T. Wright and Kevin Vanhoozer. What we do is interpret the grand narrative of God and follow the guidance it offers. Improvisation, favored by Wright and Vanhoozer however, "suggests a *lacuna* in the guidance, a space left bare to allow the performer to take over from the dramatist."[98] The freedom to act is understood differently by O'Donovan. He argues, "Neither narrative nor description has any direct reach into the future."[99] What the practical reason does in moral deliberation is think about future acts, and this is more than what hermeneutics can do.[100]

Chaplin, "Political Eschatology and Responsible Government."

93. O'Donovan, *Resurrection and Moral Order*, xviii.

94. O'Donovan, *Resurrection and Moral Order*, xvi–xvii; O'Donovan, *Desire of the Nations*, 133; O'Donovan, "Christian Moral Reasoning," 123.

95. O'Donovan, *Resurrection and Moral Order*, 200.

96. O'Donovan, *Desire of the Nations*, 22.

97. O'Donovan, *Resurrection and Moral Order*, 200; O'Donovan, "Evangelicalism and the Foundations," 100; O'Donovan, *Desire of the Nations*, 21–22; O'Donovan, "Scripture and Christian Ethics," 124–25; O'Donovan, *Church in Crisis*, 76–77; O'Donovan, *Self, World, and Time*, 80–81. On the discussion whether O'Donovan's architectonic hermeneutic is sufficiently canonical, see McConville, "Law and Monarchy," 73–74; Moberly, "Use of Scripture," 63; Bartholomew, "Time for War," 91.

98. O'Donovan, *Entering into Rest*, 182.

99. O'Donovan, *Entering into Rest*, 182.

100. O'Donovan, *Entering into Rest*, 179–83.

PARTICIPATION AND SCRIPTURE   167

O'Donovan thus distinguishes narrative, interpretation, and hermeneutics on the one hand and moral deliberation about the decisions we have to make concerning our acts in time on the other. Scripture or the drama of Scripture should not abolish moral thinking.

Moral understanding in the light of the narrative of Scripture implies the dual task of discerning the text and discerning our moral situation. First, we ask the following: What does Scripture mean? To answer this question we turn to the text before us. We read the text on its own terms, trying to understand it in its historical context. As far as O'Donovan is concerned, good interpretation cannot be a deconstructive reading that "struggles against the text."[101] Next, we move from discernment of the text to discernment out of the text. The second question is difficult and existential: "What does the situation we are facing mean?"[102] To answer this question is a matter of conscience (understood as an informed conscience, shaped by a Christian moral understanding). Now the text is behind us and sheds light upon our situation. Consequently, it would be backward to interpret Scripture in light of our situation. We need the categories, analogies, and questions of the texts, first, so that we can accurately discern our situation in their light. Under the guidance of the Holy Spirit, we now come to a judgment of ourselves in the given situation. Scripture's authority helps us in our search for freedom, authorizing us to judge and live as disciples of Christ. Although Scripture, having informed us about truth and falsehood, facilitates that judgment, it is still our judgment.[103]

What we do when we "think from Scripture" is phrased by O'Donovan in a beautiful but dense passage in *Self, World, and Time*:

> A biblical story, command, or counsel presents us with a train of moral thought, a discursive argument that runs, though sometimes we need exegetical insight to make it explicit, from some A to some B, led by its practical question, grounding itself on some principles of action, observing some contextual constraints and reaching some resolution. That whole course of thinking, from A to B, is laid before our attention as we seek to fashion a course of thinking of our own, from some X to some Y, led by our own practical question, observing our own contextual restraints

---

101. O'Donovan, *Finding and Seeking*, 136. Further: O'Donovan, "Scripture and Christian Ethics," 124–27; O'Donovan, "Moral Authority of Scripture," 168–71; O'Donovan, *Church in Crisis*, 58–59, 71–72.

102. O'Donovan, "Scripture and Christian Ethics," 125; O'Donovan, "Moral Authority of Scripture," 168; O'Donovan, *Church in Crisis*, 59.

103. O'Donovan, "Scripture and Christian Ethics," 124–27; O'Donovan, "Moral Authority of Scripture," 168–71; O'Donovan, *Church in Crisis*, 59, 66–67, 71–72.

and finally reaching our resolution of the matter that is in our view.[104]

Or, in a formula: "[A → B] → [X → Y]." This enables O'Donovan to clarify how on the one hand our moral thinking has to obey Scripture: we have "to achieve a correspondence of the *whole train of thought* of the text from A to B and the *whole* train of our thought from X to Y."[105] On the other hand, he warns against moral thinking that does not respect the complexities of both the original and our situation. This happens in a literalism that ignores our situation and takes the form of [A → B → Y]. Or in a principle-thinking that just takes biblical principles from a text and ignores what the principles imply in the original situation, taking the form of [A → X → Y].[106] Moral thinking has to be both scriptural as well as thoughtful; it has to respect both the obedience to Scripture as well as the freedom of moral reflection and deliberation.

Language has a mediating role in meaningful experience, thinking, and communication. As we saw in the preceding chapter, experience is mediated through signs, which means that someone experiences something as something. Following Lacoste, O'Donovan writes, "The distinctive thing that members of the human species do is to *correct* their language."[107] And critical reflection on our description of reality is necessary, O'Donovan emphasizes. When someone communicates meaning to another, this person "offers the reference to reality."[108] As reality exists independently of us, "our 'meaning' is not something that we bring into being."[109] Our words matter and how we phrase experience and meaning is a question to be addressed in moral thinking. Although our attention to the world is "both affective and evaluative, 'existential,'" O'Donovan has a special interest in moral description.[110] Our activity of describing reality meaningfully is part of something greater. He adds, "Our meanings, then, are nested within the meaning originally communicated to us, a meaning which our new meanings echo and respond to, a meaning that originates with the Creator and Redeemer of a meaningful world."[111] Meaning and truth are complex, as we use words to form sentences, and sentences to tell narratives and to compose arguments.

---

104. O'Donovan, *Self, World, and Time*, 79.
105. O'Donovan, *Self, World, and Time*, 79.
106. O'Donovan, *Self, World, and Time*, 79–80.
107. O'Donovan, *Entering into Rest*, 163.
108. O'Donovan, *Entering into Rest*, 165.
109. O'Donovan, *Entering into Rest*, 164.
110. O'Donovan, *Common Objects of Love*, 13.
111. O'Donovan, *Finding and Seeking*, 170.

These texts have a certain architecture.[112] But despite these complexities, the words and statements we use to describe the world do matter.

Thinking "out of the Scripture" implies that concepts that mediate our experience need to be evaluated in the light of Scripture.[113] For good descriptions, we need true words, and for good theories, we need true concepts. True concepts give access to the moral order so that we can identify moral questions and develop a robust moral theory. To think morally, we need words that make "attention to the world intelligible, a word that will maintain the coherence and intelligence of the world."[114] Misconceptions will mislead us, bringing us to wrong views and actions. O'Donovan warns that in our time we combine many ideas and concepts although they are inconsistent with each other; moreover, "the world-shaping, cultural sins have to do with bad descriptions."[115] Our conceptions are based on experience and observations of particulars. Because human knowledge is both incomplete and provisional, concepts need to be open to further clarification, and criticism of community and tradition. Observations can be exegetical, made when we read the stories of the Bible. This brings us to another function of (theological) concepts: they mediate between a reading of the narrative and theoretical thinking. The narrative provides concepts with meaning and content, and the concepts found in the story provide theoretical thinking with shape.[116]

Reading the story of God's acts will allow us to find true concepts. Good concepts are authorized in the history of God's dealings with the world because God's handling of a specific moral area discloses his purposes with it and its true nature. We consequently receive our words from God's Word, since we learn them from his story. Yet his acts also judge creation by shedding light upon our world and our conceptions. In view of the luminous proclamation of God's acts in Christ, we may judge the fragments of moral knowledge and the moral concepts we find in our world. This human moral knowledge can be appreciated, reframed, criticized, or rejected as distorted knowledge. Theological moral knowledge must always retain priority over natural moral knowledge. In conclusion, having a true concept of

---

112. On these complexities, see, e.g., O'Donovan, *Entering into Rest*, 185–87.
113. O'Donovan, "Response to Respondents," 96.
114. O'Donovan, *Self, World, and Time*, 12.
115. O'Donovan, *Desire of the Nations*, 14.
116. O'Donovan, *Resurrection and Moral Order*, 79–81; O'Donovan, *Desire of the Nations*, 13–15; O'Donovan, "Christian Moral Reasoning," 122–24; O'Donovan, "Response to Respondents," 92–93, 95–96; O'Donovan, "Deliberation, History and Reading," 128–30; O'Donovan, "Scripture and Christian Ethics," 122, 127; O'Donovan, *Self, World, and Time*, x–xi, 10–12, 32; O'Donovan, *Entering into Rest*, 171–74.

something does justice to God's dealing with it, is authorized by Scripture, and discloses the character and significance of its reality.[117]

The process of grasping a concept is difficult to analyze rationally. According to O'Donovan himself, words in Scripture are like flags on a map signaling the presence of concepts. Their identification is part of the exegetical task. Concepts—as well as heuristic instruments like the four-moment analysis of the history of Christ—are not discovered in exegesis, but rather the concepts justify themselves in exegesis and facilitate the reading of the text. However, the "recognition of a kind in a particular" is "one of the most mysterious acts there is: it seems that it either happens or does not happen."[118] The invention of concepts to facilitate the understanding of a story is a mysterious gift.[119]

The gift of good concepts is closely related to the difficult, and equally mysterious moral question: What does the situation we are facing mean? To gain sensitivity and wisdom in dealing with this question, we need life forms, such as the community of the church, reading the Scriptures, praying, worshiping, and celebrating the sacraments, to influence the moral formation of our character and to shape our moral thinking. Our Christian life is not formless but must refer to God's work and recapitulate the Christ-event. Here we return to the importance of our participation in Christ for our moral knowledge. Our lives must be formed by the Christ-event and the work of God. In this way, we mirror God's action in our increasing Christ-likeness. Liturgy as well as ethics concerns actions that are structured and shaped by language. The language of liturgy forms our persons and our characters. In the liturgy, moral categories are articulated, but these categories are also integrated into a moral vision, which itself stands in the light of an interpretation of the world as God's world. Furthermore, according to O'Donovan, prayer is important as we saw. The fact that the Lord's prayer is the heart of the Sermon on the Mount (Matt 5–7) illustrates a deep spiritual truth. The heart of moral teaching is learning to pray and learning "to act

---

117. O'Donovan, *Resurrection and Moral Order*, 89–90; O'Donovan, "Christian Moral Reasoning," 123–24; O'Donovan, "Response to Respondents," 95; O'Donovan, *Ways of Judgment*, x, 16–17; O'Donovan, *Church in Crisis*, 72; O'Donovan, "Moral Authority of Scripture," 170–71; O'Donovan, *Self, World, and Time*, 7, 12.

118. O'Donovan, *Ways of Judgment*, 18.

119. The complexity of the invention of concepts is shown where O'Donovan realized that his own triad of concepts related to authority in *The Desire of the Nations* can be traced back to Ramsey's analysis of authority; see O'Donovan, *Desire of the Nations*, 142. Further O'Donovan, *On the Thirty-Nine Articles*, 54; O'Donovan, *Desire of the Nations*, 15–16; O'Donovan, "Response to Respondents," 93–95, 97–98; De Bruijne, *Levend in Leviatan*, 153–54.

and to live our lives before and for God."[120] Together the Scriptures, church, liturgy, and prayer enlarge our conformity to God's acts and purposes, which in turn give access to the world.[121]

David Kelsey has analyzed how theologians use Scripture. He has shown that theologians differ regarding what aspect they take as authoritative, that their uses of Scripture depend on their construction of "Scripture" and their characterization of how God is present in our lives. He distinguishes several options: the content of Scripture can be authoritative as (i) revealed doctrine, or as (ii) revealed concepts. In narrative approaches, we can see (iii) the history of salvation as revelatory or (iv) the narrative being read as something used by God to transform us. Furthermore, we can focus more on language and focus on (v) images that symbolize a mystery, (vi) symbols that contain answers to existential questions, or (vii) myths seen as performative statements with performative power.[122] In O'Donovan's work, we find a combination of several of these options, although the functions of Scripture in his theology do not fit neatly in Kelsey's uses. According to O'Donovan, the authority of Scripture has to be seen in the light of the authority of Christ and the active presence of the Spirit. It is not primarily language, but the triune God who transforms us, using Scripture. Scripture is used to transform us, to make us participate in Christ, and to renew our moral thinking. Important is the narrative of Christ in which we participate and that transforms us. Furthermore, the narrative of Scripture helps us to find true concepts. In the light of the moral thinking of Scripture, its narratives, and its concepts, we discern our world and learn to think morally ourselves, sharing in the mind of Christ. So, Scripture is used to enable us to think morally ourselves.

5.6 EVALUATIVE REFLECTIONS

In this book, I am searching for a systematic theological approach to hermeneutics and Scripture that is an alternative to an epistemological approach to these themes with an interest in (absolute) certainty. In this search, the problems of secularization and the noetic consequences of sin are spotted and taken seriously. Dalferth's hermeneutical theology or theological

---

120. O'Donovan, "Prayer and Morality," 33; O'Donovan, *Self, World, and Time*, 38–39, 64.

121. O'Donovan and Vasey, *Liturgy and Ethics*, esp. 4–6, 8, 14; O'Donovan, *Desire of the Nations*, 174–75; O'Donovan, "Prayer and Morality"; O'Donovan, *Church in Crisis*, 59; O'Donovan, *Entering into Rest*, 197–98.

122. Kelsey, *Proving Doctrine*.

hermeneutics provides a good starting point: Trinitarian (God gives us new understanding in Christ through the Spirit), soteriological (new understanding is part of salvation), and radical (God offers us a radical new perspective, requiring a reversal from old to new). In God's self-identification, we receive a new orientation *coram deo*. However, his approach has some problems or needs further elaboration, as we saw. He risks a dualism of eschatological newness and worldly immanentism; he rejects the Protestant doctrine of Scripture possessing attributes like unity, perfection, sufficiency, and clarity but evokes questions about criteria. Participation in Christ and the way the new perspective in Christ is embodied in the Christian and ecclesial life deserves more development.

In this chapter, I turned to Oliver O'Donovan. In his work, the gospel is the starting point. This leads to a twofold approach, of (a) resurrection and moral order, and (b) Pentecost and moral agency. Both Easter and Pentecost, Christ and Spirit, receive attention in O'Donovan's work. Just as Dalferth's theology, O'Donovan's theology also is Trinitarian, soteriological, and valuable for developing theological hermeneutics. Christ is our representative and the Spirit makes us participate in Christ so that we receive, e.g., the mind of Christ. O'Donovan relates this transformation of the moral subject to the formation of Christlikeness as Dietrich Bonhoeffer develops this in his *Ethik* (ethics as formation).[123] More than Dalferth, O'Donovan has developed a doctrine of creation and relates his doctrine of creation to his soteriology. Furthermore, O'Donovan portrays the new life as it is embodied in a Christian believer, the Christian community, and Christian moral thinking. At the same time, he rejects perfectionism and acknowledges the eschatological tension of the present time. The risen Christ and the perfect newness of life are still hidden, so that the renewal of our life, our mind, and our acts will remain incomplete. Thus, O'Donovan helps to move beyond the tension between eschatological newness and worldly immanentism. Given this positive evaluation, more can be said.

5.6.1 Scripture, Modernity, and the Renewal of the Mind

O'Donovan especially shows how Scripture has a role in the renewal of the mind. Furthermore, he demonstrates how the Scriptures, having received coherence in Christ, function in practice in this process of renewal. Although he does not reflect on Scripture and its role as a criterion, he shows how Scripture plays its role as canon. This evokes the question about the

---

123. Jacob Phillips offers an interesting overview of Bonhoeffer's thoughts on human subjectivity "in Christ," see Phillips, *Human Subjectivity "in Christ."*

nature of Scripture. What kind of book is Scripture that it can have this canonical role? In the next chapter, dealing with Herman Bavinck, I will delve more into that question. Still, O'Donovan clarifies well what Scripture does in Christian practices.

Whereas in postmodernism the end of "grand narratives" was proclaimed, O'Donovan is among those theologians who rehabilitate the grand narrative of Scripture. Three other scholars involved in this enterprise are N. T. Wright, who has done this in the field of New Testament studies, e.g., in his book *Paul and the Faithfulness of God*; Vanhoozer who does something comparable in systematic theology with his concept of "theodrama"; and Charles Taylor who shows how also in the field of philosophy the narratives we tell each other about ourselves and our culture remain crucial.[124] To O'Donovan, the grand narrative of Scripture is important, and the conceptual framework he develops is closely related to this narrative. Again and again, he returns to the story of God, of creation and Adam, of Israel, of Jesus Christ and his life, death, resurrection, and ascension, of the Holy Spirit, Pentecost, and the church. The Christian life is a participation in the story of Jesus Christ. Moreover, this grand narrative is the first source of his own thinking, his own concepts, and his moral views. Living with the story of Scripture, he develops a train of thought whose coherence is dependent on the coherence he finds in the biblical narratives. Furthermore, this story enables him to analyze critically the stories other people tell in our society.

Conceptual analysis is not new in the field of systematic theology and (Christian) ethics. Important in O'Donovan's contribution, however, is that he relates the quest for "true" concepts to the story of the Scriptures. Much of his work is devoted to concepts, in order to provide practical reason with good descriptions of reality. Characteristic of O'Donovan is the emphasis on the Scriptures as the place to find good concepts, necessary for good thinking. Here, in his dealing with the stories and concepts of the Christian faith in confrontation with stories and concepts of our modern secular world, in the way he relates "participation in Christ" to epistemology and the Scriptures, lies a great strength of O'Donovan's contribution to our understanding of the mind of Christ.

Important is, further, his critical analysis of modernity and its effect on moral thinking: the inability of modernity to understand moral deliberation. Just as modern epistemology had been searching for epistemic certainty, modern ethics had its quest for moral stability. In early modernity, God as *absolute will* was placed over against an unsituated self, detached from

---

124. Wright, *Paul and the Faithfulness of God*; Vanhoozer, *Drama of Doctrine*; Taylor, *Secular Age*.

God's love and grace. Later in the development of modernity, the divine absolute will was secularized. The problem remained: the moral imperative was absolute, and the mediation and explanation of a moral imperative by rational thinking became difficult. Not only does Karl Barth's ethics suffer from this problem, but a Biblicist version does as well when the biblical precepts are considered to completely describe what we have to do and our moral deliberation is seen as a threat to the obedience to the divine command. According to O'Donovan, our obedience has to be thoughtful and our moral thinking is essential to our human freedom. This human freedom is restored in Christ and the Spirit. The self is not unsituated or detached; instead, it receives the love and grace of God and is renewed by it, learning to be responsible and to think morally in freedom. The problem that O'Donovan signals along with his solution has an analogy in the orthodox modern foundationalist attitude toward hermeneutics. Just as moral deliberation, hermeneutics is seen as a threat to our obedience. As a result, it becomes difficult to do justice to what the self has to do when it listens to the word of God, toward the renewal of the mind of Christ.

O'Donovan emphasizes that moral thinking comprises both reflection and deliberation. Here, he emphasizes the borders of hermeneutics. In moral deliberation, we do more than interpretation. The renewal of our understanding is important, but to live a new life is more important. Hermeneutics is not able to make moral decisions, moral deliberation is. This is important for discussion about Scripture and the ordination of women, or about homosexuality. Often, the expectation is for hermeneutics to make moral decisions. According to O'Donovan, this is a wrong expectation. Hermeneutics only helps to interpret and to understand, not to decide or to act.

5.6.2 Secularization, Plurality, and Formation

O'Donovan's theology is an important contribution to preventing a Christian perspective from collapsing under the pressure of late modern secular pluralism. At the same time, his position evokes questions: does his approach do sufficient justice to our pluralistic situation? Is a (rational) theology what we need for the formation of the mind of Christ?

O'Donovan is well aware of the situation of pluralism, but he focuses on the development of his Christian perspective. For this focus on a particular perspective, O'Donovan has been criticized repeatedly and several alternative proposals have been made. Schweiker proposes a more dialogical model, intentionally bringing in the voices of other viewpoints; Colwell and McIlroy favor a pneumatological epistemology, claiming that the Holy Spirit is at work in other perspectives outside the church; similarly, Baker argues for a christological epistemology, suggesting that all true moral knowledge is the result of participation in Christ.[125]

In my view, however, the strength of O'Donovan's constructive project is that he accepts the limitations of a human participant's perspective and does not opt for a God's-eye or an outsider's approach. Hence, he does not make any theological claim about the overall value of other perspectives and leaves open how God is working in a non-believer. To be sure, he is no relativist but takes seriously the nature of true convictions. The justified belief that in Christ God is truly restoring his creation as an ordered world has a universal impact. Vanhoozer distinguishes a "hermeneutics of conviction," declaring "Here I stand" from a "hermeneutics of humility," asking "How does it look from where you stand?"[126] O'Donovan's work is indeed more in line with a hermeneutic of conviction, which is even critical of other perspectives. Using a vast knowledge of history, O'Donovan deconstructs concepts and narratives that hinder a Christian life. In the process, he builds a conceptual framework that counters the pressures of modern secularity and advances a vital Christian life form. From his standpoint, however, conversation with other perspectives is very well possible, as we share the same reality of God's world.

His awareness that we share the reality of God's world, and the importance of discernment, can be seen first in his twofold understanding of moral thinking as reflection and deliberation. Thinking from Scripture, we have to discern our world in the light of Scripture. The path of moral thinking goes from the self (in faith) to the world (in love) to our acts in time (in hope). Second is the development from "resurrection and moral order" to "Pentecost and moral agency," which is also a development toward a more "phenomenological" approach (influenced by Jean-Yves Lacoste). It is important to note that this approach differs from the phenomenology criticized by Dalferth. In Dalferth's concept, phenomenology is characteristically blind to God and his acts. What O'Donovan does in his analysis of moral waking, perspective, agency, and thinking is thoroughly theological. If his approach is phenomenological, then it is a theological phenomenology

---

125. Schweiker, "Freedom and Authority," 122–26; Colwell, *Living the Christian Story*, 243; McIlroy, *Trinitarian Theology of Law*, 210–14; Baker, "Transformation of Persons," 143–50. According to McIlroy, O'Donovan views the work of the Spirit especially as subjective. However, O'Donovan's treatment of the filioque shows that he does not limit the work of the Spirit to Pentecost and the subjectivity of Christian believers, see O'Donovan, *On the Thirty-Nine Articles*, 44–48.

126. Vanhoozer, *First Theology*, 229.

that perceives phenomena *coram deo*. The result is a description, a discernment of reality (which is universally accessible as reality) from a particular perspective (which we all necessarily have as humans). This approach to reality is open to dialogue with other perspectives and open to what God is doing out there. According to Sarah Coakley, a contemplative theology needs nonreductive sociology to observe what God is doing "in the field" and how the water of the sea of faith is present as it "seeped back in across marshes, via backwaters and underground channels."[127] O'Donovan's theology can be used as an analogous particular perspective on how God is actively present in his world. The development of O'Donovan, from "Easter and moral order" to "Pentecost and moral agency" reminds a theological hermeneutics of the necessity to do two things: listen carefully to the gospel of Jesus Christ, and develop attentive discernment to what God is doing and saying in his creation, no matter how messy this might be.

To conclude, O'Donovan does two important things. First, he develops a coherent conceptual framework closely connected to the narrative of Scripture. This conceptual framework is like a backbone that gives strength to a Christian perspective. Second, he gives a careful and wise presentation of the genesis of moral agency, our moral perspective, and the path of moral thinking. This is important when we want to live as Christian believers in a pluralist society, feeling the pressure of secularization and post-Christendom.

For theological hermeneutics, this implies the invitation to investigate further the formation of the mind of Christ and the path of reading, interpretation, and transformation in a secular and pluralist world. For such a formation, be it moral, spiritual, or hermeneutical, practices are important as well. To prevent the collapse of a Christian moral or hermeneutical perspective, participation in Christian practices is indispensable. An emphasis on practices can be found in the narrative thinkers that were mentioned earlier. For Wright, narrative is just one aspect of his worldview model, together with practices, symbols, and central questions concerning life issues.[128] Vanhoozer deliberately opts for "drama" instead of narrative, to include the performance of the narrative in the life of Christians with all its aspects.[129] Taylor emphasizes that in the choice for or against, e.g., the Christian faith, moral judgments about the plausibility of life forms play a role together with anger about negative experiences with Christians, and narratives that are present in the background of our lives as subconscious

---

127. Coakley, *God, Sexuality, and the Self*, 70, 85.
128. Wright, *Paul and the Faithfulness of God*, 63–68.
129. Vanhoozer, *Drama of Doctrine*, 1–33.

"unthoughts."[130] O'Donovan agrees that (liturgical) practices and the life form of the church are important. Frequently, O'Donovan mentions Christian practices: reading of the Scriptures, prayer, sacraments, and the liturgy of the church in general. From his work, it is clear that these practices are important to the Christian life and our participation in Christ. Investigating further the formation of the mind of Christ to enable a new understanding of God, self, world, and the other, our practices and our acts will need our attention as well.

But first another question needs to be answered: what kind of book is Scripture that as a canonical book, it can have the important role that O'Donovan ascribes to Scripture? To answer this question, I turn in the next chapter to Herman Bavinck.

---

130. Burger, "Zelfverstaan en wereldverstaan," 29–33.

6.

Sola Scriptura and Solus Christus
The Decisiveness of Jesus Christ as the Word of God for Understanding Scripture

6.1 INTRODUCTION

In West-European theology from the second half of the Middle Ages onward, the doctrine of Scripture has been developed out of an interest in epistemology and certainty. In this chapter, I will search for an alternative doctrine of Scripture, with a clear interest in the soteriological use of Scripture by the triune God, as well as in the relationship between Jesus Christ and Scripture. Such a doctrine of Scripture has to explain the nature of the book that we want to understand, and what God does in Scripture. In our reading of Scripture, God meets us and uses Scripture to renew our understanding and transform us into the likeness of Christ. Hermeneutics and the doctrine of Scripture do not exclude but need each other.[1] While attempting to keep these together, I will keep in mind Dalferth's critical questions about the Protestant doctrine of Scripture. Dalferth warns of a view of Scripture that is misled by the invention of book printing and has made the Bible, as a printed book, too important. Furthermore, the inconsistencies he signals in the work of Gerhard Ebeling, who works with a mixture of a non-intentionalist model of a Word-event and a personal intentionalist model of the Word of a personal God, urge us to strive for consistency. At the same time, Dalferth's approach has problems as well. It has to be clarified how God was active in Israel's history and how we can prevent what John Webster has

---

1. Cf. Watson, "Hermeneutics and the Doctrine of Scripture."

called a "curious textual equivalent of adoptionism."[2] Furthermore, in Dalferth's work, Scripture loses its criteriological role. Even though O'Donovan does not reflect explicitly on this criteriological role, O'Donovan provides a criteriological role to Scripture as canon. But it needs to be clarified in which way Scripture serves as canon with this criteriological function in theology. Moreover, the question of what makes Scripture, with its human words, so special that God can use Scripture for the soteriological purpose of participation in Christ needs to be answered.

In this chapter, Herman Bavinck (1854–1921) with his doctrines of revelation and Scripture is my primary dialogue partner. To connect my reflections on Jesus Christ, hermeneutics, and Scripture explicitly with my own tradition, Bavinck (as a predecessor in Kampen) with his *Gereformeerde dogmatiek* is most appropriate. On the one hand, his approach is modern in the sense that he shows an interest in certainty. As James Eglinton shows in Bavinck's biography, Bavinck was an orthodox Reformed theologian who wanted to participate fully in modern society, embracing some elements of modernity while rejecting others.[3] He shared the modern interest in epistemology and certainty. Looking back and seeing the crisis of modernity, more than a century after Bavinck, a critical evaluation in necessary. On the other hand, he will prove to be a valuable dialogue partner to develop a soteriological approach to Scripture and to move "beyond Bavinck." According to Bavinck's Trinitarian and Christocentric doctrine of Scripture, the Reformed *sola scriptura* only can be understood as a consequence of the *solus Christus*.

Reflecting on Scripture as a dogmatic theme, answers to several problems have to be found. These problems have been raised in discussions about Scripture in the last century. The first problem concerns the relationship between Christology and the doctrine of Scripture. In Dutch Reformed theology, warnings have been issued for linking the doctrine of Scripture too closely with Christology, and several theologians have pleaded to understand Scripture in the light of pneumatology instead. In their criticisms, the analogy Bavinck saw between the incarnation of Christ and the inscripturation of the word of God plays an important role. Jan Veenhof, who analyzes Bavinck's use of the analogy, proposes a pneumatological understanding of revelation in his inaugural address. Based on this proposal,

---

2. Webster, *Holy Scripture*, 24.

3. Eglinton, *Bavinck*. Eglinton rejects the idea of "two Bavincks." It is good to see that his students again ask whether the result of Bavinck's eclecticism and his use of a variety of sources did in fact result in a coherent theology, and whether Bavinck was a modern theologian. See, e.g., Brock and Sutanto, "Herman Bavinck's Reformed eclecticism"; Sutanto, *God and Knowledge*, 178; Pass, *Heart of Dogmatics*, 112–28.

he argues that revelation continues in the present.⁴ Further, the Reformed theologian A. van de Beek states explicitly that the doctrine of Scripture should not be localized in Christology but in pneumatology (although the canon does have an important function in keeping the church close to Christ). Theologians like Bavinck and Warfield who by their concept of the organic inspiration join Scripture and Christology, "thus move away from the orthodox tradition which places the Scripture into pneumatology," Van de Beek writes.⁵ The parallel between incarnation and inscription seems illuminating, but he rejects the parallel because of the difference between Christology (the incarnation is about the eternal God who identifies himself with the human person of Jesus) and pneumatology (when the Spirit dwells in someone, there is only a communion of persons, no identification).⁶ Gijsbert van den Brink and Kees van der Kooi defend a similar position.⁷ The analogy of incarnation and inscripturation will receive due attention in what follows.

In a lecture, Ad van der Dussen adds that from a pneumatological perspective, it is easier to do justice to the human character of the Scriptures.⁸ Thus, the first problem is connected to the second, the relationship between the human words of prophets, apostles, and others in the Scriptures and the divine Word. As we saw, Dalferth distinguishes between the Bible (the written or printed text), Scripture (the practice of reading the canonical texts in the liturgy of the church to hear the Word of God), and Word of God (the revealing act of the triune God, disclosing his loving presence to someone); a distinction connected to the problem of "textual adoptionism." It is not my aim to solve this problem completely in this chapter, but something needs to be said about it. In any case, in linking Christology and Scripture, we have to do justice to the human character of the Scriptures and the Word of God. How this should be done is an open question in this chapter.

The third problem concerns the attributes of Scripture in the classic Protestant doctrine. According to Dalferth, attributes of the Word of God have been attributed wrongly to the Bible as a printed book. Similarly, the

---

4. Veenhof, *Parakleet*, 21–28. See further Veenhof, *Kracht die hemel en aarde verbindt*, 128–42; and on Bavinck's analogy Veenhof, *Revelatie en inspiratie*, 442–45. See further on the analogy Berkouwer, *Holy Scripture*, 195–212; Meijers, *Objectiviteit en existentialiteit*, 72–80; Pass, "Upholding Sola Scriptura Today," 527–30; Pass, *Heart of Dogmatics*, 132–44.

5. "Maar ze bewegen zich daarmee af van de orthodoxe traditie die de Schriftleer in de pneumatologie plaatst." Van de Beek, *Lichaam en Geest van Christus*, 328.

6. Van de Beek, *Lichaam en Geest van Christus*, 326–28.

7. Van der Kooi and Van den Brink, *Christian Dogmatics*, 533–71.

8. Van der Dussen, "Bijbel als het Woord."

Dutch literary scholar Lambert Wierenga criticizes the doctrine of the attributes of Scripture. Clarity, for example, in his view, is not an attribute of the text, but the effect of experienced clarity on hearers or readers. If we find unity in the Bible, it is the unity of its "close and dense intertextual network."[9] The authority of Scripture should be understood as the authority of God.[10] For theological hermeneutics, it is important to clarify what hearers and readers of Scripture can expect from Scripture. What unifies the books of prophets, apostles, and others to a canonical Scripture (which, in a sense, is a unity)? And if we have many books in Scripture and many readers with different interpretations of Scripture, what should we say about the clarity of Scripture? Here, an important question concerns the contribution of the relationship between the Scriptures and Christ as the incarnate Word of God to solving this problem.

Fourth, the authority of Scripture evokes other questions as well. To our contemporaries, late modern, postmodern, or post-Christian, the idea of an authoritative Scripture evokes particular resistance. "Who are you to tell me what to think or what to do, based only on a holy book?" According to Bavinck, starting with G. E. Lessing (1729–81), theologians taught that it is wrong to believe in authority. Bavinck writes, "A thing is not true because it is in the Bible, but it is in the Bible because it is true."[11] In the last century, both the German theologian Dietrich Bonhoeffer (1906–45) and the Dutch theologian Harry Kuitert (1924–2017) were sensitive to this (fourth) problem.

In his letters from prison, Dietrich Bonhoeffer writes about Karl Barth's "positivism of revelation."[12] In the end, the result of Barth's doctrine of revelation is a "Friss Vogel, oder stirb," "eat bird, or die," i.e., "like it or lump it." All parts of Christian doctrine "must be swallowed whole or not at all," without any differentiation.[13] The problems with Barth's theology, for Bonhoeffer, are that Barth does not differentiate sufficiently between faith and theology and that the focus of theology is too internal, interpreting revelation for the church, not living in the world. Such an internal focus leads to a focus on knowledge, doctrine, and dogmatics.[14]

---

9. "Z'n hechte en dichte intertekstuele netwerk." Wierenga, *Macht van de taal*, 117.

10. Wierenga, *Macht van de taal*, 93–135.

11. Bavinck, *Gereformeerde dogmatiek*, 1:430; Bavinck, *Reformed Dogmatics*, 1:461.

12. See his letters from April 30, 1944 (Bonhoeffer, *Letters and Papers from Prison*, 364); May 5, 1944 (p. 373); June 8, 1944 (p. 429). Cf. "Outline for a Book" (p. 500).

13. Bonhoeffer, *Letters and Papers from Prison*, 373.

14. Van 't Slot, *Negativism of Revelation?*, 220–26.

Harry Kuitert, more recently, begins his book *Wat heet Geloven?* on the propositions of the Christian faith with a sketch of what he sees as the central problem: "like it or lump it" ("slikken of stikken" in Dutch). The central question is whether we are obliged to believe some Christian or religious truths. This problem becomes urgent with the crisis of credibility that the Christian faith faces. According to Kuitert, in the end, many theologians seem to imply that to believe is to share the truth claims of propositions, even when they no longer believe that those propositions are revealed.[15]

Both Bonhoeffer and Kuitert struggle with the idea that to believe is to share doctrinal propositions. In the background stand the problems of Western theology that have been described in chapter 2, which color the question of authority in the modern period: what is the authoritative source for the knowledge of God for Christian doctrine or Christian practice? Is it revelation and Scripture, church and tradition, or reason and experience? The question of religious epistemology has become a question of conflicting authorities. Is it possible to move beyond these problems with a soteriological approach to Scripture and its authority?

The fifth and final problem concerns the hermeneutical significance of the church and tradition, which has been emphasized by many in recent decades. Learning from the positive reevaluation of tradition in Gadamer's hermeneutical philosophy, and reacting to (post)modern individualism and relativism in the Christian life, and also to the consequences of a historical-critical reading of Scripture in theology, postliberal theologians (and others in their footsteps) have been engaged in reconsidering the role of the interpretative community and its tradition.[16] The theme of Scripture and tradition has been a controversial one between Reformed theology and Roman Catholicism. According to Vroom, Bavinck does ascribe an important role to tradition.[17] In this chapter, I will explore how Bavinck understands the relation between Scripture and tradition, and use his position to develop my own approach to this topic.

In what follows, I will first analyze Bavinck's doctrine of revelation and Scripture (6.2). Then, I will sketch my own view of revelation and Scripture,

---

15. Kuitert, *Wat heet geloven?*, 20–56, especially 27.

16. To mention some examples of the literature on this theme: Adam et al., *Reading Scripture with the Church*; Braaten and Jenson, *Reclaiming the Bible for the Church*; Houtman, *Schrift wordt geschreven*; Jenson, *Canon and Creed*; Paddison, *Scripture*; Peckham, *Canonical Theology*; Sarisky, *Scriptural Interpretation*; Treier, *Introducing Theological Interpretation of Scripture*; Treier, "What Is Theological Interpretation?"; Vanhoozer, *Drama of Doctrine*; Yong, *Spirit-Word-Community*.

17. Vroom, "Gelezen schrift als principium theologiae," 134–39.

dealing with the described problem, and bringing together elements from chapters 4, 5, and 6 (6.3). The chapter closes with a short conclusion (6.4).

6.2 HERMAN BAVINCK

Dealing with Bavinck, I will first explain in 6.2.1 his Trinitarian understanding of the principles of dogmatics (and of all knowledge). In the next three subsections I will analyze Bavinck's view of the external principle, focusing on his doctrine of revelation (6.2.2), his view of the relationship between Christ and Scripture (6.2.3), and his treatment of the attributes of Scripture (6.2.4). In the final subsection, I will turn to the internal principle (6.2.5).

6.2.1. Trinity and Principles of Dogmatics

In his *Gereformeerde dogmatiek*, Bavinck develops his doctrine of Scripture in the section on the principles of dogmatics. This fits well within the Reformed tradition as we saw in chapter 2. The doctrines of revelation and Scripture have been developed from an epistemological interest, explaining the nature of theology as an academic discipline and of theological knowledge.[18] Bavinck writes about the principles in general (section 6), principles in the academic disciplines (section 7), and principles in religion (section 8). The closing of these three sections shows what in Bavinck's theological mindset is crucial: a Trinitarian framework. He ends each of these three sections with a Trinitarian conclusion.[19]

In section 6, Bavinck's exposition of the principles, in general, serves to show that dogmatics has its own principles. These principles are the foundation of dogmatics and legitimize the independent position of dogmatics from the position of faith.[20] For Bavinck, all theology depends on God and his self-knowledge. Thus, God himself is the *principium essendi* of all knowledge of God (its principle of being or its essential foundation), and God's self-revelation or self-communication is the *principium cognoscendi*

---

18. Cf. Van Keulen, *Bijbel en dogmatiek*, 70, 133, 153.

19. Bavinck, *Gereformeerde dogmatiek*, 1:186, 207, 254; Bavinck, *Reformed Dogmatics*, 1:213-14, 233, 279. On the principles, see Van den Belt, *Authority of Scripture*, 236-50; Bremmer, *Herman Bavinck als dogmaticus*, 155-81; Heideman, *Relation of Revelation and Reason*, 141-46; Huttinga, *Participation and Communicability*, 86-91, 102-5; Van Keulen, *Bijbel en dogmatiek*, 70-132; Oliphint, "Bavinck's Realism, the Logos Principle."

20. Bavinck, *Gereformeerde dogmatiek*, 1:180-82; Bavinck, *Reformed Dogmatics*, 1:208-10.

of our knowledge of God (the principle by which we know).[21] It is central to Bavinck's concept of God's revelation that revelation is self-revelation.[22] God is absolute and his infinite self-knowledge is non-communicable to a finite consciousness. However, God's self-revelation is accommodated to our human comprehension.[23] Revelation is Bavinck's answer to the question of the existence and knowledge of God, which became urgent in modernity.[24]

According to Bavinck, we have to differentiate, within the principle of knowledge, between a *principium cognoscendi externum* (the external principle of knowing) and a *principium cognoscendi internum* (the internal principle of knowing). The external principle concerns God's self-revelation or self-communication (insofar as this self-revelation is deposited in Scripture, Scripture has an instrumental function), and the internal principle concerns illumination, regeneration, faith, and the working of the Spirit of God.[25] The Spirit brings God's self-communication into our human consciousness, thus together with the Son guaranteeing correspondence between divine self-knowledge and human knowledge of God. God's self-revelation depends on God's triune being.[26] "It is the Father, who through the Son as *Logos*, imparts himself to his creatures in the Spirit."[27]

In section 8, Bavinck proves that what is true in theology, is true in religion as well. God knows himself in his own divine consciousness, and only God can disclose his self-knowledge by revelation and by bringing this self-knowledge into the human consciousness. Religion is the answer of the entire human being to God's revelation. Religion depends on God's existence and revelation, and revelation and religion are inseparable. Bavinck emphasizes that all these three principles presuppose that it is God himself who acts in knowledge, revelation, and illumination.[28] Theological knowl-

---

21. Bavinck, *Gereformeerde dogmatiek*, 1:183–85; Bavinck, *Reformed Dogmatics*, 1:211–13.

22. Bavinck, *Gereformeerde dogmatiek*, 1:313; Bavinck, *Reformed Dogmatics*, 1:341.

23. Bavinck, *Gereformeerde dogmatiek*, 1:185; Bavinck, *Reformed Dogmatics*, 1:213.

24. Bavinck, *Gereformeerde dogmatiek*, 1:257; Bavinck, *Reformed Dogmatics*, 1:285–86.

25. Bavinck, *Gereformeerde dogmatiek*, 1:184–85; Bavinck, *Reformed Dogmatics*, 1:212–13.

26. For the influence of Bavinck's Trinitarian doctrine of revelation on Karl Barth, see Vissers, "Karl Barth's Appreciative Use."

27. Bavinck, *Gereformeerde dogmatiek*, 1:186; Bavinck, *Reformed Dogmatics*, 1:214.

28. Bavinck, *Gereformeerde dogmatiek*, 1:212–17, 250–55, 321–22; Bavinck, *Reformed Dogmatics*, 1:241–45, 276–79, 284, 349. Bavinck's understanding of revelation and religion does not presuppose sin; against Van Keulen, *Bijbel en dogmatiek*, 160, 172; see Bavinck, *Gereformeerde dogmatiek*, 1:250–55; Bavinck, *Reformed Dogmatics*, 1:276–79.

edge and the absolute certainty of religion both rest on the notion of *"Deus dixit."*[29]

In section 7 of his dogmatics, Bavinck deals with scientific principles in general. After a discussion of rationalism, empiricism, and realism, Bavinck argues that not just in theology but in all sciences, the thoughts in God's mind are the source of all knowledge (*principium essendi*), and the thoughts of God are embodied in his creation (*principium cognoscendi externum*), whereas our intellect discovers these thoughts in our knowledge of the truth (*principium cognoscendi internum*). On the one hand, Bavinck differentiates between (i) God's thoughts and God's self-knowledge; (ii) creation as the embodiment of God's thoughts and as God's general revelation, which is the external reality to us; and (iii) our mental representations of the external world. On the other hand, Bavinck does not separate the three: it is the divine *Logos* who unites the three principles.[30] This combination of Christocentrism (*Logos*-doctrine) and Trinitarian (three principles) is typical for Bavinck.[31]

Recently, Bavinck's epistemology has generated a lot of discussion, concerning its relation to Thomas Aquinas's, German idealism, and Abraham Kuyper's, and concerning the differences between Bavinck's position and Reidian epistemology.[32] Leaving this discussion for what it is worth, it is still noteworthy that, according to Henk van den Belt, the differentiation of one *principium cognoscendi* into an external and an internal principle is a distinct innovation on Bavinck's part.[33] Van den Belt, understands this in the

---

29. Pass, *Heart of Dogmatics*, 96. In the English translation, this characteristic *"deus dixit,"* used by Bavinck in its original Latin form, is muted by the editor's preference to render it in English; see Bavinck, *Reformed Dogmatics*, 1:30, 46, 590. In Dutch, see Bavinck, *Gereformeerde dogmatiek*, 1:5, 22, 559.

30. Sutanto has shown that Bavinck uses the work of Eduard von Hartmann to differentiate epistemologically between external reality and mental representations, while ontologically claiming correspondence between the two. See Sutanto, *God and Knowledge*, 101–49. Heideman suggests in his interpretation of Bavinck to follow the Dutch philosopher A. E. Loen, "that concepts are not to be related immediately to being, but that being and concepts are both related to the Word (although not immediately)." See Heideman, *Relation of Revelation and Reason*, 144.

31. On Bavinck's christocentrism, see Pass, *Heart of Dogmatics*.

32. For an entrance to these discussions, see Oliphint, "Bavinck's Realism, the Logos Principle"; Brock and Sutanto, "Herman Bavinck's Reformed Eclecticism"; Sutanto, *God and Knowledge*.

33. Van den Belt, *Authority of Scripture*, 248. One can doubt whether this differentiation is really an innovation. According to Van den Belt, Kuyper only had one principle. Vroom, however, mentions a comparable differentiation in Kuyper, between the *principium theologiae materiale* (Scripture) and the *principium theologiae formale* (listening in faith). See Vroom, *Schrift alleen?*, 69–72; Vroom, "Gelezen schrift als principium

light of Bavinck's discussion with the ethical theology movement: Bavinck "fences his position off from subjectivism, but the *principium internum* enables Bavinck to give the religious subject a positive place and acknowledge an element of truth in Ethical Theology."[34] Bavinck himself refers to Herbert Spencer, Schopenhauer, Kant, and Ritschl in the first section of his chapter on the internal principle. Accordingly, Bavinck's innovation can be interpreted as an acknowledgment of an element of truth in the post-Kantian turn to the subject. At the same time, his Trinitarian position enables him "to address the subject-object dichotomy."[35]

Bavinck's doctrine of the principles shows that his theology is not only Christocentric, Trinitarian, and modern, but also holistic. One could say that Bavinck's organic way of thinking implies a holistic anthropology and soteriology. An objective, rationalist understanding which some Protestant scholastics and many Hegelians favor is insufficient, and so is a moralist or mysticist understanding of the followers of Kant or Schleiermacher. Revelation, religion, and salvation concern the human being as a whole—human knowledge, as well as, the human moral and spiritual life.[36] We will see that in his view of special revelation, Bavinck emphasizes that revelation communicates both knowledge and life.

However, again and again, Bavinck emphasizes the primacy of the objective. He chooses normative formulations that make this very clear.[37] Knowledge comes first and we receive this knowledge by hearing.[38] Religious human beings need the objective Word of God, and revelation and religion should not be conflated.[39] Religion needs true ideas, and religious ideas need the authority of God as their foundation.[40] This emphasis on the

---

theologiae," 120.

34. Van den Belt, *Authority of Scripture*, 249.

35. Pass, *Heart of Dogmatics*, 34–35.

36. Bavinck, *Gereformeerde dogmatiek*, 1:227–43, 252–53, 259, 312–13, 320; Bavinck, *Reformed Dogmatics*, 1:254–69, 278–79, 287, 341–42, 348. Further Pass, *Heart of Dogmatics*, 67, 86.

37. Bavinck, *Gereformeerde dogmatiek*, 1:210–11; Bavinck, *Reformed Dogmatics*, 1:239: wet, regelen, eischen, vorderen, willen, bepalen, plicht; Bavinck, *Gereformeerde dogmatiek*, 1:215–16; Bavinck, *Reformed Dogmatics*, 1:244: bepalen, willen; Bavinck, *Gereformeerde dogmatiek*, 1:250–51; Bavinck, *Reformed Dogmatics*, 1:276–77: willen, gezag, eischen; Bavinck, *Gereformeerde dogmatiek*, 1:253; Bavinck, *Reformed Dogmatics*, 1:279: willen.

38. Bavinck, *Gereformeerde dogmatiek*, 1:242; Bavinck, *Reformed Dogmatics*, 1:268.

39. Bavinck, *Gereformeerde dogmatiek*, 1:321–24; Bavinck, *Reformed Dogmatics*, 1:349–51.

40. Bavinck, *Gereformeerde dogmatiek*, 1:61, 241, 348; Bavinck, *Reformed Dogmatics*, 1:85, 268, 377.

objective makes it possible to give Scripture its relative independence from its subjective counterpart.

Furthermore, Bavinck proves to be Protestant as the emphasis falls entirely on the acts of God. In his self-revelation, the triune God has the primary role, Scripture and church only a secondary. Bavinck writes, "We must add to this only that if that self-revelation of God is deposited in Scripture or the church, that Scripture and that church can have only instrumental—hence, in a sense, incidental, provisional—significance. At best, therefore, Holy Scripture is the instrumental efficient cause of theology."[41] Because only God can reveal God, Bavinck writes, "The internal word (*verbum internum*) is the principal word (*verbum principale*), for it is this which introduces the knowledge of God into human beings."[42] Accordingly, the mediating role of Scripture is relativized, although Scripture is necessary for secondary reasons. It would be wrong to suggest that Bavinck objectifies Scripture or isolates Scripture from God's acts, which is the fear of Barthian theologians.[43] Moreover, Bavinck relativizes the mediating role of community or tradition. He leaves open the question of whether God's revelation comes to individual human beings or humanity in general, and does not deal with the polarity of the community and the individual.[44]

Finally, according to Bavinck, God's revelation (the revelation of God's archetypal knowledge) can convey "in human beings made in his image an ectypal knowledge that reflects this archetypal knowledge (*cognitio archetypa*) in his own divine mind."[45] These divine thoughts can be embodied and mediated by these embodiments. God displays his thoughts "to the human mind in the works of his hands. The world is an embodiment of the thoughts of God."[46] History "is above all the realization of the thoughts of God, the

---

41. Bavinck, *Reformed Dogmatics*, 1:213. "Alleen zij er de opmerking aan toegevoegd, dat, indien die zelfopenbaring Gods is neergelegd in de Schrift of in de kerk, die Schrift en die kerk alleen kunnen hebben een instrumentele, en dus in zekere zin toevallige, voorbijgaande betekenis. De H. Schrift is dus hoogstens causa efficiens instrumentalis van de theologie." Bavinck, *Gereformeerde dogmatiek*, 1:184.

42. Bavinck, *Reformed Dogmatics*, 1:213. "Het verbum internum is het verbum principale, want dit brengt de kennis Gods in de mens, en dat is het doel van alle theologie, van heel de zelfopenbaring Gods." Bavinck, *Gereformeerde dogmatiek*, 1:185.

43. Cf. Pass, *Heart of Dogmatics*, 140–42.

44. Bavinck, *Gereformeerde dogmatiek*, 1:184–85; Bavinck, *Reformed Dogmatics*, 1:212–13.

45. Bavinck, *Reformed Dogmatics*, 1:233. "Doch het is zijn welbehagen, om van deze cognitio archetypa in zijn goddelijk bewustzijn een ectypische kennis over te brengen in de mens, die naar zijn beeld is gemaakt." Bavinck, *Gereformeerde dogmatiek*, 1:206.

46. Bavinck, *Reformed Dogmatics*, 1:233. "Door ze in de werken van zijn handen uit te spreiden voor de geest van de mens. De wereld is een belichaming van gedachten

expression of a divine plan for his creatures; ... the bearer of the thoughts of God, the revelation of God's intent."⁴⁷ God's self-revelation includes the revelation of thoughts and as a result, we can develop true thoughts about God in our human consciousness. This possibility of the embodiment of God's revelation in creation (or in Scripture) marks a difference between Bavinck's concept of revelation and concepts of revelation with a Barthian flavor where a lasting embodiment of God's revelation is impossible—a difference that is important in light of the problems that we discovered in Dalferth's theology (chapter 4).⁴⁸

6.2.2. External Principle: the Doctrine of Revelation

Having given this general overview of the three principles, I will now analyze in more detail the external principle. Bavinck develops this conceptual framework of the external and internal principles as an answer to the epistemological question. However, in his explanation of the external and internal principles, epistemology and soteriology become inseparable. As all religions have three centers—God, humanity, and salvation—and as we need revelation for all these three centers, revelation and grace are closely related, according to Bavinck.⁴⁹ Moreover, revelation communicates both knowledge and life.⁵⁰

This is, of course, clearer in the special revelation, where revelation receives a soteriological character. Bavinck's understanding of special revelation and soteriology are almost identical: revelation is the gift of new life. God's special revelation is a dynamic and historical process with Christ as its center and the recreation of the entire world as its soteriological aim.⁵¹ Whereas in his conceptual framework, Bavinck carefully distinguished the

---

Gods." Bavinck, *Gereformeerde dogmatiek*, 1:206.

47. Bavinck, *Reformed Dogmatics*, 1:379. "Verwezenlijking van gedachten Gods, uitwerking van een raad Gods over zijne schepselen ... draagster der Godsgedachten; de apocalypse van Gods voornemen." Bavinck, *Gereformeerde dogmatiek*, 1:350–51.

48. Heideman, *Relation of Revelation and Reason*, 134–62; Pass, *Heart of Dogmatics*, 132–33, 140–42.

49. Bavinck, *Gereformeerde dogmatiek*, 1:258–59; Bavinck, *Reformed Dogmatics*, 1:286–87.

50. Bavinck, *Gereformeerde dogmatiek*, 1:262, 317–18; Bavinck, *Reformed Dogmatics*, 1:290, 343–45.

51. Bavinck, *Gereformeerde dogmatiek*, 1:209–10, 259; Bavinck, *Reformed Dogmatics*, 1:237–38, 287. Revelation is "one single historical and organic whole, a mighty world-controlling and world-renewing system of testimonies and acts of God"; see Bavinck, *Gereformeerde dogmatiek*, 1:311; Bavinck, *Reformed Dogmatics*, 1:340.

objective and the subjective, in his explanation of the history of salvation, the emphasis is more organic (which implies, holistic). The difference between the objective communication of knowledge and the subjective communication of life becomes less important. Here, Bavinck's formulations are less normative, and he chooses more relational and soteriological formulations.[52] Special revelation is inseparably connected to the subjective change of human beings, for it is sin that makes special revelation necessary.[53]

It is the same picture that Bavinck sketches when he deals with the means of special revelation, theophany, prophecy, and miracles, but also when he later explains his view of special revelation. Special revelation is the organic process of the history of salvation, in which God aims at re-creation and salvation from sin. The purpose of theophany is that God is present in his creation; the end of prophecy is that all believers receive the anointing of the Spirit and are God's prophets; the culmination of miracles is that God reveals his miraculous power in the unity of the kingdom of God and the kingdom of the world. Here, the communication of knowledge and the communication of life are one.[54]

Accordingly, Van Keulen signals two different lines in Bavinck: the line of the completed communication of knowledge and the more dynamic line of the communication of life. In the first, the emphasis is on the formal aspect of authority, and in the second the emphasis is on the material.[55] We could say that in the first line, Bavinck is more interested in epistemology and certainty, and in the second line, his interest is more focused on soteriology and transformation.

Bavinck understands the process of special revelation in the light of the Trinity: "But in the works of grace, God comes to us as Father in the

52. Some examples: Bavinck, *Gereformeerde dogmatiek*, 1:298; Bavinck, *Reformed Dogmatics*, 1:327: zoeken, scheppen, behouden, verkiezen, wetten geven, roepen en bekwamen, zenden, afzonderen, komen tot en zoeken van den mensch; Bavinck, *Gereformeerde dogmatiek*, 1:316; Bavinck, *Reformed Dogmatics*, 1:344: zoeken Gods van en komen Gods tot den mensch, zich aan den mensch gelijk maken, in onze natuur en in onzen toestand ingaan, schikken, leiden; Bavinck, *Gereformeerde dogmatiek*, 1:318; Bavinck, *Reformed Dogmatics*, 1:346: aan de macht der zonde ontworstelen en de heerlijkheid Gods weer te doen schitteren.

53. Bavinck, *Gereformeerde dogmatiek*, 1:209-10, 213, 259; Bavinck, *Reformed Dogmatics*, 1:237-38, 241-42, 287.

54. Bavinck, *Gereformeerde dogmatiek*, 1:300-301, 306-7, 310-11; Bavinck, *Reformed Dogmatics*, 1:329-30, 335-36, 339-40. Clearly, Bavinck is stimulated by the newer concept of revelation that he discusses critically; see Bavinck, *Gereformeerde dogmatiek*, 1:263; Bavinck, *Reformed Dogmatics*, 1:291-92.

55. Van Keulen, *Bijbel en dogmatiek*, 95, 116, 138, 155-56. Meijers worked with another tension, between objectivity and existentiality; see Meijers, *Objectiviteit en existentialiteit*.

entirely unique sense of the Son, and as Father, he consequently also reveals himself to us by that Son, more precisely by the Son who became incarnate in Christ and by the Spirit acquired by that Christ."[56]

Bavinck distinguishes two dispensations—christological and pneumatological. In the first, the economy of the Son, God's revelation is objective. In the history of salvation, God prepared for his own coming in the flesh. Then Christ comes, in whom God gives everything that we need, in whom God fully reveals himself. Everything leads to Christ who saves us from sin. The completeness of the revelation and work of God in Christ leads directly to the completeness of the Scriptures. Just as Christ has become head of the communion of the church, so God's revelation is completed in the Scriptures. No new constitutive elements can be added: both Christ's work and God's revelation are finished. Bavinck understands the completion of the canon as a consequence of Christ's completed work. But after Christ is formed as head of the church, now what is present in Christ has to be worked out in the entirety of creation, so that the revelation reaches its goal. Thus, after the economy of the Son, the church entered a new dispensation, the economy of the Spirit. The church is now formed as the body of Christ by the Holy Spirit. The work of the Spirit is to glorify Christ and to make us share in Christ. Just as the objective revelation embraces word and deed, the work of the Spirit recreates the entire human being. In the economy of the Spirit, the content of revelation has to be realized in the life and consciousness of humanity. The Spirit does not reveal new mysteries, but rather, applies the treasures of salvation. Prophecy and miracles are no longer necessary and cannot enrich God's revelation with new elements that add to the objective facts of the revelation in Christ. The ultimate goal, however, is the complete re-creation of the world into a kingdom of God. The completion of revelation is not the completion of God's work. God's aim is the new creation, in which God will live with his people.[57]

6.2.3 External Principle: Christ and Scripture

To better understand the external principle, I will now focus on the relationship between Christ and Scripture. Because Christ is the center of God's

---

56. Bavinck, *Reformed Dogmatics*, 1:342. "Maar in de werken der genade komt God tot ons als Vader in geheel eenigen zin van den Zoon, die daarom ook door dien Zoon, nader nog door den in Christus vleeschgeworden Zoon en door den door dien Christus verworven Geest zich aan ons openbaart," Bavinck, *Gereformeerde dogmatiek*, 1:314.

57. Bavinck, *Gereformeerde dogmatiek*, 1:316–21, 323–24, 354–57, 461–62, 471, 557–58; Bavinck, *Reformed Dogmatics*, 1:344–48, 350–51, 382–85, 490–91, 505–6, 587–88. Cf. Pass, *Heart of Dogmatics*, 50–51.

revelation, he is also "the central focus and main content of Holy Scripture," and "the midpoint of Scripture."[58] God's special revelation comes to us in Christ. Bavinck writes,

> All the revelations and words of God, in nature and history, in creation and re-creation, both in the Old and the New Testament, have their ground, unity, and center in him. He is the sun; the individual words of God are his rays. The word of God in nature, in Israel, in the NT, in Scripture, may never even for a moment be separated and abstracted from him. God's revelation exists only because he is the *Logos*.[59]

It seems that Bavinck wants to closely relate Christ as the incarnate word of God and God's revelation, without completely identifying the two.

Bavinck elaborates on this close connection in two ways. The first one we find in a consideration of God's coming in the incarnation of Christ. God's coming to humankind begins already at creation in the *Logos*, continues in the angel of the LORD and in the prophecy which has Christ as its content, and finds its conclusion and end in the person of Christ. In Christ's incarnation, in his person, lies the central fact and content of special revelation. Bavinck draws a string of revelatory facts: "Israel is the preparation, Christ the center, the church the consequence, and the *parousia* the crown—that is the cord that binds the facts of revelation together."[60] The incarnation is thus part of a history, and it is precisely in the incarnation that the Son enters into history and thus inserts himself into the organism of humanity. In that history, we see God coming to his people, with Christ as the content and center. Thus God becomes part of history.[61]

---

58. Bavinck, *Gereformeerde dogmatiek*, 1:87; Bavinck, *Reformed Dogmatics*, 1:110. According to Bavinck in this passage, Christ cannot be the starting point for theology. Bruce Pass understands Bavinck's christocentrism as a fruit of his organic thinking. Interestingly, he states that in Bavinck a development can be seen toward a theology that has Christ as its starting point. See Pass, *Heart of Dogmatics*, 23–56.

59. Bavinck, *Reformed Dogmatics*, 1:402. "Alle openbaringen van God, alle woorden van God, in natuur en geschiedenis, in schepping en herschepping, onder Oude en Nieuwe Testament hebben in Hem hun grond, hun eenheid en middelpunt. Hij is de zon, de bijzondere woorden van God zijn zijn stralen. Het woord van God in de natuur, onder Israël, in het Nieuwe Testament, in de Schrift mag geen ogenblik van Hem worden losgemaakt en afgedacht. Er is alleen openbaring Gods, omdat Hij de Logos is." Bavinck, *Gereformeerde dogmatiek*, 1:372.

60. Bavinck, *Reformed Dogmatics*, 1:376. "Israël de voorbereiding, Christus het centrum, de kerk de uitwerking, de parusie de kroon—dat is het snoer, dat de openbaringsfeiten met elkaar verbindt." Bavinck, *Gereformeerde dogmatiek*, 1:347.

61. Bavinck, *Gereformeerde dogmatiek*, 1:316, 319, 323, 351, 354; Bavinck, *Reformed Dogmatics*, 1:344, 346–47, 350, 379, 382–83.

It is important to note that for Bavinck the unity of Scripture is not an attribute of a text, as Wierenga suggests (see 6.1).[62] Bavinck does not give a separate discussion of the unity of Scripture, although he writes that Scripture is a unity.[63] Scripture is a unity because of the unity of God's acts in the history of his revelation. The ground of this unity is christological.[64]

Here then the second way in which Bavinck connects Christ and God's revelation with each other announces itself. After all, "the bearer of the ideal goods of humanity is language, and the *sarx* of language is the written word."[65] To enter into the consciousness of people, a new step must be taken after the incarnation: revelation must be written down. Only in this way can Christ come to dwell in his church. The way to people's hearts is through their heads and consciousness, and thus such a means as Scripture is necessary. Revelation, therefore, cannot exist and be soteriologically effective without Scripture as the special revelatory act of God. Bavinck writes, "Divine revelation is now an ineradicable constituent of this cosmos in which we live and, effecting renewal and restoration, continues its operation."[66] The soteriological path of special revelation needs to be mediated by the embodiment of revelation by Scripture.[67]

Revelation and Scripture grew up together. Explanations of Christ's place in Scripture constitute the second way in which Bavinck elaborates how Christ and revelation relate to each other. In this context, Bavinck addresses both the relationship of Jesus to the writings of the Old Testament and the writings of the New Testament. Bavinck emphasizes that the canon of the Old Testament had divine authority for both Jesus and his disciples. Bavinck shows how the New Testament treats the Old, and how it demonstrates that according to Jesus and his disciples, the dispensation of the Old Covenant

---

62. Wierenga, *Macht van de taal*, 73, 108–10.

63. Bavinck, *Gereformeerde dogmatiek*, 1:363, 372; Bavinck, *Reformed Dogmatics*, 1:395, 402.

64. Pass writes, "The soteriological purpose of Scripture constitutes the biblical organism and confers unity on its diverse parts." Bavinck's organic thinking, his Christocentric theology, and the soteriological purpose of God's special revelation give unity to Scripture. See Pass, "Upholding Sola Scriptura Today," 523.

65. Bavinck, *Reformed Dogmatics*, 1:380. "De drager van de ideale goederen der mensheid is de taal, en de sarx van de taal is het schrift." Bavinck, *Gereformeerde dogmatiek*, 1:352.

66. Bavinck, *Reformed Dogmatics*, 1:443. "Zij maakt thans een onuitroeibaar bestanddeel uit van deze kosmos waarin wij leven, en zet vernieuwend en herstellend daarin haar werking voort." Bavinck, *Gereformeerde dogmatiek*, 1:414.

67. Bavinck, *Gereformeerde dogmatiek*, 1:352, 354, 539; Bavinck, *Reformed Dogmatics*, 1:380–82, 570.

finds its fulfillment in Jesus and the New Covenant.[68] Jesus himself did not leave behind any writings, but he made sure, according to Bavinck, "that his true witness was passed on pure and unalloyed to humankind."[69] Given this task, he chose apostles to testify of him. Through them, the Spirit testifies so that the apostles are also able to testify of him reliably and authoritatively.[70] These expositions of Jesus's relationship to the Old and New Testament writings, incidentally, are found almost at the beginning of Bavinck's section on inspiration. His views on inspiration have a Christocentric core.[71]

Bavinck thus characterizes Christ (the incarnation of God's Word) as the culmination of both revelation and Scripture. Twice, the same movement is drawn, of God coming to ultimately bring his knowledge into human consciousness and even to dwell in people. The Son takes on the form of a servant; revelation must also take on the form of a servant. The inscripturation "results from God's incarnation in Christ, and is in a sense its continuation, the way by which Christ makes his home in the church, the preparation of the way to the full indwelling of God."[72]

This double servant form, of the weakness of Christ and the weakness of Scripture, brings Bavinck to the parallel between incarnation and inscription. Since this parallel has been criticized, it is important to see for what purposes Bavinck does and does not use this parallel.

> 1. The parallel has an epistemological significance. Bavinck is aware of the difference between divine and human knowing, as we observed in the doctrine of the *principia*. Important in the parallel between incarnation and inscripturation is that both are necessary to bring God's absolute and divine self-knowledge close to the level of human

---

68. In 1886, Bavinck's colleague Maarten Noordtzij (1840–1915) gave a rectorial address with the title *De leer van Jezus en de Apostelen over de H. Schrift des O. Testaments. Rede bij de overdracht van het rectoraat aan de Theologische School te Kampen, den 17 December 1885, Kampen*. Bavinck could have referred approvingly to this lecture, but he did not.

69. Bavinck, *Reformed Dogmatics*, 1:398. "Dat zijn waarachtig getuigenis onvervalst en zuiver aan de mensheid werd overgegeven." Bavinck, *Gereformeerde dogmatiek*, 1:367.

70. Ridderbos's *Heilsgeschiedenis en heilige schrift van het Nieuwe Testament* could be seen as an elaboration of these thoughts about the New Testament. See Ridderbos, *Heilsgeschiedenis en heilige schrift*.

71. Bavinck, *Gereformeerde dogmatiek*, 1:354, 363–69, 423; Bavinck, *Reformed Dogmatics*, 1:382–83, 394–400, 455.

72. Translation slightly modified. Cf. Bavinck, *Reformed Dogmatics*, 1:380–81. "Zij vloeit voort uit de menswording van God in Christus, zij is in zekere zin de voortzetting ervan, de weg, waarlangs Christus woning maakt in zijn gemeente; de praeparatio viae ad plenam inhabitationem Dei." Bavinck, *Gereformeerde dogmatiek*, 1:352.

consciousness. For Bavinck, the human character of Scripture is linked to the character of our human knowing. It is about the "communication of the divine thoughts," as he states the second time when he draws the parallel: "The Word (Λογος) has become flesh (σαρξ), and the word has become Scripture."[73] Both the incarnate Word of God and the written word of God embody and mediate the divine self-revelation to the human consciousness.[74]

2. Bavinck sees a parallel between the foolishness of Christ crucified and the foolishness of human Scripture. The same servant's stature, the same humility, the same weakness, "in order that the excellency of the power, also of the power of Scripture, may be God's and not ours."[75] Everything is from God and everything is grace, including our knowledge of God. But there is a spiritual battle to be fought: "Scripture has at all times encountered contradiction and opposition," and thus shares as a "handmaiden" in the "defamation" of Christ the Lord.[76]

3. Elaborating on the parallel, it is important that Bavinck uses pneumatology to explain how biblical authors could "serve as an organ of the divine."[77] For the character, individuality, and activity of the biblical writers to be maintained and sanctified, Bavinck connects their activities not with Christology but emphatically with pneumatology.[78] It seems to me, therefore, that Berkouwer is right to observe, "In my opinion, Bavinck rightly saw at this very point that the traditional analogy between incarnation and inscription was not the center of the discussion concerning Scripture."[79] It is precisely in his organic doc-

---

73. Bavinck, *Reformed Dogmatics*, 1:434. "Mededeling van de gedachten van God"; "De Λογος is σαρξ geworden, en het woord is Schrift geworden." Bavinck, *Gereformeerde dogmatiek*, 1:405.

74. Cf. Pass, *Heart of Dogmatics*, 132.

75. Bavinck, *Reformed Dogmatics*, 1:434–35. "Dit alles is geschied, opdat de uitnemendheid van de kracht, ook van de kracht van de Schrift, van God zij en niet uit ons." Bavinck, *Gereformeerde dogmatiek*, 1:405.

76. Bavinck, *Reformed Dogmatics*, 1:440. "Op zichzelf behoeft het dus niet de minste verwondering te baren, dat de Schrift te allen tijde weerspraak en bestrijding heeft ontmoet. Christus heeft een kruis gedragen, en een dienstknecht is niet meerder dan zijn heer. De Schrift is de dienstmaagd van Christus. Zij deelt in zijn smaad." Bavinck, *Gereformeerde dogmatiek*, 1:411.

77. Bavinck, *Reformed Dogmatics*, 1:442. "Om tot orgaan te dienen van het goddelijke." Bavinck, *Gereformeerde dogmatiek*, 1:414.

78. Bavinck, *Gereformeerde dogmatiek*, 1:405, 414; Bavinck, *Reformed Dogmatics*, 1:438–39, 443.

79. Berkouwer, *Holy Scripture*, 209. In the Dutch original, Berkouwer refers to Haitjema, who writes that in the inscriptuation we are facing the self-humilation of the

trine of inspiration that Bavinck shows that the doctrine of Scripture cannot do without pneumatology.[80]

4. Bavinck connects the analogy with remarks about the divine and human character of Scripture. Comparing the weakness and lowliness of Christ and Scripture, Bavinck writes, "But just as Christ's human nature, however weak and lowly, remained free from sin, so also Scripture is 'conceived without defect or stain'; totally human in all its parts but also divine in all its parts."[81]

The suggestion is that the analogy helps to understand that despite the activity of the human writers, Scripture still can be divine. Bavinck's *organic* understanding of inspiration implies that the human could become an *orgaan* (instrument) of the divine.[82] However, here the problem is that Bavinck overlooks the difference between the incarnation of the Son and the relation between his divine and human nature on the one hand, and the work of the Spirit in the human writers and the nature of Scripture on the other. The hypostatic union of the two natures in Christ does not clarify the character of the inspiring work of the Spirit in the human authors of Scripture. Furthermore, the analogy wrongly suggests that Scripture is in some sense free from sin and thus more or less inerrant, infallible, or perfect.

Remarkably, Bavinck does not write that Scripture is inerrant or infallible.[83] Dealing with the attributes of Scripture in section 14, he focuses on authority, necessity, clarity, and sufficiency (or perfection). Important for Bavinck was the historical reliability of Scripture. At the same time, Bavinck shows awareness of the problems raised by historical criticism. Moreover, he emphasizes that the purpose of Scripture is religious and ethical. All the facts Scripture teaches, relevant as they might be for all sciences, stand in a specific perspective: "All those facts in Scripture are not communicated in isolation and for their own

---

Holy Spirit; see Berkouwer, *Heilige Schrift II*, 126–27.

80. Thus, Bavinck's use of the parallel between incarnation and inscripturation in his doctrine of the organic inspiration does not justify the thesis of A. van de Beek that the doctrine of the organic inspiration connects the doctrine of Scripture with Christology. See Van de Beek, *Lichaam en Geest van Christus*, 328. Bavinck's organic doctrine of inspiration is both christological and pneumatological.

81. Bavinck, *Reformed Dogmatics*, 1:435. "Maar gelijk het menselijke in Christus, hoe zwak en nederig ook, toch van het zondige vrij bleef, zo ook is de Schrift sine labe concepta. Menselijk geheel en in al haar delen, maar ook evenzo θεια παντα." Bavinck, *Gereformeerde dogmatiek*, 1:406.

82. Bavinck, *Gereformeerde dogmatiek*, 1:414; Bavinck, *Reformed Dogmatics*, 1:442.

83. Pass, "Upholding Sola Scriptura Today," 519–21.

sake but with a theological aim, namely, that we should know God unto salvation."[84] Thus, Bavinck shows modesty in elaborating on the sinlessness of Scripture. He does not give a clear answer to the question of what it means that Scripture is "conceived without defect or stain," *sine labe concepta*.[85] Did he feel the problematic character of his claim?

5. The analogy has soteriological significance. Incarnation and inscripturation have the same purpose, the indwelling of Christ in the church, and the indwelling of God in his creatures so that creation again reveals God's glory. For Bavinck, God's acts of revelation and salvation, the incarnation of Jesus Christ, the inscripturation of God's word, the mystical union with Christ, and the final revelation of God's glory in the re-creation are closely connected. Bavinck writes, "We have no fellowship with Christ except through fellowship in the word of the apostles."[86] Therefore, Christ and the New Testament or his apostles must not be played off against each other. If we approach the witness of the apostles with distrust, we lose Christ. For the church after the apostles, Scripture is the only way to know God's revelation in Christ. This thought also returns in the discussion with Rome, almost as a refrain: "There is no knowledge of Christ apart from Scripture, no fellowship with him except by fellowship in the word of the apostles."[87] Here, it becomes clear again how for Bavinck the doctrine of Scripture is set in a Trinitarian framework, but also how Scripture is the channel of his Trinitarian soteriology. The Scriptures were written by the Spirit so that the Spirit could use them in building up the body of Christ. God comes to his people in the Bible. And the Bible binds us to the living Lord in the heavens. Christ, the *unio mystica* of the Holy Spirit, and God's witness in his Word are inseparable to our consciousness. Church and sacraments play a secondary role. Through Christ, we

---

84. Bavinck, *Reformed Dogmatics*, 1:445. "Ook al die feiten worden in de Schrift niet op en voor zichzelf meegedeeld, maar met een theologisch doel, opdat wij God zouden kennen tot zaligheid." Bavinck, *Gereformeerde dogmatiek*, 1:416.

85. See Veenhof, *Revelatie en inspiratie*, 455–73; Van Keulen, *Bijbel en dogmatiek*, 109–11; Pass, "Upholding Sola Scriptura Today"; Pass, *Heart of Dogmatics*, 135–37.

86. Bavinck, *Reformed Dogmatics*, 1:382. "Geen gemeenschap met Christus dan alleen door de gemeenschap aan het woord van de apostelen," Bavinck, *Gereformeerde dogmatiek*, 1:354.

87. Bavinck, *Reformed Dogmatics*, 1:472. "Er is geen kennis van Christus dan uit de Schrift, geen gemeenschap met Hem dan door gemeenschap aan het woord van de apostelen," Bavinck, *Gereformeerde dogmatiek*, 1:442.

come to Scripture, and Scripture brings us to Christ. Faith in Christ and trust in Scripture strengthen each other.[88]

Given Bavinck's view of special revelation as the communication of knowledge and life, and his emphasis on the role of Scripture in the *unio mystica* with Christ, it is no surprise that Bavinck writes that "theopneustie" (inspiration) is a permanent attribute of Scripture. Scripture was God-breathed (passive) when it became a book, but the book itself remains inspired. Scripture is God-breathing (active), for it is the inspiration that keeps Scripture alive and effective.[89]

Both in subsections 95–97 (on special revelation) and 104–5 (on revelation and holy Scripture), Bavinck shows that the inspired Scripture is part of one dynamic and historical movement, in which God reveals himself in creation, history, and specifically in the history of Israel and Jesus Christ, to complete this revelation in his saved creation when Christ returns in glory. Scripture as the embodiment of God's self-revelation in the history of Israel and Jesus Christ is a necessary means in this historic process, to renew the image of God in human beings, transforming them into the image of Christ. This is the opposite of "textual adoptionism," the danger in modern accounts of Scripture signaled by John Webster. Scripture grows together with the history of Israel and Jesus Christ. Scripture as *God-breathing* text has Christ as its center and has a central role in our union with Christ and our transformation into the likeness of Christ.

One might expect that in Bavinck's doctrine of inspiration (the following subsections 106–17), the emphasis is both on the communication of knowledge and life. However, in his doctrine of inspiration, Bavinck moves back from his dynamic view of the process of salvation to his epistemological starting point, not stressing the nature of inspiration as a present reality, but the role of the Spirit in the inscripturation. When Bavinck discusses 2 Tim 3:16, he points out that the Greek *theopneustos* can mean both "God-breathing" (active) and "God-breathed" (passive). Explaining the work of the Spirit in the organic inspiration of Scripture, he prefers the latter. Bavinck uses inspiration not as a functional category, but as a category of origin. Dealing with the inspiration of Scripture, he returns to the emphasis on epistemology and certainty. Scripture is the word of God because God

---

88. Bavinck, *Gereformeerde dogmatiek*, 1:352, 354, 357, 393, 397, 408, 442, 538–39; Bavinck, *Reformed Dogmatics*, 1:380–82, 385, 423, 427, 437, 472, 569–70.

89. Bavinck, *Gereformeerde dogmatiek*, 1:357; Bavinck, *Reformed Dogmatics*, 1:385. See also Trimp, "Heilige Geest en Heilige Schrift," 114–27. In the English translation, the difference between "inspiratie" and "theopneustie" has disappeared. Van Keulen has shown that an important difference exists between these two words, see Van Keulen, *Bijbel en dogmatiek*, 99–106.

inspired its authors. Because of the combination of revelation and inspiration, Scripture is God's Word with divine authority.[90]

6.2.4 The Attributes of Scripture, Christ, and the Church

The relationship between Christ and Scripture is important to Bavinck's explanation of the attributes of Scripture. In his discussion of these, we find elements of both the lines that Van Keulen distinguished: formal arguments when Bavinck has an epistemological interest in certain knowledge, and material arguments when Bavinck's focus is soteriological. Christ plays a role in both lines of argument.

According to Bavinck, the attributes of Scripture have been developed in Reformed theology in discussion with Rome and the Anabaptists. Bavinck's view of Rome is determined by the council of Vatican I (1870), the council that had declared the church infallible with the pope as "the subject of infallibility."[91] For Bavinck, a theologian born in 1854, this decision (reached in 1870) was a relatively recent one. This declaration implies that "the relation between church and Scripture has been reversed. The church, more concretely the pope, has precedence over and stands above Scripture. . . . Like Scripture in the Reformation, so the church, the magisterium, or really the pope, is the formal principle, the foundation of faith, in Roman Catholicism."[92] Bavinck emphasizes the primacy of Christ and Scripture.

Christ plays a central role in Bavinck's argument for the authority of Scripture. The Old Testament had divine authority for Jesus because of its inspiration. Within the New Testament, the testimony of Jesus is divine and infallible. Jesus gave his apostles the task of being his witnesses, inspired by the Holy Spirit. Because of Christ, we believe in the inspiration of Scripture.[93] Further, Bavinck parallels objections against Scripture with objections against Christ: they share in the same hostility. And in our attitude to Scripture and Christ, we need the same obedience and self-denial.[94]

---

90. Bavinck, *Gereformeerde dogmatiek*, 1:432–34; Bavinck, *Reformed Dogmatics*, 1:463–65.

91. Bavinck, *Gereformeerde dogmatiek*, 1:421; Bavinck, *Reformed Dogmatics*, 1:453.

92. Bavinck, *Reformed Dogmatics*, 1:453–54. "Daarmee is heel de verhouding van kerk en Schrift omgekeerd. De kerk, of meer concreet de paus, gaat voor en staat boven de Schrift. . . . Gelijk de Schrift bij de Reformatie, zo is de kerk, het magisterium, of eigenlijk de paus het formele principe, het fundamentum fidei in het Romanisme." Bavinck, *Gereformeerde dogmatiek*, 1:422.

93. Bavinck, *Gereformeerde dogmatiek*, 1:363–64, 367–68, 408, 423; Bavinck, *Reformed Dogmatics*, 1:394–95, 397–99, 437, 455.

94. Bavinck, *Gereformeerde dogmatiek*, 1:397, 408, 410–12; Bavinck, *Reformed*

Remarkably, in this Christocentric argument the grounds for the authority of Scripture are formal (we believe Christ because he is the climax of revelation) and not material (we believe Christ because of the content of his person, narrative, gospel).

Bavinck's central thesis in his defense of the authority of Scripture is that the Christian faith and preaching need divine authority. We need a divine word, but we also need a divine testimony that Scripture is the word of God. Consequently, it is insufficient to assert with Roman Catholicism that Scripture is dependent on the church. For Bavinck, it is the other way round: the church exists because of Scripture. Similarly, the authority of Scripture cannot consist in a subjective acknowledgment of the fact, as many of his modern contemporaries argued. Human reason, morality, or religiosity cannot give us the deep rest that only the divine witness can. Bavinck maintains this same position when he explains his view of the internal principle. Neither historical apologetics, rational speculation, the empirical reality of religiosity, nor moral psychology can give the absolute certainty that religion needs.[95] To be sure, this divine authority is not one of force but of invitation. Bavinck writes, "It is not human but divine. It is sovereign but still operates in a moral manner. It does not resort to coercion, yet manages to maintain itself. It is absolute, yet resistible. It invites and pleads yet is invincible."[96] However, this statement on the character of divine authority does not change the formal nature of Bavinck's argument.

According to Bavinck, the authority of Scripture depends on her inspiration; and faith, worked by the Holy Spirit, is the internal principle. Faith gives its own certainty, for it has its own grounds. The only solid foundation for faith can be the divine testimony, the *deus dixit*. Scripture is *autopistos* and the testimony of the Holy Spirit brings us to a free and spontaneous acknowledgment of its authority.[97]

Apart from the authority, Bavinck discusses the necessity, the clarity, and the sufficiency of Scripture. Is Scripture necessary to the knowledge of religious truth or the church? Does Scripture need the interpretation by the magisterium of the church, or does Scripture possess the "'power

---

Dogmatics, 1:427, 437, 439–41. See also Bavinck, *Gereformeerde dogmatiek*, 1:537–39; Bavinck, *Reformed Dogmatics*, 1:568–71.

95. Bavinck, *Gereformeerde dogmatiek*, 1:423–34, 472–531; Bavinck, *Reformed Dogmatics*, 1:455–65, 507–59.

96. Bavinck, *Reformed Dogmatics*, 1:465. Het is souverein en werkt toch op zedelijke wijze. Het dwingt niet, en weet zich toch te handhaven. Het is absoluut, en wordt toch weerstaan. Het nodigt en bidt, en is toch onoverwinnelijk." Bavinck, *Gereformeerde dogmatiek*, 1:434.

97. On Bavinck's view of *autopistia*, see Van den Belt, *Authority of Scripture*, 229–99.

of interpreting itself' and is [it] the 'supreme judge of all controversies'"?[98] Is Scripture sufficient or do we need the supplement of the tradition of the church? Here, he returns frequently to the theme of the relationship between Scripture and church (including the tradition). Thus, it is good to delve a little deeper into Bavinck's view of tradition and the church.

Bavinck's view of tradition is determined by the difference between the two dispensations of the economy of Christology and pneumatology, leading him to a differentiated concept of tradition. Before the completion of the canon, tradition and Scripture were like two streams of water, flowing side by side. But like the incarnation, revelation has to adopt the humble form of Scripture. When the process of inscripturation came to an end, these two streams became one. Now we only come to know the truth through the reading of the Scriptures. Tradition cannot add anything to the word of God, just as nothing can be added to the person and work of Christ. The Holy Spirit's special work of inspiration has come to an end.[99]

Nonetheless, Bavinck does emphasize the hermeneutical significance of tradition. This tradition flows from the Scriptures as a river from its source and has to be shaped by them. The tradition "is the method by which the Holy Spirit causes the truth of Scripture to pass into the consciousness and life of the church."[100] We inherit everything from the preceding generations. We always read the Scriptures within the perspective that we received from the communion of the church in which we were raised. Theologians "look at Scripture with the aid of the glasses that their churches have put on them."[101] Living in a fractured church with many traditions, the best each can do to serve the unity of the church is by trying to think "through the faith of his own church and make[s] the most accurate presentation of it."[102] Reading Scripture, we start with the perspective of the confession and the life of our own church, but we need to read in unity with the worldwide catholic communion of the church. Bavinck believed that despite aberrations, the Christian tradition does make progress in interpreting the Bible.

---

98. Bavinck, *Reformed Dogmatics*, 1:480. "Vanwege deze *perspicuitas* heeft de Schrift ook de *facultas se ipsam interpretandi* en is zij *supremus judex controversiarum.*" Bavinck, *Gereformeerde dogmatiek*, 1:450.

99. Bavinck, *Gereformeerde dogmatiek*, 1:65, 318–21, 355, 452, 455–56; Bavinck, *Reformed Dogmatics*, 1:88, 346–48, 383, 482, 485–86.

100. Bavinck, *Reformed Dogmatics*, 1:494. "Zij is de weg, waarlangs de Heilige Geest de waarheid van de Schrift doet overgaan in het bewustzijn en leven van de gemeente." Bavinck, *Gereformeerde dogmatiek*, 1:465.

101. Bavinck, *Reformed Dogmatics*, 1:82. "Beziet dus ook de Schrift met de bril, die de kerk hem voorhoudt." Bavinck, *Gereformeerde dogmatiek*, 1:58.

102. Bavinck, *Reformed Dogmatics*, 1:85. "Als elk het geloof zijner eigen kerk indenkt, en op 't zuiverst voorstelt." Bavinck, *Gereformeerde dogmatiek*, 1:63.

In summary, the apostles' christological tradition came to an end. Nothing can be added to the objective revelation of God's truth. Pneumatologically, however, tradition is a tradition of interpretation that is needed if we are to understand revelation. Hermeneutically, the tradition is very significant, for in the tradition it is the Holy Spirit who guides in all truth.[103]

Consequently, Bavinck's concept of tradition is differentiated, in the first place by two dispensations, the economy of Christ and the Spirit; and in the second place pneumatologically by the distinction between inspiration and illumination.

Due to his christological emphasis on the completeness of Scripture, Bavinck is critical of a concept of tradition that sets it alongside Scripture as a second source. In line with Jesus and the apostles, he argues that the Christian church never acknowledged the Jewish tradition as we find it now in *Mishna* and *Gemara*. Unjustly, this Jewish tradition had become a second source alongside the *Tanakh*, suggesting its insufficiency. During the genesis of the Old Testament, revelation and Scripture were two different streams. Still, to preserve God's revelation and to protect it against human sinfulness, it had to become Scripture. The same is the case with the New Testament: the apostles' oral tradition had to be written down to make it lastingly available in an uncorrupted form. As such, the tradition of the apostles became part of Scripture. Bavinck claims that until the Council of Trent, the church always acknowledged the supreme authority of Scripture, at least theoretically.[104]

But this was changed by the Council of Trent, and this change was affirmed, in turn, by the First Vatican Council of 1870, as we saw already. In Bavinck's view, Rome teaches the insufficiency of the Scriptures, which need to be flanked by another source, namely, the tradition of the church. Rome claims the continuity of the apostolic tradition in the church, which, according to Bavinck, causes the difficulty of selecting who determines what counts as infallible tradition: the bishops, or a council? As such, Bavinck sketches a development in which Rome ultimately decided to proclaim the infallibility of the pope to create clarity and certainty. The church and the tradition replace the Scriptures, and the pope replaces Christ, leading

---

103. Bavinck, *Gereformeerde dogmatiek*, 1:58, 61–63, 70, 93–95, 350–52, 464; Bavinck, *Reformed Dogmatics*, 1:82, 85–87, 93, 119–20, 379–80, 493. Despite its significance, according to Bavinck, in reproducing the thought of the church, theology should not start with tradition to go back to the Bible, but begin with the source and then follow the river that proceeds from it, see Bavinck, *Gereformeerde dogmatiek*, 1:70; Bavinck, *Reformed Dogmatics*, 1:93.

104. Bavinck, *Gereformeerde dogmatiek*, 1:372–77, 420–21, 439–42; Bavinck, *Reformed Dogmatics*, 1:402–8, 452, 470–72.

Bavinck to conclude that the infallible pope is the *principium formale* of Roman Catholicism.[105]

This particular conclusion sheds light on why only twice Bavinck briefly presents a positive concept of tradition in his doctrine of principles.[106] In the introduction to his dogmatics, in which Bavinck gives a general overview of the field, he develops a concept of tradition more directly. When dealing with the principles of theology, however, Bavinck seems reluctant to do so.

Closely related to his differentiated concept of tradition is Bavinck's view of the relationship between Scripture and the *church*. Bavinck acknowledges the hermeneutical significance of the church. At the same time, he maintains the unique position of the Scriptures. He argues, "Pedagogically, the church is prior to Scripture. But in the logical order, Scripture is the sole foundation (*principium unicum*) of church and theology."[107]

In this context, Bavinck quotes Augustine's dictum several times: "I indeed would not have believed the gospel, had not the authority of the church moved me."[108] Of course, the church and tradition cannot be separated here. As has already been seen, it is in the church that we receive our perspective for reading the Scriptures. Bavinck emphasizes over against Rome that the "church" does not refer to the pope or an institution but to the communion of believers. In the first place, this starts with one's own local denomination, but in the end, has in view the entire catholic church. To understand the length, depth, height, and breadth of the love of God, we need the communion of all saints. Further, in the church as an organism, objective revelation becomes part of the consciousness of humanity. Christ and the Spirit, revelation and illumination, word and consciousness belong closely together, as do Scripture and the church. In the dispensation of the Spirit, "revelation . . . is continued jointly in Scripture and in the church. . . . Scripture is the light of the church, the church the life of Scripture. Apart

---

105. Bavinck, *Gereformeerde dogmatiek*, 1:87, 420–23, 439–42, 451–55, 458–59, 463–64; Bavinck, *Reformed Dogmatics*, 1:81, 452–55, 470–72, 481–85, 487–88, 492–93. Marcel Sarot confirms this analysis, comparing the infallibility of the pope with the doctrine of the inerrancy of Scripture, seeing both as forms of foundationalism. See Sarot, "Christian Fundamentalism."

106. Bavinck, *Gereformeerde dogmatiek*, 1:350–52, 463–64; Bavinck, *Reformed Dogmatics*, 1:379–80, 493.

107. Bavinck, *Reformed Dogmatics*, 1:86. See also 93. "Pedagogisch gaat de kerk aan de Schrift vooraf. Maar naar logische orde is de Schrift het principium unicum van kerk en theologie." Bavinck, *Gereformeerde dogmatiek*, 1:63. See also 70.

108. Bavinck, *Gereformeerde dogmatiek*, 1:424, 477; Bavinck, *Reformed Dogmatics*, 1:456, 510; Van den Belt, *Authority of Scripture*, 260–62; Chen, "Herman Bavinck and Augustine on Epistemology."

from the church, Scripture is an enigma and an offense. . . . Conversely, the life of the church is a complete mystery unless Scripture sheds its light upon it. Scripture explains the church; the church understands Scripture."[109] As such, the church remains important for believers throughout their lives. The Holy Spirit prepares the *parousia*, keeping Scripture and the church closely together. In conclusion, Bavinck highly values the hermeneutical significance of the church.[110]

At the same time, it is Scripture, and not the church, that is the principle of theology. Scripture is *autopistos*, but the church is not. Bavinck is very keen to maintain the right order of Scripture and church. The church lives under the authority of the Scriptures. The Scriptures did not come into existence within the church but are God's gift to the church. However, he argues, Rome increasingly changed this order by claiming that temporally and logically the church precedes the Scriptures. According to Bavinck, Rome makes the Scriptures dependent on the church and even denies that the church needs the Scriptures. Due to their obscure character, the Scriptures need the church as its interpreter. Particularly on the issue of Scripture and church, he believes, Rome is the model of error. In this context, Bavinck often mentions Schleiermacher and Rome together, accusing Schleiermacher of vigorously supporting Rome by changing the order of Scripture and church, in the process giving primacy to the church. To reinforce Rome's claim on this particular point, it seems, was perhaps the worst thing a Protestant could do.[111]

This overview of Bavinck's thoughts about Scripture, church, and tradition helps us to understand Bavinck's understanding of the necessity, clarity, and sufficiency of Scripture. The starting point for Bavinck is that only in Christ do we find everything we need for our salvation, and that the word of salvation is mediated through Scripture. In our union with Christ and our participation in Christ, Scripture, tradition, and the church all play an important role. Scripture, however, has the primacy for it does not share in the ambivalence of tradition and the church. Scripture safeguards the *extra nos* of salvation and is dependent on the *solus Christus*. Scripture is

109. Bavinck, Reformed Dogmatics, 1:384. ". . . zet de openbaring zich in deze bedeling voort in de Schrift en in de kerk te zamen. . . . De Schrift is het licht van de kerk, de kerk is het leven van de Schrift. . . . En omgekeerd is het leven der kerk een verborgenheid, als de Schrift er haar licht niet over schijnen laat. De Schrift verklaart de kerk, de kerk verstaat de Schrift." Bavinck, Gereformeerde dogmatiek, 1:356.

110. Bavinck, Gereformeerde dogmatiek, 1:5–6, 23, 59, 61–63, 318–19, 355–57, 425–27, 471–72; Bavinck, Reformed Dogmatics, 1:31, 46, 83, 85–86, 346–47, 383–85, 457–58, 505–6.

111. Bavinck, Gereformeerde dogmatiek, 1:5, 64–65, 77, 423–25, 437–43, 446, 457–59; Bavinck, Reformed Dogmatics, 1:30, 88, 100, 455–57, 468–69, 471, 476, 487–88.

necessary to unite us with Christ and our salvation in him (without Scripture, we could not know Christ), Scripture is a clear text because its core message about salvation in Christ is clear (without Christ, Scripture would be a diverse and open book), and Scripture is sufficient because God has revealed his salvation definitively in Christ (nothing new can be revealed about our salvation). Church and tradition have an important role, too. Still, they cannot replace Scripture.

6.2.5 Internal Principle

Bavinck's Trinitarian approach to theology has led him to the formulation of three principles of theology. This Trinitarian frame for doing theology implies that Scripture is embedded within the acts of the triune God. Consequently, an analysis of Bavinck's view of Scripture would be incomplete without the internal principle of knowing. After the analysis of the external principle, we now turn to this internal principle.

Bavinck relates this *principium* to the acts of the triune God. In the human consciousness, the Spirit works faith (or rebirth, purity of heart, love for the will of God). The acts of the *Logos* result in divine revelation as we find it, especially, in the Scriptures. The Spirit is also active in the *testimonium spiritus sancti*. Scripture is *autopistos* and the testimony of the Holy Spirit brings us to a free and spontaneous acknowledgment of its authority in faith.[112] Faith as *fides salvifica* is the "soul's union with the person of Christ according to the Scriptures and with the Scriptures as the Word of Christ." Its object was "the grace of God in Christ; its foundation the witness of God in his Word; its author the Holy Spirit."[113] Salvific faith has its own unshakable certainty due to the work of God ("*deus dixit*") both in the revelation and in the *testimonium spiritus sancti*.

---

112. Van den Belt fears that the subjective element will lead to subjectivism, due to the dualism of an objective and subjective approach to faith. See Van den Belt, *Authority of Scripture*, 290–94. However, it is important to notice that, according to Bavinck, the religion of the sinner who becomes Christian is the result of God's Trinitarian act. The subjective testimony of the Holy Spirit as well as faith are the results of what God has done in a sinner. Bavinck, *Gereformeerde dogmatiek*, 1:252–54, 533–34, 538–39, 556–61; Bavinck, *Reformed Dogmatics*, 1:278–79, 565–66, 570, 587–91.

113. Bavinck, *Reformed Dogmatics*, 1:573. "Een band van de ziel was aan de persoon van Christus naar de Schriften en aan de Schrift als het woord van Christus. . . . Gods genade in Christus was haar voorwerp, het getuigenis van God in zijn woord was haar grond, de Heilige Geest was haar auteur." Bavinck, *Gereformeerde dogmatiek*, 1:542. Cf. Dalferth's emphasis on the eschatological character of the Christian faith, to distinguish faith in Jesus Christ from a doxastic (or affective or fiducial) understanding of faith. See Dalferth, "Über Einheit und Vielfalt."

Unlike reason, feeling, or will, the *principium cognoscendi internum* is not a natural, anthropological given. Human reason, morality, or religiosity cannot give us the deep rest that only the divine witness can. Neither historical apologetics, rational speculation, the empirical reality of religiosity, nor moral psychology can give the absolute certainty that religion needs.[114] Because of the unshakable certainty of faith, the testimony of the church can also never be the ground of faith. Faith is more than believing that what the church and the Scriptures say is true. Consequently, Bavinck is critical of the Roman Catholic concept of faith. This is no more than a *fides historica*, a rational assent of a suprarational, mysterious doctrine. According to Bavinck, in the end, Rome and Reformation both acknowledge that only the Holy Spirit can give strong convictions of faith. Again, Bavinck acknowledges the role of the church but sees its pedagogical function as embedded in the work of the Spirit. The *testimonium spiritus sancti* is threefold: first, it is the testimony of the Spirit about the Scriptures as divine in content and form; second, it includes the testimony of the Spirit through the church; and third, the Spirit testifies about the Scriptures in the heart of every individual believer.[115]

6.3 BAVINCK AND BEYOND

As we have seen, in Bavinck's doctrine of revelation and Scripture, two lines can be distinguished. On the one hand, a more formal line with an epistemological interest in certain knowledge. This line fits well within the development of the doctrine of Scripture from the medieval period, through the premodern formation of Reformed orthodoxy, until the modern Neo-Calvinism of Abraham Kuyper as sketched in chapter 2. On the other hand, there is a more material line with a soteriological interest in the formation of the organism of the new creation. Here, epistemological questions are important but have a secondary character. Epistemology is not an activity

---

114. Bavinck, *Gereformeerde dogmatiek*, 1:472–531; Bavinck, *Reformed Dogmatics*, 1:507–59.

115. Bavinck, *Gereformeerde dogmatiek*, 1:431, 531–32, 540–55, 559–63, 566–68; Bavinck, *Reformed Dogmatics*, 1:462, 559, 563, 571–86, 589–93, 596–98. On the internal principle, see further Van Keulen, *Bijbel en dogmatiek*, 122–33. On the *autopistia* of Scripture, see Van den Belt, *Authority of Scripture*, 250–300. According to Bavinck, the bond of the soul to Scripture as the word of God is beyond consciousness and mystical by nature (Bavinck, *Gereformeerde dogmatiek*, 1:560; Bavinck, *Reformed Dogmatics*, 1:590). Bavinck does not connect the testimony of the Spirit and the bond of the soul to Scripture to the mystical union with Christ. He relates Christ to objectivity and the Spirt to subjectivity. The importance of the mystical union in his theology does not undermine this scheme at this point of his theology.

with a foundational character, its nature is only critical-reflective. The reconstruction of the doctrine of Scripture that I am pursuing in this book has a soteriological focus and is not primarily guided by epistemological interests (although they can be important at some moment). In the final section of this chapter, I will give a sketch of a doctrine of Scripture, building on Bavinck's soteriological motivated view of revelation and Scripture. In doing so, I want to integrate the strengths of Dalferth's approach, answer his criticisms of the orthodox Protestant doctrine of Scripture, and solve the problems of his proposal (see chapter 4). Moreover, this section has to explain why Scripture can be a book that is used by God to make us participate in Christ and to renew our minds as we saw it in the work of O'Donovan (see chapter 5).

As my starting point for this section, I will take what I see as the strength of Bavinck's position. Scripture is a result of the work of the triune God (in the first dispensation) and a necessary means in the continuation of the activity of God (in the second dispensation). Scripture thus is embedded in the acts of the triune God to save the organism of creation. The first dispensation has its center and climax in Jesus Christ. In the second dispensation, the Holy Spirit uses Scripture as a means to unite us to Christ in a mystical union and to transform us into the likeness of Christ. Bavinck's imaginative construction of the "mode in which God is present among the faithful" is Christocentric.[116] In this section, I will presuppose that such a Christocentric reading of Scripture is justified. In the next chapter, I will deal with the position of Christ within the grand narrative of Scripture.

First, I will discuss the concept of revelation (6.3.1). In the next step, I will focus on Scripture as a book with a history (6.3.2). Having done so, I will present my view of the differences between the concepts of God's Word, Scripture, and the Bible (6.3.3). Then, I will turn to the attributes of Scripture (6.3.4). Finally, the role of tradition and the church will receive attention.

6.3.1 Revelation

A comparison of Dalferth and Bavinck concerning revelation leads to the question of how to evaluate Barth's view of revelation.[117] Dalferth follows

---

116. Cf. Kelsey, *Proving Doctrine*, 159–63. Kelsey mentions "three families of ways to construe the mode in which God is present." In his overview, this Christocentric element is missing.

117. On differences between Bavinckian and dialectic or Barthian views of revelation, see Heideman, *The Relation of Revelation and Reason*; Pass, *Heart of Dogmatics*, 132–33, 141–42. Webster rejects "an objectified account of revelation," in which an entity like Scripture "embodies... the presence of God." See Webster, *Holy Scripture*, 33.

Barthian lines. For Barth, the triune God reveals himself as Lord and God in his Son (the Word of God) and in his Spirit. He is the Revealer, the Revelation, and the Revealedness.[118] Because Barth wants to respect that God is free in his self-revelation, he opposes the objectification of God's revelation in a written book or the isolation of the book from God's acts of self-revelation. Scripture has to be distinguished from God's revelation, for only "by the Holy Spirit it became and will become to the Church a witness to divine revelation."[119] Barth is opposed to the orthodox Protestant doctrine of Scripture and excludes the possibility of the fixation of God's revelation in text. Thus, the embodiment of God's revelation in the Bible is not possible for Barth. Only Jesus Christ is the embodiment of God's revelation, which makes Barth critical of general revelation and natural theology. Moreover, Barth's emphasis on the transcendence of God makes it difficult for him not to imprison God in vertical relationships. Thus, it becomes problematic to understand God's presence in the horizontal plane, in creation, in the history of salvation, or in the existence of the church and the believers. Against the background of Barth's theology, difficulties in Dalferth's work concerning God's presence in his creation and the embodiment of the life of Christ in church and believers (see 4.4) can be understood.[120]

Elements from Bavinck's theology can be used to correct Barthian weaknesses, and Barthian interests can make us critical of Bavinckian problems. According to Bavinck, God's self-revelation is also the act of the Father, Son, and Spirit. Revelation comprises both the communication of knowledge and life. Bavinck sketches God's revelation as a large and dynamic movement, of creation and recreation. Thus, after the entrance of sin in creation God's revelation has a soteriological and eschatological character. It is only complete when the re-created world shows God's glory again.

For Dalferth, revelation started with an experience of a personal address (someone experiences Jesus in the Spirit as the Christ and thus as God's address). However, his focus is on the identification of God and an impersonal language event. For Bavinck, revelation is God's self-revelation, However, he is primarily interested in revealed knowledge about God. In both theologies, the element of a personal encounter fades into the background.

---

118. Barth, *Church Dogmatics*, I/1, 297.

119. Barth, *Church Dogmatics*, I/2, 466.

120. On Barth's transcendentalism, Bonhoeffer's critique of Barth and his own alternative, see Phillips, *Human Subjectivity "in Christ"*; Van 't Slot, *Negativism of Revelation?* According to Van 't Slot, Barth's christological concentration does not solve all the problems of his transcendentalism. Van 't Slot, *Negativism of Revelation?*, 229–35.

How important their emphases might be, it is good not to forget that revelation starts with a personal encounter as a source experience.[121]

Important for Bavinck's understanding of revelation is his organic view of the history of salvation with Jesus Christ as its climax. God's revelation is a historical process, in which he repeatedly speaks his Word and makes himself to be understood in his Spirit. We could say that in the history of Abraham and his people Israel, God builds a horizon within which his final revelation can be understood. God does not reveal himself in isolated words, metaphors, or propositions, but in histories and narratives in which we get to know him, his character, and his intentions more and more. Over the centuries, he creates his analogies and builds a reservoir of images and symbols that can be (re)used to reveal himself to us.

Another valuable element is the possibility of the embodiment of God's thoughts for our human consciousness in creation, the history of salvation, Jesus Christ, a text like Scripture, or the church and the believers. In these embodiments, the divine *Logos* has a central role. Still, God's transcendence is safeguarded, because this embodiment presupposes the difference between God's archetypal self-knowledge and the ectypal revealed knowledge. This concept of embodiment brings a solution to various Barthian problems. The possibility of embodiment in creation leads to a positive doctrine of general revelation, but not to a naïve natural theology: what is embodied in God's good creation is no longer perceived in an unproblematic way after the entrance of sin. Sin has corrupted both creation and our consciousness.

More nuance is needed where Scripture is concerned. The epistemological interest of medieval scholasticism, Protestant orthodoxy, and modern, foundationalist, Protestant theology was too limited and has led to a focus on revealed propositions. But knowledge about God or knowledge about God's salvation is not the sole purpose of revelation. Inspired by Barth, Reformed theology should give primacy to Bavinck's more dynamic, soteriological, sketch of revelation, rather than his epistemological line of thought. Hence, a concept of revelation should start with God's self-revelation, an encounter full of love and grace, and the communication of life. Thus understood, it is impossible to separate God's revelation from the acts of the Father, Son, and Spirit; and also from the freedom of God to make himself present to us in Christ and the Spirit and to grant us an encounter with him. Moreover, revelation is an eschatological concept. Christ and the salvation present in him still have to be revealed in glory (cf. Col 3:1–4).

---

121. For the emphasis on revelation as encounter, see Van Manen, *Ontmoeting met God*.

Only when Christ is revealed, will the new humanity and the re-created cosmos embody God's glorious self-revelation again.

Still, God has revealed the mystery of his salvation in Christ (cf. Rom 16:25–26; Eph 3:3–12; Col 1:26–27; 1 Tim 3:16). The revelation of this mystery of salvation in the incarnation, cross, and resurrection of Christ shows that knowledge is communicated as well. God's thoughts can be embodied in Jesus Christ, Scripture, and human believers, even if salvation in Christ is still partly hidden, and has mysterious aspects. This is how God seeks to relate himself to humans, communicating to our human consciousnesses, to transform human beings into the likeness of Christ by the renewal of their minds. Accordingly, the mediating role of Scripture, as the inscripturation of God's revelation, is indispensable in the current phase of salvation history. It is important to emphasize now that the text of Scripture only embodies thoughts, not God's presence or the communicated life (the church is the life of Scripture). But we need Scripture in our relationship with Christ and with God. Given this possibility of embodiment, for Bavinck, Scripture has a criteriological role.

Investigating Dalferth, we saw that he takes as criterion not a text, but the actual disclosure of God's loving presence in Christ and by the Holy Spirit. With Fickert, I concluded that a more positive appreciation of ecclesiological norms is necessary (see 4.4.2). Bavinck's idea of the embodiment of the divine thoughts in a human text is a first step toward the understanding of the criteriological role of Scripture in theology. However, this is only the first argument for the possibility of the function of Scripture in a criteriological discourse. As Maarten Wisse has argued, Scripture is often used in theology selectively, following specific theological interests. It is important to reflect explicitly on these theological interests and the selective mechanisms, whereas the Reformed tradition refuses to do so, leaving the *sola scriptura* unqualified.[122] Consequently, more has to be said on how Scripture functions as a theological criterion.

Nevertheless, concerning revelation the following can be concluded, following Gerben van Manen: we can speak of revelation based on the Bible, in the context of the daily reality of our "experience"/"Erfahrung" (which is not closed to God but in which God in his general revelation can meet us), and from our personal experience understood as "believing"/"Erlebnis" (which has become closed to us by the noetic consequences sin but is opened by God when he speaks to us in Christ and enlightens us by the

---

122. Wisse, "Contra et Pro Sola Scriptura."

Holy Spirit).[123] But what kind of book is the Bible? I will deal with this question in the next subsection.

6.3.2 A Human and Historical Book

After more than two centuries of historical-critical research, it is important to emphasize that justice should be done to the historical origin of the books of the Bible.[124] Historical research is good and it is useless to deny the human form of Scripture. Bavinck intended the same with his doctrine of organic inspiration. Without the epistemological focus on certain knowledge and the nineteenth-century interest in historiography, however, the existential tension disappears from the discussion of the historical reliability of Scripture.[125]

At the same time, for Christian believers and Christian theology, it is essential that the Scriptures emerged following the traces of God's acts—speaking, promising, giving guidance, liberating, judging, and justifying. Without God's acts in the history of Israel (the exodus) and the history of Jesus Christ (incarnation, cross, resurrection) the stories of the Bible lose their roots in the historical reality. It is not by accident that we read these books, as Webster emphasized, warning for a "textual equivalent of adoptionism."[126] God has sanctified all the historical processes and inspired the prophets and apostles.[127] These texts are the fruits of the purposeful acts of God in the lives of the fathers, the people of Israel, Jesus of Nazareth, and the first Christian believers. This divine activity extends not only to what they experienced, but also how they went about writing and editing their texts, and how God preserved these texts so that they received canonical recognition. Only from an epistemological interest in certain knowledge does it become urgent to explain as precisely as possible the genesis of Scripture. Though we face uncertainties about the origin of the Scriptures, the Scriptures are, nevertheless, powerful and wonderful books. These texts testify of God's acts, tell us what has happened from the perspective of God's acts, give a theological interpretation in these stories, receive their center and fulfillment in Jesus Christ, and have a soteriological purpose—the transformation of human existence. The Nicene Creed relates the Scripture both to

---

123. Van Manen, *Ontmoeting met God*.
124. Cf. Sarisky, *Reading the Bible Theologically*, 63.
125. Cf. Van Bekkum, "Zekerheid en schriftgezag."
126. Webster, *Holy Scripture*, 24.
127. For the combination of sanctification and inspiration, see Webster, *Holy Scripture*, 17–39.

the Son (". . . rose again on the third day in accordance with the Scriptures") and to the Holy Spirit ("who has spoken through the prophets"). Also in their origin, these texts are embedded in the acts of the triune God, who uses them to the present day to relate to us and to speak to our hearts.

"Holy Scripture is human discourse commissioned and confirmed as the servant form of God's communicative initiative," Kevin Vanhoozer writes.[128] With Nicholas Wolterstorff, God's word can be understood as divine discourse: a divine speech-act of God, who has sent and authorized human beings as prophets and apostles to speak in his name, and who uses the canonical texts of Scripture also to speak to us today.[129] Accordingly, I differ from Dalferth who opts for a consistent non-intentionalist event-model of God's word. Instead, I prefer an intentionalist model of divine speech-acts and personal encounter. As a result of divine discourse in the past and as a means of divine discourse in the present, we read the canonical Scriptures as God's word.

Modern historical discussions on the canon tended to focus on the final decision about the closure of a canonical corpus of texts. Van Bruggen, Dalferth, Webster, Bartholomew, and Peckham in different ways all relativize this approach and make a case for a more theological approach. When the formation of a corpus of normative texts has followed historical events like the exodus and the life, death, and resurrection of Jesus Christ, the primary interest will shift toward these originating events. As Bartholomew argues, it is reasonable to expect that the priest in the temple preserved carefully a growing collection of normative texts. The history of the early church shows a process of "recognizing intrinsic authority [that] related back to the Christ and his apostles rather than imposing authority on texts."[130] Thus, Dalferth writes about the church: "It does not declare Scripture to be authoritative, but it confesses the normativity of Scripture by acknowledging that it expresses God's Word, to which it owes its existence, in an authoritative way."[131]

---

128. Vanhoozer, "Holy Scripture," 49.

129. Wolterstorff, *Divine Discourse*. See further Vanhoozer, "Apostolic Discourse and Its Developments."

130. Bartholomew, *Introducing Biblical Hermeneutics*, 263.

131. "Nicht sie erklärt die Schrift für verbindlich, sondern sie bekennt sich zur Normativität der Schrift, indem sie anerkennt, dass diese Gottes Wort, dem sie sich verdankt, in verbindlicher Weise zum Ausdruck brengt." Dalferth, *Wirkendes Wort*, 214. On canonicity, see further Bartholomew, *Introducing Biblical Hermeneutics*, 251–78; Peckham, *Canonical Theology*, 16–47; Van Bruggen, *Kompas van het christendom*, 16–67; Webster, *Holy Scripture*, 58–67. On canon formulas in Deuteronomy, see Versluis, "'And Moses Wrote His Torah.'" On the process of reinterpretation and reuse of normative texts in the prophetic book of Isaiah, see Dekker, "Sacra Scriptura Sui Ipsius Interpres."

Without being able to clarify exactly the relationship between divine and human activity, we receive these texts as the fruit of the triune divine activity. As Christians, we read these inspired, sanctified, canonical texts as Scripture and the word of God. What does it mean to say that these books are Scripture or the word of God?

6.3.3 Jesus Christ, Word of God, Scripture, Bible

Clarification is necessary concerning the use of the terms "Word of God," "Scripture," "Scriptures," and "Bible." Bavinck does not reflect on his use of these words. He prefers the singular "Scripture" (more than 1400 times in vol. 1 of the *Gereformeerde dogmatiek*) and only uses "Scriptures" when he refers to a plurality (19 times). Furthermore, for Bavinck, Scripture is the Word of God. Sometimes he uses "Bible" as well (29 times).[132] Clearly, for Bavinck, the Scriptures have become one Holy Scripture. Furthermore, Bavinck does not distinguish between Scripture as the "word of God" and Jesus Christ or the Son as the "Word of God." Learning from Dalferth (and following Karl Barth's impulses), it is good to distinguish the use of these words.

"Word of God" is related to the acts of triune God himself. First, it is important to differentiate between the "Word of God" and the "word of God." In my proposal, we use "Word of God" to refer to the eternal Word of God, who we know as the incarnate Word of God, Jesus Christ. "Incarnation" has become a technical term in christological discussions. However, that Jesus Christ is the incarnation of the Word of God means more: he is the fulfillment, embodiment, and realization of what God has to say.[133] In him, God communicates a fullness of life and knowledge (life and knowledge deliberately reversed relative to Bavinck's order). Accordingly, as the personal incarnation of what God has to say, he is the key to understanding the Scriptures. For his apostles, this implies that he is the fulfillment of the *Tanakh* of Israel. The perspective of Easter (resurrection) and Pentecost (Holy Spirit) makes the Scriptures a book with a clear purpose, to transform us into the likeness of the Son. In him, we hear the Word of God most clearly and from him, the Scriptures receive their unity and clarity. The "Word of

---

132. Numbers based on a word count in a pdf of the first volume of the *Gereformeerde dogmatiek*, searching for the Dutch words "Schriften," "Schrift" and "Bijbel." https://www.neocalvinism.space/.full_pdfs/Gereformeerde%20Dogmatiek%20I.pdf (accessed the 29th of April 2022).

133. Cf. Jenson, *Systematic Theology*, 1:166.

God" himself is God and belongs to the Trinity, distinct from the speaking God and God's Spirit who makes us understand.

As a consequence, the "Word of God" as the second person of the Trinity can never be reduced to a book or a text. The Word of God is a person and, as Dalferth emphasizes, He remains external to the text of Scripture. He communicates love, salvation, and new life, and not just information. In the word of God, the Word of God communicates himself. Accordingly, an approach to Scripture from an exclusively textual or literary perspective as Lambert Wierenga practices, has blind spots.[134] For the Christian faith and theology, the person of the Word of God is necessary for understanding the text of the word of God. Christ precedes Scripture: because of Christ, we receive Scripture; in the light of Christ, we understand Scripture; what is in Christ, is communicated by Scripture; the role of Scripture in the Christian life and theology depends on Christ himself. This is not to play off Scripture against Jesus Christ: Christ is the Christ of the Scriptures. Only by remaining in the word can we remain in the Word.[135] From Bavinck we can learn the necessary role of Scripture as a means, indispensable for the present times, to know Christ, be united to Christ, live in mystical union with Christ, and be transformed into the likeness of Christ.

It is also important not to forget that the "word of God" is embedded within the work of the triune God. This means that the "word of God" refers to the Scriptures used in the divine discourse, the divine speech-acts addressed to us today.[136] That it is possible within the Neo-Calvinist tradition to understand this becomes clear in what Abraham Kuyper wrote in his *Encyclopedia of Sacred Theology*: "To him who does not feel that, at the moment when he opens the Holy Scripture, God comes by and in it and touches his very soul, the Scripture is not yet the Word of God, or has ceased to be this; or it is this in his spiritual moments, but not at other times, as

---

134. Wierenga, *Macht van de taal*.

135. This was emphasized by Bavinck's colleague Lucas Lindeboom, see Lindeboom, *Blijf in het Woord van God*. Others do play off against each other Christ and Scripture, see Dalferth, "Mitte ist aussen," 190–91; Weder, "Externität der Mitte."

136. According to Jenson, the action of Father, Son and Spirit has to be understood as a "mutually single act." Consequently, it is too easy to say that Father, Son and Spirit do "different things" (Jenson, *Systematic Theology*, 1:111). Accordingly, we should be careful to identify the locution of the divine speech act too strictly with the activity of the Father, the illocution with the Son's act, and the perlocution with pneumatology. Father, Son and Spirit speak; Jesus Christ, God and man, cannot be understood without the Spirit; and in the perlocution the ascended Christ is active together with his Spirit.

Relating Father, Son and Spirit with locution, illocution and perlocution, Vanhoozer's formulations differ; sometimes he formulates more openly, sometimes more strictly. See Vanhoozer, *First Theology*, 154–55, 200–202, 227–28; Vanhoozer, *The Drama of Doctrine*, 66–68.

when the veil lies again on his heart, while again it is truly such when the veil is taken away."[137] This connects easily with the actual nature of Scripture as *"theopneustos"*—breathing the Spirit of God when we listen or read.[138] In the dialogue with Pentecostal and Charismatic theology, it is noteworthy that Scripture can play a mediating role in the fulfillment, along with the Holy Spirit.

"Scriptures" and "Scripture" refer to what has been inscripturated, the written texts that we read in the community of the church. The plural "Scriptures" implies that it is not just one book with one author written during the lifetime of one human being. Within the Scriptures, we find the Torah, a long history of Israel—preceded by Israel's fathers and with its climax as Israel's Messiah. Moreover, we have in the Scriptures the prophetic books, poetry and wisdom, and apostolic letters. The *Tanakh* we read together with the Jewish people, and the other books we read as the community that follows Jesus as the Messiah or Christ. Many prophets and apostles have been active in writing and editing these texts. While the plural "Scriptures" implies the question of how to understand this plurality as a unity, the singular "Scripture" implies that in Christ these books find their center.

"Bible," finally, refers to the scrolls of the Scriptures, collected as printed books in one volume. "Bible" is the designation that is most used in our secular world and thus the most neutral designation. Given the possibility of making printed books widely available, "The Bible" is most open to secular and non-theological use. It refers to the book of Christians, without assigning significance to this book. Anyone can go to a bookstore, buy a Bible, and read it.

That this is book is holy and has divine qualities, is a contested claim. A clarification of the terms "Word of God," "Scripture," or "Bible" does not solve this problem. Thus, it is necessary to discuss the attributes of Scripture in the next subsection.

6.3.4 The Attributes of Scripture

As already mentioned in the introduction of this chapter, the attributes of Scripture—in this subsection authority, clarity, necessity, and sufficiency—have been criticized by Wierenga and Dalferth. They cannot be understood as attributes of the texts. Instead, according to Dalferth, the attributes of Scripture are the attributes of God's Word that he clearly distinguishes from Scripture.

137. Kuyper, *Encyclopedia of Sacred Theology*, 364.
138. Trimp, "Heilige Geest en Heilige Schrift," 114–19.

Bavinck's approach to the attributes of Scripture is more nuanced. Bavinck only discusses the authority, necessity, perspicuity or clarity, and the sufficiency of Scripture. The criticism of Wierenga and Dalferth is a reason to reconsider the authority of Scripture, and to reconstruct it as the authority of God who makes use of Scripture in the exercise of his authority over us. The necessity and sufficiency of Scripture, however, regard the mediating role of Scripture and its function as a means in our relationship with the triune God. Scripture cannot be missed, and Scripture gives us everything we need. Given the fact that Bavinck argues that Scripture only has a mediating role and that this mediating role only is temporary, here Dalferth's criticism does not apply to Bavinck. These two attributes have a role for Bavinck in the dispute of Rome and Reformation about tradition. In the case of the attribute perspicuity or clarity, Bavinck deals with the hermeneutical role of tradition. Regarding the clarity of Scripture, the criticisms of Wierenga and Dalferth are still valid.

In what follows, I will argue that the nature of Scripture (and possibly its attributes) can only be understood in the light of Christ. In Scripture, we encounter the authority of Christ. Scripture becomes a book with a clear purpose when we see Scripture together with Jesus Christ, the incarnation of the Word of God. Scripture cannot be missed because the Holy Spirit uses Scripture to unite us to Christ. And finally, Scripture is sufficient, because in Christ we have everything we need.

Strictly speaking, it is difficult to say that for Bavinck the *sola scriptura* can only be understood in the light of the *solus Christus*. Bavinck never uses the expression "*sola scriptura*" in volume 1 of his *Gereformeerde dogmatiek*. Henk van den Belt has argued that the triad *sola gratia, sola fide,* and *sola scriptura* are not older than 1917. In the Dutch context, it was used for the first time in 1917, by Herman Bavinck.[139] Still, Bavinck's understanding of the attributes of Scripture shows that he materially affirms the *sola scriptura*. And as I have shown, for Bavinck, in many respects, the attributes of Scripture can only be understood in the light of Christ. On the material level, here Bavinck is in line with Dalferth. Because of the *solus Christus*, Scripture is necessary and sufficient. The authority and clarity of Scripture demand a more extensive discussion.

The Authority of Scripture

Regarding the authority of Scripture, we need to remember that in the late modern period, the limitations of a doctrine of Scripture guided by

---

139. Van den Belt, "Problematic Character of Sola Scriptura," 39–42.

epistemological interests have become clear. Moreover, the Reformed doctrine of Scripture was developed amid a dispute on authority. At the same time, modernity and its turn to the subject have raised a critical awareness or even an allergy to authority. To argue that Scripture has authority because of revelation, inspiration, and illumination does not work any longer in the present Western context. In this argument, the authority of Scripture is isolated from God's acts and God's authority, and the authority of Scripture is presented in a rather formal manner. Only after someone has become convinced of the authority of Scripture does Christ come into view. This approach evokes criticisms similar to those found in Bonhoeffer and Kuitert. Moreover, when God himself has become an open question, or when in a pluralist society Christianity is just one religion among many, an appeal to divine revelation does not suffice.

To develop a more material and soteriological approach, the specific content of Scripture could be the starting point. The gospel is the message of Jesus Christ who has triumphed as God's king. O'Donovan's reflections on the authority of God's kingdom can help to further develop an understanding of authority. In O'Donovan's model of political authority, he identifies four leading terms.

>   a. Salvation: It is connected to a positive understanding of power. God's kingship is established when he delivers his people from their enemies. This victory of God's righteousness shows his loyalty to his covenant people. As a result, God's people receive freedom and space to live.
>
>   b. Judgment: It is connected to what is right. In his righteous judgment, God distinguishes between good and evil, between right and wrong. This distinction and God's ability to carry out his judgment create a new public situation where his people can live peacefully. Add to this judgment the law of God, which gives some permanence to this peaceful situation.
>
>   c. Possession: This is connected to tradition. To sustain a community, it should be possible for possessions to be handed down from generation to generation. Life can flourish when people continually have possessions to live with.
>
>   d. Acknowledgment: This is connected with praise. Authority has to be answered by the recognition of the people. The worship of God confirms his kingship and gives kingship its effect.[140]

---

140. O'Donovan, *Desire of the Nations*, 36–49.

According to O'Donovan, God's kingdom has triumphed in the death and resurrection of Jesus Christ. First, this implies that God has conquered our deepest enemies—sin, death, and evil—which is important for all humanity. Second, God's judgment means that God separates us from our evil and gives us a new existence, wherever and whenever we live. Third, we receive a new nature in which a transformed life can grow and flourish in all different contexts. And fourth, this leads to a new life as a living sacrifice for God's glory. God's authority is a saving, judging authority that creates a new peaceful and stable situation: God's universal kingdom. It evokes our free acknowledgment and praise.

To understand Scripture as part of the exercise of God's authority means, first, to understand the message of Scripture as good news about his salvation and his coming reign to people living their lives in various contexts. Second, we hear in Scripture God's condemning and justifying judgment, and in its light, we learn to distinguish within our own existence between where God speaks his condemning *no*, of dying with Christ, and where his justifying *yes*, of rising with Christ. Following God's judgment, we learn to distinguish, corporately and individually, between good and evil, right and wrong. Third, we listen to God's Word to hear a word of transformation, renewing our patterns of thought and our mindset, so that the Spirit and mind of Christ can bear fruit in our lives. And finally, this word evokes our praise of God because we are saved and adopted by God, our loving Father.

With this concept of authority in place, we can say that, first, a personal encounter with Jesus Christ, his salvation, or his followers brings the joyful acknowledgment of Jesus as Christ and Lord. Furthermore, this encounter is followed by the experience of participation in Christ and of transformation in the Spirit. Scripture is an important means used by God to renew us. The good news of Jesus Christ and the Scripture, in which we find this message, prove themselves as impressive, convincing, and too good to be made up. It has a renewing, liberating, and transforming effect. Accordingly, the acknowledgment of Scripture is only a consequence of the acknowledgment of Jesus as Lord and Savior. Questions concerning Scripture or concerning God's existence are not answered with an isolated proof of God's revelation or God's presence. An answer to this question is implied when someone has come to confess Jesus Christ as Savior and Lord.

The gospel of the triumph of God's kingdom not only brings us to Easter but to Pentecost as well. At Pentecost, the Holy Spirit is given as the "firstfruits" (Rom 8:23) of redemption. Looking from Pentecost, Keener states that the readings of Scripture will be experiential, missional, eschatological, diverse, and contextualized.¹⁴¹ In many different ways, people have and will come to the Spirit-filled experience of Jesus Christ as the risen Lord and king. Reflection on the authority of Scripture, experienced in many different contexts and translated into many different languages, cannot be separated from this saving presence of the Holy Spirit.¹⁴² At the same time, Scripture is an important means in the experience of the Holy Spirit.

Consequently, I understand the authority of Scripture as part of God's authority: the powerful, judging and sustaining authority of God's king, Jesus Christ. How Jesus Christ exercises his authority in our lives, is by uniting us with himself, giving us his Word and his Spirit. He identified with us, we identify with him. He lives in us, we live in him. This mysterious union cannot be separated from his Spirit in us, nor Scripture. Scripture is a fruit of God's dealings with humanity, in Israel, and its climax in Jesus Christ. We remain in Christ by remaining in his word. And when his word remains in us, Christ remains in us. The mystery of our union with Christ is the mystery of the Spirit and the mystery of the word. We read Scripture as his disciples and in the imitation of Christ. Scripture is for us the way to Jesus Christ, but Jesus Christ also is for us the way to Scripture. We accept Scripture because we came to believe in Jesus Christ and follow him.

The Clarity of Scripture

The clarity of Scripture confronts us with several problems. First of all, it is important to realize that the clarity of Scripture is confessed because it is disputed. Sometimes, Scripture is difficult and we do not understand the meaning of Scripture. The confession of the clarity of Scripture does not mean that this is not the case but explains what makes passages from Scripture to be understood as a clear and meaningful Word of God. Let us presuppose that the clarity of God's Word could be analyzed in this way:

> Something (a text from Scripture) is clear to someone (one or more persons) leading to a better discernment (of a life situation).

This shows that the theme of clarity comprises more than one problem and we will see that the person of Jesus Christ contributes in various ways to the solution of these problems.¹⁴³

---

141. Keener, *Spirit Hermeneutics*.

142. On the illumination by the Spirit and its hermeneutical implications, see Witzier, *Lezen in het licht*.

143. Of course, the same is true of the Holy Spirit. See Witzier, *Lezen in het licht*.

Clarity is clarity of *something*:

a. Does Scripture as a whole have a clear message? We have many human books in the Bible. Is it possible and justified to read these many books as part of one story with one direction, or even with one message? These questions concern the unity of Scripture. If Christ contributes to an answer to these questions, he does so as the center or climax of the story of the history of salvation. According to Bavinck, Christ is the center of Scripture that gives unity to Scripture. In chapter 7, I will investigate further whether good arguments can be given to justify this position.

b. Do passages of Scripture have a clear sense? Is the sense of the text of Scripture as a property of the text itself stable? Complicating this further, in Scripture we find passages that are reused and reinterpreted along typological, analogical, and spiritual lines. These questions concern the interpretation of specific passages of Scripture. A possible justification for these interpretations is christological. Now, Christ gives not just clarity by his role within the history of salvation, but the question is whether Christ is present in the text of Scripture. This question will be discussed in chapter 7.

But furthermore, clarity is clarity of something to *someone*:

c. What is the role of the community to make Scripture clear to an individual person? Does the individual reader need a community to come to understand Scripture or to test her interpretation intersubjectively? Now, we are dealing with the hermeneutical significance of the church. For Bavinck, the church has this hermeneutical significance. Christ comes in through his body, that is the church, within which the members of the body, limited as they are in understanding, need each other to learn from each other and to complement. However, this has evoked questions in the history of theology concerning the relationship between Scripture, the church, and the tradition. I will deal with this problem in 6.3.5. The theme of the hermeneutical significance of the community will return in chapter 8.

d. How does Scripture become clear to sinners? If sin has noetic consequences (see chapter 3), even a clear Scripture will remain unclear to

---

The significance of Christ for the clarity of Scripture in its various aspects leads to analogous thoughts as developed by Sarisky following Augustine with regard to how Christ makes us enter the hermeneutical circle; see Sarisky, *Reading the Bible Theologically*, 110–11, 114–15.

sinners, for various reasons (unwillingness, fear, inability, deception, etc.). It might be hoped that conversion, faith, and sanctification have hermeneutical significance. This evokes new questions as well: how does sin influence the reading of texts of Scripture? And how does faith change our perspective on the texts of Scripture? Is a perfectly believing lay Christian a better interpreter of Scripture than an atheist academic theologian? Now, the focus is on the formation of the mind of Christ in us. I will deal with these questions in chapters 7–9 (see also chapter 5).

Finally, clarity leads to a better *discernment of a life situation*.

e. How does Scripture give us clarity in our life situations? This question concerns the practical significance of Scripture. Is it a danger to take this question too actively, pretending that we as human interpreters have to make Scripture significant and relevant. Scripture could imply a call to faith, hope, and love. Still, it is a question of how we learn to discern our situations in the light of Scripture, how we discern God's presence in our situation, how our self-image and worldview are transformed, and whether we see possibilities to act. These final questions concern the formation of the mind of Christ in us to develop our discernment. I will deal with these questions in chapters 8–9 (but also chapter 5 is important).

Concerning the necessity and sufficiency of Scripture, finally, it is said that Scripture is an essential means (necessity) and the primary means (sufficiency) in God's saving acts in our lives, in the work of the Spirit, in our relationship, in the Spirit, with Jesus Christ, and in the Spirit and Christ with the Father. Believers can have no faith in Christ, no unity with Christ, and no participation in Christ without Scripture. As we saw, for Bavinck these two attributes depend on the *solus Christus*. Here, just as with the clarity of Scripture, theological interests at stake concern the relationship between Christ, Scripture, and the church. To these questions, I turn in the next subsection 6.3.5.

6.3.5 Church and Tradition

Does Bavinck help us to understand the relationships between Christ, Scripture, and the church? In his evaluation of Bavinck, Van den Belt asks "how this renewed emphasis on the Church can be made fruitful, without returning to the . . . position in which the church overrules the authority of Scripture."[144]

1. Essential to Bavinck's position is the relation between the completed work of Christ and the completeness of the Scriptures; and hence between the sufficiency of salvation in Christ and the sufficiency of Scripture. This christological emphasis is important to maintain: in Christ, we find everything we need. Christ is and remains our representative, who constitutes us as his represented people. Nothing needs to be added to his person or work for our salvation. The Spirit takes from Christ, but never replaces him (John 16:14).[145] This makes impossible a two-source theory of the revelation of what we need to know about our salvation, as everything we need to know concerning our salvation in Christ is contained in Scripture.[146]

2. Christ makes us participate in his identity and story through his Spirit. The head of the church is formed first, and then the body of Christ, Bavinck writes. In this process of participation, Christ and the Spirit are both active in using the Scriptures and the community of the church. Bavinck's organic thinking in connection to the mystical union with Christ makes it possible to deny primacy both to the individual and the community because both are rooted in Christ. Still, the central question now concerns the relationship between Christ, the Spirit, the Scriptures, and the church and her tradition and their respective roles in this process of participation.

3. In Bavinck's reflections, an important difference between Christ, the Spirit, and the Scriptures on the one hand, and the church and her tradition on the other, has to be noted: as far as our salvation is

---

144. Van den Belt, *Authority of Scripture*, 296.

145. Burger, *Being in Christ*, 460-64, 481, 487. O'Donovan even uses the pairing of objective/subjective to refer to what is reality in Christ as our representative (objectively), and to what is realized in us by our participation in Christ through the Spirit (subjectively). Bavinck refers twice to John 16:14 to indicate the relationship between Christ and the Spirit, see Bavinck, *Gereformeerde dogmatiek*, 1:320, 397; Bavinck, *Reformed Dogmatics*, 1:347, 427. See further Echeverria, *Berkouwer and Catholicism*, 306-7.

146. According to Echeverria, the two-source theory is now rejected by a part of Roman Catholic theology. Echeverria distinguishes a material sufficiency (all truth of salvation is contained in Scripture) from a formal insufficiency (for its interpretation, Scripture needs the church). Echeverria claims that the Council of Trent does not necessarily lead to the doctrine of such a two-source theory. However, Ratzinger's criticism of Vatican II indicates a new problem: now the primacy of Scripture is threatened, and Scripture is being swallowed up into the tradition. See Echeverria, *Berkouwer and Catholicism*, 281-83, 295-303. And further Trimp, *Betwist schiftgezag*, 192-221.

concerned, the church and her tradition cannot be trusted as infallible, whereas the Son and the Spirit and the divinely inspired Scriptures are infallible. Here the transcendence of the salvation *extra nos* and the critical otherness of God and his truth are at stake. In this critical instance, the church and her tradition need to lay bare their human ambivalence.[147] In line with John 10 and 15, Bavinck emphasizes that we have communion with Christ only through the word of Scripture. In this line, the normativity of the Scriptures as critical "*Gegenüber*" (opposite) of church and tradition has to be maintained. Scripture has primacy over the church because the church is *creatura verbi*.[148]

4. As seen before, Bavinck emphasizes that Scripture is the light of the church and the church is the life of Scripture. The importance of the church's particular mediating and formative role must be acknowledged. *Sola scriptura* can never mean *solo scriptura*, as though it should be understood as an "anti-tradition principle."[149] Bavinck also sees the *testimonium spiritus sancti* working through the church. We can understand this role of the church as we consider the work of the Spirit as the communion of the Spirit and the church as Christ's body through which he works.

5. Using the difference between Christology and pneumatology, Bavinck develops a differentiated concept of tradition. In the christological economy, an oral stream of tradition existed alongside the Scriptures. At the end of this economy, this stream of tradition (in its entirety) became part of the Scriptures and disappeared. In the pneumatological economy, a new stream of tradition flows from Scripture as the source, connecting us with the Scriptures. In this tradition, we find a perspective from which to understand the Scriptures. This second tradition, however, does not provide us with new information, or with new revelation of divine mysteries. Bavinck is very hesitant to reflect on prophecy and the guidance of the Spirit.

However, this concept of tradition is not sufficiently nuanced. First, Bavinck's idea of the two rivers of tradition and Scripture flowing together until the canon was finished, does not clarify the interaction between tradition and the growing Scriptures. Texts resulting from revelation were

147. In a comparable way Berkouwer, see Echeverria, *Berkouwer and Catholicism*, 311–16; and further 275–76, 304, 309.

148. Dalferth, *Wirkendes Wort*, 7, 172; Webster, *Holy Scripture*, 44–47. On canonical theology as an alternative to communitarian approaches to theology, see also Peckham, *Canonical Theology*.

149. Echeverria, *Berkouwer and Catholicism*, 303–4, and further 276–78.

preserved, read, interpreted, and handed down within a living community. During the christological dispensation, the community already maintained a perspective on the Scriptures within which they understood Scripture. Moreover, texts produced within the Jewish community that did not become part of the Christian Scriptures nonetheless influenced the genesis of other parts of the Christian Scriptures: for example, we cannot understand the genesis of parts of the New Testament without acknowledging the role of intertestamental Jewish literature.

Second, within this view of tradition as the handing down of a perspective for reading, we need to distinguish between three points: (a) basic convictions about the triune God who acts to save us in Christ and the Spirit, uniting us to Christ, and realizing his kingdom; (b) the central elements of the Christian faith as we find them in the Apostolic and Nicene Creeds; and (c) specific, confessional or exegetical subtraditions, like the Reformed tradition or a particular exegetical school. These distinctions are necessary to acknowledge that within the Christian tradition, readers of Scripture can recognize each other as fellow Christians, even as orthodox Christians, while at the same time perhaps understanding passages differently within their Christian subtraditions.[150]

Third, the reality of Christ is more comprehensive and mysterious to us than what we know and find in Scripture. We do not know what it is to share in Christ completely. Our knowledge is sufficient for our present Christian lives, but it is not comprehensive. Christ himself is hidden in heaven until he will be revealed in his glory. As the first letter of John says, "Dear friends, now we are children of God, and what we will be, has not yet been made known. But we know that when he appears, we shall be like him, for we shall see him as he is" (1 John 3:2). For fear of Anabaptist or Roman Catholic derailments, Bavinck does not leave room for eschatological newness within the pneumatological economy. Nonetheless, if the Spirit makes us participate in Christ, he can reveal secrets in the lives of individual persons, in prophecy, or in guiding the church. And the Spirit completely will reveal what this eschatological newness comprises when Christ appears in his glory at his *parousia*.

This necessitates a reconsideration of the relationship between Christ, Scripture, Spirit, and the church. From Bavinck, we can learn that nothing

---

150. Peckham notes that there is no unanimity among the theological traditions on what comprises the *regula fidei* as a rule for reading Scripture. He defends that Scripture itself is the *regula fidei*. See Peckham, *Canonical Theology*, 109–39. Even if no consensus about the *regula fidei* exists, it remains important that in the tradition of Jesus's disciples, a perspective of reading is handed down, starting with faith in Jesus as the Messiah.

constitutive for our salvation can or has to be added, by the Spirit or the church, to what we have in Christ. Scripture contains sufficiently what we need to know about salvation in Christ. However, we need to maintain openness to what the Spirit can do if he lives in us, unites us with Christ, and makes us share in who Christ is and what he has done. Here we face a difficult problem: how can we maintain openness toward prophecy as a gift of the Spirit, without creating openness toward wrong enthusiasm, new dogmas (for example, the ascension of Mary or the infallibility of the pope), or a liberal movement away from the Scriptures in the name of progress?[151] While it is impossible to solve this problem completely, some guidelines can be given based on the previous discussion. The words of Jesus, "It is finished," should guide us here. Our salvation is complete, and a prophecy in the name of the Holy Spirit, Mary, or a bishop of Rome cannot add anything to Christ as our Messiah. As our Lord and our representative substitute, he constitutes our identity as well as our destiny. Furthermore, nothing else than conformity to Christ, as we know him through the canonical writings of his apostles, is the aim of the Christian life. The canonical Scriptures remain normative and thus have the "epistemic primacy,"[152] and prophecy has to be tested in the light of Scripture. Keener warns that things go wrong "with those who supplant the text's message by interpretations that do not flow from it."[153] The canon is a "measuring stick for testing other claims to revelation."[154] At the same time, we cannot know in advance what will happen if the Spirit makes us share in Christ and how he will speak to us today. Our knowledge of what it is to be conformed to Christ, and our life in conformity to him, increase together. Hence, *solus Christus* should be the final word.

Following this, within a concept of tradition, we need to differentiate between these four aspects:

> a. Tradition as a source of knowledge flowing from God's interaction with his people, culminating in his revelation of the mystery of salvation and coming to an end in the completion of the texts of the canonical Scriptures.
>
> b. Tradition as the noncanonical writings and oral traditions stemming from the first Christians that might be conserved partly in early Christian writings, but that cannot claim canonical normativity.

---

151. Houtman maintains an openness of the canon when moral issues are concerned; a comparable movement can be made as well in doctrinal discussions. See Houtman, *Schrift wordt geschreven*, 456–507.
152. Keener, *Spirit Hermeneutics*, 104.
153. Keener, *Spirit Hermeneutics*, 106.
154. Keener, *Spirit Hermeneutics*, 107–8.

c. Tradition as a perspective of faith in God our creator and Father, in his Messiah as the fulfillment of the Scriptures, and in his Holy Spirit who spoke through the prophets, passed down through the generations. Here, the Apostolic and Nicene Creeds play an important role, identifying the three persons of the Trinity "by biblical names for the *dramatis personae*" of the divine drama.[155]

d. Tradition as a history of the effect of the Scriptures in the life of the church.

In conclusion, the christological character of Bavinck's emphasis on Scripture can be appreciated within a soteriological framework. When the Father, Son, and Spirit make us share in Christ, God uses the Scriptures. If God does so, the church is formed in conformity with Christ, the head of the church. In this process of transformation, Bavinck rightly saw the mediating role of church and tradition. Scripture, church, and tradition belong together in the unity of the Spirit. However, in the church, we need the saving transcendence of Christ and his word, the canonical Scriptures. Here Bavinck's distinction between Christology and pneumatology reminds us of something important: Christ and the Spirit are divine, and Scripture is canonical, but while church and tradition are important, they remain ambivalent.[156]

6.4 SHORT CONCLUSION

In Bavinck's doctrine of Scripture, we discovered two lines of thought: an epistemological and a soteriological one. Whereas we should no longer give primacy to the epistemological line, the soteriological line remains the more important to understand the nature of Scripture in the economy of salvation. Bavinck's work can help us understand the role of Scripture as a necessary means in the various aspects of our relationship with Jesus Christ. The triune God encounters us in Scripture so that we come to know God in Jesus Christ; we come to confess him as Savior and are filled with his Spirit; we are united to Christ in a mystical union; we participate in him and thus are transformed into Christlikeness.

Especially when discussing the clarity of Scripture, something like a new agenda opened up. Now that a soteriological frame for understanding Scripture has been developed in dialogue with Ingolf Dalferth (Trinity),

---

155. Cf. Jenson, *Canon and Creed*, 45, and further 43–50.

156. This ambivalence of church and tradition is an important argument in Peckham's defense of canonical theology, see Peckham, *Canonical Theology*, 103–8.

Oliver O'Donovan (participation in Christ), and Herman Bavinck (Scripture), it is time to turn to the practice of reading and understanding. The first step concerns the position of Christ within the narrative of Scripture.

7.

Literal and Spiritual
Faith in Jesus Christ and the Reading of Scripture

7.1 INTRODUCTION

Those who enter the Saint Vitus Church in Naarden, the Netherlands, where I grew up, will see its wooden barrel vault, painted between 1510 and 1518 with large images of biblical scenes. On the north side, we find representations of scenes from the story of the cross and the resurrection of Jesus Christ. On the south side, ten scenes from the Old Testament are pictured that are related typologically to the New Testament scene. Some of these typologies have roots in Scripture itself. For example, the crucifixion together with the copper snake in the desert (John 3:14), and the burial of Jesus together with Jonah in the huge fish (Matt 12:40). Some other prefigurations are not rooted in Scripture: e.g., the flogging of Jesus together with the martyrdom of the Maccabees. These paintings were probably inspired by the printed works with illustrations of biblical stories, explanations of these stories, and typologies: the *Biblia Pauperum* (1460) and the *Speculum Humanae Salvationis* (1470).[1]

---

1. On the painted ceilings, see Den Hertog and Holtrop, *Hemelbestormers*. These are the ten painted prefigurations: (1) Jesus on the Mount of Olives, together with Moses praying on the hill; (2) the kiss of Jude, together with Joab betraying Amasa or Abner; (3) the flogging of Jesus, together with the martyrdom of the Maccabees; (4) the mockery of Jesus, together with the mockery of Elisha; (5) Jesus bearing his cross, together with Abraham going to sacrifice Isaac; (6) the crucifixion, together with the copper snake in the desert; (7) the burial of Jesus, together with Jonah in the huge fish; (8) the resurrection (the painting on the cover of this book), together with Samson, carrying

These late medieval paintings show something of what has been through the centuries characteristic of Christian reading of the Bible: faith in Jesus Christ somehow regulates or determines the reading of the books of the Bible as Holy Scripture. The source experience of a personal encounter with Jesus Christ in Scripture evokes a practice of a Christian reading of Scripture. In the preceding chapters, we saw that this is the case also with Ingolf Dalferth, Oliver O'Donovan, and Herman Bavinck, although in different manners. For Dalferth, Jesus Christ is the theological key point in a plural collection of texts. In O'Donovan's view, Christ gives narrative coherence to different stories with moral incompatibilities. According to Bavinck, Christ is the center of one large movement of God's revelation in the history of salvation. The ceilings of the church in Naarden demonstrate a reading of Scripture that finds typological relations between passages from the Old and New Testament. The practice of allegorical reading, finally, reads Scripture with the conviction that Christ is present in Scripture everywhere and thus can be found in Scripture. In this chapter, I will focus on the regulation of the Christian reading of Scripture by faith in Jesus Christ. Doing this, I move from reflection on hermeneutics and Scripture to reflection on the reading of Scripture itself.

An implication of the relation between Christian faith and the Christian reading of Scripture is that theological hermeneutics as critical reflection on the processes of understanding includes reflection on specific beliefs that regulate the Christian reading of Scripture. These specific regulative beliefs might sometimes be implicit in a practice of reading; it is well possible to formulate them explicitly, reflect critically on them, and discuss them. Significantly, a naturalistic reading of Scripture also has hidden regulative beliefs: a commitment to a naturalistic ontology, as Sarisky notes.[2] It is important to discuss these regulative beliefs explicitly, to protect theologians from laziness, and to explain what we prioritize in Scripture and how we weigh the various parts of its diverse collection.[3] The discussion of these regulative beliefs should be a part of theological hermeneutics.

---

the doors of the city gates of Gaza; (9) the ascension, together with the ascension of Elijah; (10) the outpouring of the Holy Spirit, together with Moses, receiving the law.

2. Sarisky, *Reading the Bible Theologically*, 163–71.

3. Cf. the discussion of *sola scriptura* in Wisse, "Contra et Pro Sola Scriptura." Peckham defends a canonical approach of theology, using the ambivalence of church and community as an argument against communitarian approaches. At the same time, he signals the hermeneutical diversity that will exist in such a canonical approach. He does not explain how to deal with this hermeneutical diversity. Discussing the mechanism of selection is an important step in dealing with the hermeneutical diversity among theological approaches. Cf. Peckham, *Canonical Theology*, 139, 162–64, 258.

For Christian believers, the canonical Scripture is one of the means used to keep us close to Jesus Christ.[4] We read Scripture, believing that the triune God uses them to make Christ known to us, live in union with him, participate in who he is, and transform us into the likeness of Christ. That also means that we read the Scriptures to devote ourselves to the teaching of the apostles (Acts 2:42) and to live in the perspective opened by the resurrection of Jesus Christ at Easter, to which we are enabled by the Holy Spirit given at Pentecost. Thus, we are "being committed to receiving (theological) beliefs" instead of being a reader operating "solely on the basis of his own internal resources."[5] What does all that mean regarding beliefs that are regulative for the reading of Scripture? Which are these beliefs that should guide us in reading and interpreting Scripture?

Seeking an answer to this question, I will take several steps. First, I will take Klaas Schilder's meditations on the suffering of Christ as an example of a reading of Scripture that is guided by beliefs (7.2). Second, I will answer the question of whether Scripture can be read as one story and what it means to speak about the narrative coherence of Scripture (7.3). Third, I will discuss the allegorical reading of Scripture, as it was traditionally propagated in the *quadriga*. Here, I will enter a dialogue with Hans Boersma (7.4). In the final section, I will look back and relate the reflection on these beliefs to the renewal of the mind. I will argue that the renewal of the mind partly regards the formation of beliefs and that public theological reflection has a role in this renewal of the mind (7.5).

7.2 THE EXAMPLE OF KLAAS SCHILDER

As an example of a rich theological perspective on Scripture, I take the Dutch theologian Klaas Schilder (1890–1952) in his trilogy *Christus in zijn lijden* (Christ in His Suffering).[6] Primary to his theocentric perspective is the conviction that God has to reveal himself, and God has revealed himself, although sometimes in a hidden way in a *mashal* (parable). This *mashal*

---

4. Van de Beek, *Lichaam en Geest van Christus*, 275–338.
5. Sarisky, *Reading the Bible Theologically*, 167–68.
6. Schilder, *Christus in zijn lijden*. Schilder played an important role in the Dutch church history of the first half of the twentieth century, and took a leading position in the Reformed Churches Liberated (Gereformeerde Kerken [vrijgemaakt]), which were established in 1944, after Schilder was dismissed by the Synod of the Reformed Churches in the Netherlands. See on Schilder and this trilogy Dee, *K. Schilder*, 182–206; De Bruijne, "Schilders vroege spiritualiteit," esp. 68–71; Schaeffer, "Schilder mysticus," 223–48.

brings crisis, to reveal the heart: whether it hides friendship or enmity.[7] God's revelation and the mystery of Christ's suffering surpass our understanding.[8] Moreover, sin makes it difficult to understand God's revelation. Not according to the flesh, only according to the Spirit, that is, in faith, can we see God's actions and understand the meaning of Christ's suffering. To see, one has to be in Christ and one has to learn to observe in the light of Scripture.[9] Hence, the renewal of our knowing is fundamental to Schilder. His hermeneutic is a soteriological hermeneutic.

God's revelation is a unity and Christ is its center. Repeatedly, Schilder demonstrates that Christ, through his actions and suffering, is the fulfillment of Scripture. When after the celebration of Passover Christ and his disciples sing the psalms of the *Hallel*, the author (i.e., the Word of God himself) sings his own psalms, Schilder points out.[10] Dogmatics helps to see this unity. When we read Scripture with Schilder, we read with a theologian who uses dogmatic concepts to explain what he reads. As such, we get access to the Word of God. Then we see Christ, who performs the plan of salvation that Father and Son made together in the eternal covenant of redemption. We see Christ in his threefold ministry of prophet, priest, and king. Schilder especially emphasizes God's justice and God's wrath on sin. As the mediator and second Adam, Christ fulfills the requirements of God's covenant. The moment of substitution, the unique sacrifice of Christ is thus heavily emphasized. At the same time, at the end of many chapters, Schilder asks us to reflect on ourselves, our reactions, and our position. Faithful knowledge of Christ has to touch and change us.

Schilder's theological reading is guided by a whole range of important beliefs: about God and his revelation, human sin and misunderstanding, the necessity of regeneration to understand properly, the value of dogma, the unity of Scripture, the central place of Christ within Scripture, readers who do not stay apart as spectators but are existentially involved because God addresses them, the person of Christ, and the significance of Christ's death in the light of God's eternal counsel.

Such an approach has the danger that we come to read Scripture in the light of a dogmatic system. This is what Schilder does: he interprets Scripture using classical Reformed doctrines of Christology, covenant, and soteriology. Recently, Jamieson and Wittman have formulated christological

7. On the *mashal*, see Schilder, *Christus in zijn lijden*, 2:80–100.

8. See, e.g., Schilder, *Christus in zijn lijden*, 1:12, 52–53.

9. On the epistemic influence of sin on the one hand, and on being in Christ, faith and Scripture on the other hand see Schilder, *Christus in zijn lijden*, 1:27–29, 31, 55–56; 2:182, 216, 266, 269, 285. Cf. Schaeffer, "Schilder mysticus," 224–26.

10. Schilder, *Christus in zijn lijden*, 1:320.

and Trinitarian rules for reading and exegeting Scripture. For them, the glory of Christ is the central focus of reading Scripture. As a result, they read the Old Testament only in the light of the New, have trouble doing justice to suffering and brokenness, and ignore the historical developments of the Scriptures. Moreover, a certain version of Trinitarian and christological doctrine determines their reading of Scripture.[11]

Despite this danger, theological hermeneutics needs to reflect explicitly on the regulative beliefs implied in the Christian faith, for these beliefs are important in the Christian practice of reading Scripture. These regulative beliefs concern the acts of the triune God, Jesus Christ as the Word of God, the narrative of the Old and New Testament, and the involvement of Christian readers.[12]

> 1. *God's Trinitarian acts*: Schilder wanted the readers to see the acts of God in the dramatic story of the Bible and their own lives. As we saw earlier, modernity suffered from an "eclipse of God's agency,"[13] and as a result, the consciousness that we have to read Scripture as embedded in God's Trinitarian act is at risk of being lost. When we lose this consciousness, we lose the Word of God.[14] Vanhoozer has demonstrated the relationship between our understanding of God's interaction with his people and our views of Scripture.[15] We should see God act, the one God who has bound himself to Abraham and his seed, in the way the creed identifies him threefold as Father, Son, and Spirit.[16] The one God is the main character of the stories of the Bible who unites them into one drama. As Robert Jenson says, the Father, Son, and Spirit, the "*dramatis dei personae*" (the "characters of the drama of God") "make an internal structure of the one God's personal name," and "the three identities are one God."[17] This fits well with what we saw earlier: as Father, Son, and Spirit, he is the one God who addresses us, who restores our relationship with himself in Christ and his Spirit, and who re-creates his image in us, in conformity to Christ, by his Spirit. Hence, we need to understand Scripture as embedded in God's Trinitarian

---

11. Jamieson and Wittman, *Biblical Reasoning*.
12. Cf. the theses 3–7 in Huijgen et al., "Biblical Exegesis and Systematic Theology," 189–92.
13. Bowald, *Rendering the Word*, 14.
14. Bowald, *Rendering the Word*, 1–23.
15. Vanhoozer, *First Theology*, 127–58.
16. Jenson, *Canon and Creed*, 2010, esp. 45–46.
17. Jenson, *Systematic Theology*, 1:75; Jenson, *Canon and Creed*, 2010, 45.

act. We read Scripture because God, in Christ and his Spirit, uses this book to exercise his saving authority over our lives.

2. *Christ as the extratextual center*: "The text alone" is not sufficient. Texts, separated from their author and original context do not have a stable meaning.[18] Texts can be interpreted and reused differently, depending on the reader and its context. A clear example is the difference between a Jewish reading of the *Tanakh* and a Christian reading of the same books as the "Old Testament." These books form an open text with a story that can be continued in different ways. Thus, it is an important question of how we come to read Scripture as one story (see 7.3). To Schilder, it was obvious that Christ is both the author and the fulfillment of Scripture. We already discussed that God acted in Christ *extra-textually*, so that the center of Scripture remains *extra-textual* as well and the Scripture-principle has to be understood in the light of the *solus Christus* (see 4.3.4 and 6.3.3–4). In this chapter, I will further investigate which beliefs this implies and how they can be justified.

3. *Old and New Testament as one narrative*: Schilder just tells the story of Christ in his suffering. At the same time, the way he uses the Scriptures demonstrates that he reads the Old and New Testaments as a unified whole that tells one grand narrative. This third element follows from the first two: if the one God of Israel fulfills his word in his Son Jesus Christ, the incarnate Word, then the Scriptures receive coherence. This is not self-evident, for the Scriptures tell many different stories and contain more than stories. It would be wrong to suggest that we only read the Old Testament in the light of the New. Thus, it is an important question of how we come to distinguish this grand narrative and how we see the relationship between this grand narrative on the one hand, and on the other all these small stories, prophecies, poetry, and wisdom.

4. *We, as the body of Christ, share in that story*: Often, Schilder ends his chapters with a question concerning ourselves. This shows that we are involved and that we somehow share in the story of Jesus Christ. Christians read Scripture as a book with the intended effect that we will become part of the new covenant and live as a member of the same. As Vanhoozer argues, "What God does with Scripture is covenant with humanity by testifying to Jesus Christ (illocution) and by bringing about the reader's mutual indwelling with Christ (perlocution)

---

18. Wisse, *Scripture between Identity and Creativity*, 146–57.

through the Spirit's rendering Scripture efficacious."[19] In Christ's body, we learn to understand Scripture and actively embody our role within God's grand narrative, together. The Christian faith is not about text, but about communal life in which our lives are reshaped in conformity to Christ. As we saw in chapter 6, Bavinck writes that Scripture is the light of the church and the church is the life of Scripture.[20] In chapter 8, I will deal further with our participation in Christ, in the community, and practice of the body of Christ.

These four elements imply (a) the creed that identifies Father, Son, and Spirit as the God in whom we believe, and (b) the canon of the one Scripture as Old and New Testament, whereas the life in the body of Christ implies ordained ministers. Although I will not delve into a discussion of the three instruments that the early church had to keep the church close to Christ (canon, creed, and episcopate), I do want to mention the relationship between these four elements and the three instruments.[21]

In what follows I will further investigate the beliefs that follow from faith in Jesus Christ and should regulate the Christian reading of Scripture. In 7.3, I focus on the grand narrative of Scripture, and in 7.4, I will deal further with beliefs about the relationship between Christ and Scripture.

7.3 ONE STORY?

As I already mentioned, the *Tanakh* has an open end. The *Tanakh* is a diverse collection, with the *Torah*, the *Nevi'im* (a diversity of prophetic books), and the *Ketuvim* (the writings with poetry, wisdom, the five *Megillot*, and some other books). It all starts with the *Torah*, but does it imply a story that continues? How will God fulfill the promises to Abraham and his people Israel? Will God restore the kingship of David's house, or will Israel be restored from its division and exile completely? The prophets give reason to expect this. And does this imply hope for the gentiles as well?

This diversity of texts is read differently, and an important issue is the question of whether the New Testament is the continuation of the *Tanakh*. Here, Jewish and Christian readings of the *Tanakh* differ. Emphasizing the difference between the *Tanakh* and the New Testament as well as between Jewish and Christian readings of Scripture, Notger Slenczka has proposed a

---

19. Vanhoozer, *First Theology*, 200.

20. Cf. Vanhoozer's emphasis on the performance of the theodrama of Scripture, Vanhoozer, *Drama of Doctrine*.

21. For a discussion of these three instruments, see Van de Beek, *Lichaam en Geest van Christus*, 195–391; Jenson, *Canon and Creed*.

radical separation: leave the *Tanakh* to the Jewish community of the synagogue, and let the church confine herself to reading the New Testament in her liturgy.[22]

The Nicene Creed, however, confesses about Jesus Christ that "the third day he rose again according to the Scriptures." This implies a closer relationship between the history of Jesus Christ and Israel's *Tanakh*. The Nicene Creed implies that the God of Israel has raised the crucified Jew Jesus of Nazareth as the fulfillment of what has been written in the law and the prophets.[23] It also implies that the Holy Spirit given at Pentecost is the same Spirit who has spoken "by the prophets" of the *Tanakh*; and finally, the God of Israel is the Father, Son, and Spirit. This is what we already saw, in Klaas Schilder and Robert Jenson (see 7.2).

The unity of Scripture is contested, by historical criticism, under the influence of postmodernism, and due to the dialogue with the Jewish synagogue. Historical criticism has emphasized the historical diversity of Scripture, postmodernism has criticized the oneness of the Christian grand narrative, and the dialogue with the synagogue has questioned the relationship between the *Tanakh* and the New Testament. However, I will follow the canonical emphasis of the Christian tradition.[24] At the same time, I will not posit unity in advance as if the confession of a certain form of unity should not confirm itself in reading. Theological hermeneutics should respect the diversity of perspectives of biblical books and authors, the historical developments, and the tensions present therein.[25] Systematic theology should not hinder the work of biblical theology or the historical investigations of biblical exegesis, for historical consciousness is valuable.[26] It is primarily the task of biblical theology to reconstruct this metanarrative. With Richard Bauckham and Christopher Wright, I will search for a nonmodern metanarrative that is not suppressive but hospitable to diversity.[27] If Ricoeur is right that a narrative is characterized by "discordant concordance," defined as "the synthesis of the heterogeneous," a narrative is not necessarily

---

22. Slenczka, "Kirche und das Alten Testament." See further Slenczka, *Vom Alten Testament*.

23. Cf. Van de Beek, *Kring om de Messias*, 22, 44–45.

24. Cf. Bartholomew, *Introducing Biblical Hermeneutics*, 52–61.

25. Here, I differ from Jamieson and Wittman, who formulate as the first rule for reading Scripture "read Scripture as a unity . . . as a harmonious testimony to God and his works." They ignore the diversity of perspectives and the development within the history of salvation. See Jamieson and Wittman, *Biblical Reasoning*, 54–57.

26. Cf. Sarisky, *Reading the Bible Theologically*, 57–63, 170–71.

27. Bauckham, *Bible and Mission*, 90, 93; Wright, *Mission of God*, 64.

totalizing.[28] Moreover, I will try to do justice to the Israelite character of Scripture.

In this book, I have a special interest in the significance of Jesus Christ for understanding Scripture as a unity. Thus, it is promising that Craig Bartholomew, referring to both Brevard Childs and Henri de Lubac, writes that "a view of the canon as a whole basically originates in the Christ event itself."[29] To explain this, I first turn to Jesus Christ himself.

7.3.1 Jesus in Luke 24

In Luke 24, we can sense something of the hopes and expectations that Jesus evoked. Two disciples walk back from Jerusalem to Emmaus and tell the stranger they meet about Jesus of Nazareth that he was "a prophet, powerful in word and deed." They "had hoped that he was the one who was going to redeem Israel" (Luke 24:19, 21). Whatever the hopes of Jesus's Jewish contemporaries, his preaching of the coming kingdom of God did resonate with their expectations. Would Jesus be the one who will restore Israel, as the prophet, "Rabbi," "Messiah," "Son of man," "Son of David"?

The continuity between Jesus and Israel's Scriptures can also be seen in Jesus's teaching. I do not intend to solve all questions about the historical Jesus and the authenticity of the gospels. However, to mention some aspects of Jesus's teaching, it is clear that for Jesus, Moses and the Torah were important. According to Matthew, Jesus has said, "Do not think that I have come to abolish the Law or the Prophets; I have not come to abolish them but to fulfill them" (Matt 5:17). Jesus is critical of the human heart, but teaches a way of life in which outward practice and a renewed heart come together. This resonates with the expectations of a new covenant and the circumcision of the heart, as we find it in Deuteronomy, Jeremiah, and Ezekiel. Jesus's words when he celebrates the feast of the unleavened bread suggest that his coming death will bring a new exodus, the new covenant, and forgiveness of sins (Matt 26:27–28; Mark 14:24–25; Luke 22:20). Here, we see that Jesus enacts the coming kingdom in the eating of bread and wine, just as he enacted some days earlier the coming of the king to the temple, evoking the prophecy of Zechariah (Zech 9:9). To conclude, Jesus teaches his disciples to highly respect the law and the prophets, and to expect their fulfillment in his person and ministry—a clear continuity between Israel's Scriptures and himself.[30]

28. Ricoeur, *Oneself as Another*, 141.
29. Bartholomew, *Introducing Biblical Hermeneutics*, 54.
30. On Jesus and the Scriptures of Israel, see Blomberg, "Reflections on Jesus's View";

In Luke 24, we hear about Jesus himself, after his resurrection, teaching his disciples again, regarding what is said in Moses and all the prophets, concerning himself, his death, and his resurrection. Because of what the prophets have spoken, Christ had "to suffer these things and then enter his glory" (Luke 24:25-27). The cross of Jesus is no reason to lose all hope as Cleopas and his wife or friend did, but the fulfillment of Israel's Scripture and something that had to happen to redeem Israel.

Later in Luke 24, Luke tells us that Jesus comes to his disciples in Jerusalem and sketches the beginning of a narrative line. This is all not immediately evident, for Jesus first "opened their minds so that they could understand the Scriptures" (Luke 24:45). At the same time, they should have understood this earlier, for Jesus reproaches them that they were "foolish" and "slow of heart to believe" (Luke 24:25). In this chapter, I am especially interested in beliefs about Scripture related to faith in Jesus Christ that regulate the Christian reading and interpretation of Scripture. Nevertheless, it is significant to note that the two walking to Emmaus as well as the apostles, both needed another person, or even Jesus himself and his Spirit, to open their eyes. The source experience of a personal encounter with Jesus results in these regulative beliefs. Reading on their own, they did not see. This has two aspects: it shows the need for a guide (against reading as an individual; the aspect of the community) and it also shows the need for illumination (to counter the noetic consequences of sin; the aspect of renewal).

What Jesus sketches presupposes that "everything must be fulfilled that is written about me in the Law of Moses, the Prophets, and the Psalms" (Luke 24:44). Then Jesus continues (Luke 24:46-49):

> This is what is written: Christ will suffer and rise from the dead on the third day, and repentance and forgiveness of sins will be preached in his name to all nations, beginning at Jerusalem. You are witnesses of these things. I am going to send you what my Father has promised but stay in the city until you have been clothed with power from on high.

The lines Jesus sketches both presuppose a continuation with the Scriptures of Israel and its fulfillment in his death, his resurrection, the gift of the Holy Spirit at Pentecost to empower the disciples for their mission, and the mission to the nations to bring them also the good news of repentance and forgiveness of sins.[31] Thus, to be a disciple of the risen Jesus Christ implies a

---

Greijdanus, *Schriftbeginselen ter schriftverklaring*, 66-83; Keener, *Spirit Hermeneutics*, 205-18. See further Wright, *Jesus and the Victory of God*, 274-97, 405-28, 553-63.

31. On Luke 24 and its hermeneutical significance, see Bartholomew, *Introducing Biblical Hermeneutics*, 54-56; Keener, *Spirit Hermeneutics*, 35, 42-43, 49; Vanhoozer,

new metanarrative with a messianic and missional perspective on the Scriptures of Israel. Christian believers read the Scripture of Israel as part of a new metanarrative in the *imitatio Christi*, as followers of Christ.

7.3.2 The New Testament Writers

The writers of the New Testament continue and elaborate on this teaching of the risen Jesus Christ regarding Scripture. His teaching introduces a second direction to the reading of the *Tanakh*: we can follow the order of its books from Genesis until its fulfillment in Jesus as the Messiah, and we can reread the *Tanakh* in the light of its fulfillment in Jesus the Messiah.[32] The Gospels, especially Matthew and John, emphasize repeatedly that something happened with Jesus concerning the fulfillment of the words of Scripture.[33] At the beginning of his Gospel, Matthew gives his understanding of the history of Israel. In his genealogy of Jesus, Matthews demonstrates that he takes the Scriptures of Israel together as one story. He divides the story into three parts: from Abraham to David, from David to the exile, and from the exile to Jesus Christ. Abraham, David, the exile, and Jesus Christ represent crucial moments in this story. Where Matthew tells the story of Israel, Luke's genealogy tells the story of the whole of humanity, thus implying that Jesus has significance for all humanity. Luke traces Jesus through the history of Israel back to Genesis and "the son of Adam, the son of God" (Luke 3:38).[34]

About Paul's understanding of Jesus and the Scriptures of Israel, much has been written. Paul, an educated Pharisaic scribe well acquainted with the Scriptures of Israel, often alludes to the Old Testament, especially to Isaiah, Psalms, Deuteronomy, and Genesis. What God has done in Jesus Christ is a climax in Israel's history. Paul's intertextual play with the Scriptures of Israel is based on his belief that the stories of Israel can be read typologically, as a prefiguration of the Christ event and the community of Christian believers. It is the same God who acts in the history of Israel and the *kairos*-moment

---

Drama of Doctrine, 120, 210, 221–22; Wright, *Mission of God*, 29–31, 41, 60, 66, 247, 303. Vanhoozer takes Acts 8 as a starting point for his reflections on the Christocentric reading of Scripture, see Vanhoozer, *Drama of Doctrine*, 116–20.

32. Rereading the *Tanakh* in the light of Christ does not make superfluous the first reading that follows the direction of the *Tanakh*. In the approach of Jamieson and Wittman, however, this first reading does not play a role and seems forgotten. See Jamieson and Wittman, *Biblical Reasoning*.

33. Matt 1:22; 2:15, 17; 4:14; 8:17; 12:17; 13:14, 35; 21:4; 27:9; and John 2:22; 7:38; 10:35; 12:38; 13:18; 15:25; 17:12; 19:24, 28, 36–37; 20:9.

34. On the Gospels, see, e.g., Blomberg, "Reflections on Jesus's View"; Greijdanus, *Schriftbeginselen ter schriftverklaring*, 83–85; Hays, *Reading Backwards*.

in his own days. Jesus is the Messiah of Israel and he fulfills the Scriptures of Israel.[35] Regarding a possible metanarrative, Gal 3 is an interesting chapter. Here, Paul mentions three persons and uses three concepts to understand Israel's story: Abraham and the promise, Moses and the law, and Christ and faith. Christ is the seed of Abraham, who bears the curse of the law and brings the blessing of Abraham to the nations (Gal 3:6–25). Now, through faith in Christ, even the gentiles will share in the promise to Abraham and receive the promised heritage, the Spirit who adopts us as children of God (Gal 3:26—4:6).

Based on Paul's writings, N. T. Wright has given a detailed reconstruction of Paul's understanding of the plots and subplots of the biblical narrative.[36] The outer story is about God and creation. God created the world with a purpose, but due to human acts things have gone wrong. God will come to judge and restore his creation. That restoring judgment of God will bring an end to the present age, and the age to come will begin.

The first subplot is about humanity, which was created to bring creation to its purpose. However, human beings failed to play their part in God's plan to reflect God's glory to his creation and bring this world to God's destiny. God's relationship with humanity is broken, and sin and death threaten us. Now, the restoration of both God's relationship with humanity and of humanity itself is necessary, so that humanity can reflect again God's glory and take its place in God's plan with creation.

Here, the second subplot comes in, the story of Abraham and his seed Israel. God's intention with Israel was to rescue humanity from rebellion, sin, and death. Abraham and his family were called to be a blessing for humanity, but they proved to be part of the problem of humanity themselves and failed due to their covenant rebellion.

The third subplot is about the role of the Torah. The Torah was given to Israel to play its part as a light for the nations. However, from the first moment that the Torah was given, it has shown Israel that it shares in the Adamic problem of humanity. The Torah has a paradoxical function in Israel's story, both as a helper and an opponent. It keeps Israel together, but also makes it more sinful so that Israel will suffer from the curse of the law instead of being a blessing unto the nations until Israel itself will be saved and restored.

The story of Jesus presents the solution to the problems of all the other stories. The crucified Messiah is God's answer to the problems of all the other (sub)plots. He is the Messiah, the rescuer of the rescue operation with

---

35. Cf. Hays, *Echoes of Scripture*.
36. Wright, *Paul and the Faithfulness of God*, 475–537.

the name Israel, who fulfills Israel's calling. He is the true Israel, the seed of Abraham, who brings God's blessing to the world. And he is last Adam, the new man who will bring creation to its purpose.

God is the one God of Israel, who is faithful to his creation and his purpose for creation; to humanity and his plan for humans in creation; to his covenant with Abraham and Israel to restore humanity and creation. He is faithful, although humans and Israel rebel against him. In Christ Jesus, he returns to his people and becomes their king again. What God does in Christ and through his Spirit shows a radical view of the problem of evil: dark powers and human sin together plunged creation into darkness. The one God of Israel, however, is willing and able to rescue his rescue operation and give the real answer to the human plight. God himself, identified with Jesus and present in his Spirit, brings the solution to the dark problem of evil.

To conclude this impressionist overview of how diverse the books of Scripture are, the New Testament presents the beginning of a metanarrative. Looking back to the *Tanakh*, this rudimentary metanarrative runs like this. It starts with Adam and creation. Adam's first sin is the beginning of a process in which evil more and more influences the entire world. This is a reason for God to make a new beginning with Abraham, to rescue and bless the world. Israel grows and is liberated from Egypt in the exodus through Moses's hand. At Mount Sinai, Israel receives the law. In the promised land, Israel receives David as its king with a promise of a house of kings for his sons. However, during Israel's history, it becomes evident that Israel shares the same problem as all of humanity: sin. Israel's prophets announce God's judgment and promise, and the restoration of Israel and the Davidic kingship. Part of this restoration will be that God will make a new covenant with Israel, including the circumcision of the heart, according to the expectation of Deuteronomy. Israel is divided into two parts and goes into exile. Only a small remnant returns to the land. Then Jesus of Nazareth comes as the fulfillment of Israel's Scriptures. According to the New Testament, he is the promised Messiah, the seed of Abraham, the king on David's throne, and the kingly high-priest according to the order of Melchizedek. He brings the new covenant with Israel, in him Israel and the nations together will be rescued, in him God's kingdom comes.[37]

---

37. For various reconstructions of the metanarrative, see Bartholomew and Goheen, *Drama of Scripture*; Burger, "God's Character and the Plot"; Goldingay, *Old Testament Theology*; Jackson, *Biblical Metanarrative*; Wright, *Mission of God*; Wright, *New Testament and the People of God*, 139–43; Watkins, *Drama of Preaching*, 31–44.

7.3.3 A Covenant-Story?

If the New Testament presents the beginning of a metanarrative, new questions rise. How should we tell this metanarrative? Should this metanarrative be constructed as a covenant-story? It seems that good reasons exist to do so. In the work of N. T. Wright, the covenant is an important theme in the story of Scripture, as seen in the title of his book *The Climax of the Covenant*.[38] In the Reformed and Presbyterian traditions, covenant is an important concept to reconstruct the story of Scripture but also to understand Scripture as such.

Standing in the Presbyterian tradition, both Michael Horton and Kevin Vanhoozer use the concept of covenant as a central concept to understanding the nature and function of Scripture. Horton emphasizes repeatedly that the covenant is the context for Scripture. Both Horton and Vanhoozer characterize the canon of Scripture as a covenant document. According to Vanhoozer, the triune God uses Scripture in the discourse of the covenant. In their approaches, "the covenant" is the central category to understanding the relationship between God and humanity.[39]

This approach presupposes that "covenant" is the central category in the relationship between God and humanity. "Covenant" is mostly used in singular. Something like a "covenant of works" or a "covenant of creation" has to exist. The distance between God and humanity has to be bridged by a covenant and the relation between God and creation has to be understood within a "covenant ontology."[40]

However, the picture changes when "covenant" should not be identified with "relationship" and when the covenant of works does not exist. In Scripture, a covenant regulates, shapes, or directs a relationship that oftentimes exists already. Often, new covenants are made as a reaction to a situation of crisis to give renewed stability to the relationship. With Arie Leder, many biblical covenants can be characterized as "redemptive instruments."[41] For many reasons, I prefer a theology without a covenant of works and a covenant ontology, but instead with an ontology of love and a series of covenants building on another.[42] Accordingly, "covenant" is not the

---

38. Wright, *Climax of the Covenant*. See further Wright, *Jesus and the Victory of God*, 274–97; Wright, *Paul and the Faithfulness of God*, 783–815.

39. Horton, *Covenant and Eschatology*; Vanhoozer, *First Theology*, 159–206; Vanhoozer, *Drama of Doctrine*, 133–50.

40. See, e.g., Horton, *Covenant and Salvation*, 182–242.

41. Leder, "Divine Presence (Part Three)," 695; cf. 691–92.

42. See Burger, "Story of God's Covenants"; Burger, "Theology without a Covenant of Works."

most fundamental category in Scripture, when the story of the relationship between God and humanity is concerned.[43]

At the same time, it is significant that at important moments in the story of Scripture, one or more covenants are made: with Abraham, Israel after the exodus from Egypt, David, and the new covenant in Christ after the exile. This chain of covenants does give access to the coherence of the biblical metanarrative and to the acts of God in the history of humanity and Israel.[44] In the covenants with Abraham, God starts his rescue operation of the world. In Abraham's seed, the world of the gentiles will be blessed. In the covenants with Israel, the relationship with Abraham's children is shaped further, with an eye to their life in the promised land. The covenant with David the king gives extra strength to the covenants with Abraham and Israel. In the new covenant, the seed of Abraham bears the curse of the law and makes God's blessing available to the gentiles, the new covenant with Israel is made, and David's royal house is restored.[45] Seeing these relationships between the covenants and the new covenant that became a reality in Christ, the coherence of the history of salvation and the position of Christ within that history can also be seen.[46]

7.3.4. Participation in Christ

Until now, we have seen that according to Luke 24, Jesus Christ himself sketches lines through Scripture that suggest the reconstruction of one metanarrative (7.3.1). Furthermore, at several moments the writers of the New Testament suggest building blocks of such a reconstruction (7.3.2). And finally, the chain of covenants in Scripture helps to see the coherence of the scriptural narratives (7.3.3). When dealing with Schilder, we saw that

43. See, e.g., Stek, "'Covenant' Overload in Reformed Theology"; Leder, "Presence, Then the Covenants (Part One)."

44. It is significant that recently the covenants have been used often to reconstruct the metanarrative of Scripture. See, e.g., Burger, "Story of God's Covenants"; Dumbrell, *Covenant and Creation*; Gentry, *Kingdom through Covenant*; Hahn, *Kinship by Covenant*; Horton, *God of Promise*; Leder, "Divine Presence (Part Two)"; Renihan, *Mystery of Christ*; Wright, *Mission of God*, 324–56.

45. More extensively, see Burger, "Story of God's Covenants." On Israel and the problem of supersessionism, see Burger, "Theirs Are the Covenants."

46. Here I differ from Van de Beek. According to Van de Beek, the coherence of the (meta)narrative of Scripture cannot be understood in terms of "salvation history." "In the relationship of God and human beings is no progression, only a fulfilment," he writes. In his opposition to the idea of progress, he does not see the development in the chain of covenants. See Van de Beek, *Lichaam en Geest van Christus*, 292; and further 292–96.

Schilder not only reads Scripture as one story but also thinks that the believers participate in that story.

The idea of our participation in the story of Scripture is an important regulative idea for our reading and interpretation of Scripture, but what is the justification behind that idea? When do we read stories as our stories? First, we do so if we own the story, in the sense that either the story is our story or we are part of a collective that is the owner of the story. Second, when we recognize what the story speaks of and when we identify with the persons in the story. But this can be hopeful fantasy or wishful thinking. A white male European will not read Chinese, African, or Native American mythologies as his own stories. What is the reason for reading the stories of Scripture as my stories?

In Eph 2, it is made clear that formerly, for someone who is gentile by birth and not circumcised, no reason existed to read the stories of Israel as "my story." The gentiles were "excluded from citizenship in Israel and foreigners to the covenants of the promise, without hope, and without God in the world" (Eph 2:12). Jesus Christ had made the difference: in Jesus Christ, the distance is taken away (v. 13). He has made Jew and gentile together, "to create in himself one new humanity out of the two" (v. 15). Both are "built on the foundation of the apostles and prophets, with Christ Jesus himself as the chief cornerstone" (v. 20), one building and one "holy temple in the Lord," "a dwelling in which God lives by his Spirit" (vv. 21–22).

The letters of Paul show that this has implications for how Jewish and gentile believers read and hear the story of Jesus Christ. Using the language of "into Christ," "in Christ" and "with Christ," Paul establishes a relationship between the biography of his readers and the story of Jesus Christ. Baptism marks this identification. Romans 6 can serve as a clear example. His readers were "baptized into Christ Jesus," "buried with him," their "old self was crucified with him," and they "will also live with him" and may count themselves "dead to sin but alive to God in Christ Jesus" (Rom 6:3–11).[47] This interpretation of the story of Jesus Christ implies that Jesus Christ is the substitute and representative of a new humanity and that all baptized believers participate in his story. Thus, the ministry of Jesus Christ as representative Messiah is crucial in the identification of believers with the story of Jesus Christ.

For reading the entire Scripture as "my" Scripture, however, more is necessary.[48] Identification with the story of Jesus Christ is still different from

---

47. On Paul and on participation in Christ as participation in his story, see Burger, *Being in Christ*, 158–279; Burger, *Life in Christ*, 137–72; Campbell, *Paul and Union with Christ*; Thate et al., *"In Christ" in Paul*.

48. "My" story should not be read individualistic, but signals existential involvement

identification with the story of Israel. For gentile believers, participation in Christ must be participation in the Messiah of Israel. First of all, the Jew, Jesus of Nazareth, is Israel's Messiah, and Israel's Messiah is the fulfillment of the *Tanakh* of Israel. That means that someone who is introduced in the story of Jesus Christ comes to share in Israel's story as well; gentiles are "no longer foreigners and strangers, but fellow citizens with God's people and also members of his household" (Eph 2:19). This does not mean that the gentiles replace Israel, but that according to the Jewish authors of the New Testament gentile believers are received into Israel's family. It is painful for Jews and shameful for Christians that the history of Jews and Christians has been a history of hostility, whereas the Jew Paul preached the gospel of the Messiah who has put to death hostility, making peace (Eph 2:15–16). It is only by the grace of God that gentile believers share in the new covenant with Israel, in Israel's Messiah, and in the kingdom of God.[49]

If Jesus Christ is the promised Messiah of Israel and the fulfillment of the *Tanakh*, and if the God of Israel exists as the one who interacts with human beings in history, establishes covenants with Abraham and his family (his seed), and makes promises (and I believe these to be true), the redemptive-historical approach of which the Dutch theologian Herman Bavinck was representative and which is also my tradition, the narrative approach that emerged after the linguistic turn, and the more recent theodramatic approach of Michael Horton and Kevin Vanhoozer, are complementary.[50] In Christ, the historical acts of God, the story of the history of salvation, and our dramatic participation in this grand narrative, all belong together as the world behind the text, the world of the text, and the world in front of the text. For those who participate in Christ, their context is not suffering so much from a historical distance from Jesus Christ. By union with and participation in Christ, their context is primarily the context of the new covenant with Israel, of participation in Christ in the light of Easter, and of a new heart by the inhabitation of the Holy Spirit given at Pentecost.[51]

---

which is always personal; cf. Keener, *Spirit Hermeneutics*, 237–38.

49. Cf. Burger, "Theirs Are the Covenants."

50. Horton, *Covenant and Eschatology*; Vanhoozer, *Drama of Doctrine*.

51. Sarisky writes in a similar fashion, "What secures the fundamental similarity of readers is . . . their location within one and the same saving economy . . . unified by the action of the triune God," Sarisky, *Reading the Bible Theologically*, 229.

7.3.5 The Metanarrative of Scripture and the Story of Jesus Christ

If this reconstruction of the metanarrative of Scripture is correct, Scripture speaks of a God who patiently and lovingly works toward the salvation of his creation and the coming of his kingdom, and who sends his Son Jesus Christ as the climax of his interactions with humanity and Israel. Importantly, this metanarrative is not a modern suppressive story but has to be hospitable and open to many other small stories. This is important to do justice to the diversity of human stories (think of the stories of Ruth and Esther), but also to do justice to the diversity of human experiences.

A rich Christology helps to create this hospitable openness. It is the story of Jesus Christ that interprets the Scriptures as well as the lives of believers who identify with Christ. The richer our view of Jesus Christ, the greater the diversity of stories, genres, and experiences that can be welcomed "in Christ." A rich Christology means a Christology that explains the significance of different moments of his history. Consequently, I will not follow Jamieson and Wittman who focus entirely on the glory of Christ.[52] According to Bonhoeffer, we are conformed to Christ's incarnation, crucifixion, and resurrection. This means that we become truly human (incarnation), suffer, are judged (crucifixion), and live a new life amid the old (resurrection).[53] Oliver O'Donovan adds to this the exaltation of Christ: we must speak about the resurrection (and thus about creation), about exaltation (the final redemption will come, for Christ reigns in heaven and has given the Holy Spirit as firstfruits), about the cross (which implies reconciliation), and finally advent (the appearance of Jesus as the fulfillment of Israel's promises).[54] According to Veli-Matti Kärkkäinen (following Jürgen Moltmann), it is important as well to see the significance of the earthly life of Jesus. Otherwise, we will lose "Christopraxis" (discipleship, community, care for the weak).[55] Keener warns about readings of Scripture with a strong focus on personal application that forget "God's larger kingdom agendas."[56] Frank Macchia, finally, adds from a Pentecostal perspective the importance

---

52. Jamieson and Wittman claim that the "Christian's hope . . . to see Christ's glory . . . structures our relationship with God and others and shape how we suffer, lament, pray, pursue and receive temporal goods, and more." Jamieson and Wittman, *Biblical Reasoning*, 12. However, they fail to show how their focus helps to do justice to the diversity of experiences of Christians. Their Christology is too narrow. Cf. Jamieson and Wittman, *Biblical Reasoning*, 3–22.

53. Bonhoeffer, *Dietrich Bonhoeffer Works*, 106–8.

54. O'Donovan, *Resurrection and Moral Order*, xvii. See also O'Donovan, *Desire of the Nations*, 133–46, 174–92.

55. Kärkkäinen, *Christ and Reconciliation*, 42–47.

56. Keener, *Spirit Hermeneutics*, 237.

of Pentecost and the baptism with the Spirit. This regards the inhabitation of Christ in the Spirit, our incorporation in Christ, and the resulting fruits of transformation and empowerment for mission.[57] This implies that we need a Christology that includes these moments at least:

> a. Advent: The coming of Christ to his own to fulfill Israel's promises, to be the incarnation of the Word of God, to embody God's presence in his creation, and to accomplish his mission in obedience.
>
> b. Jesus's earthly life: As a full human being, Jesus practiced the kingdom of God, preaching the good news of the kingdom, establishing signs of the kingdom, and bringing liberation, healing, and community.
>
> c. Suffering and the cross: The righteous Jesus encountered opposition and rejection, he took our sins and the consequences of our sins, he suffered God's judgment, our guilt, and the brokenness of our existence, lamented because of injustice and godforsakenness, gave his spirit back to God when he died.
>
> d. Resurrection: Christ was vindicated and justified, he was risen from the dead and transformed, and he is a hopeful beginning of the new creation.
>
> e. Ascension: Christ is exalted in majesty and glory, but he is also hidden by a cloud and no longer visible to us, direct experience of Christ is not possible at this moment, his presence now is hidden;
>
> f. Pentecost: Christ baptizes with the Holy Spirit to fulfill, incorporate, transform, and empower, as a beginning and guarantee of the final fulfillment.

In light of these different aspects of the story of Jesus Christ, we can recognize a diversity of human experiences. As Christian believers, we can learn to understand these experiences as aspects of participation in Christ. We share in his life, cross, death, resurrection, and ascension, and receive his Spirit.[58] Furthermore, this story of Jesus and our participation in this story helps to interpret the variety of biblical passages: prophecies of judgment, justice, and hope; psalms of praise, prayer, and lament; and wisdom, voicing justice and futility. It also helps us interpret various moments in the story of salvation: promise, expectation, decisive moments of salvation and fulfillment, hope for more than what has been given here and now, the

---

57. Macchia, *Jesus the Spirit Baptizer*.
58. See, e.g., Burger, *Life in Christ*.

eschatological tension of yet and not yet, and moments of contrast when we face disobedience and unbelief. Accordingly, the coherence of the metanarrative does not oppose the importance of wisdom and discernment. When a story is a "synthesis of the heterogeneous" (Ricoeur), we need the wisdom to see in which situation we refer to which part of the story to let Scripture be light on our path.

7.3.6 Christian Ethics and the Story of Scripture

If the story of Jesus Christ regulates our interpretation of the Scriptures, this is also the case in the field of Christian ethics when Scripture is used.[59] The *Tanakh* is fulfilled in Christ, which means fulfilled (a) through Christ's teaching; (b) through Christ's obedience; and (c) through participation in Christ.

> a. Christ shows us the full breadth and depth of Scripture including its commandments.[60] What this looks like, we see in the sermon on the mount (Matt 5–7).
>
> b. Christ is obedient to Scripture, both in his life and in his willingness to be obedient until the end of the death on the cross. His righteousness that makes us righteous, encompasses both this active and passive obedience, as the Reformed tradition has called them.
>
> c. Now the power of sin is broken, the Holy Spirit makes us participate in Christ, "in order that the righteous requirements of the law might be fully met in us" (Rom 8:4). When we clothe ourselves with the Lord Jesus Christ (Rom 13:14) we are both justified and transformed. In the transformation into Christlikeness, we become obedient to the law of Christ and the Spirit as well.[61]

We have to take more seriously that we are no longer under the law (Gal 3:23—4:7) than the Reformed tradition usually does. The law that came after the promise has lost its power over us. At the same time, we live with the law of the Spirit (Rom 8:2). I will not try to solve all discussions about Paul and the law.[62] But seen from Christ's death and resurrection,

---

59. On the use of Scripture in ethics, starting from God's works in Christ, see, e.g., De Bruijne, "Christian Ethics and God's Use."

60. On the importance of Christ as fulfiller and on fulfilment, see Douma, *Grondslagen christelijke ethiek*, 107–8.

61. Keener, *Spirit Hermeneutics*, 219–25.

62. See, e.g., Van Bruggen, *Paul*, 214–53; Spanje, *Inconsistency in Paul?*; Wright, *Paul and the Faithfulness of God*, 505–16.

all commandments, including the ten commandments (Exod 20), have lost their control over us.[63] It is up to Jesus Christ to determine what is still significant for us to follow. Accordingly, the Sabbath commandment is not the exception, but the paradigm for how we receive the Old Testament commandments.[64] The Torah and its commandments come to us in Christ. The teaching and the example of Christ (moral), the sacrificial death of Christ (ceremonial), and the reign of Christ over heaven and earth (civil) will help us to discern what it means to fulfill the law after Easter as followers of Christ and after Pentecost in the Spirit.[65]

Thus, I agree with Oliver O'Donovan that Christian moral thinking has to follow the history of salvation. In 5.5 we saw O'Donovan's opinion that each area of moral interest "has to be given . . . a salvation-history of its own."[66] Dealing with a moral question, we have to reconstruct the story of God's dealings with a moral area and Christ will have a central position in this story. Accordingly, De Bruijne writes, following O'Donovan's path, that the task of Christian ethics is not to "repeat the instantiations but to connect the narrative of God's work in Christ to situations and questions we face today."[67] This is in line with O'Donovan's formula of "thinking out of Scripture" as "[A → B] → [X → Y]."[68]

As a consequence, the role of hermeneutics in moral issues should not be overestimated. It is a hermeneutical insight that moral decisions today do not follow directly from biblical passages. But it is a biblical-theological, systematic-theological, and practical-theological task to reconstruct the salvation history of God's work in Christ, to reflect on moral questions, and to formulate moral decisions for a life of participation in Christ. Take as an example the ordination of women. If theological hermeneutics knows in advance what should be decided, this is a bad hermeneutics, since it prevents the interpreter from being surprised or contradicted, and it is an obstacle to moral thinking. Hermeneutics reflects critically on problems in understanding biblical passages, the history of Christian theological reflection, the contemporary and local situation, or the various (opposite) positions in the debate. The proposal by William Webb of a redemptive movement hermeneutic shows that hermeneutical reflection, the reconstruction of the

---

63. Thus, the path of "Christian Reconstruction" is a dead end street; cf. Douma, *Grondslagen christelijke ethiek*, 110–12.

64. Cf. De Bruijne, "Christian Ethics and God's Use," 177.

65. On the distinction of moral, ceremonial and civil, see Douma, *Grondslagen christelijke ethiek*, 108–10.

66. O'Donovan, *Resurrection, and Moral Order*, xviii.

67. De Bruijne, "Christian Ethics and God's Use," 176.

68. O'Donovan, *Self, World, and Time*, 79.

story of Scripture and its movement, the exegesis of scriptural passages, and the formulation of moral conclusions are all fully theological activities.[69] Further, the positions of complementarianism (man and woman have different but complementary callings and roles) and egalitarianism (the gender roles of man and woman are equal) play a role in the discussion on ordination.[70] The debate about complementarianism and egalitarianism is a theological discussion about the story of God's dealings with man and woman and about the implications for a life of participation in Christ today in a specific context. This theological debate transcends the borders of hermeneutics. And the solution to the discussion on ordination is a theological one. Not everything is hermeneutics.

7.4 QUADRIGA?

In this chapter, I have argued that faith in Christ regulates our understanding and interpretation of Scripture. Following Christ, it is part of the *imitatio Christi* to read Scripture as having one metanarrative. For Christ is the climax of a history in which God in a series of covenants acts with humanity and Israel to restore his creation and bring it to eschatological glory. As Christian believers, we understand that story in the light of the story of Jesus Christ and of our participation in Christ. Christ comes to us in Scripture and in Scripture we encounter Christ. In Christ, we learn to understand Scripture, and in Scripture, we come to know Christ better. Thus, faith in Christ is important for how we as Christian believers read the *Tanakh* or how we use Scripture in moral reflection and deliberation.

Still, it is an open question what this all implies for typological interpretations of Scripture, as this tradition is manifested in the ceilings of the Saint Vitus Church in Naarden. As I mentioned already, we find such a typological interpretation of the *Tanakh* in the New Testament itself. And what do these typological interpretations imply for the possible justification of allegory as a hermeneutical method?

In the contemporary quest for theological hermeneutics, many of the proponents of the "theological interpretation" of Scripture plead for a revaluation of the *quadriga*, the traditional idea of the fourfold sense of Scripture. One of them is Hans Boersma, who has extensively studied patristic exegesis. Boersma builds on the Nouvelle Théologie (Henri de Lubac and Jean Daniélou) as part of a larger project of the reconstruction of a sacramental

---

69. Webb, *Slaves, Women & Homosexuals*.

70. In the contemporary formulation of "complementarianism," an important publication has been Piper and Grudem, *Recovering Biblical Manhood and Womanhood*.

or participatory ontology.⁷¹ In this section, I will discuss typological interpretation, allegorical interpretation, and the *quadriga* in dialogue with his work on the interpretation of Scripture. For Boersma's view of the fourfold sense of Scripture, two important building blocks have to be distinguished: the conviction that Christ is present in the Old Testament and his Christian-Platonist participatory ontology. I will argue for an interpretation of the fourfold sense of Scripture that builds on the presence of Christ in the Old Testament but without a Christian-Platonist ontology.

I will start with an overview of Boersma's position (7.4.1). Next, I will evaluate Boersma's Platonist ontology and argue that this ontology is somewhat problematic (7.4.2). I will then give my alternative interpretation of the four senses of Scripture continuing with Boersma's other building block, the presence of Christ in the Old Testament (7.4.3). Finally, I will also explain why I continue to refer to this presence as "sacramental" (7.4.4).

7.4.1 Hans Boersma

Boersma's central thesis is that behind the exegesis of the church fathers stands one central belief: Christ and the new Christ-reality are present in the Old Testament. The use of typological, allegorical, and sacramental interpretation is not due to philosophical ideas but arises from a specific Christian perspective. Boersma writes, "The reason why the church fathers practiced typology, allegory, and so on is that they were convinced that the reality of the Christ-event was already present (sacramentally) within the history described within the Old Testament narrative."⁷² Thus, this exegetical practice requires several theological beliefs:

> 1. Christ is present in the Old Testament: What the church fathers do in their exegesis is search for Christ who is hidden in the Old Testament like a treasure hidden in the field.⁷³

This implies two further beliefs:

---

71. Boersma, *Nouvelle Théologie and Sacramental Ontology*; Boersma, *Heavenly Participation*; Boersma, *Sacramental Preaching*; Boersma, *Scripture as Real Presence*.

72. Boersma, *Scripture as Real Presence*, 12; see further xv, 15, 17, 82, 103, 130. In this point, Boersma builds on Lubac and Daniélou who both in different ways emphasized also that the spiritual reading of the Old Testament presupposed the presence of Christ in the Old Testament. See Boersma, *Nouvelle Théologie and Sacramental Ontology*, 149–90; Boersma, *Heavenly Participation*, 138, 151.

73. This image was used by Irenaeus; see Boersma, *Scripture as Real Presence*, xv, 17, 130.

1.1 In his providence, God reigns over the history of salvation in a Christ-shaped way rather than in an arbitrary way. How the history of salvation unfolds is in line with the incarnation of the eternal Word of God so that we can discern his shape already in earlier events.[74]

1.2 In a sacramental way, texts and events of the history of salvation before Christ participate in the reality of Christ. The relationship between Christ and earlier events is not merely nominal but sacramental. Just as it is believed that Christ is really present in the sacrament of the Eucharist, Christ as the *res* is present in the Old Testament texts and events as *signum*.[75]

The sacramental-christological reading involves more than just the allegorical-dogmatic reading which finds Christ himself in Scripture. The tropological-moral and the anagogical-eschatological meanings presuppose that the church, believers, and their future can also be found in the text. Consequently, this practice of reading implies more beliefs:

2. Those who are in Christ share in his reality. Christ cannot be separated from his body or from those who are incorporated in him. Christ is always the *totus Christus*.

Accordingly, this implies two further beliefs:

2.1 Where Christ is present, his church is present as well.

2.2 Because Christ or the Christ-reality is present sacramentally in the Old Testament, the church can also be found in the Old Testament.[76]

These other beliefs also concern the future:

3. Part of the reality of Christ is the eschatological goal of history, the heavenly reality of the beatific vision.

Consequently, two other convictions are implied:

---

74. Cf. Boersma, *Scripture as Real Presence*, 24–25.

75. Cf. Boersma, *Nouvelle Théologie and Sacramental Ontology*, 155–57, 174, 180–83; Boersma, *Heavenly Participation*, 149–50; Boersma, *Scripture as Real Presence*, xiii, xv, 17, 79, 96, 102–3, 178, 184.

76. Cf. Boersma, *Heavenly Participation*, 148, 151; Boersma, *Scripture as Real Presence*, xv–xvi, 19, 24, 89, 113–18, 148, 152. In this light, we can understand that not all biblical analogies are christological, as Keener signals rightly; see Keener, *Spirit Hermeneutics*, 244–46.

> 3.1 We have to read Scripture in the light of this ultimate supernatural purpose.
>
> 3.2 We have to read Scripture as part of a spiritual movement in service of the virtuous transformation of our lives and oriented toward this eschatological future.[77]

What this makes clear is that the practice of sacramental reading with the four senses (literal, allegorical, tropological, and anagogical) is an implication of beliefs about the reality of Jesus Christ as the eternal and incarnate Word of God. As the preexisting Word, he was already present sacramentally in the history of salvation before his incarnation, and the providence of God could give events their Christlike form. Moreover, since the believers share in Christ, who is now seated in heaven, they can read Scripture as part of a spiritual and transformational process of participation in Christ, searching for doctrinal truth, transforming direction in their way of life, and eschatological orientation.

For Boersma, this is closely connected with a sacramental or participatory ontology. He writes,

> The Platonist-Christian synthesis made it possible to regard creation, history, and Old Testament as sacramental carriers of a greater reality. Creation, history, and Old Testament had significance throughout most of the Christian tradition precisely because they pointed to and participated in a greater reality: what the Platonists called "Forms" or "Ideas," and what the Christians insisted was the Word of God himself.[78]

So, according to Boersma, the practice of sacramental-christological reading implies another belief.

> 4. Our reality has to be understood in terms of a sacramental and Platonic ontology, claiming the existence of the Platonic forms or ideas in the eternal *Logos*.

To be more specific:

> 4.1 As the incarnation of the eternal *Logos*, Christ is the heavenly reality.

---

77. Cf. Boersma, *Nouvelle Théologie and Sacramental Ontology*, 153–55; Boersma, *Heavenly Participation*, 138; Boersma, *Scripture as Real Presence*, xii, 19–22, 112, 122, 131–58, 249–72.

78. Boersma, *Heavenly Participation*, 38. On participation in the history of the Platonist-Christian tradition, see the overview in Huttinga, *Participation and Communicability*, 39–75.

4.2 Because the eternal *Logos* is sacramentally present in the history of salvation, he gives this history meaning, coherence, and unity.

4.3 The heavenly and eternal *Logos* has to be identified with the Platonic forms or ideas.

4.4 The entire created reality participates sacramentally in the eternal *Logos*, who gives creation its meaning, coherence, and unity.[79]

According to Boersma, a twofold coherence is necessary, although he does not make this distinction himself: the coherence in time of the history of salvation and the coherence of the created reality. For the sake of the latter coherence, Christian Platonism is necessary. In Boersma's reconstruction, the history of theology and philosophy nominalism caused both the horizontal fragmentation of history into disconnected events as well as the vertical separation of created objects from their transcendent and eternal origins.[80] The impact of this vertical separation concerns not just the interpretation of Scripture but is far deeper, leading to voluntarism and relativism in the field of ethics.

7.4.2 Is Platonism Necessary?

The question is, however, if both forms of meaningful coherence are necessary, or if it is possible to continue the practice of spiritual interpretation without Platonism. In search of an answer to this question, I will start with Ps 22. Reading Ps 22 with the story of the cross and resurrection of Jesus Christ in mind, the psalm proves to be mysterious and prophetic. The analogies between this psalm and the story of Jesus Christ are many. It is hard, if not impossible, to imagine that this psalm was written without God's hidden wisdom (cf. 1 Cor 2:7) or the inspiration of his Holy Spirit. It is, therefore, not surprising that the early church said that allusions to Jesus Christ were already present in this psalm.

It will be clear that I believe that the God of Israel is the triune God of the Christian faith and that this God is actively involved in our world which is also his creation. If we follow the tradition of the church and the Nicene Creed, God the Father is acting providentially in history, God the Son is the eternal and preexistent Word of God, and God the Spirit has inspired the

---

79. Cf. Boersma, *Heavenly Participation*, 23–51; Boersma, *Scripture as Real Presence*, 3–6, 9–12.

80. Cf. Boersma, *Nouvelle Théologie and Sacramental Ontology*, 16; Boersma, *Heavenly Participation*, 21–39, 67, 76–81, 88–94; Boersma, *Scripture as Real Presence*, 7–8, 96.

prophets that have written Scripture. Furthermore, I believe that this God gives eternal salvation in the history of Jesus Christ. If it is correct to believe this and if these convictions are true, I have no problems with the above-implied beliefs 1, 2, and 3:

1. Christ is present in the Old Testament.

2. Those who are in Christ share in his reality.

3. Part of the reality of Christ is the eschatological goal of history, the heavenly reality of the beatific vision.

When these three beliefs and their implications are true, the practice of spiritual reading can be continued.

This practice of spiritual reading is a christological reading. It presupposes that God can do things in a Christlike manner in the history of salvation before Christ and that his Spirit can inspire human authors to write scriptural texts that reveal Christ before his incarnation. Furthermore, Christ is seen as the representative of Israel and of humanity but also as the embodiment of what God has to say (the incarnation of the Word of God). Moreover, in the community of the church as the body of Christ, believers participate in Christ. This means that they receive a Christlike character more and more in a lifelong process of transformation until Christ returns on the last day. But does this practice imply a Christian form of Platonism? This is the case in belief 4 in my reconstruction:

4. Our reality has to be understood in terms of a sacramental and Platonic ontology claiming the existence of the Platonic forms or ideas in the eternal *Logos*.

Within the movement of nouvelle théologie, Jean Daniélou has claimed that we need to distinguish between typology and allegory within patristic exegesis. On the one hand, there is the good christological typology that does justice to the text. On the other hand, there is the problematic allegorical reading that gives everything a symbolic meaning and has the Platonism of Philo as its source.[81] Henri de Lubac, however, had no problems with the allegorical reading.[82] Craig Bartholomew supports Daniélou, distinguishing between typology, which follows the history of salvation and has an eschatological pull, and allegory, which has a strong tendency toward a Platonist vertical pull.[83] Both Boersma and Ypenga, however, conclude that

---

81. Cf. Danielou, *From Shadows to Reality*, 64–65, 111–12, 149, 226, 287–88.

82. On this discussion, see Boersma, *Nouvelle Théologie and Sacramental Ontology*, 180–90; Ypenga, "Sacramentum," 45–53.

83. Cf. Bartholomew, *Introducing Biblical Hermeneutics*, 130–31, 141–42.

the distinction between typology and allegory does not help understand patristic and medieval exegesis.[84] Still, apart from the terms of typology and allegory, it is important to distinguish the salvation-historical eschatological movement and the Platonic upward movement. The first is connected with the historical unity and coherence of the history of salvation, while the second is connected with the ontological unity and coherence of the created reality. Do we need both of them or can we suffice with a coherent and united view of the history of salvation? What conclusions, exactly, follow from the presence of Christ in the Old Testament? Boersma understands the presence of Christ in the Old Testament as a sacramental presence. Let us presuppose that Christ is really present in the sacrament (which I believe is the case). This implies further beliefs.

> 5. God can use elements from his creation for meaningful and saving communication and communion with human beings. God can use a psalm, an Old Testament story, or bread and wine to communicate his salvation with us.

Accordingly, it is logical to hold the following conviction, as well.

> 6. God has created this world and events in the history of salvation so that he can use them for meaningful and saving communication and communion.

Thus, God uses specific elements from the created and historical reality in specific situations to be present with us in a specific way and to communicate his saving presence with us in a specific communicative act. It is a possibility that God chooses to be sacramentally present in particular events or texts.

According to Boersma, this justifies a generalization: God is sacramentally present in the created reality as a whole, for the entire created reality participates in the eternal *Logos*. Here an important shift is made. We start with a model of *interpersonal communication*. God communicates meaningfully with humanity and uses elements of his creation to communicate personally with us. In Scripture, the Eucharist, the church, and even in creation, God's Word can be heard and read so that we can consciously live in God's presence. In this historical model, God can be seen as a dynamic God coming from the *eschaton* in Christ the redeemer.

According to Boersma, God's use of words and events in a historical event (becoming) implies a participatory, ontological relationship between

---

84. Cf. Boersma, *Nouvelle Théologie and Sacramental Ontology*, 188–90; Ypenga, "Sacramentum," 47–48, 52–53.

created words and events, on the one hand, and a divine reality (being) on the other.[85] From a model of personal interaction, a shift is made to a model of *participatory ontology*. According to this model, our creation is a meaningful one because the natural world sacramentally participates in the supernatural world, that is, the temporal participates in the eternal. Now impersonal categories are used. The danger looms that the emphasis is no longer on history but on vertical relationships between time and eternity. This is related to another impending shift of emphasis—the historical Christ becomes the eternal *Logos* who, as the mediator of creation, can be identified with the Platonic ideas or forms.

However, I have some problems with this Platonism. First, it presupposes a cycle of *exitus* and *reditus*. This reality is perceived as a cyclic movement from eternal unity to temporal plurality and back to eternal unity. Human history is replotted, accordingly, as what Oliver O'Donovan has called an "ecstatic and self-gathering movement of being" and is perceived in the light of vertical dynamics between the natural and the supernatural. O'Donovan further remarks that the return to God is a "confirmation of the *first* movement of our being."[86] This means that the origin of the movement is emphasized. In the movement, "There is self-transcendence, but it is intellectual; it is not the historical transcendence of end over beginning."[87] Furthermore, the historical character of the dynamics of God's interaction with his creation and with humanity are ignored and the possibility of eschatological newness or a surprisingly unexpected act of God's love is excluded. Moreover, the liturgical act of worship, including the Eucharistic movement of praise and thankfulness, is seen as part of this ontological cycle.

But love and liturgy are more than what is ontologically necessary. A model of interpersonal communion can do justice, more completely, to the freedom, creativity, and abundance of this "more." Love does not only do what is necessary but also what is unexpected, new, and generous. Love brings something into existence that did not exist before. This is true of the eschatological act of God as well as the Eucharistic act of the human liturgy. The sacrifice of praise and thankfulness in which the creation is sanctified is not just ontologically necessary. It is more of a free act of interpersonal communication.

Second, Platonism offers a solution to a metaphysical problem and answers the question of which world is the real world. The real world is

---

85. In the conclusion of *Scripture as Real Presence*, Boersma uses this word pair of *becoming* and *being*. See Boersma, *Scripture as Real Presence*, 237–79.

86. O'Donovan, *Entering into Rest*, 10.

87. O'Donovan, *Entering into Rest*, 11.

not our world of time and change but the world of eternity and immutability. The result of this solution is the upward pull from time to eternity that has already been mentioned. The Platonic ideas provide an ontological fundamental to our world, giving extra certainty to our existence. However, this leads to a deterministic view of our world. The immutable divine ideas determine our reality. Moreover, it does not help us understand how human uses of signs and language develop.

Our use of signs and language is our way of participating in our world, and its development is guided by changing practical and contextual interests. Our knowledge has a constructive aspect, whereas reality has a certain plasticity. More importantly, God has created a world of temporal, spatial, embodied creatures, and that world is good. We need no higher reality. Furthermore, God's creation is contingent. Although this created reality originates in God's thoughts (God's thoughts are relevant) and although God has created an ordered reality with creatures made according to their kind, his thoughts are free and more is possible than we have seen in this creation until now. God's thoughts are greater than our thoughts.

Where Platonism understands the relationship between God and his creation within a model of ontological participation, an alternative ontology is possible: an ontology of God's communicative and powerful speech acts and God's loving presence. In Scripture, we find such personal and communicative categories (Heb 1:3) as well as the importance of the presence of God's Spirit (Ps 104:30). It is enough that the Creator creates by his Word and is present in his creation, faithfully sustaining it. I do not see why before sin came into the world, an extra guarantee was necessary to give stability to the relationship between God and his creation, whether it be a platonic ontology of participation or a voluntarist covenant ontology.[88] God speaks and enters into a personal relationship of loving nearness. Consequently, that the creation bears witness to the creator should be understood in a communicative model. God wants to communicate his majesty and his loving presence. In his work of art, the artist demonstrates his creativity; in the same way, the creation is an expression of God's glory.

Thus, such a communicative model does not imply a voluntarist separation of God's will from his character and his thoughts. For Boersma, Platonism is necessary to solve the problematic consequences of modern nominalism and voluntarism in Christian ethics. That is, our preferences determine what is good or evil. Indeed, God's creation is not empty or meaningless in a moral sense. However, the work of Oliver O'Donovan shows

---

88. With the concept of the covenant of works, Reformed theology has opted for a voluntarist covenant ontology. On the covenant of works, see Burger, "Theology without a Covenant of Works."

that the problems caused by voluntarism can be solved in another way by using the concept of a created moral order instead of the Platonic theory of forms or ideas (see 5.3). With this idea of a moral order, O'Donovan maintains, on the one hand, the real existence of teleological and generic relations, and, on the other hand, the freedom of the Creator and the contingency of creation.[89]

Third, the doctrine of eternal ideas requires that the eternal *Logos* is more real than created reality. It might be the case that God is the source of reality, but, still, the significance of events in human history is great. According to the narrative of Scripture, human acts—human sin, the obedient acts of the incarnate Son in his human life on earth, and the renewal of humanity in the Spirit—have a crucial impact on the future of creation. How is it possible that events in human history have this impact, and why was the incarnation of the *Logos* important if Platonism is true?

Platonism finds the real reality above history. However, according to the narrative of Scripture, what is decisive for created reality happens in history. The fact that believers participate in the heavenly Christ does not change this. Nor should the believers' participation in the mind of Jesus Christ be understood as participation in the eternal *Logos*. All treasures of wisdom and knowledge are indeed hidden in Christ, not the eternal *logos asarkos*, but Jesus Christ, who died and rose again, the incarnate *Logos*, the embodiment of what God has to say, and in whom God's fullness dwells.

With O'Donovan, I understand Christians' participation in the mind of Christ in a non-Platonic way (see chapter 5). Following O'Donovan, my alternative proposal would be something like what follows. God has made an ordered creation with creatures created with an inherent meaning, according to their own nature. Knowing is our human way to participate in the order of creation. In the act of knowing, human beings participate constructively in the existence of reality with our linguistic acts. Thus, the reality that God has created, has a certain plasticity. Entities are partly linguistic constructions. Accordingly, the quality of our linguistic acts and our human mindset (our *nous*, in Greek biblical terms) is crucial for how we as humans, with our acts of knowing, participate in the cosmos created by God. Here sin has destructive noetic consequences. We rebuild God's reality according to our interests, following our idols. At the same time, transforming participation in the mindset or *nous* of Christ is salutary, both for human beings and for the nonhuman created reality. To conclude, it is necessary that we as human beings participate in the human mind of the incarnate Word, through whom God saves and creates.

---

89. Cf. O'Donovan, *Resurrection and Moral Order*, 31–45.

These three problems show that Platonism has a de-historicizing tendency. Platonism emphasizes the eternal reality of immutable ideas and moves away from the world of time and change. It stimulates a focus on the eternal *Logos* instead of the incarnate Son, Jesus Christ. It leads to a re-plotting of the biblical story that does not help understand the dynamics of the history of salvation and God's loving interaction with fallen humanity.[90] To offer a solution to metaphysical problems, Platonism proposes a participatory ontology, where I would prefer a model of interpersonal communication that does more justice to the creativity and abundance of God's loving interaction with humanity in history.

7.4.3 The Presence of Christ in Scripture and Multiplicity of Meaning

For modern people, deeply influenced by nominalism, the spiritual reading of Scripture seems to be an impossible practice because we do not share the view of a cosmos filled with signs that refer to a divine reality.[91] Nevertheless, I want to continue with the central conviction of the patristic exegesis, which is the other building block of Boersma's view of sacramental reading: the presence of Christ in the Old Testament. In this section, I will sketch an alternative proposal of a theological view that can support this spiritual reading.

Again, I will start with Ps 22. This psalm is a poetic prayer that later became part of the book of Psalms and Old Testament Scripture. The psalm is ascribed to David but it is difficult to reconstruct the original context of the psalm. We may suppose that the psalm was sung or recited many times before and after it was included in the Psalter. It is possible to specify in more detail the meaning of the psalm. I will distinguish between (a) sense (the meaning of an expression that is language-internal; related to the world of the text), (b) reference (the relation between an expression and an extra-linguistic entity; related to the world behind the text), and (c) significance (secondary meanings, emotional and personal associations of an expression; related to the world in front of the text).

> a. *Sense:* Together, the Hebrew words of the psalm create the world of the text.

---

90. When Boersma is dealing with some problems of (Neo)platonism for the Christian faith, he does not seem to see this problem; see Boersma, "All One in Christ."

91. Cf. Ypenga, "Sacramentum," 33.

b. *Reference*: The psalm refers to a situation of loneliness before God, enemies, illness, and threats, to an experience of liberation, and to a future generation. Every time this psalm was reread and reused it may have been used with other references.

c. *Significance*: The text has meant something to persons who read or prayed this psalm, as it evoked emotions, memories, and thoughts.

The reference and the significance of the psalm can change from situation to situation. However, the sense is relatively stable, even though changes in reference and significance also influence the sense of the text.

According to the Gospels of Matthew, Mark, and Luke, Jesus quoted the second verse of the psalm during his crucifixion. Jesus had read the Hebrew Scriptures and applied these texts to his messianic role. Several times, he used texts from Scripture to model his acts accordingly.[92] It must be presupposed that he had read Scripture to find his own destination. He may have read Ps 22 when he announced his death and found hope in it for his own resurrection after his crucifixion. In any case, Jesus knew this psalm and used it at the cross. It must have been a meaningful psalm to him.

a. *Sense*: It might be that for Jesus the words of the psalm already denoted death and resurrection.

b. *Reference*: Likely, for Jesus, the words of the psalm increasingly referred to his own future suffering, death, and resurrection, until the moment came that the loneliness, mocking, enmity, nakedness, thirst, and godforsakenness became his own experience.

c. *Significance*: The psalm must have been personally meaningful to Jesus, evoking expectations, images of his own death and resurrection, and strong emotions.

From the perspective of Easter and Pentecost, Jesus's followers have read Ps 22 as a prophetic psalm that is fulfilled in Jesus Christ. The events of Jesus's death and resurrection have influenced their understanding of the meaning of the psalm.

a. *Sense*: The sense of the psalm is influenced slightly. For example, abandonment by God became a reality in a special way during Jesus's crucifixion. Moreover, verse 16 says that something happens with "my hands and my feet," which is difficult to interpret. They are "dug

---

92. Examples are Zech 9:9–10 (Mark 11:1–8), Ps 110 (Mark 12:35–37), the exodus-narrative (Mark 14:22–25), and Dan 7:13–14 (Mark 14:62). Cf. Wright, *Jesus and the Victory of God*, 490–93, 507–9, 527–28, 554–63, 586.

through" or "pierced." Read in the light of Jesus's crucifixion, the sense of these words becomes more specific.

b. *Reference*: The psalm can be used to refer first to the events of Jesus's crucifixion, death, and resurrection, but it can still be used to refer to other experiences of suffering, as was the case before Jesus. But, in the second half of the psalm, other possible references come into view, like the worldwide mission, a worldwide people praising God, the universal kingship of Jesus, and an eschatological meal.

c. *Significance*: For different people in different situations of more or less suffering, the psalm will have a variety of meanings. It might help to connect one's suffering to Christ's suffering, to hope for God's answer to suffering, or to praise God for his salvation. Paul can serve as an example: he has used elements of the psalm to refer to his own life, looking back on his career as an apostle (2 Tim 4:16–18).[93]

This confirms what I argued already in 7.3. Within the historical processes of the use and reuse of the text, the figure of Jesus is crucial. It is important to see what he does and who he is when he acts. The Gospels recount how Jesus used passages from Scripture, applied them to himself, or modeled his life accordingly to claim a connection between himself and words from Scripture. At the same time, what happens during Jesus's life goes beyond what he can actively model as a human person. This becomes clear in the fulfillment of the prophetic Ps 22: Jesus quotes verse 2 on the cross, but it was beyond his human capabilities that the soldiers acted in accordance with verse 18, dividing his clothes and casting lots. According to Luke, after his resurrection Jesus said to his disciples that the Law of Moses, the Prophets, and the Psalms wrote about him (Luke 24:27, 44). The apostolic Gospels and letters substantiate this in a variety of ways. The New Testament shows him as the Messiah of Israel who represents his people and, as such, embodies, fulfills, and realizes their Scriptures. Jesus the Messiah is the fulfillment of the Law, the Prophets, and the Psalms. Moreover, as the incarnation of the eternal Word of God, he is the decisive embodiment of what God has to say. God spoke his Word to Israel but Israel had a mission to be a blessing to the world. As the representative of Israel, Jesus is also the last Adam who represents a new humanity.[94] His reality includes the reality of the renewed Israel, renewed humanity, and renewed creation.

This has several implications for the relationship between Jesus Christ and the meaning of Scripture, confirming what I already argued in this

---

93. Houwelingen, *Timoteüs en Titus*, 234–35.
94. See Burger, *Being in Christ*, 457–64.

chapter. First, Jesus the Messiah is the climax of the story of Israel, the fulfillment of the Scriptures of Israel, and the definitive embodiment of what God has to say. Within the salvation-historical process, Jesus the Messiah gives the Scriptures of Israel their final meaning. Without Jesus as the Messiah, Israel's Scriptures have an openness and ambiguity that disappears in Jesus. As fulfillment and embodiment of the Word of God, he gives the Scriptures their final and definitive meaning. But, Jesus himself is a living person and not a text; he remains extra-textual, Scripture receives its meaning in its relationship with this extra-textual person, the living Christ.

Second, if Jesus Christ is the definitive embodiment and fulfillment of what God has to say, he is also the incarnation of the preexistent eternal Word of God. Thus, he can be found in the words of the *Tanakh* and is already present in those words.[95] The one who is the final fulfillment of Scripture can already be found in ambiguous but still Christomorphic passages, like Ps 22. Accordingly, in the interpretation of passages like Ps 22, it can be argued that a christological interpretation is not arbitrary. This implies the belief that God who fulfills the Scriptures of Israel in Christ was already in the eternal Word involved in the formation of the *Tanakh*.

Third, Jesus Christ, the Word of God himself, is no text. As we saw in chapter 4, Dalferth emphasizes correctly that Christ as the center of Scripture remains extra-textual, external to the book. However, this leads, in his theology, to a tension between Christ and Scripture. This tension is solved when we see that Christ is sacramentally present for us in Scripture. Christ resolves the ambiguities and openness of the *Tanakh* and gives the Scriptures a clarity that goes beyond the text alone. Once one knows Jesus as the Messiah, one can find Jesus in the Scriptures of Israel.

---

95. When Peter Enns writes about the interpretation of the Old Testament in the New Testament, he emphasizes that the authors of the New Testament follow the interpretative methods of the Second Temple and gives this eschatological hermeneutic the label "christotelic." What he fails to see in his historical approach is that Christ as the eternal Word of God can be present sacramentally already in the Old Testament before his incarnation. See Enns, *Inspiration and Incarnation*, 103–52.

In the theological tradition of Kampen (both Boersma and I come from that tradition), a christological reading of the Old Testament was suggested that emphasized the historical relationship to Jesus Christ and the similarity between the (character of) the God of the Old Testament and the God whom we get to know in Jesus Christ. Still, this leads to a historical distance between the church and the Old Testament reality that has to be bridged. More recently, this has been done by narrative means. Boersma's emphasis on the sacramental presence of (the reality of) Christ in the Old Testament repairs the problems of this Kampen approach at a more fundamental level. See Boersma, *Scripture as Real Presence*, xiv. On the Kampen approach of the Old Testament, see Van Bekkum and Kwakkel, "Theologische boodschap."

Thus, we can read Scripture in two directions. We can read Scripture in a literal or historical reading where we follow the direction of time, trying to reconstruct the meaning of a text in its original context. In this reading, we follow the dynamics of the history of salvation with its tensions, disappointments, hopes, surprises, and unexpected newness.[96] Hence, the *sensus literalis* of a passage is a combination of the sense that this passage had in the original situation, the first reference (the reality the human author of the text wanted to refer to when he produced the text), and the significance that the text had for the original audience. This reading of Scripture is important, for it is necessary to discern the historical form of the texts of Scripture to understand its significance. Because God spoke and acted in the history of salvation, no opposition exists between history and theology.[97]

In a spiritual reading, we look back, knowing the story of Jesus the Christ. This spiritual or sacramental reading of Scripture is fundamentally a christological reading. It is a reading in the light of Easter and the Spirit at Pentecost, a reading in the light of the fulfillment of Israel's Scripture in Jesus the Messiah. Still, the reality of Christ is a complex reality for several reasons. First, Christ is God and man who exists eternally as the Word of God. Second, Jesus is the Messiah and embodiment of Israel, and consequently also the representative of the new humanity and the head of the new creation.[98] Third, the differentiation of head and body results both in a diversity of persons and, an eschatological tension. What is already the case with the head, living with a spiritual body in the heavenly glory of God is not in the same way it is with the members of his body. And, fourth, this eschatological tension is connected as well with the time differences between Christ's first coming and his representative act, the time of the church (the "in between" with its tension of the "already but not yet"), and Christ's second coming with the completion of history.

Accordingly, a christological reading is a reading with various interests, as the *quadriga* demonstrates. The allegorical-dogmatic reading is interested in the reality of Christ, the new covenant, the new Israel, and the church as the fulfillment of Scripture. The moral-tropological reading

---

96. For interesting examples of such a reading, see Talstra, "God"; Talstra, "Spirit as Critical Biblical Scholar." 23–35. Strange enough, Jamieson and Wittman ignore this direction of reading, see Jamieson and Wittman, *Biblical Reasoning*.

97. In his series "Christian Origins and the Question of God," N. T. Wright demonstrates that historical research and biblical theology belong together. See Wright, *New Testament and the People of God*, 6–28. God acts and speaks in history, as is emphasized by Michael Horton; see Horton, *Covenant and Eschatology*. See also Van Bekkum and Kwakkel, "Theologische boodschap"; Sarisky, *Reading the Bible Theologically*, 243–67.

98. For a contemporary rendition of the spiritual reading, it is a challenge to develop a non-supercessationist version that does not forget Israel.

searches for the ongoing realization of the mysterious unity with Christ in the life of the congregation and the believers. Finally, the anagogic-eschatological reading longs to perceive the complete and public fulfillment of participation in Christ in the eschatological kingdom of God. De Lubac has emphasized that the four senses of Scripture constitute an organic whole.[99] The four senses refer to the coming of God in Christ and the realization of the Christ-reality. Consequently, the four senses can be understood as various reading strategies that follow each other as part of a mystagogical path: the discovery of Christ and the mystery of life in union with him (faith), the ongoing transformation by participation in him (love), and the desire for the eschatological life with him (hope).[100]

Because this complexity leads to a multiplicity of meaning it is important to further analyze this multiplicity.

> 1. The literal-historical reading of the biblical texts evidences that Christ is not the only hermeneutical key to understanding these texts. The exegetical work of Jewish authors, the diachronic work of historical-critical scholars, and the synchronic analyses with a literary focus all provide valuable insight into the meaning of biblical texts. Reading these texts following the direction of historical developments necessitates such approaches.
>
> If it is true that Jesus Christ is the final Word of God, the embodiment of what God has to say, the incarnation of the eternal *Logos*, a christological reading is evoked. Now, these biblical texts are read as part of the saving activity of the triune God, to make us participate in Christ and transform us into Christlikeness. Christian believers discover that these texts are "able to make you wise for salvation through faith in Christ Jesus," and "useful for teaching, rebuking, correcting and training in righteousness, so that the servant of God may be thoroughly equipped for every good work" (2 Tim 3:15–17). New meanings come into view, given this Christ-reality.
>
> 2. Christ and his reality can be present in various ways in a text. Firstly, this variety is related to different references, as a rich Christology helps to distinguish (cf. 7.3.5). The text can be used to refer to Christ, to his cross and resurrection, to the restoration of Israel, to the church, to a life of participation in Christ, and the kingdom of God. Further, it is important to note that the reuse of texts started already before

---

99. Lubac, *Exégèse médiévale*, 643–56; Ypenga, "Sacramentum," 35.

100. Cf. De Jong-Van Campen, *Mystagogie in werking*, 106–12, 307–10; Van Bruggen, *Kompas van het christendom*, 170–72.

Christ in Scripture itself (e.g., the use of the exodus to refer to a future liberation)[101] and in Jewish exegesis (e.g., the reading of the Song of Songs to refer to the relationship between God and Israel).[102]

Secondly, the variety of genres is important as well. In historical texts, persons (David) or events (exodus) can be a type. Legal prescriptions can be fulfilled in a moral or public life in Christ. Cultic laws can be a sign of the fulfillment of Christ as a high priest. Promises or prophecies can refer more or less explicitly to restoration or Christ. Psalms, Proverbs, or the Song of Songs evoke their own way of spiritual or mystagogical reading.[103]

In some passages, the text itself explicitly speaks about a future figure like Christ.[104] In other passages, the christological relecture or reuse of the passage is like the use of words in a metaphor, creating new meaning by using the passage in a christological context.

3. At the level of the sense of the text, the change of meaning is the smallest. Still, during the process of the development of Scripture in the work of editors, the reuse of texts in later books of Scripture, or the translation of the Septuagint, the sense of passages has undergone changes. The use of a text with new references influences its sense as well, as in the example of the pierced hands and feet in Ps 22:16.[105] This means that the sense of the text as a feature of the text itself is not completely stable.[106]

---

101. Boersma, *Scripture as Real Presence*, 83–92; Danielou, *From Shadows to Reality*, 153–60.

102. Boersma, *Scripture as Real Presence*, 190.

103. Cf. Lubac, *Exégèse médiévale*, 173–74. Hans Boersma shows in his book how the variety of genres in Scripture colors the sacramental reading of Scripture, see Boersma, *Scripture as Real Presence*.

104. On the development of Messianic expectations and Messianic reinterpretations of passages in the Old Testament, see Rose, "Messiaanse verwachtingen in het Oude Testament."

105. Other examples: compare 1 Cor 15:55 with Hos 13:14; but also "virgin" in Matt 1:23 with "virgin" in Isa 7:14; "son" in Matt 2:15 with "son" in Hos 11:1. On the influence of the LXX and how this translation made a christological use easier see, e.g., Wright, *Resurrection*, 147–50.

106. Relating the sense of the text to authorial intention, several theologians have defended the stability of the sense of a text. Walter Kaiser and Moisés Silva follow Hirsch and emphasize the stability of the intended sense by the author, see Kaiser and Silva, *Introduction to Biblical Hermeneutics*, 30, 34–37, 45. Vanhoozer gives a reconstruction of meaning as a property of the text, understanding a text as embodiment and enactment of an intentional speech act. The text can be read within the canon as a divine speech act with a divine author. However, he does not deal sufficiently with the change

If it is true that Jesus Christ is the center of Scripture, this development of sense receives its endpoint in the work of the authors of the New Testament. As the definitive Word of God, Christ adds new meaning to the *Tanakh* that cannot be found yet in the Old Testament. Thus, the christological meaning of the Old Testament is not static, although Christ is present in the old words. The christological meaning can only be understood completely as the result of a salvation-historical process in which old words receive new meaning. At the same time, this development finds its end in Christ. In him, God has said what he wants to say. Accordingly, the closure of the canon implies that within the intertextual web of the canon, the sense of a passage receives its final stability.

4. More change of meaning is possible at the level of reference. Passages can be used to refer to the reality of Christ with all its aspects: his person, the events of his life, his present role as high priest and king, the new Israel and the church, his presence in the life of believers participating in him, and the future to be revealed at his return. Still, the number of new possible references is not endless. They all must be concerned with the reality of Christ.

5. By far, most new meanings emerge at the level of significance. In new contexts and new situations, passages from Scripture speak to many people who receive instruction, wisdom, consolation, encouragement, empowerment, inspiration, etc., from Scripture.[107] It would be misleading to search for a variety of meanings, especially within the text. The variety of meanings that can be found in the practice of spiritual reading is not text-immanent. Only the sense of a text is a feature of the text itself. Reference and significance are a result of the relecture or reuse of text in a variety of situations by many different persons.[108] They only slightly influence the sense of the text.

---

of the sense of words in the reuse of passages within the canon; see Vanhoozer, *Is There a Meaning?*, 246–65. Wisse critically discusses authorial discourse interpretation and concludes that this can be a useful but limited interpretation strategy. Moreover, he argues that is not fruitful to counter the postmodern idea of the instability of a sign by claiming an unchangeable sense, see Wisse, *Scripture between Identity and Creativity*, 146–57, 166–75.

107. The diversity of meaning is emphasized especially in Pentecostal and charismatic hermeneutics and theology. See, e.g., Keener, *Spirit Hermeneutics*. But see also Macchia, *Jesus the Spirit Baptizer*, 56–64.

108. Theo Hettema argues similarly that rehabilitation of the model of the fourfold sense of Scripture is possible if the plurality of meaning is not seen as text–immanent but as referential; cf. Hettema, "Viervoudige schriftzin."

Finally, this multiplicity of meanings is not arbitrary, allowing every reader to create her own meaning. In the first place, the practice of spiritual reading has a clear theological legitimization in the sacramental presence of Christ in the text. Secondly, this practice has a clear theological purpose—to live in communion with Christ.

7.4.4 Sacramental Reading without Platonism

The practice of spiritual reading in search of a christological meaning can be continued today. To do this an alternative to the Platonism of the patristic and medieval theologians is necessary. Since the reading practice is a combination of several reading strategies motivated by theological convictions about Jesus Christ and the new reality that can be found in him, it is important to be explicit about these theological beliefs.

Fundamentally, God can communicate with us, that he can act within history, and that he can use elements of his creation (words, events) to communicate with us. Without this divine interaction with us at a personal level, the practice of sacramental reading is meaningless. Moreover, the practice of spiritual reading presupposes that Jesus is the risen Messiah, the decisive embodiment of what God wants to communicate with us, and the incarnation of the eternal preexistent divine Word.

Still, it has to be decided whether this reading practice is "sacramental." This is not the case if the Reformed tradition is followed. According to the Reformed tradition, a sacrament is a material sign and seal of the Word of God that follows the Word and is instituted by Jesus Christ himself.[109]

However, an alternative approach is possible. Originally, the word "*sacramentum*" is the translation of *mysterion* in 1 Tim 3:16. It refers to Christ, who is the mystery of salvation. Following Walter Kaspar and Eberhard Jüngel, Jesus Christ can be conceived of as "Ursakrament," the primordial sacrament.[110] Consequently, "sacrament" is a christological and soteriological concept. Moreover, it is a communicative concept. The sacrament communicates the mystery of salvation and gives the knowledge, wisdom, and life that is in Jesus Christ.[111] Thus, a sacrament can be understood as a sign that refers to the mystery of salvation in Jesus Christ, the primordial sacrament, and that mediates and communicates the presence of Christ and his salvation, thus enabling us to live in union with Christ and to participate in

---

109. For a Reformed understanding of sacraments, see, e.g., Billings, "Sacraments."
110. Jüngel, *Wertlose Wahrheit*, 273, 315, 333; Kasper, *Theologie und Kirche*, 245.
111. Jüngel, *Ganz werden*, 274–87.

him. In this communication of the mystery of salvation in Christ, Christ is represented and present in Scripture, the church, the proclamation of the gospel, and baptism and the Eucharist. Accordingly, these means of communication can be called sacraments that all refer to Christ as the "Ursakrament." This does not mean that all divine communication is sacramental or even that human speakers are sacramentally present in their texts. What is present and what is communicated in the sacraments, is more specific: in them, Christ is sacramentally present, and Christ is communicated sacramentally with those who receive him in faith. Such a concept of the sacrament does not contradict the *solus Christus*, the *extra nos* of Jesus Christ, or the *prima scriptura* of the Reformation. Because Christ is sacramentally present in Scripture, a spiritual and christological reading of Scripture can be called a sacramental reading as well.

God's sacramental presence in particular persons, moments, events, and texts, and his communication and presence with us in Christ means that he comes, shows his merciful love, makes himself present to us, and even chooses to live in human beings by his Spirit. This coming is part of God's saving acts and always implies a response to human sin. Theologically speaking, it is part of soteriology and eschatology. This has to be distinguished from ontology or protology. Sacrament is a soteriological concept, not metaphysical or ontological. Consequently, God's sacramental presence in his word, in baptism and the Eucharist, or in his people does not imply a sacramental ontology. Neither does participation in Christ imply a participatory ontology. Instead of a Platonic ontology that understands everything in the light of an "ecstatic and self-gathering movement of being"[112] and that understands humanity in the light of the first movement of our being, I would propose an eschatological ontology. In such an ontology, God, his Word, and his Spirit are coming from his future that is full of creativity, newness, and surprise. At the same time, this loving God is the eternal God. Coming from the *eschaton*, he is already present from the beginning. For this reason, his eternal Word already is present in Scripture before his incarnation. If this is all true, it is possible to continue the practice of sacramental reading in search of a christological meaning. At the same time, it is possible to avoid the problems of a Platonic worldview—a worldview with a "gravitational pull" that is "upward"[113] and not helpful to understand the salvific historical dynamics of Scripture.

The three reading strategies of the three christological readings in the *quadriga* make clear that it is not just faith in Jesus Christ that influences

112. O'Donovan, *Entering into Rest*, 10.
113. Bartholomew, *Introducing Biblical Hermeneutics*, 141.

the Christian reading of Scripture. As Darren Sarisky has emphasized and demonstrated through Augustine's hermeneutic, a theological reading of Scripture implies not just faith in Jesus Christ, but a theological ontology as well: "For Augustine, a theological ontology leads to an ethics of biblical interpretation: how the reader and text are understood in relation to God determines how the text ought to be read."[114] Sarisky focuses on God, the text, and the reader. Jesus Christ is important as well. The christological reading of Scripture implies a view of Jesus Christ and Scripture in relation to Jesus Christ. Jesus Christ is the incarnate Word: the fulfillment of what God has spoken in the *Tanakh*, the embodiment of what God has to say, and as such he is more than Moses (cf. John 1:17), the realization of what God says in the new humanity (he is the *autobasileia*). Scripture is a mysterious book wherein Jesus Christ already is prefigured before his incarnation (he is the Word of God), in which Jesus Christ comes to us (Scripture is the word of Christ) and with which the Holy Spirit renews us into Christlikeness (participation in Christ). A christological reading and interpretation of Scripture will align to this theological ontology, to serve the practice of the triune God.

7.5 RENEWAL OF THE MIND AND THE ROLE OF PUBLIC THEOLOGICAL REFLECTION

The noetic consequences of sin constitute an important argument for a soteriological approach of theological hermeneutics instead of a doctrine of Scripture developed with epistemological interests. Due to sin, we have problems in becoming good hearers and readers of Scripture. That does not mean that only Christian believers can read and interpret the Bible. But when someone reads Scripture with an interest in Christ, as the Savior who comes to us in Scripture to save us from sin and all its consequences, sin will prove to be problematic.[115] Luke's story about Jesus in Luke 24 shows this when Jesus says, "How foolish you are, and how slow of heart to believe all that the prophets have spoken! Did not the Christ have to suffer these things and then enter his glory?" (vv. 25–26). But Jesus not only has the critical diagnosis, but he also provides the healing solution. This solution has two aspects. First, "he opened their minds so they could understand the Scriptures" (v. 45). And second, he teaches again and explains the Scriptures. The first aspect we all have to experience personally, and the second

---

114. Sarisky, *Reading the Bible Theologically*, 106. And further Sarisky, *Reading the Bible Theologically*, 44–56.

115. Cf. Sarisky, *Reading the Bible Theologically*, 196–97.

we can learn as well by reading about his teaching. These two aspects are important for understanding the renewal of the mind in relation to the reading of Scripture.

In the next chapter, I will deal with the renewal of the mind more extensively. However, I want to make a few preliminary remarks about the renewal of the mind here, because the formation of beliefs about Scripture as a consequence of faith in Jesus Christ is an aspect of the renewal of the mind. It might seem that the illumination and renewal of the mind will result in an irrational, fideistic hermeneutics that shies away from public justification and discussion. However, when we want to learn to read Scripture no longer "from a worldly point of view" (2 Cor 5:16) and when we want not to "conform any longer to the pattern of this world, but [to] be transformed by the renewing of [our] mind" (Rom 12:2), this renewal of the mind has the following two aspects. First, it is the work of Christ and his Spirit to open our minds and this transcends our rational capacities. Second, the beliefs that regulate our reading and interpretation of Scripture are open to rational and public discussion. Furthermore, if it is true that "the noetic effects of sin generally are expected to be most evident in the knowledge of God, less evident in the knowledge of human beings, and least evident in the knowledge of impersonal aspects of creation,"[116] this will be the case in the renewal of the mind as well. The more we deal with the worship of the triune God and the transformation into Christlikeness, the more the interests of sin will rebel.

Regarding the textual history, semantic, grammatical, and narrative analysis, the influence of sin and renewal often will not be visible, although theological interests sometimes may interfere with such analyses. In these historical reconstructions of the history of Israel and Jesus, worldview and philosophy can play a role. It does make a difference whether one believes that God does not exist or is a deistic God who does not act in history, or that God is actively involved in the history of his people.[117] The same is the case in biblical-theological reconstructions: the degree of existential involvement will influence one's view of what is at stake theologically. Speaking about the divinity of Jesus Christ, the significance of his death, or his resurrection, the conflict of interpretations is influenced by sin and transformation. And this touches immediately on the relationship between Jesus and the *Tanakh*. Is Jesus the fulfillment of the Scriptures of Israel, the promised Messiah, the seed of Abraham, the son of David, or not? And

---

116. Moroney, *Noetic Effects of Sin*, 37.

117. Cf. Bartholomew, *Introducing Biblical Hermeneutics*, 206–25; Bowald, *Rendering the Word*, 1–23.

finally, only when someone believes that Jesus is the promised Christ, that in faith we are united with Christ and participate in him, reading Scripture will include a christological reading with the aim of transformation into Christlikeness by the Holy Spirit.[118]

Whether someone has a worldview that is open to God's active presence or not, whether someone believes in Jesus as the promised Messiah or not, is a matter of faith. First of all, faith is a gift of the Holy Spirit who can open our minds and give illumination. And which regulative beliefs someone has, is linked to faith in Jesus Christ, and thus depend on the divine activity that transcends our mind.[119]

However, that does not make the renewal of the mind irrational or esoteric. Mysterious and intellectual aspects are not mutually exclusive, indeed, they need each other. In a contemplative, transformative theology, the theologian and interpreter of Scripture has to be both intellectual and mystic. Transformation by a contemplative, mystic, life of prayer with the triune God and intellectual reflection go well together.[120] That means that we need both the opening of our minds and the intellectual reflection on the beliefs that regulate our reading. Luke 24 shows that following the risen Jesus Christ, we will find both. Thus, the renewal of the mind has an aspect of intellectual discussion of our beliefs. More specifically, the renewal of the mind with regard to the reading of Scripture has an aspect of the public discussion of the beliefs that regulate a Christian reading of Scripture.

Thus, it is an aspect of the renewal of the mind to discuss critically the beliefs that regulate a Christian reading of Scripture, and that follow from faith in Jesus Christ. In this chapter, I have discussed several of these beliefs: that Jesus Christ is the fulfillment of the *Tanakh*, that the story of Jesus Christ makes Scripture a unity, that Jesus Christ is the incarnation of the Word of God, that Jesus Christ is present in the *Tanakh*, that Christian believers participate in Jesus Christ, and that Christian believers read Scripture to be conformed to their Lord. Whether one shares these beliefs is a matter of faith. The explanation of these beliefs, however, is a public activity. The critical discussion of these beliefs by Christian believers is rational as well, open to anyone interested.

Furthermore, faith in Jesus Christ and a resulting renewal of the mind (at least the beginning of this renewal) is a prerequisite of a Christian

---

118. Koert van Bekkum, analyzing the importance of theology for biblical studies on different levels, distinguishes between craftsmanship, methodologies, and narrative frameworks. See Huijgen et al., "Biblical Exegesis and Systematic Theology," 180.

119. Cf. Sarisky on the naturalistic view of readers of the Bible and the alternative theological view, Sarisky, *Reading the Bible Theologically*, 164–69, 179–83, 188–96.

120. Cf. Coakley, *God, Sexuality, and the Self*, 182.

hearing and reading of Scripture. At the same time, hearing and reading Scripture in faith will lead to a renewal of the mind. In the light of Christ, we can read Scripture, and in Scripture, we come to know Christ. In Scripture, we find the teaching of Jesus and his apostles. Thus, a Christian reading of Scripture will foster a further transformation of our thinking, willing, and feeling in accordance with our participation in Christ.

In this seventh chapter, I have dealt with the significance of faith in Jesus Christ for our hearing and reading of Scripture, with a focus on our beliefs. Still, the renewal of the mind embraces more than rational beliefs. In Christ, the Word of God has become flesh. To be human is to live an embodied life. If Scripture is the light of the church, and the church is the life of Scripture as Bavinck wrote, the Christian practice has significance for hermeneutics, for our reading of Scripture, and for the renewal of the mind. Accordingly, in the next chapter more has to be said about the Christian life and practice, individual and communal in the church.

8.

Community and Practice
Reading and Transformation in Ecclesial, Moral, and Spiritual Practices

8.1 INTRODUCTION

In a soteriological approach to theological hermeneutics, the transformation of the hearer and reader of the word of God has to be a central theme. Because this is a book on hermeneutics and Scripture, with a special interest in verbal communication through texts, I will focus on the renewal of the mind, which is the opposite of the noetic consequences of sin. The resurrection of Jesus Christ at Easter and the baptism with the Holy Spirit at Pentecost together open a new perspective. This new perspective and new understanding are both a precondition and a consequence of our hearing and reading Scripture. Chapter 7 finished with a section on the renewal of the mind. However, more has to be said on this, because humans are more than their beliefs.

Transformation or renewal is an important and complex theme. First, it is an important theme. As we saw in chapter 2, an epistemological approach to Scripture and hermeneutics tends to forget the reader. Moreover, Sarisky has shown that in recent approaches to theological hermeneutics, the reader also is often forgotten.[1] However, critical reflection about understanding and interpretation has to face the question of who is understanding and interpreting. This is even more pressing because it is not self-evident that our perspective is open to God, as our discussion of Taylor's works made

---

1. Sarisky, *Reading the Bible Theologically*, 190–96.

clear. This is what we call secularization, but we are confronted with the noetic consequences of sin as well (see chapter 3). As hearers and readers of the word of God, we need salvation. Moreover, to a significant degree, the salvation of the hearers and readers of the word of God is the theme of Scripture. Their renewal is an aspect of their salvation.

Second, it is a complex theme for several reasons. It is complex because of our context. In the Western secularized world, a perspective that is open to God is possible, but the Christian life is under heavy pressure as well (see 3.2). Still, the transformation toward openness is necessary and possible. Moreover, it is complex for anthropological reasons. Human existence is narrative, social, affective, and embodied (see 3.3). Consequently, how we live and how we understand Scripture influence each other reciprocally. This brings me to another aspect of this complexity: the circularity of understanding that occurs in several ways. First, due to the noetic consequences of sin. As a consequence of sin, we are deaf and blind to Scripture. By God's grace, we receive a new perspective, leading to insight into Scripture. By understanding Scripture, our perspective is transformed further. This continuous transformation also leads to the ongoing growth of our understanding of Scripture. Second, the relationship between Christ and Scripture causes complexity. Faith in Christ determines our perspective on Scripture, whereas our relationship with Christ is mediated by Scripture. And because Christ is the embodiment of the Word of God, Scripture as *theopneustos* is used by the Holy Scripture to transform us into Christlikeness. The formation of the mind of Christ in us is a mind that is soaked in Scripture. In an ongoing interaction, one reinforces the other: faith in Jesus Christ, knowing Jesus Christ, living with Jesus Christ, following Jesus Christ, discerning Scripture, the formation of Christlikeness in us, understanding everything in the light of Scripture and with the mind of Christ, and thinking and feeling and acting with the mindset of Christ. This implies a third aspect of the complexity caused by the circularity of understanding. We discern Scripture and we discern everything in the light of Scripture, looking at and looking through the text (see 5.5 on O'Donovan).[2] The renewal of understanding also concerns our images of God, the self, and the world, as Dalferth emphasizes (chapter 4). Understanding Scripture and understanding everything in the light of Scripture and experiencing its truth, leads to a better understanding of Scripture, and so on.

Summarizing, we hear the words of Scripture in the proclamation of the good news of Jesus Christ, in the light of Easter and Pentecost. We understand Scripture from faith in Christ and with the mind of Christ, but

---

2. Cf. Sarisky, *Reading the Bible Theologically*, 94-95, 98-99, 267-72.

we come to know Christ in Scripture and we receive the mind of Christ by reading Scripture. We remain in Christ by remaining in the Word, and by remaining in the Word we remain in Christ. Understanding Scripture and Christlikeness mutually reinforce each other. Moreover, we understand everything else (God, the world, and the self) in the light of Scripture, from faith in Christ and with the mind of Christ. At the same time, living a Christian life, with God and our neighbor, in God's world, will deepen our understanding of Scripture.

In this chapter, I will further explore the complexity of reading, interpretation, and transformation in the community of the church based on empirical research into Bible reading (8.2). Next, I will show that participation in Christian practices influences Bible reading and can deepen your understanding, taking as an example, practices of mercy (8.3). Furthermore, I will discuss *Sunesis Pneumatikè*, a text by John Owen, to further investigate the renewal of the mind (8.4). In the final section, I will bring together observations from this chapter and present some reflections on the renewal of the mind (8.5).

8.2 READING SCRIPTURE AS AN ECCLESIAL PRACTICE

The church has an important role as a hermeneutical community. Ideally, the church is a community where believers learn to listen to Scripture as God's word, understand, and live in obedience to God. That means that the church has to be a formative community—learning to understand Scripture and to discern in the light of the Word of God, and being formed in the mind of Christ to live a life of participation in Christ. This is a beautiful vision. However, Sarah Coakley has warned theologians not to envision concepts in abstraction from the reality of life. Theology should not limit itself to its safe orthodoxy, but rather it should confront itself with the messy reality where God is present. Thus, theology needs the social sciences and their empirical studies.[3] The idea of the church as a hearing and reading community is part of the so-called "ecclesial turn," emphasizing the importance of the church as an alternative community embodying the Christian life. This turn has been criticized for idealizing the church.[4] To apply this criticism to the church as a listening and reading community, we must ask: Is the real church in a position to have this important role as a hermeneutical community? What happens when members of the church listen to the

---

3. Coakley, *God, Sexuality, and the Self*, 71.

4. For a short overview of the ecclesial turn and criticisms, see De Jong, "Church Is the Means," 7–19.

Scriptures? Does it result in more Christlikeness or less? Is the church able to be a formative community that fosters the renewal of the minds of its members?

The empirical reality of the church differs from the ideal situation. Significantly, the Dutch Protestant church published, in 2019, the small booklet *De Bijbel in het midden: het geloofsgesprek te midden van verschillen* (*The Bible in the Middle: The Conversation of Faith amid Differences*).[5] In the church, it is difficult to read Scripture together. Wisse signals several causes for this. First, the plurality within the Protestant church. Further, he mentions the decline of the catechetical culture. Moreover, due to the rise of the leisure culture along with the culture of experience, reading Scripture has become similar to a hobby. Can the church bear fruit as a hearing and reading community? To prevent reflections on church and hermeneutics from becoming utopian programs, this section will investigate what significant insights can be learned from the practice of the church as a community that hears and reads Scripture.

When it comes to empirical hermeneutics, the Bible-reading project led by Hans de Wit cannot be ignored. In this intercultural project of empirical hermeneutics, John 4 was read in groups, after which an exchange took place with a group elsewhere in the world. Reading together and comparing lectures appeared to be an enriching experience that reinforces solidarity, although it remained difficult to read through someone else's eyes. The role of a group leader was crucial in this process of reading together. In this project, special attention was given to the contrasts between (critically) trained professional readers and "ordinary readers." Awareness of historical distance turned out to make applying the text to one's life more complicated.[6] Still, I will not delve further into this project, because it does not say much about the significance of a church community with regard to reading the Bible.

Instead, I will now turn to several recent publications on the reading of Scripture in the Netherlands. Next, the results of three British and American studies in empirical hermeneutics will be investigated. The research in this overview was done before the COVID-19 pandemic that began in December 2019. It is interesting that the 2022 version of the yearly American report *State of the Bible* shows that "the pandemic turned out to be a major change agent, and we're still experiencing the fallout. Many spiritual practices—in homes and churches—were disrupted."[7] The interaction with

---

5. Wisse, *Bijbel in het midden*.

6. For reflections on the tension between historical distance and application, see Sarisky, *Reading the Bible Theologically*, 217–32.

7. Fulks et al., *State of the Bible: USA 2022*, 52.

the Bible in 2021 decreased in an unprecedented way, e.g., a decrease of 10 percent in Bible users. Also, Scripture engagement and the spiritual impact of the Bible show a decline. The report suggests the influence of the COVID-19 pandemic, political polarization, and other disruptions. Also, the influence of social distancing and online services on ecclesial practices is mentioned.[8] How reading practices have developed since the COVID-19 pandemic is open to further investigation.

8.2.1 The Netherlands

What do we know about the reading of the Bible in the Netherlands? The survey, *God in Nederland 1966–2015*, shows the influence of secularization in the changing beliefs about Scripture, and the decrease in church membership. In 2015, fewer Dutch people saw Scripture as the word of God (56 percent in 1966, 14 percent in 2015). Between 1979 and 2015, the group of regular readers diminished from 15 percent to 9 percent, and the group of nonreaders grew from 27 percent to 67 percent.[9] Regular readers are especially found in smaller Protestant denominations.[10] The KASKI report "Godsdienst, Kerk en Bijbel in Nederland" (2005; not public) observes that "the most frequent and fervent Bible-readers are to be found among Evangelical rather than orthodox Protestant Christians (i.e. conservative Calvinist)."[11]

The volume *De Bijbel in Nederland* (2018) brings together observations and experiences of theologians, ministers, and other workers in the church.[12] Several authors signal a longing for the otherness of the world of Scripture, although Scripture is a difficult book.[13] For that reason, Erik Borgman and Bram van Putten, emphasize the importance of a community where a culture of reading can be practiced.[14] Concerning youth in conservative-Protestant circles, a longing for spiritual experience is signaled, together with a lower reading frequency, a more fragmentary way of reading, and a

---

8. Fulks et al., *State of the Bible: USA 2022*, x, xiii–xvi.

9. Bernts et al., *God in Nederland 1966–2015*, 74 (table 3.13).

10. Bernts et al., *God in Nederland 1966–2015*, 74 (table 3.14). See further Foppen et al., "Most Significant Book," 111–12.

11. This report is mentioned in Foppen et al., "Most Significant Book," 113.

12. Barnhoorn et al., *Bijbel in Nederland*.

13. Schol-Wetter, "Bijbel: verhaal en tegenverhaal," 33–34; Nieuwpoort, "Omwille van de vrije Bijbel," 40–42.

14. Borgman, "Ziel van het geloof," 52; Van Putten, "Stemmen met de voeten," 99. Cf. Van der Graaf, "Bijbel in het Leven," 161–62.

loss of the self-evidence of the authority of Scripture.[15] Further is mentioned the loss of the use of the Bible as a physical book, due to the influence of smartphones and projectors.[16]

Finally, in 2021, Annemarie Foppen, Anne-Mareike Schol-Wetter, Peter-Ben Smit, and Eva Coster-Van Urk published the results of their research conducted together with the Dutch Bible Society.[17] Already in 2017, these results were published in the report "NBG-Onderzoek Bijbelgebruik in Nederland."[18] This report again shows the diversity of readers of the Bible in the Netherlands. It turned out that not membership of a denomination, but practices and attitudes were determinative factors in Bible usage. The report uses two variables: active or passive reading habits (practices), and a radical or liberal attitude (attitudes) toward the Bible. Based on these two variables, the researchers distinguished five groups of readers:

> a. radical-active (heavy users; the motive to read is the relationship with God; 100 percent of this group affirms that Scripture is, literally, God's word; churchgoing; especially Reformed-Evangelical-Protestant);
>
> b. radical-passive (light users; the motive to read is the longing for consolation and affirmation; 100 percent of this group affirms that Scripture is, literally, God's word; less frequent church attendance; mostly Roman Catholic or Protestant);
>
> c. liberal-active (heavy users; the motive to read is the hope for wisdom; 8 percent of this group affirms that Scripture is, literally, God's word; church-going; primarily Protestant, Roman Catholic, or Reformed);
>
> d. liberal-passive (light users; the motive to read is the expectation of lessons for life; 4 percent affirms that Scripture is, literally, God's word; not very church-going; predominantly Roman Catholic, Protestant).
>
> e. lateral (non-users; the motive to engage with the Bible is the education of the next generation; zero percent affirms that Scripture is, literally, God's word; rarely going to church; 63 percent Roman Catholic).

These reports and views from everyday life give a first impression of the church as a reading community. However, more thorough empirical

---

15. Van Putten, "Stemmen met de voeten," 89–100; Van Wijngaarden and Van Vreeswijk, "Een slag apart," 104.

16. Van der Graaf, "Bijbel in het Leven," 160.

17. Foppen et al., "Most Significant Book."

18. "NBG-Onderzoek Bijbelgebruik in Nederland."

research about the church as a hermeneutical community in the Netherlands is still lacking.[19]

8.2.2 Empirical Research in Great Britain and the United States

This is different as far as the Anglo-Saxon world is concerned. Andrew Village (2007) and Andrew Rogers (2015) both did empirical research in British churches, and James Bielo in American churches (2009).[20] Andrew Village, an Evangelical-Charismatic Anglican, did his research mainly in eleven different Anglican congregations. A passage from Scripture, Mark 9:14–29, where Jesus casts out a spirit from a boy, functioned prominently in his questionnaire. Village developed a Bible scale, measuring the beliefs and attitudes toward the Bible from a liberal to a conservative position. Predicting factors were tradition (Anglo-Catholic, Broad church, or Evangelical), frequency of church attendance, and level of education. Beliefs about the importance of Scripture influence the reading frequency, except for Anglo-Catholics.[21]

Next, Village investigated the level of literalism, the belief that events in the Bible happened as described. Factors that influence literalism were tradition, education, theological training (both correlated with less literalism), participation in charismatic practices, and frequency of Bible reading (both correlated with more literalism). For Evangelicals, education had less influence. The level of literalism was influenced by the plausibility of the worldview of the biblical story. The less plausible this worldview seemed, the less literalist it was understood. The Charismatic experience was a factor that increased this plausibility.[22]

Another set of issues connects to the concept of *horizon*. Generally, lay people tend toward a preference for the horizon of the reader; education leads to a higher preference for the horizon of the author. Horizon separation is influenced by beliefs about literalism and supernaturalism. Literalism especially led to a preference for the horizon of the text, and not so much to a higher degree of application. Non-literalists preferred the horizon of the author because the text seemed to be too unfamiliar. Application reached the highest level when readers expected that the same could happen today. For example, in response to Mark 9, they would conclude that God could

---

19. Smit, "Contextuele bijbelinterpretatie bestaat niet," 80.

20. Bielo, *Words upon the Word*; Rogers, *Congregational Hermeneutics*; Village, *Bible and Lay People*.

21. Village, *Bible and Lay People*, 36–53.

22. Village, *Bible and Lay People*, 62–74.

do miracles today. Membership of a congregational healing team was correlated positively with application. Familiarity with the text also leads to less horizon separation.[23]

The influence of the tradition and/or the congregation was especially clear regarding the degree of literalism. Furthermore, feeling at home in a church, and being comfortable with the way Scripture was read and with the teaching in that church, are correlated. Therefore, according to Village, "there is some evidence of a 'community effect' that goes beyond the effects of individual difference, but this effect is by no means overarching."[24] Moreover, Village shows that congregations are by no means uniform communities.[25]

Finally, Village examined the influence of charismatic belief. Charismatic belief is correlated positively with literalism, the frequency of Bible reading, belief in supernatural healing, and a conservative attitude toward morality. For members of healing teams, the belief in God's healing presence is shown to be stronger than experience, which is often a mixed outcome.[26]

James S. Bielo, an American anthropologist, did ethnographic research in six Protestant congregations in the Lansing area (Michigan). In his research, Bielo wanted to analyze group Bible study, as "a crucial institution in the cultural life of Evangelicals."[27] He focused "on the life of social institutions, the practices of collective reading and interpretation, and the discourse that gives life to these processes."[28]

Bielo shows the relationship between textual ideology ("the expectations that guide how individuals and groups read specific texts") and a textual practice where these expectations are formed, negotiated, and cultivated. Importantly, he emphasizes that literalism "functions primarily as a signifier of theological and religious identity," but not as a hermeneutical method ("a self-conscious or tacit means of actually reading and interpreting biblical texts").[29] Furthermore, Scripture is seen as relevant, e.g., because of its revealing and transforming quality.[30] A third element of this "textual ideology" is the belief that the Bible can be read as a unified text.[31] Moreover,

23. Village, *Bible and Lay People*, 81–94.
24. Village, *Bible and Lay People*, 137.
25. Village, *Bible and Lay People*, 130–35, 141–42.
26. Village, *Bible and Lay People*, 147–54.
27. Bielo, *Words upon the Word*, 157.
28. Bielo, *Words upon the Word*, 16.
29. Bielo, *Words upon the Word*, 49.
30. Bielo, *Words upon the Word*, 59–60.
31. Bielo, *Words upon the Word*, 64.

it was considered important to apply passages from Scripture to everyday life, whereby "an extremely close relationship between text and action" was asserted.[32] Apart from beliefs about Scripture itself, beliefs about God also shape the reader's interpretation of Scripture. If it is believed that God always keeps his promises, this determines what can be read as a promise and what not.[33]

Reading is a social activity. Hence, the social imaginary of the group is important. Bielo emphasizes both the importance of the "subtext for reading" and the "textual economies." He shows that in the discursive-ideological subtext, the awareness of the historical distance between the first Christians and the present situation is used to highlight the difference between then and now.[34] Accordingly, reading the Bible together gives rise to dialogue about the reader's world. Another social reality is the "textual economy" within which the Bible is read. The community of Evangelical Bible readers is influenced by books about the Bible and Christian beliefs, written by respected authors. Although this textual economy is fluid because the popularity of authors varies, this textual economy still makes a significant contribution to how the Bible is read.

Furthermore, Bielo's analyses show that Bible study groups can vary in their focus from meeting to meeting. Doing Bible study, Evangelicals deal with questions concerning God's presence, cultivating intimacy with God and with Jesus, or they read the Bible as preparation for witness.[35] Furthermore, a social interest that can influence Bible reading is the articulation of religious identity when affirming the differences with other religious groups.[36] Thus, Bielo's analyses demonstrate that Bible reading is influenced by expectations and beliefs about Scripture ("textual ideology"), and by expectations and beliefs about what God gives. Reading also is socially embedded and influenced by social imaginary ("discursive-ideological subtext") and "textual economy"; lastly, his research shows that reading is a social activity, regulated by common interests and common longings, but also by identity politics.

Andrew Rogers, a British Evangelical, did ethnographic research in two independent Evangelical congregations in London. In his research, Village observed that theological education often deliberately destroys the

---

32. Bielo, *Words upon the Word*, 50.
33. Bielo, *Words upon the Word*, 54–58.
34. Bielo, *Words upon the Word*, 97–99, 105–9.
35. Bielo, *Words upon the Word*, 91, 120–21.
36. Bielo, *Words upon the Word*, 138, 152.

"first naivety," leaving students in the "desert of criticism."[37] Rogers wants to construct a proposal for an "intentional, corporate, and virtuous hermeneutical apprenticeship," stimulating the "growth in hermeneutical virtue."[38] However, in this chapter, I am primarily interested in the descriptive part of his project. In his analyses, he focuses on tradition, practices, epistemology, and mediation.

In Rogers's research, tradition means congregational tradition, consisting "of patterns of discourses, actions, artifacts, and mediators over time."[39] Tradition's "potential for shaping" the reading community consists of "guiding one's interpretation, of providing interpretative emphases, or through providing boundaries to possible interpretations."[40] Every congregation has such a tradition, and Rogers emphasizes that it is important to relate to this tradition in a self-conscious and self-critical manner. Our reading is shaped by our congregational tradition, and also by the critical question of whether readings of Scripture are not only affirmative but also disruptive.[41]

Rogers places hermeneutical practices under the heading of "Hearing God Speak through Scripture," and analyses them using the concepts "horizon" and "fusion."[42] In the hermeneutical philosophy of Hans Georg Gadamer, understanding a text means a fusion of the horizon of the text and the horizon of the reader. How do processes in these practices build connections between the horizons of the text and the congregation? The ways to connect horizons Rogers found were premodern (christological readings), text-linking (placing text after text so that they interpret each other), a "this is that" reading (Pesher) and allegory, and finally modern (the grammatico-historical method and a reading in two steps: then and now). These reading strategies remained often implicit and each congregation has its own hermeneutical tradition.[43]

Interestingly, Rogers makes epistemology a central category as well. Epistemological positions were found "to be a key feature of their horizons that shaped hermeneutical practices."[44] One congregation was more modern, foundationalist, and objectivist; and the other was more late-modern, less foundationalist, and understanding the text with a subjective

---

37. Village, *Bible and Lay People*, 90, 93, 160.
38. Rogers, *Congregational Hermeneutics*, 2, 12, 36.
39. Rogers, *Congregational Hermeneutics*, 67.
40. Rogers, *Congregational Hermeneutics*, 89.
41. Rogers, *Congregational Hermeneutics*, 92.
42. Rogers, *Congregational Hermeneutics*, 63, 95.
43. Rogers, *Congregational Hermeneutics*, 100–116.
44. Rogers, *Congregational Hermeneutics*, 119.

kind of realism. This epistemological difference is typical of two groups of Evangelicals: a position of common sense rationalism with an emphasis on inerrancy and certainty, and a more postmodern, critical realism seeing Scripture as authoritative and trustworthy.[45]

Mediation in this study refers to "the process of transmitting hermeneutical practices through a variety of mediators."[46] Rogers lists internal mediators (sermons, Bible display, liturgical use, congregants, house groups, church Bible studies) and external mediators (visiting preachers, friends and family, songs, books, material to support Bible reading, other Christian organizations, events, and courses). Rogers signals the international influence of songwriters and best-selling authors.[47] Again, this shows the complexity and the diversity of the hermeneutical field. Regarding the mediatory dynamics and the tension between heterogeneity/homogeneity, Rogers sketches two complexes: (a) affirmative readings, connected with strong, stream-down, mediatory dynamics and a more homogeneous mediation; (b) disruptive readings, connected with weaker, trickle-down, mediatory dynamics, and a permeable congregation with more external mediation. Too much affirmation and homogeneity lead to a rigid tradition that loses its vitality, too much disruption and heterogeneity lead to a loss of stability in a tradition and an undervaluing of the Bible. Scripture needs a healthy tradition that is both stable and dynamic.[48]

8.2.3 Reflections

What significant insights can be learned from these investigations into the practice of the church as a community that hears and reads Scripture, to arrive at a better view of reading Scripture as an ecclesial practice that transforms members of the congregation into Christlikeness?

In a secular, pluralist, post-Christian world, (the formation of) a mindset and worldview that is open to God and not immanentist, is under pressure. At the same time, facing the crises of our time, Christian formation is important. Thus, the church must be an embodied community where relations, practices, and social imaginary foster the understanding of Scripture as the word of God, the formation of the mind of Christ, and Christlikeness. This review of empirical research shows the importance of the church as a hermeneutical community. In real life, congregations do

---

45. Rogers, *Congregational Hermeneutics*, 56–58, 135–40.
46. Rogers, *Congregational Hermeneutics*, 141.
47. Rogers, *Congregational Hermeneutics*, 141.
48. Rogers, *Congregational Hermeneutics*, 168.

function as a hermeneutical community. Scripture always is read within a perspective, constituted by a community with its tradition and practices. Active participation in a congregation and active engagement with the Bible help to understand the Bible. The community, its leadership, and hermeneutical apprenticeship within the community have hermeneutical significance.[49] At the same time, congregational life is as ambivalent as the reality of the church is. The church is a plural community, showing differences and even divisions. Accordingly, it is important to critically reflect on the church as a hermeneutical community. For more detailed reflections, I will deal successively with the congregation, mediators, individual readers, Scripture, and God.

Congregation: Congregations consist of a variety of people, participating in a variety of practices, where some people have special mediatory roles and where various mediators are used. In a congregation, we find a culture of reading, teaching, and guidance, but this can also be a catechetical culture in decline. The Dutch situation shows a plurality of readers. Bielo's analysis shows that reading groups can read with different interests. Such mixed communities have to manage the tension between heterogeneity and homogeneity. Sometimes this will cause problems and persons will leave the group on account of these differences.[50]

Traditions of Bible reading imply views of Scripture, attitudes, hermeneutical virtues, practices, and behavior. Textual practices are inseparably connected with textual ideologies, but they are also embedded in social imaginaries and background beliefs. This pluriformity evokes the question of whether a community has a unifying center and a resource to handle differences. Rogers warns, "There is a dark side to community when it is not aligned with a Christian *telos*. Community can be an excuse for a hermeneutical free for all or for authoritarian policing of congregational boundaries."[51]

However, it is impossible not to be part of a tradition, and a tradition of reading is necessary to learn to listen to Scripture. Rogers is right that it is best to embrace one's tradition in a self-critical way (and as a result to learn together how to listen to each other).[52] Village refers to Stephen Fowls's idea of a "vigilant community," where readers work together toward

---

49. On community and hermeneutical reflections, see the concluding chapter of Rogers, *Congregational Hermeneutics*, 199–224.

50. For two examples, see Bielo, *Words upon the Word*, 85, 162.

51. Rogers, *Congregational Hermeneutics*, 205.

52. Rogers, *Congregational Hermeneutics*, 89–93.

"charity in interpretation."[53] To do so, a church will find resources for dealing with differences in her identity as the body of Christ. It is the Spirit of Christ who unites us in Christ and makes us share in Christ. In a self-critical Christian community, readers have to be aware of the noetic consequences of sin, longing to use their gifts of understanding to build the body of Christ in a Christlike manner. They need to strive for a healthy dynamic of Word and Spirit, of affirmation and disruption. To reach this goal, clarity about a shared faith in Christ, to follow him as his disciples, is important, with a clear focus on the basics of this Christian faith: love for the triune God and hope for his kingdom. It is important to remind here what we started in chapter 4: the most important actor in the hermeneutical field is the triune God. If the triune God is active in this world, hope exists for the church as a listening community.

Mediators: It is good to be aware of the "textual economy" (Bielo) and the complexity of the mediation processes, as Rogers's analysis shows. Rogers focuses on impersonal categories, such as activities and objects. However, the analysis shows repeatedly how important living people are in the mediation processes such as learning to listen to the Bible, facilitating the reading process, dealing with differences, and stimulating reading "with the eyes of another," in the formation of persons and communities.

Thus, the training of ministers, pastors, or group leaders is fundamentally important, so that they can be guides in the hermeneutical and mystagogical processes of listening to Scripture. These mediators have to be spiritual guides who are themselves transparent toward God before they can help interpret experiences (see 8.3 as well).[54] They have to resemble Sarah Coakley's ideal leader, a "mystic" type with "the intense personal passion to spiritual depth, the drive to intellectual comprehension, the willingness to offer somewhat uncomfortable leadership beyond what an existing group already entertained."[55] Congregations need mediators who embody their message and live the basics of the Christian faith. They should not follow a strategy of control, but help a congregation to deal with plurality and to grow as a community in "charity of understanding" with a healthy dynamic of Word and Spirit, practicing a life both after Easter and Pentecost. As such, they can help others to understand the Bible, by offering possible interpretations and applications. Their guidance should be characterized by openness

---

53. Village, *Bible and Lay People*, 140.
54. De Jong-Van Campen, *Mystagogie in werking*, 75, 87–90, 285–87.
55. Coakley, *God, Sexuality, and the Self*, 185, cf. 181–82.

and faithfulness, interpreting between affirmation and disruption, as Rogers stresses.[56]

Individual readers: People read, understand, and apply what they holistically hear in the Bible. Personality, education, beliefs, attitudes, behavior, and practices, all influence one's reading of Scripture. Readers have undergone their own formation. For Western people, education often implies the formation of a critical-argumentative mindset, sometimes even a "desert of criticism" after the loss of a first naivety.[57] This can be a problem, although the example of Evangelicals shows that Christian beliefs can correct this mindset of criticism. De Jong-Van Campen's study of mystagogical processes sees the transformation of this mindset as part of a mystagogical process.[58]

Rogers shows the influence of one's (implicit) epistemological assumptions, which is part of the reader's mindset. Readers with a foundationalist epistemology will have problems with interpretative uncertainties and plurality, "since different interpretations of Scripture threaten the stability of the noetic structure."[59] The difference between foundationalist and nonfoundationalist epistemologies shows the necessity of a discourse in which these differences can be bridged, based on a shared commitment to Jesus Christ. The soteriological approach offered in this book could help to offer what Rogers is looking for, emphasizing humility and confidence.[60] All readers have their personalities, beliefs, attitudes, and experiences. Hopefully, they learn to see their strengths and weaknesses and share themselves with their congregation. Village encourages churches to "accept and use individual differences."[61]

Finally, De Jong-Van Campen reminds us of something that seems to be a blind spot of the research of Village, Bielo, and Rogers: the intention and openness of the reader matter as well. Thus, it is important to investigate further the mystagogical processes (see 8.3). Moreover, it is important to recall again the activity of the triune God. While human beings can influence their intentions and openness only to a certain extent, the renewing work of the Holy Spirit can reach us where no human being can (cf. 8.4).

Scripture: As Bielo has written, textual ideology and textual practice influence each other; or in Village's terms, one's relationship with the Bible

56. Rogers, *Congregational Hermeneutics*, 168–69.
57. Village, *Bible and Lay People*, 160.
58. De Jong-Van Campen, *Mystagogie in werking*, 85–87, 96–101, 109–12.
59. Rogers, *Congregational Hermeneutics*, 137.
60. Rogers, *Congregational Hermeneutics*, 139–40.
61. Village, *Bible and Lay People*, 122.

has been shaped by one's attitudes toward and beliefs about the Bible. These are shaped by personal growth and experience, but also by participation in practices, reading traditions, and congregational interactions. As far as experience is concerned, it can be expected that positive experiences with listening to Scripture and God's use of Scripture to speak his Word to us will influence the reading of the Bible positively.

Clear differences in beliefs about the Bible exist between liberal and conservative (or radical) Christians. About the Bible, Reformed, and Evangelical Christians differ significantly from Roman- and Anglo-Catholic Christians. This polarization presents a danger. Interestingly, Bielo mentions that literalism is more an identity marker than a regulative idea for the interpretation of Scripture.

The influence of historical criticism is also important. Both the projects of De Wit and Village show that the larger the historical consciousness and awareness of historical-critical problems, the smaller the preference for the horizon of the reader and the ability to apply the text within that horizon. Here, beliefs about and expectations from God will have a necessary positive corrective influence. Furthermore, it is good to remember that everyone can read the Bible, irrespective of one's beliefs about the Bible. It is true for all Christians that the frequency of reading has a positive influence on one's relationship with the Bible. The growing significance of synchronic approaches to the Bible in theological education is helpful as well. We all can search for the meaning of the world of the text. Moreover, we have the world behind the text only in a variety of historical reconstructions, based on the text. Thus, they have a secondary character. This focus on the world of the text might help readers to find the second naivety (a renewed naivety beyond critical thinking) that is so necessary according to Village.[62]

God: That the reading of Scripture is influenced by beliefs about and expectations from God, is confirmed in this survey of empirical research. For modern readers, a secularized practice of reading the Bible is a real danger, leaving the individual reader with just a book and an absent or nonexisting God. Therefore, a church must embody a different perspective. Only in God's presence can the Scripture be truly understood as a Word that transforms into Christlikeness.

Village warns Evangelicals of the danger of being Word-dominated churches, forgetting the work of the Spirit. Both the Word and the transforming work of the Spirit are important for theological hermeneutics. Village is right in emphasizing the importance of charismatic renewal. His research interestingly shows that participation in charismatic practices,

---

62. Village, *Bible and Lay People*, 90–91.

actively living with the Holy Spirit, fosters a mindset that expects the active presence of God here and now.[63] Similarly, Bielo highlights the influence of expectations from God on the reading of Scripture. Generally, the expectation of God's active presence and the interpretation of experiences in the light of God's active presence will help us understand the Bible as God's word. This is confirmed by studies on how mystagogy "works": the offer of a Christian view of reality is important to let mystagogy into the mystery of God's presence.[64]

8.3 THE RENEWAL OF THE MIND AND MYSTAGOGY IN PRACTICES OF MERCY

The renewal of the mind is not just a matter of reading and understanding Scripture better, but also of the transformation of our views of everything else in the light of Scripture. This concerns our image of God, neighbor, self, and world. We have seen that human existence is narrative, social, affective, and embodied. Thus, it is reasonable to expect that the renewal of the mind does not just concern our cognitive beliefs, the narrative frames we use, or our participation in a community. It also concerns our participation in practices and the spiritual impact this has on our inner lives. In this section, I will further investigate the role of participation in practices in the complex process of the renewal of the mind. I will do this by delving into mystagogical processes and their influence on the renewal of the mind. As a case study will serve the participation in practices of mercy and mystagogical processes as a consequence of participation in these practices. In this section, my focus will not be on the understanding of Scripture, but on the understanding of mercy. Our understanding of mercy is more or less informed by Scripture and connects to our views of God, the neighbor, the self, and the world. Does participation in practices of mercy influence the transformation of our views of mercy? And what is the role of biblically informed views of God's mercy?

A Christian understanding of mercy concerns God's mercy as well as human practices in which we show mercy to our neighbors. Divine mercy is the horizon and the source of human acts of mercy.[65] At the same time, more relationships exist between the two. A few biblical examples illustrate these relations. Firstly, the parable of the king and his servants in Matt 18

---

63. Village, *Bible and Lay People*, 153–56.

64. De Jong-Van Campen, *Mystagogie in werking*, 293–98.

65. Brock, "Mercy, Compassion, and the Flesh"; Ulrich, "Mercy: The Messianic Practice."

relates God's mercy to the mercy of his servants. Furthermore, the Gospel of John relates Jesus's love and mercy to the love and mercy of his disciples. The story of Jesus washing his disciples' feet implies this relation, when we hear Jesus say, "I have set you an example that you should do as I have done for you" (John 13:15). Explicitly, Jesus's sacrificial love is presented as an example in these words of Jesus: "Love each other as I have loved you. Greater love has no one than this: to lay down one's life for one's friends. You are my friends, if you do what I command" (John 15:12-14; cf. 1 John 3:16). God's mercy can be seen as a horizon, a source, and an example of human mercy. Furthermore, practices of mercy may have a formative effect. But how are we to understand these relations between God's mercy and human mercy more precisely?

To analyze the relationship between God's mercy and human mercy, one could, in a Barthian fashion, start with the revelation of God's mercy. This will guarantee a theological perspective, seeing human mercy in the light of God's mercy. However, to explore the relations, we also need an anthropological perspective, seeing God's mercy in the light of human mercy. To explore the relations in both directions, the mystagogical significance of practices of mercy will be taken as the starting point. Referring to the works of De Jong-Van Campen (on mystagogy) and Meeuws (on the mystagogical significance of diaconal practices), I will show the mystagogical significance of these practices.[66] Provided that the conditions are right, diaconal practices can have a function in mystagogical processes. They can not only help us to become aware of God's presence, but they can also serve to see ourselves and our neighbor in the light of God's presence.[67] Based on this mystagogical significance, I will distinguish hermeneutical and formative relations. Building on De Jong-Van Campen and Meeuws, I will proceed to analyze, in more depth, these different relations between God's mercy and our practices of mercy.

8.3.1 The Mystagogical Significance of Practices of Mercy

In *Mystagogie in werking*, De Jong-Van Campen describes how mystagogy takes place in Christian communities. Meeuws builds on her book, focusing more on diaconal work. According to De Jong-Van Campen, mystagogy concerns the initiation into mysteries, and living with God's mercy in

---

66. De Jong-Van Campen, *Mystagogie in werking*; Meeuws, *Diaconie*.

67. De Jong-Van Campen, *Mystagogie in werking*, 85-88, 125-26, 135-37, 294-96; Meeuws, *Diaconie*, 88; 366-415.

Christ is ultimately a mystery.[68] De Jong-Van Campen defines mystagogy as "initiation in personal faith and the community of faith."[69] In mystagogical processes, the mystagogical offer of the community and the mystagogue has a threefold character. First, the offer of a Christian view of reality, which is aimed not only at a Christian frame of reference but also at spiritual and symbolic awareness. This implies that a theological perspective creates the possibility of a human perspective on mercy. Second, the evocation of spiritual experiences is required. And third, these experiences need to be interpreted.[70]

She understands the aim of mystagogy as a spiritual process of inhabitation and transformation. In the mystagogical process, the myste (the person being spiritually guided) "discovers himself as a temple, in which more and more space comes into existence (transformation) for God to live in (inhabitation)."[71] Formulated in a way that can be understood christologically, it is "a process in which the image of God unfolds and conjugates in and between human beings."[72] Mystagogy aims at transformation toward becoming truly human before God's presence.

Further, De Jong-Van Campen distinguishes three corresponding domains of being human in which the mystagogical process of transformation takes place: in the mental domain, the formation of a Christian view of reality and a symbolic consciousness; in the physical domain, the application of the spiritual distinction between flesh and spirit to observe reality with a spiritual vision, and to learn how to act motivated by this vision and as the expression of this vision; and finally in the communicative domain, to make contact with reality, learning to deal with the emotional nature of this contact.[73] De Jong-Van Campen emphasizes the strong relationship between these dimensions of contemplating on, experiencing, doing in, and having contact with reality.[74]

De Jong-Van Campen shares the view that mystagogy is a "paradigm for the entire pastoral praxis."[75] She assumes that mystagogical processes

68. De Jong-Van Campen, *Mystagogie in werking*, 30–31; Meeuws, *Diaconie*, 358.
69. De Jong-Van Campen, *Mystagogie in werking*, 68.
70. De Jong-Van Campen, *Mystagogie in werking*, 85–94, 296–98, 312.
71. "In het mystagogisch proces zichzelf ontdekt als tempel, waarin steeds meer ruimte ontstaat (omvorming) voor God om er te wonen (inwoning)." De Jong-Van Campen, *Mystagogie in werking*, 299; cf. 94–95.
72. "Een proces waarin het beeld van God zich ontvouwt en vervoegt in en tussen mensen." De Jong-Van Campen, *Mystagogie in werking*, 95.
73. De Jong-Van Campen, *Mystagogie in werking*, 94–105; cf. 296, 299.
74. De Jong-Van Campen, *Mystagogie in werking*, 299.
75. "Een paradigma voor de hele pastorale praxis." De Jong-Van Campen,

can take place in all pastoral fields, including diaconate.[76] However, in her analysis of stories to flesh out her understanding of the mystagogical process, she has found no stories of mystagogy in the field of the diaconate. The interesting question is why she did not find them, and what that implies.

According to De Jong-Van Campen, diaconal practices can lead to mystagogical processes if both the mystagogical offer, as well as the mystagogical openness, are present. The second was present in her research, but the first was lacking. To start with the first: both concerning the view of reality and the interpretation of experiences, the offer of the mystagogue was defective. For mystagogical processes in diaconal practices, a context is needed in which the divine dimension can become "visible"; symbols that can be used in the interpretation of spiritual experiences; and spiritual guides who help to interpret experiences and are themselves transparent for God.[77]

The second requirement, mystagogical openness, is also important. In this respect as well, it is not self-evident that participation in diaconal processes results in mystagogical processes. The specific character of diaconal practices becomes clearer when we compare them to liturgy. Liturgical and diaconal practices can both play their role in mystagogical processes, but they differ in an important respect: liturgy has an inherent mystagogical potency, and diaconal practices have this potency only if one participates in this practice with a spiritual motivation. Mystagogical openness is needed.[78]

This mystagogical openness has different aspects. First, the diaconal practice must be performed with a spiritual motivation. Second, this openness presupposes for the myste and the surrounding community the presence of a frame of reference and a symbolic, spiritual awareness of having and understanding spiritual experiences. Third, required is the willingness to learn and have spiritual experiences. In addition to De Jong, Meeuws emphasizes that a Christian community active in diaconate can become the mystagogue and subject of her mystagogical process. In sharing the gift of God's mercy, the experience of the flowing source of life deepens the understanding of God's mercy.[79]

From the analysis thus far, we reach some conclusions concerning the mystagogical significance of human practices of mercy. We have seen that

---

Mystagogie in werking, 68.

76. De Jong-Van Campen, *Mystagogie in werking*, 68, 119, 125.

77. De Jong-Van Campen, *Mystagogie in werking*, 135–37, 294–96; Meeuws, *Diaconie*, 368.

78. De Jong-Van Campen, *Mystagogie in werking*, 87–90; Meeuws, *Diaconie*, 368–71, 376.

79. Meeuws, *Diaconie*, 383; and more general Meeuws, *Diaconie*, 375–83.

participation in practices of mercy can result in mystagogical processes. These processes include a transformation of the mindset of the myste: they can result in a deepened thinking about God's mercy, experience of God's mercy, acting in accordance with God's mercy, and living focused on God's mercy. This requires that the myste and his/her community or mystagogue share, firstly, a conceptual and symbolic framework for understanding experiences as an expression of God's mercy, secondly, a spiritual intention behind their acts of mercy, thirdly, an openness for spiritual experiences, and, lastly, the ability to interpret experiences and acts of mercy as expressions of God's mercy. In our acts of mercy, it is possible to experience God's mercy as the source of them.[80] The mystery of God's mercy in Christ increasingly becomes a reality to live in and to share. In this mystagogy, the theological and the anthropological perspective both are necessary.

8.3.2 Different Relations between Divine and Human Mercy

We have seen that participation in practices of mercy can have mystagogical significance, transforming our understanding of the mystery of God's mercy. In a second step, I now want to analyze more precisely this mystagogical significance to understand better the relationships between divine and human mercy: what kinds of relationships can we now discern between God's mercy and our acts of mercy? Although I start this analysis in practices of mercy, the character of this analysis has a more general character and is not limited to practices of mercy.

De Jong distinguishes three domains of transformation: the mental, the physical, and the communicative. These three domains encompass different transformative processes: the formation of a Christian view of reality, the observation of reality in the light of a spiritual vision, the growing ability first to act in line with such a spiritual vision, second to deal with emotions in the contact with reality, and third to stand in contact with reality. Consequently, this transformation involves someone's understanding of reality, someone's personal formation, and someone's contact with reality itself. In my analysis, I will focus on understanding and formation, and distinguish hermeneutical relations and formative relations.[81]

---

80. Compare what Brock writes, using Illich's analysis of the parable of the Good Samaritan. According to Brock, in the pedagogy of the Spirit our neighbor "is thus a divine emblem of God's grace as well as a concrete invitation to embrace the divine mercy and in doing so to discover what it means to love the God who is all in all." See Brock, "Mercy, Compassion and the Flesh," 48.

81. In an article, I also distinguished a third type of relationship, normative relations. However, because these normative relations do not contribute really to my

1. *Hermeneutical relations*

Hermeneutical relations concern our understanding of mercy. We can discern three hermeneutical relations.

1. We can understand our acts of mercy in the light of God's merciful acts. Language about God's mercy based on God's merciful acts in the Bible and tradition provides us with the possibility to understand what mercy is.

2. In the light of our practice of mercy, we understand God's mercy. Participation in practices of mercy offers us the opportunity to acquire a deeper understanding of this language about God's mercy.

3. The relationship of personal involvement, which we encounter in the mystagogical process via notions such as openness and intention. Understanding God's mercy and human mercy in the light of God's mercy is possible only in the case of personal involvement.

According to De Jong-Van Campen, the first hermeneutical relation has primacy above the second: only if we have a view of God's mercy, our view of God's mercy can be deepened by spiritual experiences in human practices of mercy. This highlights the importance of language, concepts, and symbols for experience. As we saw in the chapter on Dalferth, we experience something as something (see 4.2).[82] If we have no adequate words, our experiences change and we are unable to articulate our experience.[83] We can learn our words for mercy from different traditions, but how do we come to know adequate concepts of mercy and how do we learn to distinguish them? And how will our experiences of mercy bring us closer to God? According to De Jong-Van Campen, we need a Christian view of mercy to gain a deeper understanding of God's mercy through a mystagogical process. Theologically, this underlines the truth of the starting point of Barth's doctrine of revelation: we learn to understand what mercy is if God reveals his mercy.[84] First, God has to act mercifully and his acts of mercy have to be described as merciful acts. We need both God's acts and texts that tell

---

argument here, I will not deal with these normative relations in this chapter. See Burger, "God's Mercy and Practices of Mercy."

82. Apart from Dalferth, cf. Heidegger, *Sein und Zeit*, 62, 82, 149–51.

83. We know more than we can articulate, as Meek and Clark emphasize, using the work of Polanyi. According to Clark, this is partly due to the fact that we live as bodies and experience as bodies more than we can articulate linguistically. See Meek, *Loving to Know*, 69–76; Clark, *Divine Revelation and Human Practice*, 174.

84. On Barth, see Clark, *Divine Revelation and Human Practice*, 1–35.

about God's mercy, as we believe them to be found in the Scriptures. Hence, reading the Scriptures is important to learn to use the word "mercy" and to find an adequate concept of mercy. From O'Donovan, we learned how reading the Bible can be a source of theological concepts (see 5.5). Within the liturgical context of worship in the church, our language is reshaped by the word of God.[85] This implies that participation in practices of mercy has to be accompanied by the offer of a Christian view of reality (and mercy), be it within a practice of mercy or in other Christian practices. The formation of an adequate concept of mercy in the mental domain is indispensable. The more we have such an adequate concept of mercy, the more we can learn to distinguish what a practice of mercy looks like.

Learning to use adequate words means at the same time that we discover other concepts as less adequate or misguiding. We need to revise our concepts of mercy in the light of God's mercy. Here hermeneutical relations touch on relations of transformation, and the first hermeneutical relation touches on the third one (personal involvement). Learning to use the word "mercy" adequately might imply a moment of conversion (we saw already that conversion has hermeneutical implications, see 4.3.2 and 5.5). Moreover, learning to use the word mercy is inseparably linked with the formation of a view of reality *coram deo* in the light of God's mercy. Both from a spiritual and a moral perspective, we need the transformation of our minds so that we can learn to act mercifully.[86]

In this first hermeneutical relation, God's mercy is the starting point for understanding human acts. In the second hermeneutical relation, we find the reverse direction. Although the first relation has primacy, these two relations cannot be separated in time. To learn to use a word, we need the word first, and we need good concepts to perceive correctly; in that sense, the offer of language and a Christian view of reality has primacy. Especially, when the mystagogical significance is concerned, using the word "mercy" can bring us only closer to God if we learn to relate "mercy" and "God" in the concept of "God's mercy." But at the same time, we learn to use words better when we use them in real life and examples are presented. Hence, participation in human practices of mercy with a Christian intention is a good position to learn to use the word "mercy" and this participation leads also to a (deepened) understanding of God's mercy. When we embrace people hospitably, when we serve people and care for them, we can better

---

85. Clark speaks here with Torrance of "commandeering of language"; see Clark, *Divine Revelation and Human Practice*, 63-65.

86. On the moral perspective, see, e.g., Wright, *After You Believe*, 135-80. On the spiritual perspective, see Willard, *Renovation of the Heart*, 95-116; Vanhoozer, *Drama of Doctrine*, 106, 255, 331.

understand God's hospitality and God's care. The fact that De Jong-Van Campen emphasizes the importance of a Christian intention, shows the importance of existential intentionality, which correlates with the third hermeneutical relation of personal involvement.

This indicates all the more that the three relations belong together. We can understand this using the concept of a sign as developed by C. S. Peirce and others. According to them, a sign is a triadic relation between, first, the sign bearer, second, a sense, and third, a reference.[87] The relations between the three are not static. For Dutch people, the word "koningin" ("queen") has the sense of "wife of the head of state," and refers specifically to a person with the name "Máxima Zorreguieta." In the past, the word "koningin" denoted "head of state" and was used to refer to a person named "Beatrix van Oranje." Furthermore, a word with its sense and reference might evoke significance and subjective meaning. For those who love royalty, the words "queen" or "koningin" have a different meaning than for a republican. In 7.4.3 I have already used these concepts of sense, reference, and significance (see figure 1). They can be connected to the world of the text (sense), the world behind the text (reference), and the world in front of the text (significance).

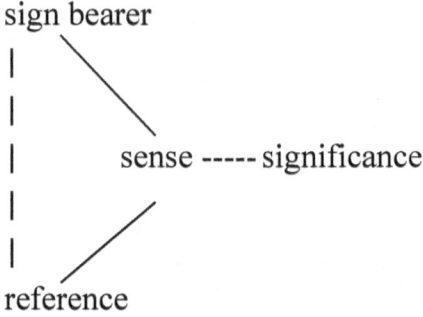

Fig. 1 Sign

From the mystagogical offer and the Scriptures, we learn to use the sign "mercy." Stories about and experiences of God's mercy can become sign bearers for us. Using these sign bearers we can both refer to God's mercy (seeing God's mercy in the light of what we already know about God's mercy)

---

87. Chandler, *Semiotics*, 32–36; De Pater and Swiggers, *Taal en teken*, 122–51. For C. S. Peirce's theory of signs, see Short, "Development of Peirce's Theory of Signs"; Vetter, *Zeichen Deuten Auf Gott*, 26–146.

or to human mercy (seeing human mercy in the light of God's mercy). This is what we do in the first hermeneutical relation (see fig. 2).

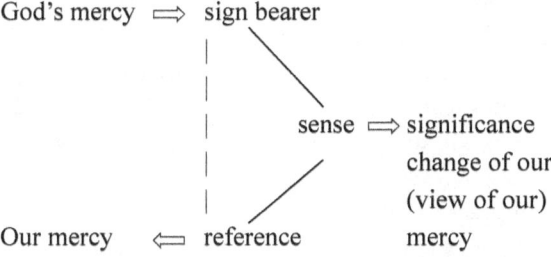

Fig. 2 First hermeneutical relation

However, the opposite is possible as well. Living with a reality in practice and experiencing its presence and its influence is essential for understanding this reality.[88] Experiences with and practices of human mercy can lead to an understanding of mercy that is more fleshed out. Stories and memories of human mercy can become sign-bearers as well. Now, we can refer to God's mercy (as well as other human acts of mercy) in the light of what we now know from human mercy. This is the second hermeneutical relation: seeing divine mercy in the light of human mercy (see fig. 3).

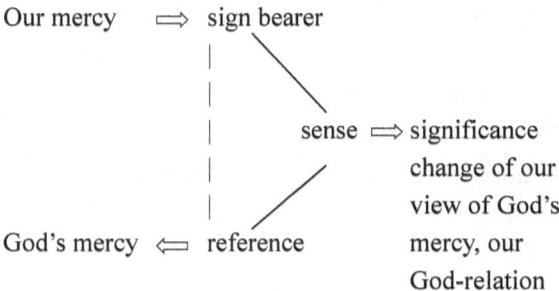

Fig. 3 Second hermeneutical relation

88. In reference to Polanyi, both Meek, and Clark emphasize the importance of participation for our understanding; Meek in her "covenant epistemology" and Clark in his plea for (semantic) participation in understanding divine revelation. See Meek, *Loving to Know*; Clark, *Divine Revelation and Human Practice*, 145–96. See further on the importance of canonical practices, covenantal forms of life, and *sola scriptura* as a practice Vanhoozer, *Drama of Doctrine*, 211–42.

In both cases, however, we have a sign bearer (the word "mercy"), a reference (divine or human acts of mercy), and a sense (see fig. 2 and 3). This sense is intersubjective; however, it is attached to a (more subjective) significance for someone. The third hermeneutical relation of personal involvement has to do with the difference between the linguistic concept of "sense" and the more personal concept of "significance." As persons with consciousness and a will we relate to ourselves and our world. We act intentionally and our will determines whether we are open to reality or not. Consequently, De Jong-Van Campen and Meeuws found that the diaconal intention behind practices of mercy and further the mystagogical openness of both the mystagogue and the myste play an essential role. Learning about mercy and arriving at a deepened understanding of mercy is possible only if I as a subject am willing and open to learn more about mercy. Our existential involvement in our acts influences our understanding and the change of our understanding of God's mercy. Willingness or unwillingness, love or hatred, determine how we see, understand, interpret, and think. Especially when God and God's mercy are concerned, the concept of sin is important. As human beings, we no longer love God with all our hearts, which influences our knowledge of God and his mercy. On the other hand, the renewal of our lives in Christ implies that our participation in Christ has a positive effect on our understanding of God and his mercy. To summarize, we have three hermeneutical relations:

> 1. a relation between God's acts of mercy and our acts of mercy: we understand our acts and practices of mercy in the light of God's mercy;
>
> 2. a relation between our acts of mercy and God's mercy: our understanding of God's mercy is influenced by our acts, practices, and experiences; and
>
> 3. the relation between ourselves and human or divine acts of mercy: our openness and willingness to learn to influence the transformation of our understanding.

1. *Formative relations*

Closely related to these hermeneutical relations, I distinguished *formative* relations as well. Practices of mercy can have a transforming effect. We are transformed increasingly into the image of Christ and consequently into the image of God. Moreover, in these transforming relations we encounter the mystery of our participation in Christ.

However, I am not just speaking of a transforming *effect*, but of formative *relations* between God's mercy and our mercy. How should we reconstruct such a formative relation between God's mercy and our mercy? Building on the hermeneutical relations, we could say that, in general, the act of knowing often has a formative effect, by opening a new perspective, and new perspectives have an impact on our lives.[89] Applied to mercy, new knowledge of mercy transforms our lives. We gain a better perspective on God's mercy and in the light of God's mercy on everything else. It makes a difference when we see everything with a merciful eye and listen with a merciful ear. Here the formative and hermeneutical relations are identical.

But as human beings, we are more than the concepts and thoughts we have in our minds. Our existence is narrative, social, affective, and embodied. We have feelings, a will, and a body, and we are social beings.[90] We live in and with reality, participating bodily in communities and practices. Continuing the thoughts of De Jong-Van Campen and Meeuws, we could say that if practices of mercy have a mystagogical effect, they result in the inhabitation of Christ and the transformation of our person and acts. Phrased differently, they have an intensifying effect on our participation in Christ. But then, we focus only on the transforming effect of diaconal practices.

We encounter God's mercy in richly differentiated ways. First, we hear the proclamation of God's mercy and read about it in the Holy Scriptures and other Christian texts. Second, we worship God's mercy in the liturgy, singing spiritual songs and celebrating the sacraments. The Christian self is a singing and a liturgical self.[91] Third, as Christians, we experience God's mercy as a present reality through the inhabitation of Christ and his Holy Spirit in ourselves. And fourth, if Christians intentionally act mercifully, they experience that they pass on God's mercy in Christ to someone as a present reality that has become a source within themselves. Bodily embedded in practices of mercy, we experience ourselves as an instrument of God's mercy, receiving God's mercy as a source.[92] This can have a transforming effect both on the subject of the act as well as on the person receiving mercy. It is this complex of living with God's mercy that has a formative effect on our

---

89. This is an important emphasis of Meek's covenant epistemology: knowledge is transforming. See, e.g., Meek, *Loving to Know*, 46, 60, 63, 70, 94, 100, 125–26, 273.

90. Cf. Willard, *Renovation of the Heart*, 32–42.

91. According to David Ford, the Christian self is a worshipping self, a singing self and a eucharistic self. See Ford, *Self and Salvation*. See on formation by participation in the liturgy further Smith, *Desiring the Kingdom*; Smith, *Imagining the Kingdom*.

92. Volf emphasizes that it is Christ in us who is giving and forgiving if we give and forgive. See Volf, *Free of Charge*.

person, our knowledge and character, our community, acts, and practices (see fig. 4).

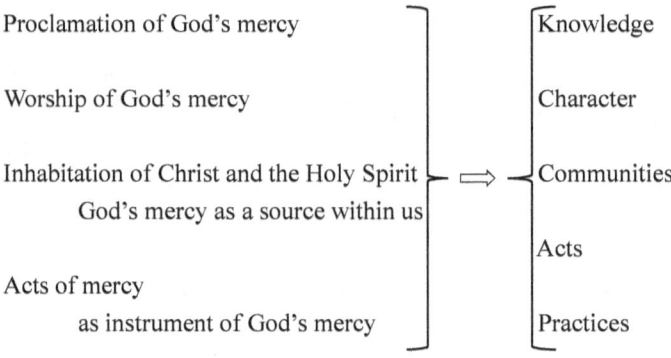

Fig. 4 A formative relation

This implies that hermeneutical relations are embedded in this complex formative relation. A combination of verbal activities (preaching, reading, singing), practices and acts (worship, diaconal practices, acts of mercy), and the real presence of the Spirit of Christ within us has a transforming effect on our mind, our character, our communities, acts, and practices. It is this combination of the Word of God, liturgical and diaconal practices, and the presence of the risen Christ in his Spirit that has a transforming effect.

Theologically, this transformation has different aspects. Individually, we are transformed in the direction of Christlikeness by the inhabitation of his Spirit. The formation of the image of Christ in us implies the restoration of the image of God in us, for Christ the Son of God is the true image of God. It means that Christ's mercy becomes a trait of our character. As a communion, the church as the body of Christ is transformed into a community where our eyes are the eyes of Christ's mercy; our mouth speaks words of his mercy; our hands and feet act in the service of his mercy. Finally, more and more, our acts and practices become bearers of God's mercy that receives in this way a public manifestation. As it is said in 1 John 4:12 of God's love, it is true of God's mercy as well: "No one has ever seen God; but if we love one another, God lives in us, and his love is made complete in us." This public manifestation has significance both for potential givers of mercy as well as for potential receivers of God's mercy.

8.3.3 Conclusion

The purpose of this section was to clarify the influence of participation in Christian practices on the transformation of the mind and the renewal of our understanding. To do this, I focused on the mystagogical significance of practices of mercy, investigating the relations between God's mercy and human acts of mercy. I found two different kinds of relations: hermeneutical and formative relations. Regarding the first, I distinguished three different hermeneutical relations, concerning the understanding of mercy:

> 1. a relation between God's acts of mercy and our acts of mercy: we understand our acts and practices of mercy in the light of God's mercy;

> 2. a relation between our acts of mercy and God's mercy: our understanding of God's mercy is influenced by our acts, practices, and experiences; and

> 3. the relation between ourselves and human or divine acts of mercy: our openness and willingness to learn to influence the transformation of our understanding.

The formative relation concerns personal formation. This relation is more complex, for it is a combination of verbal activities (preaching, reading, singing), practices and acts (worship, diaconal practices, acts of mercy), and the real presence of the Spirit of Christ within us that has a transforming effect on our mind, our character, our communities, acts, and practices. All these clarify the complexity of the interaction between Scripture, our understanding of Scripture, our understanding of God, our neighbor, self, and world in the light of Scripture, our participation in practices, our personal transformation, and the importance of our existential involvement in all of this.

Reading Scripture will lead to participation in Christian practices, to renewed understanding in the light of Scripture, and to Christian formation. Participation in practices will not only contribute to more understanding in the light of Scripture and to Christian formation but also a better understanding of Scripture. It all enforces our remaining in Christ and our transformation into Christlikeness. Remaining in Christ and transforming into Christlikeness on the other hand will influence positively our understanding and participation.

In terms of the interaction between the world of the text, the world behind the text, and the world in front of the text, we can say that what we do in front of the text (like participation in Christian practices) helps to understand the world of the text and the world behind the text. It is also our participation in the world behind the text because the text refers to the practice of the triune God and the participation of believers in Christ. When we read Scripture and understand better the world of the text, we will understand better the world behind the text and our world in front of the text will be transformed, so that we are more able to participate in Christian practices and are transformed personally as well. By understanding the world behind the text (in which we participate in Christ and the Spirit), we will understand the world of the text better and participate in Christian practices in the world in front of the text.

Until now, I have reflected on several aspects of the renewal of our understanding: the renewal of our beliefs about Scripture, the influence of the ambivalent ecclesial practice, and the role of participation in Christian practices. Traditionally, Reformed theology started its reflections on the work of the Holy Spirit in the believer. That will get also my attention in the next section of this chapter.

8.4 LEARNING TO UNDERSTAND THE MIND OF GOD

The Reformed and Puritan traditions know that the ability to understand is not natural, but is a spiritual gift of the Holy Spirit that has to be fostered. We have seen the importance of the community of the church and participation in practices. In this section, I will focus on a Puritan vision of the renewal of the mind as part of the work of the Holy Spirit. I aim to show how these recent emphases on community and practice connect to the Reformed tradition of reflection on the renewal of the mind.

The English Puritan John Owen (1616–83) has written a book with an intriguing subtitle: *Sunesis Pneumatikè: The Causes, Ways, and Means of Understanding the Mind of God as Revealed in His Word, with Assurance Therein* (1678). *Sunesis Pneumatikè* (spiritual insight) is a diptych together with *The Reason of Faith* (1677), that has already been discussed in 2.3. We saw that both works, included in his two-volume work on the Holy Spirit, have the aim "to declare the work of the Holy Spirit in the illumination of the minds of man."[93] *Sunesis Pneumatikè* deals with the understanding and the interpretation of Scripture, or more specifically, understanding the mind of God when we read and interpret Scripture.[94]

John Owen deals with spiritual illumination, causes of spiritual ignorance, and means for understanding the mind of God. Although John Owen is primarily focused on understanding Scripture, these themes have a larger

---

93. Owen, *Works*, 4:7.
94. Owen, *Works*, 4:7.

importance in his work. When one learns to understand the "mind of God" and overcomes spiritual barriers, this will change one's mindset and way of understanding in a more general manner.[95] In 8.4.1, I begin with a description of the knowledge of the mind of God as Owen's aim. In 8.4.2, I focus on the renewal of the mind by the Holy Spirit. I conclude this section with an evaluation, in 8.4.3.

8.4.1 Owen's Aim: Knowledge of the Mind of God

In a seventeenth-century theological landscape, Owen tried to navigate between the position of the Roman Catholic church, which in his view overemphasized the role of the church, the theologies of Arminians and Socinians, who expected too much of human capacities, and the influence of the Quakers whom he saw as "enthusiasts," who despised the role of the means for the interpretation of Scripture.[96] Owen defends the perspicuity of Scripture and the importance of the work of the Holy Spirit.

In *Sunesis Pneumatikè*, Owen is not just interested in understanding a text, but in a theological understanding of Scripture and a spiritual understanding of the text.[97] Believers need "knowledge of the things themselves designed in them," that is "the mind and will of God in them."[98] Owen is convinced that we need the Spirit's illumination, a "special work of the Holy Spirit on our minds" so that we can "understand the Scriptures in a right manner, or to know the mind of God in them."[99] In *Sunesis Pneumatikè*, Owen tries to clarify the nature of illumination and show the implications for the (spiritual) practice of reading Scripture.

Owen presents a Trinitarian understanding of the revelation of the mind of God. The Son of God has given believers an understanding of the mind of God. God the Father and the Son share their divine knowledge because of their essential unity. God's eternal counsel and his eternal life are in the Son. Because believers are in the Son, the Son communicates with them this knowledge and eternal life, including the ability to understand this knowledge. To know the mind and will of God means that this life-giving

---

95. On this treatise and more in general Owen's view of illumination and hermeneutics, see Leslie, *Light of Grace*; Trueman, *Claims of Truth*, 75–99; Webster, *Domain of the Word*, 51–53, 59–63; Zimmermann, *Recovering Theological Hermeneutics*, 87–104, 109–11, 115–19.

96. Trueman, *Claims of Truth*, 65–67, 75, 78; Zimmermann, *Recovering Theological Hermeneutics*, 93, 101–2, 109.

97. Owen, *Works*, 4:122; cf. 124.

98. Owen, *Works*, 4:156; cf. 163.

99. Owen, *Works*, 4:127.

knowledge of God is communicated in the Son and by the Spirit with the believers.[100] All these have a Christocentric focus. The truths of Scripture are the "mysteries of divine truth, wisdom, and grace ... with their especial respect unto Jesus Christ."[101] This knowledge concerns remaining in Christ, and "whatever is needful unto our communion with Christ and our obedience to him."[102]

Consequently, this knowledge transforms and gives wisdom for life. It transforms, because this knowledge of the mind and will of God "affects the heart, and transforms the mind in the renovation of it unto the approbation of the 'good, and acceptable, and perfect will of God,' as the apostle speaks, Romans 12:2," and this capacity of discernment is "valuable and desirable, as unto all spiritual and eternal ends."[103] Knowledge of God's mind and will makes us wise to discern and to be able to be obedient. As Zimmermann writes about Owen, "Sanctification, the increasing restoration of the human being to the image of God, it the goal of Biblical hermeneutics."[104] Further, Owen clearly would agree with O'Donovan that discernment of Scripture and discernment out of Scripture have to come together. Thus, Owen's reflections on the formation of the mind of God have a larger significance for the formation of the ability to discern.

Reading and even studying Scripture does not automatically lead to knowledge of the mind of God. Knowledge without illumination causes pride, according to Owen.[105] Moreover, Owen is aware of the "god of this world" who can blind people and fill them with prejudices against the good news of Christ.[106] Owen dedicates an entire chapter to the causes of spiritual ignorance. Owen also writes about the noetic consequences of sin. Due to the depravation of sin, the mind is blinded and darkened. As a consequence, "the mind is kept off from discerning the glory and beauty of spiritual, heavenly truth, and from being sensible of its power and efficacy."[107] Furthermore, the fallen mind is dominated by corrupt affections. The mind is no longer attached to God, but "inclined unto all things that are vain, curious,

---

100. Owen, *Works*, 4:164.
101. Owen, *Works*, 4:129.
102. Owen, *Works*, 4:146.
103. Owen, *Works*, 4:157.
104. Zimmermann, *Recovering Theological Hermeneutics*, 116.
105. Owen refers to 1 Cor 8:1. Owen, *Works*, 4:156.
106. Owen, *Works*, 4:169.
107. Owen, *Works*, 4:176.

superstitious, carnal, suited unto the interests of pride, lust, and all manner of corrupt affections."[108]

Although Thomism had some influence on Owen, in his anthropology he was no Thomistic intellectualist. As a Reformed theologian, he was a "soteriological voluntarist." As a Puritan, he was aware of the affective dimension of humanity. And both the will and the affections are "more corrupted than the understanding."[109] These corrupted affections hinder a good understanding of the mind of God and underline for Owen the importance of the work of the Holy Spirit to enlighten the darkened mind.

8.4.2 The Holy Spirit and the Formation of the Renewed Mind

As Owen tries to navigate between Arminians and Socinians, Quakers and other enthusiasts, as well as Roman Catholicism, he sketches an overview of the work of the Spirit that includes the study of Scripture, the role of other believers, the use of reason, and the use of other means.[110] Still, the emphasis on the work of the Spirit is very clear. In *Sunesis Pneumatikè*, Owen wants to show that

> there is an especial work of the Spirit of God on the minds of men, communicating spiritual wisdom, light, and understanding unto them, necessary unto their discerning and apprehending aright the mind of God in his word, and the understanding of the mysteries of heavenly truth contained therein.[111]

Owen gives three enumerations to clarify this work of the Spirit. First, he gives a list of scriptural expressions to indicate what the Spirit does. It is the work of the Spirit "to open one's eyes," "to translate out of darkness into

---

108. Owen, *Works*, 4:176.

109. Owen, *Works*, 4:268. See Leslie, *Light of Grace*, 98. Furthermore on Owen between intellectualism and voluntarism, see Leslie, *Light of Grace*, 95–102; Trueman, *Claims of Truth*, 79–83. Rehnman writes, "He is firmly rooted in Renaissance scholasticism and modified Thomism with a stricter Augustinian and Scotist orientation in the context of his Reformed theology." See Rehnman, *Divine Discourse*, 45. Leslie, Rehnman and Trueman characterize the position of Owen and many other Reformed theologians of that age as "Scotistically modified Thomism," see Leslie, *Light of Grace*, 34; Rehnman, *Divine Discourse*, 62–63; Trueman, *Claims of Truth*, 58–60. On the influence of Thomism in Owen's work see Cleveland, *Thomism in John Owen*. On the role of affections in spiritual life, see Ferguson, *John Owen on the Christian Life*, 38, 53–54, 84–85, 127, 135; King, "Affective Spirituality of John Owen."

110. Owen, *Works*, 4:125–26, 161, 167–68. See further Trueman, *Claims of Truth*, 65–67, 75, 78.

111. Owen, *Works*, 4:124.

light," "to give a new understanding," "to teach and to guide into the truth," and "to shine into one's heart."[112] Second, Owen uses the images of light, understanding, and wisdom to clarify the effect of this work of the Spirit.[113] Finally, conceptually expressed, the Holy Spirit has to do three things to our mind according to Owen: "communicate a spiritual light"; "deliver and purge our minds from corrupt affections and prejudices"; and "implant in our mind a new spiritual habit and principle, leading to a new attitude of humility, meekness and being teachable."[114] I will continue my discussion of Owen's understanding of the renewal of the mind following this threefold distinction because this conceptual distinction influences Owen's interpretation of the scriptural expressions and images.

1. *Communication of spiritual light*

Leslie and Cleveland have shown the influence of Thomism on Owen's anthropology and epistemology.[115] Within the Platonist-Thomistic tradition, to know is to participate in the divine light. This light is an inner light. To know the supernatural divine truth, the natural mind has to be enabled by grace to understand what transcends the capacity of the natural mind. For Owen, this implies a special interest in the subjective element of the process of knowing. Knowing the mind of God and thus participating in the divine light is only possible due to inner enlightenment. Humanity was created with a natural, inner light. The fall into sin implies a darkening and blinding of the mind, which is the same as the loss of this inner light. The Spirit does two things: "the expulsion of spiritual darkness" and "the introduction of spiritual light."[116] It is important to hear the influence of the Thomistic framework here. The gracious communication of a supernatural light has a double effect: it restores the natural capacities of the mind and elevates the mind to enable an understanding of the divine supernatural truths.[117]

Within this framework, Owen reads passages in Scripture about illumination. The divine light is shining. Christian believers pray that their eyes may be opened, or that the covering of their eyes may be taken away. Owen reformulates this as a prayer for inner, subjective enlightenment. In

---

112. Owen, *Works*, 4:162–70.
113. Owen, *Works*, 4:171–73.
114. Owen, *Works*, 4:184–85.
115. Cleveland, *Thomism in John Owen*, 69–120; Leslie, *Light of Grace*, 69–77, 81–102, 119–20.
116. Owen, *Works*, 4:172; cf. 163.
117. See, e.g., Owen, *Works*, 4:125–26, 129–30.

his view, the enlightenment is twofold: the objective enlightenment of the objective revelation, and a corresponding subjective inner enlightenment.

He discusses Ps 119:18: "Open thou mine eyes, that I may behold wondrous things out of thy law." The psalm presupposes an outer light and blindness. Owen, however, expects that the psalm deals with an inner light. In the end, this opening of eyes is understood as the "communication of spiritual light" and as "supernatural illumination."[118] Owen, furthermore, deals with 2 Cor 3. Here, Paul writes about a double veil, causing blindness, that has to be removed. Owen, again, understands this removal of the veil as the illumination of the mind.[119] In 2 Cor 4, Paul continues that when the veil is taken away, it is possible to see the glory of God in the face of Jesus Christ so that his light shines in the hearts. Owen understands this as a twofold light, the objective light of the gospel itself and the subjective light in our hearts, a divine light implanted in the mind by a distinct divine act.[120] This light in the mind "is a spiritual ability to discern and know spiritual things."[121]

Due to his understanding of light primarily as an inner light, Owen has to presume a twofold light: objective and subjective. Scripture suggests a different picture: the light shines in Christ or God's word, but due to blindness, a veil covering the eyes, or a closed mindset, humans are unable to see this light so that the light does not shine into their hearts. The removal of this problem does not presuppose a second light, but the opening of the eye, mind, and heart for the reception of the light that shines—no extra source of light but the gift of a capacity to see.[122] The emphasis on an inner light minimizes the illuminating role of the personal encounter with Christ in Scripture.

2. Renewal of Affections

Owen emphasizes our responsibility: "It is, indeed, our *duty* so to purify and purge ourselves,"[123] At the same time, "It is by the grace of the Holy Spirit that we do so."[124] It goes beyond our capacities to free our minds from corrupt

---

118. Owen, *Works*, 4:130.
119. Owen, *Works*, 4:133.
120. Owen, *Works*, 4:170.
121. Owen, *Works*, 4:171.
122. Cf. Webster, *Domain of the Word*, 57. Webster refers to Barth, *Church Dogmatics*, IV/2, 509.
123. Owen, *Works*, 4:184.
124. Owen, *Works*, 4:185.

affections and prejudices. Remarkably, this remains an underdeveloped theme in *Sunesis Pneumatikè*. Though Owen writes that the mind receives "an experience of the power and efficacy of the truth known or discovered, so as to transform the soul and all its affections into it," here he seems especially interested in the resulting "full assurance of understanding."[125] Within Owen's work, the impact of communion with the triune God on the affections is an important theme. Believers live in union with Jesus Christ and can have communion with the Father, Son, and Spirit, which touches our affections. This gives the impression that Owen was more focused on the work of the Holy Spirit in the renewal of the mind than on the process of the renewal of affections.[126]

3. A New Habit

Another concept that Owen takes from Thomism is the concept of infused habits.[127] Due to sin, humans suffer from the power of "vicious, depraved habits" which the Holy Spirit has to take away.[128] Various forms of Reformed theology have been criticized for their understanding of illumination or the gift of a new habit. Illumination can be understood in a subjectivist manner, as the ground of faith, detaching faith from the word of God as possible ground of faith. The gift of a new habit can be presented as a mysterious act in which the agency of the mind is excluded and in which the Word of God as the seed of regeneration plays no role. This is even stronger when the gift of a new habit as the ability to understand can be given long before someone hears the Word of God.[129]

According to Leslie, Owen's understanding of the gift of a new habit does not suffer from these conceptual disadvantages. According to Owen, the infused habit is "a formal copy of the gospel."[130] Furthermore, Owen closely connects the gift of habit with spiritual illumination. Leslie writes

---

125. Owen, *Works*, 4:156. Accordingly, it is too much honor when Zimmermann writes that "Owen thus clearly advocates an 'affective' hermeneutics," Zimmermann, *Recovering Theological Hermeneutics*, 102.

126. On the process of sanctification and communion with God, see, e.g., Ferguson, *John Owen on the Christian Life*, 54–98. On communion with Father, Son and Spirit, see Kapic, *Communion with God*, 147–206.

127. See Cleveland, *Thomism in John Owen*, 69–121; Leslie, *Light of Grace*, 105–34.

128. Owen, *Works*, 4:184.

129. Leslie, *Light of Grace*, 116, 122. So, e.g., Herman Bavinck, see Bavinck, *Gereformeerde dogmatiek*, 4:56, 61–63, 67–72; Bavinck, *Reformed Dogmatics*, 4:80–81, 85–87, 91–95; Burger, *Being in Christ*, 126–27.

130. Leslie, *Light of Grace*, 116.

that "through the infusion of the habit and its likeness to the gospel, the mind is furnished with a new 'spiritual light' whereby it is prepared to receive the truth of the Word."[131] Symmetry exists between "the subjective intellectual light of illumination and the objective light of Scripture."[132] Furthermore, the infusion of the new habit and the presentation of the saving message of the gospel take place simultaneously.[133] As a consequence, Leslie claims, Owen can "preserve the effectual agency of the Word in regeneration" and prevents an understanding of illumination or regeneration as "some secret persuasion."[134]

Still, the twofold understanding of light influences Owen's conceptuality here. Although Owen maintains the simultaneity of the presentation of the external word and the gift of the ability to understand the word, and although a similarity exists between inner and outer light (a likeness exists between word and habit), it is not the light of Christ that shines in our heart. And I wonder whether Owen succeeds in connecting the effectivity of the Spirit with the effectivity of the Word of God who speaks and it happens.[135]

Nevertheless, Owen is right that something has to happen to us. God has to do an effectual work on one's mind to give the ability to understand and discern the mind and will of God. The mind has to be opened, the blindness has to be taken away, and the veil has to be removed. God speaks and gives us the capacity to understand his word.[136] Both the discernment of Scripture and the discernment out of Scripture are possible only if the Spirit has opened one's eyes, mind, and heart. The Spirit has to give understanding and wisdom.[137] This does not imply a gnostic idea of enlightenment or the suggestions of an infallible insight. According to Owen, we don't need "any new divine affiliations, or immediate prophetical inspirations," and he does not propagate "enthusiasm."[138] Owen argues that "No new things are revealed unto our minds," "but our minds are enabled to discern the things that are revealed already."[139]

---

131. Leslie, *Light of Grace*, 117.

132. Leslie, *Light of Grace*, 118.

133. Owen, *Works*, 4:167.

134. Leslie, *Light of Grace*, 122.

135. Cf. Owen, *Works*, 4:167–68. Here, Owen writes that the teaching of God is distinguished from the proposition of the word in the outward dispensation of it.

136. Cf. Webster, *Domain of the Word*, 57–61.

137. Cf Owen, *Works*, 4:172–73.

138. Owen, *Works*, 4:125–26; cf. 161.

139. Owen, *Works*, 134.

Owen wants to foster the ability of believers to understand the written word, using the means that we have received to do so. While emphasizing the primary importance of the work of the Holy Spirit, Owen also recognizes that the Spirit integrates other means and we have to make good use of them. This is already indicated by the fact that Owen recognizes differences, among believers, in receiving the gifts of Christ, according to their duty, work, and obedience.[140] The Spirit demands meekness and humility, but also continual prayer, meditation, and study of the Word.[141] And the gift of the new habit leads to these virtues and to the willingness to be obedient.[142] The importance of all of this for Owen is manifested in the fact that he devotes four chapters to the other means.

First, Owen emphasizes the relevance of how Scripture is composed. The variety of genres enables the church to discern the mind and will of God in different situations for different persons.[143] Second, the fact that Scripture is thus composed, makes the frequent and diligent reading of Scripture important for all believers.[144] Third, he mentions three types of means designed for the improvement of our reading of Scripture: spiritual, disciplinary (like languages and logic), and ecclesiastical means.

As spiritual means, Owen mentions the following.

1. The first spiritual means is prayer. Owen writes, "*Fervent and earnest prayer* for the assistance of the Spirit of God revealing the mind of God" is necessary.[145] Owen tempers the expectations of his readers and warns them not to expect perfect knowledge of all spiritual truths. Owen argues that he who prays for this spiritual guidance "shall be preserved from pernicious errors, and attain that degree in knowledge as shall be sufficient unto the guidance and preservation of the life of God in the whole of his faith and obedience."[146]

2. Secondly, Owen writes about the "readiness to receive impressions from divine truths as revealed unto us."[147] The more our soul is conformed to the revealed truth, the more powerful our understanding

---

140. Owen, *Works*, 4:143.
141. Owen, *Works*, 4:154.
142. Owen, *Works*, 4:185–86.
143. Owen, *Works*, 4:187–99.
144. Owen, *Works*, 4:199–201.
145. Owen, *Works*, 4:201.
146. Owen, *Works*, 4:204.
147. Owen, *Works*, 4:205.

of spiritual things will be. For this reason, believers should long for an experience of its transforming power.

3. The third spiritual means, according to Owen, is obedience to God. Because humans learn by doing, and doctrine and life belong together, believers grow in knowledge only when they practice what they believe.

4. The fourth discipline is "a constant design for growth and a progress in knowledge, out of love to the truth and experience of its excellency."[148] Those who pretend to know everything, will not discover much. Admiration for the treasures of divine wisdom is necessary.

5. Finally, Owen mentions participation in spiritual worship as well as a spiritual means.

The final chapter of *Sunesis Pneumatikè* is devoted to what can be learned from the ministry of the church, and ecclesiastical means. For Owen, it is clear that believers are dependent on the Spirit and not on the church for their knowledge and assurance. Church ministers are like other believers; not "lords of their faith," although they can be "helpers of their joy."[149] Owen brings in the Reformed Scripture-principle, as Trueman has stated.[150] Thus, Owen starts with a critical discussion of the catholic or universal tradition and the consent of the fathers and then concludes:

> We say, therefore, that the sole use of ecclesiastical means in the interpretation of the Scripture is in the due consideration and improvement of that light, knowledge, and understanding in, and those gifts for the declaration of, the mind of God in the Scripture, which he hath granted unto and furnished them withal who have gone before us in the ministry and work of the gospel.[151]

8.4.3 Evaluation

In *Sunesis Pneumatikè*, Owen is focused on the understanding of Scripture. Because he is interested in spiritual discernment of Scripture, not of the words but of the divine things in Scripture, his reflections have a larger

---

148. Owen, *Works*, 4:206.
149. Owen, *Works*, 4:123, 148.
150. Trueman, *Claims of Truth*, 88. See further Zimmermann, *Recovering Theological Hermeneutics*, 107–15.
151. Owen, *Works*, 4:228.

relevance. He who discerns the mind and will of God in Scripture is transformed and receives a renewed way of discerning in the light of Scripture. Owen shows spiritual and psychological insight. Sin has consequences on the human mind and affections. When the mind is no longer attached to God, corrupted affections will attach it to something else, serving sinful interests. As a consequence of sin, our mind is darkened and blinded, no longer able to discern wisely, especially where the heavenly truths are concerned. He not only knew of the noetic consequences of sin, but he also emphasized the renewing work of the Holy Spirit. Only the light of the revelation of the triune God can remove the darkness and heal our blindness.

Positioning himself between Roman Catholics with their emphasis on community and tradition, Arminians and Socianians with their high trust in human capacities, and Enthusiasts who minimized the role of Scripture and study, Owen does two things. First, he emphasizes the decisive character of what God does, and second, he connects this to the church and her tradition, formative practices, and rational activities like the study of theology. The renewal of the mind is principally the work of the Spirit, but because the Spirit uses the word, it is important to listen carefully to the word of God. Because the Spirit works through the community of believers, believers must learn to discern together with all saints. Because the Spirit works in our spirit, prayer, desire, obedience, and participation in the liturgy are important. And finally, because the Spirit restores our capacities, our reason and the use of scholarly methods cannot be missed.

Despite this lasting value of his reflections, his theological elaboration of illumination has several problematic aspects. First, Owen follows the Platonist-Thomistic tradition that understands knowledge as participation in the divine light, emphasizing the importance of inner subjective light. In Scripture, God's light is revealed to us as the light of Christ and the gospel. In 2 Cor 3 and 4, our problem is imagined as a veil that covers the eyes or as spiritual blindness. Once this problem is cured, God's light shines in our hearts (2 Cor 4:3–6). Owen, however, differentiates between an objective and a subjective light. The problem of a veil, blindness, or a closed mindset is understood by Owen as the absence of inner subjective light. Although he tries to keep the objective and subjective light closely together, still it is no longer the outer light that shines in the heart. Objective and subjective are thus separated. In an early modern setting, this separation of objective and subjective easily becomes a separation of the inner and outer world, and thus a separation of the inner work of the Holy Spirit and the external mediation by which the Spirit works.

Second, this separation of the inner and outer works of the Holy Spirit interferes with the order he chooses. Owen's primary emphasis is on the work of the Holy Spirit, and only secondarily he connects the work of the Spirit with community, tradition, practices, and scholarly methods. What is said first, receives the emphasis. What is said at a later moment, is easily forgotten, or the connection is lost with what has been said earlier. Accordingly, the chosen order reinforces the first problem, of the (unintended) separation of the work of the Holy Spirit from the external means.

Third, because the community is not in view from the beginning and the work of the Spirit in believers is mentioned first, Owen does not avoid the impression that the transformation of believers is an individual process.

Fourth, Owen understands illumination as the work of the Spirit who infuses a new habit in the believer. According to Leslie, Owen tried to connect this new habit with the effective power of the Word. As mentioned in the third point, he does not connect the formation of the new habit with the role of the community and its practices. Moreover, we saw that Owen does not reflect on the process of affectual renewal which is an aspect of the transformation of the mind. Maybe to prevent the idea that the formation of the new habit is the result of our participation in the church and our efforts to transform of affections, he does not reflect on the role of the church in the gift of the new habit and in the process of affectual renewal that is part of the formation of the new habit.

Fifth, as in a Platonic, pre-Christian understanding of illumination, Christ does not play a role in it. Moreover, Owen connects the decisive work of the Holy Spirit with the gift of a new habit. Against this background, it is not surprising that Owen does not understand the transformation of the mind as the result of a personal encounter with Christ, participation in Christ, and the formation of the mind of Christ in us. In other words, it is surprising that Owen with all his emphasis on communion with the Father, Son, and Spirit does not make the connection between this communion and the transformation of the mind. He knew about the affective impact of communion with God on the believer. Nevertheless, he has an obvious blind spot regarding the transformation of the mind as participation in the mind of Christ and his affective life.

Thus, I propose an alternative that starts with Christ and participation in him. Furthermore, I will modify the (*substantialist*) model of the renewal of the mind as the gift of a new habit more dynamically and relationally, beginning with the inhabitation of the Holy Spirit. The renewal of the mind should be understood primarily as a result of a personal encounter with Christ in Scripture, as participation in the mind of Christ, mediated in the church, as a gift of the Holy Spirit.[152]

---

152. Cf. Burger, *Being in Christ*, 554–56; Lehmkühler, *Inhabitatio*. This proposal

8.5 PARTICIPATION IN CHRIST, MEDIATED IN THE CHURCH, AS A GIFT OF THE HOLY SPIRIT

Theological hermeneutics has to reflect on the transformation of the hearer and reader of Scripture and the renewal of the mind. In this chapter, we have investigated the renewal of the mind and the role of the community of the church, the participation in practices, and the work of the Holy Spirit in believers (illumination). In this section, I will bring this all together in concluding reflections on the renewal of the mind.

Luke 24 gives a richly variegated image of illumination and the renewal of the mind. The presence of the risen Christ is central. Further, nowhere in Luke 24 is the change in the disciples an individual process. When the disciples recognize the risen Jesus, they are together. Furthermore, his instruction that is publicly accessible cannot be missed. This instruction evokes something in his disciples. The two disciples who walked to Emmaus ask each other (Luke 24:32): "Were not our hearts burning within us while he talked with us on the road and opened the Scriptures to us?" Still, this was not the moment that he was recognized by them. In Jerusalem, the two tell the other disciples "how Jesus was recognized by them when he broke the bread" (Luke 24:35). Finally, when Jesus appears again to his disciples, he has to do something apart from showing himself, eating and giving instruction (Luke 24:45): "he opened their minds so they could understand the Scriptures."

After Pentecost, the Holy Spirit has to be mentioned as well. About the Holy Spirit, Jesus promises his disciples that "he will be in you" (John 14:17). The Spirit "will teach you all things and will remind you of everything I have said to you" (John 14:26). He is "the Spirit of truth" who "will guide you into all truth" (John 16:13). Furthermore, "he will prove the world to be in the wrong about sin and righteousness and judgment" (John 16:8). Opening our minds to the reality of sin and forgiveness has an effect on the noetic effects of sin.

Owen's basic interest is justified: the act of God is decisive in the transformation of the mind. This important Reformed insight is to be preserved. God has to open our eyes and ears so that his light will shine into our hearts.[153] At the same time, Jesus's teaching that we now find in Scripture, the community of disciples, and the meal with the broken bread play a role as well. Here, the Reformed tradition risks the danger of minimizing the mediating role of community, sacrament, practice, and tradition. The risk

---

differs from Horton, *Covenant and Salvation*, 232–42; Leslie, *Light of Grace*, 108–13.

153. Cf. Keener, *Mind of the Spirit*, 115, 128, 133, 180–81, 196–98; Oldhoff, "Soul Searching with Paul," 173, 175, 192–93, 200, 202, 206, 226.

of an isolated and immediate work of the Spirit has to be avoided. The same is true of an individualistic and disembodied view of transformation and sanctification. Thus, the order of theological topics in the theological narrative matters, as "misapprehension of their place in the *systema* of Christian teaching" results in "theological difficulties."[154]

Both the order of this chapter—church, practice, illumination—and the order of the title of this section—participation in Christ, mediated in the church, as a gift of the Holy Spirit—have been chosen deliberately. What God does in the Holy Spirit is decisive, but the Spirit uses mediation. What we receive is participation in Christ and transformation into Christlikeness. Where and how we receive this, is in the context of the church where Christ is mediated to us through the Word, sacrament, community, practice, and ministry. And in all these meditations, it is the Spirit who gives this participation in Christ and transforms us into his image. In what follows, I will present some reflections on the process of transformation, following this order: Jesus Christ, the various means used by the Spirit (Scripture, community, mediators, practices), the Holy Spirit, the transformation of the believer, and the formation of hermeneutical virtues.

Participation in Christ

The Christian life begins with an encounter with Christ, mediated by the Word of Christ. It is a life in Christ, a life in union with Christ as he lives in us and we in him, a life of participation in Christ and his story, and a life of transformation into the likeness of Christ. The Gospel of John tells us about the mutual indwelling of Christ and the believers. We will receive a fullness of life and fruitfulness when we remain in Christ (cf. John 6, 10, 15). Paul, in his letters, returns repeatedly to our participation in the story of the representative Messiah. The believers will be conformed to the likeness of the Son (Rom 8:29). The process of renewal includes the believers putting on the Lord Jesus Christ (Rom 13:14) and being transformed by the renewing of their minds (Rom 12:2). That means the Holy Spirit will give them "the mind of Christ" (1 Cor 3:9) so that their "attitude should be the same as that of Christ Jesus" (Phil 2:5). Where we face the problem of the noetic consequences of sin, the gospel of Jesus Christ promises the healing of our minds, by participation in Christ, as a gift of the Holy Spirit.

---

154. Webster, *Domain of the Word*, 52.

Scripture

In this process of renewal, Scripture is the first mediator that has to be mentioned. The *solus Christus* and the *extra nos* of salvation are closely connected to the primacy of Scripture (cf. chapter 6). Christ is "the Christ of the Scriptures." In the New Testament, Christ and the Word belong together. In John 8:31 Jesus says, "If you hold to my teaching [literally, if you remain in my word], you are truly my disciples." Similarly, in the passage on the true vine, Jesus says, "If you remain in me and my words remain in you" (John 15:7). In the Pauline letters, we find similar passages. Romans 10:17 joins faith in Jesus Christ with the word of Christ: "Faith comes from hearing the message, and the message is heard through the word of Christ." Moreover, faithfulness to the message of Jesus Christ (which we now find in the New Testament) is emphasized in 2 Tim 3:14 (continue in what you have learned and have become convinced of . . .). Thus, Lucas Lindeboom was justified when he, in a lecture in 1888, explained how we remain in Christ when we remain in the Word.[155] The importance of Scripture cannot be understood without mentioning the active presence of the Holy Spirit in the Word. Scripture is the inspired Scripture, "*theopneustos*" (2 Tim 3:16), which says something both about the *origin* of Scripture and about *how* God uses this book in the present. In faith, i.e., with an open and receptive attitude, we experience the transforming breath of the Spirit when we hear Scripture as God's Word to us.

The role of Scripture is important to understand that the activity of Christ and the Spirit are publicly accessible. We are not discussing an esoteric spirituality, but we can "give the reason" (1 Pet 3:15) for the interpretation of Scripture and its effects on our mindset. On the role of Scripture in the transformation of our beliefs, interpretations, and participation in Christ, already much has been said in chapters 5 and 7 (section 7.5). After discussing John Owen's *Sunesis Pneumatikè* it is good to be reminded of this. The Spirit renews us so that we can understand Scripture. And in reading Scripture, the Spirit works to renew us. The cooperation of the Word and Spirit is like a hermeneutical circle, where the Spirit, the text of Scripture, and our minds together have the same *telos*: faith in Jesus Christ, union with Christ, and participation in Christ with all its richness (cf. 7.3.5).

---

155. Lindeboom, *Blijf in het Woord van God*.

Community

A life in Christ and the Spirit, in which we listen to Scripture, is a community life—in the body of Christ and the temple of the Holy Spirit. Together we breathe an atmosphere that is open to God, filled with the Word and Spirit. Together, we live a life of faith in Jesus Christ that provides us with the necessary perspective for a Christian reading of Scripture. Furthermore, the tradition of the church is the tradition of the effective history of Scripture that connects us to Scripture itself. Within this hermeneutical community, we learn to understand and undergo the necessary transformation.

Reformed theology gives the impression that sanctification and transformation is an individual process. Thus, it is important that the *nous* in the New Testament "is (also) a communal concept," as Martine Oldhoff has shown.[156] It is a mistake to conceive of the mind as an isolated, strictly personal entity. Our mindset, thought patterns, emotional life, and (fundamental) mood, are related to our neighbors with whom we live together. Accordingly, "the mind is a corporate instrument to be trained in a communal setting."[157] Thus, the work of the Spirit to renew and transform has a place: the community of the body of Christ, which is at the same time the temple of this Spirit of God.

We live in a context different from John Owen's early modern context. We experience the downside of the turn to the subject in modernity. We face the plurality of a secularized and post-Christian world that puts pressure on the faith of believers. This gives the "ecclesial turn" its theological urgency. The revaluation of community, tradition, and embodiment in twentieth-century philosophy underlines the importance of the community and her (liturgical) practices. The themes discussed in 8.2 and 8.3 confirm the role of community and practice (as Owen and Bavinck did in their context although they gave it another place in their theologies).

Thinking about communities, it is important to be realistic. Communities are plural and ambivalent, as empirical research discussed in 8.2 demonstrates. Communities and their practices have to embody Christ and his Spirit, but it is no automatism that they do so. Instead, they are in a continuing process of renewal and transformation, just as individual believers. The process of participation in the death and resurrection of Christ takes place on a collective and individual level. Communities have to be characterized by a mixture of thankful continuity (as part of a tradition) and discontinuity

---

156. Oldhoff, "Soul Searching with Paul," 225.

157. Oldhoff, "Soul Searching with Paul," 225. Concerning this communal aspect, she is critical of Keener who has a blind spot in this respect. See Oldhoff, "Soul Searching with Paul," 174; Keener, *Mind of the Spirit*, 199.

(open to the Spirit who wants to transform us further into Christlikeness); "vigilant communities" as Village designates them.

Mediators

An interesting outcome of 8.2 and 8.3 is the role of ministers, office bearers, and mystagogues. This corresponds to Dru Johnson's emphasis on authoritative voices and the failure to listen to them as (a consequence of) sin.[158] In hermeneutics and mystagogy, we need good guides who combine spiritual depth (existential involvement), intellectual capacities (theology), pastoral sensitivity (open to the other), and the ability to open fresh perspectives (transforming impulses). Within a community, we need living persons who guide and lead us, knowing where to go. To be such living mediators, these guides themselves have to live a life of participation in Christ, a life in the Spirit.

Practices

The formative role of practices is confirmed in this chapter. In this chapter, I focused on practices of Bible reading in congregations and on diaconal practices. Of course, other practices could have been chosen as well. That liturgical practices matter has been demonstrated already by others, like James K. A. Smith.[159] All these practices contribute to the (trans)formation of believers and their understanding of Scripture.

Through various practices, we participate in the reality of God by the enactment of that reality. We remain in a reality and thus enlarge our understanding of it, not only in conscious thoughts but also in "tacit knowledge" as Polanyi puts it. Participation enlarges our involvement and creates more openness to this reality in which we are involved. By participation, we follow God in his practices as his fellow workers. We learn by doing, as disciples of Jesus, to grow in the imitation of Christ.[160] In a Johannine phrase, by loving one other, we remain in God's love; and when we remain in God's love, we remain in God (cf. John 15:10; 1 John 4:7-8; 12:16). Of course, practices differ and what a practice "does" depends on the practice and what this practice embodies of God's reality.

---

158. Johnson, *Biblical Knowing*.

159. Smith, *Imagining the Kingdom*; Smith, *Desiring the Kingdom*.

160. For comparable emphases, see Clark, *Divine Revelation and Human Practice*; Meek, *Loving to Know*; Vanhoozer, *Drama of Doctrine*.

a. In *liturgical practices,* we experience what it is to be a "worshiping" and a "singing self."[161] Through singing and praying, we practice worship of God (instead of idols), surrender, and dependency. We dedicate our lives not to idols and no longer pretend autonomy but lay our lives in the hands of God.

b. In *sacramental practices* like baptism and eucharist, we face the reality of participation in Christ, by being baptized into Christ, or eating his flesh and drinking the cup of his blood. By coming and doing, we enact faith and union with Christ. We live as a "eucharistic self."[162]

c. In practices where we read Scripture together, we listen to Scripture and grow in our knowledge of the reality Scripture speaks about and its significance. Scripture can be read together in many different ways (see 8.2). The impact of these different practices will vary accordingly.

d. In *diaconal practices,* we participate in God's practice of love as God's fellow workers. We experience actively the reality of God's love, including the vulnerability and suffering implied in it.

e. In *charismatic* practices of speaking in tongues, healing, or prophecy, we experience the active presence of God's Spirit and enact the reality of God's coming kingdom. As we saw, this enlarges our understanding of God's active presence here and now and creates a worldview that is more open to God.

f. In *ministerial* practices, like preaching, pastoral work, or Christian education, we share in God's practice. We experience more intensely the reality of what we embody in our acts.

g. In *missionary* practice, we discover more about what matters most and what is really important.

This list is not exhaustive, but it demonstrates the variety of its formative effects. Nevertheless, we are more able to participate in these practices when we understand them in the light of Scripture. Conversely, in the light of these practices, we can understand better what Scripture says. Furthermore, in these practices, we receive the formation of ourselves in the direction of growing likeness to Christ. As our mind is transformed during this formation, we are enabled further to understand.

---

161. Ford, *Self and Salvation*, 73–136.
162. Ford, *Self and Salvation*, 137–66.

Holy Spirit

In these mediations of the reality of Christ and in all these practices that make us participate in that reality, humans have to be involved actively. However, Scripture, the church, her tradition, ministers, and practices have no significance for us when the Holy Spirit does not use them and make them fruitful. What the Holy Spirit does in all this is essential. It is the Spirit who brings Jesus to us, gives faith, lives within us, unites us to Christ, makes us participate in Christ, and transforms us into Christlikeness. The Spirit is more than Scripture, more than the church and her reality. Nevertheless, after Easter and Pentecost, the work of the Spirit cannot be separated from Jesus Christ, Scripture, and the church.[163] The Spirit works to make us participate in Christ. Within the activity of the Spirit, Scripture has primacy. It is in the church with her liturgy, tradition, and other practices that the Spirit works. (Nevertheless, the Spirit is present in all creation and works outside the church as well.)

Transformation

In the process of transformation, we are primarily passive and receptive. It starts with Jesus Christ who loves and identifies with us, who lived our lives, suffered, died, was buried, rose again, and gave us the Holy Spirit abundantly. In him, God's kingdom is present. Transformation begins where we encounter him, where faith is evoked, and where we receive him as "our righteousness, holiness, and redemption" (1 Cor 1:30). According to Volf, the wrongly centered self has to be crucified. However, I am not erased, but the inhabitation of risen Christ results in a re-centered self. As Volf argues, "The center is Jesus Christ crucified and resurrected, who has become part and parcel of the very structure of the self."[164] In Christ, we are freed from sin and guilt, but also the powers that controlled us are broken and inner healing begins.

This happens in Christian communities, where the new life begins to be embodied, where we experience something of his love and hospitality, where the gospel of Jesus Christ is preached, and where we together

---

163. Van de Beek discusses pneumatology within his ecclesiology. However, because the Spirit precedes the church (also in the Nicene Creed), I will not follow him in this respect. Moreover, Beek emphasizes that pneumatology needs a christological paradigm, because in the church the Spirit and Christ cooperate in the united work of God. Here, I follow Van de Beek. See Van de Beek, *Lichaam en Geest van Christus*, 392–410, 431–36.

164. Volf, *Exclusion and Embrace*, 70.

listen to Scripture (8.2). This happens when other Christians introduce us to the mystery of Christ and our union with him, and when we learn to understand God, our neighbors, ourselves, and our world in the light of the gospel of Jesus Christ. This happens when we participate in practices that make participation in Christ accessible because we together enact here the new life (8.3). This happens when the Holy Spirit gives us new life from above (birth *anōthen*; John 3:3, 7), is present in the church as his temple, breathes in our lives when we read Scripture, fills us, and leads us. The Spirit enters the self and renews it in the image of Christ.[165] Without the Spirit, we remain spiritually dead, but in the Spirit, we receive new life (Rom 8:9-11). More and more, we become active participants during this process, clothing ourselves with Christ (Gal 3:27; Rom 13:14).

Consequently, regeneration and conversion have hermeneutical significance, as Dalferth and O'Donovan show as well (see 4.3.2; 5.3). As a result of Easter and Pentecost, a new perspective opens. In the light of Scripture, we learn to distinguish between the old and new, "to discern what is best" (Phil 1:10), and to think about "whatever is true, whatever is noble, whatever is right, whatever is pure, whatever is lovely, whatever is admirable" (Phil 4:8). Thus, "transformed by the renewing of [y]our mind," we will "be able to test and approve what God's will is" (Rom 12:2). This requires that we "demolish arguments and every pretension that sets itself up against the knowledge of God, and we take captive every thought to make it obedient to Christ" (2 Cor 10:5).

Justification has implications for our understanding as well. In 3.4.5 I have quoted Volf: "Both the 'clenched fist' and the 'open arms' are *epistemological stances*: they are *moral conditions of moral perception*."[166] When we are justified, our sins are forgiven, our relationship with God is restored and we receive "the peace of God, which transcends all understanding" (Phil 4:7), our hands and arms are opened. We were banned from the garden and no longer lived in the safe environment of God's loving presence (3.4.4). Justified by faith, we are safe again in Christ. When we have no need anymore to justify ourselves and when our selves receive new stability and inner freedom, our mind is changed. Our new identity in Christ has hermeneutical relevance.[167]

---

165. Volf, *Exclusion and Embrace*, 92.

166. Volf, *Exclusion and Embrace*, 216.

167. As we saw in 3.4.4, Jüngel writes beautifully about the (noetic) consequences of sin in his book on justification. This implies that justification is liberating in noetic respect as well, although he elaborates less on this implication of justification. See Jüngel, *Evangelium von der Rechtfertigung*, 191-92, 202-6, 221-25.

In this process of transformation, the renewal of our self-understanding and the development of our understanding of Scripture mutually influence each other. We learn to understand ourselves in the light of Scripture, and in learning to live as new selves, our understanding of what Scripture tells about the new life deepens. However, the renewal of the mind is more than a matter of changing beliefs, understandings, and interpretations. Our thought life, our feelings and emotions, our will and our choices, our attitudes, and our body where we embody who we are, all share in this process of transformation.[168]

Sin and salvation both have noetic consequences. If this is true, all humans are equally in need of this noetic transformation. We have further seen that the greater the existential import of a subject, and the more a subject is related to knowledge of God, the stronger we will experience the noetic consequences of sin (3.4.5). So the reverse is true as well, regarding the transformation of the mind. First of all, our relationship with God changes, and this influences who we are and transforms our regulative beliefs. But this does not necessarily give us more craftsmanship, or make us better scientists or more creative technicians. With regard to Scripture, everyone can learn Hebrew and Greek, read and interpret, and study the history of the civilizations of the ancient Near East. The more our reading of Scripture touches upon our relationship with God, faith in Jesus Christ, and life in the Spirit, the more the dynamic of sin and salvation will make itself felt. Finally, we have to face here, the tension between the "already but not yet." Sin does not change us into monsters, nor does salvation make us perfect, instantly. The renewal of the mind remains incomplete, and hence I do not propose hermeneutical perfectionism. As the apostle Paul said, "Now we see only a reflection as in a mirror; then we shall see face to face. Now I know in part; then I shall know fully, even as I am fully known" (1 Cor 13:12).

In hermeneutics, virtues are important as well. As Vanhoozer writes, "The mind of Christ is the set of moral, intellectual, and spiritual habits or virtues that serve as the mainspring for all the particular things that Jesus does and says."[169] For believers who know about their sins, a self-critical attitude is important. And "to practice criticizability, however, knowers must become intellectually honest and evince epistemic humility," Vanhoozer writes.[170] Here, we could think of the theological virtues of faith, hope, and love. In faith, we expect a truthful voice in the text we read. In hope, we long

---

168. On the transformation of the self, see, e.g., Collicutt, *Psychology of Christian Character Formation*; Willard, *Renovation of the Heart*.

169. Vanhoozer, *Drama of Doctrine*, 256.

170. Vanhoozer, *Drama of Doctrine*, 303.

to receive insight and understanding, to arrive at a good interpretation. In love, we are in a good and open relationship with the reality we are facing.[171] Furthermore, it is important to think about interpretative, intellectual, and hermeneutic virtues. Based on his empirical research, Rogers presents the following set of virtues: honesty, faithfulness, openness, courage, humility, confidence, and community.[172] These virtues foster the restoration of our cognitive functioning and stimulate our attentiveness. But servanthood matters as well. Macaskill has shown that (epistemic) humility is opposed to intellectual pride and arrogance. Humility is patient and thankful, and first of all willing to serve the interests of others.[173]

In the process of transformation, we learn to look, think, feel, desire, and act differently. Often when we try to influence these processes, we speak words and communicate in language. Correspondingly, we think when we consciously reflect on these processes. What we embody and feel can be communicated as well, and often we translate this into verbal language. Hence, important in the transformation of the believer are the renewal of the mind and its thinking, the use of Scripture and language, and the critical reflection of hermeneutics. Participation in Christ begins with the Word of Christ.

---

171. Vanhoozer, *First Theology*, 231–32.
172. Rogers, *Congregational Hermeneutics*, 171–97.
173. Macaskill, *New Testament and Intellectual Humility*, 168–69, 192.

9.

Christ and Scripture
Transformation into the Image of Christ and the Use of Scripture in the Ecological Crisis

9.1 FROM EPISTEMOLOGY TO SOTERIOLOGY

My aim in this book is to develop a coherent vision of theological hermeneutics and Scripture, starting from the notion of participation in Christ, as an alternative to proposals of a doctrine of Scripture that were developed out of an epistemological interest and in interaction with modern foundationalism. Christ, hermeneutics, and Scripture are closely connected. Without (faith in) Christ, we will not find a fruitful perspective on Scripture. Without Scripture, we will not know Christ or live in union with Christ. Scripture has to be understood primarily as part of the salvation economy of the triune God. God uses Scripture to bring us to Christ and transform us into the likeness of Christ. At the same time, living as a Christian deepens our understanding of Scripture. Reading Scripture, we receive the mind of Christ. And the more we share in the mind of Christ, the better we will understand Scripture. Theological hermeneutics as a reflection on processes of understanding, both understanding Scripture as well as understanding of God, the world, neighbor, and self in the light of Scripture, is itself part of the reflection on the transformation of believers into the likeness of Christ (which includes, having the mind of Christ). To conclude, a soteriological approach to the doctrine of Scripture is fruitful.

A soteriological approach to hermeneutics and Scripture has primacy over an epistemological approach because it brings theological reflection more directly to the heart of God's use of Scripture. God does not just inform us, he transforms us and he has to do so because as sinners we are blind and deaf to God and what he says, does, and gives. Epistemology can be important, but our faith does not depend on it. Accordingly, theology does not depend on epistemology. Epistemology is only a reflective discipline and not an absolute one (epistemology should not be identified with knowledge). A theological epistemology will reflect on Scripture. But the reverse is not true: a systematic theological doctrine of Scripture is not necessarily epistemological. An epistemological approach to Scripture is not the best entrance way to understanding Scripture and the role of Scripture in the life of the community of believers.

In our context, an epistemological approach to Scripture is no longer the most effective. The Christian faith no longer is the default option in Western countries. Epistemology often has pretended a neutral starting position. This neutrality has always been an illusion. In today's Western context, the Christian faith cannot build any longer on common ground with others concerning, e.g., God's existence. Due to the noetic consequences of sin, neutrality never existed in reality. To give an epistemological justification for the presence of God already includes faith and (secretly or openly) presupposes divine activity. Moreover, the pluralist and secularized nature of the Western post-Christian world puts pressure on a Christian perspective. It is always contested and alternatives are available. Confronted with this pressure, an appeal to revelation and inspiration, as we find in the classical Reformed approach of the doctrine of Scripture, is no longer sufficient to justify the Christian faith. The content of the Christian faith itself, the experience within a Christian community, and testimonies about what God does in the lives of believers cannot be missed. This signals that an epistemological approach is too narrow to do justice to the social, bodily, and affective nature of human existence. Furthermore, if an epistemological approach is connected with an ideal of absolute certainty and with modern foundationalism, such an approach is an obstacle to hermeneutical honesty. Finally, it is not helpful to isolate Scripture first from the economy of God's salvation. This makes it more difficult to understand the nature of Scripture. This is the negative part of my proposal: I have deliberately not chosen an epistemological approach to Scripture.

The aim of this book, however, is positive: to offer an alternative, soteriological approach to hermeneutics and the doctrine of Scripture. To demonstrate what the preceding chapters have accomplished, I turn in this final chapter to a specific case: the ecological crisis.[1] Discussing the eco-

1. Unfortunately, often the impression is given that we face only a climate crisis. The model of the planet boundaries offers good help to see the elements of this crisis. See Rockström et al., "Planetary Boundaries"; Steffen et al., "Planetary Boundaries."

logical crisis, I will give a final overview of my soteriological approach to hermeneutics and Scripture.

9.2 HERMENEUTICS, SCRIPTURE, AND THE ECOLOGICAL CRISIS

An epistemological approach to Scripture leads to a focus on the truth of propositions that can be found in biblical texts. Concerning the ecological crisis, passages about creation and the human role within creation are especially of interest. From an epistemological viewpoint, there will be a particular interest in questions concerning whether and how God has created: the debate on creation or evolution, the understanding of the days of creation, and the age of the earth.[2] Moreover, questions concerning the human position within the order of creation, and the instructions God has given to humans about their role in creation will also prove crucial. An epistemological approach following *sola scriptura* suggests implicitly or explicitly, that in Scripture we will find all necessary propositions about creation and that we can understand them as part of Scripture. What difference will my soteriological and more holistic approach make to hermeneutics and Scripture?

Hermeneutics is a critical reflection on processes of understanding, both of texts as well as of God, the world, the neighbor, and the self in the light of these texts. The ecological crisis evokes the question of how we see our world and our role within our world. An epistemological approach might have difficulties in acknowledging that the crisis is a reason for re-reading Scripture. From a soteriological viewpoint, it is not strange that we could have misunderstood Scripture, given the noetic consequences of sin. Thus, the ecological crisis is a good reason to critically question our understanding of Scripture, creation, and humanity in the light of Scripture. This regards the understanding of humanity and the world that contributed to this crisis, but also a renewed and hopeful understanding of humanity and the world that could perhaps help to solve the ecological crisis.

We need this hope. The ecological crisis is frightening and maddening, as Bruno Latour has emphasized in *Facing Gaia*.[3] Where do we find the courage and honesty to face this crisis? This is a hermeneutical question. We need the hopeful perspective of God's coming kingdom to prevent us

---

2. In Dutch Neo-Calvinism, the Geelkerken-conflict in the 1920s presents an example of the interests of an epistemological approach. See, e.g., Van Bekkum, "'Naar de klaarblijkelijke bedoeling.'"

3. Latour, *Facing Gaia*, 1–40.

from anxiety, despair, or rage. Moreover, we need the forgiveness of our sins and the justification in Christ, to live with the burden of our ecological guilt. Knowing and understanding are part of life processes. From the beginning, salvation cannot be missed.

Pope Francis signals in his encyclical *Laudato Si'* greed, aggression, and selfishness behind the human exploitation of our world.[4] This attitude determines not only human actions, but also how humans see the world and their position within the world. The work of Sally McFague at least partly is an attempt to correct such an understanding. In *Super, Natural Christians* she wants to correct an arrogant eye. Instead, we need a loving eye and a caring attitude.[5] *Life Abundant* offers an alternative worldview that corrects our economic approach to the planet.[6] Her hermeneutical approach to ecotheology is a strong indicator of the necessity to transform our views when we search for the flourishing of God's creation. Facing the ecological crisis, hermeneutics urges critical self-reflection, which confronts us with the noetic consequences of sin.[7] Our knowing and understanding need salvation.

However, the practices of our Western way of life interfere with this required transformation of our mindset. Our lives are embodied and our practices shape our minds and desires. Technology, economic interests, globalization, urbanization, and hedonism all contribute to a mindset that alienates us from God's creation. This can start very small: the use of a plow has changed the attitude toward the soil and creation.[8] In the present, this has grown into a complex that can hardly be overseen. Modern agriculture with its large and heavy machines, fertilizers, pesticides, and genetically engineered seeds is a complex system where several large multinationals have great economic interests. The same is true of the food industry and the supermarkets, that sell what we the Western people need for our mass consumption of meat and dairy products. We enjoy the luxury of our globalized consumer culture, are accustomed to flight vacations and city trips, and are attached to the comfort that it offers us. We live in an urbanized world, where air conditioning ensures that the indoor climate remains pleasant. Many no longer have the time or attention for gardening, and hence, cover their garden with tiles to avoid having to work in their garden. Many of us practice a life of distance from animals, insects, birds, soil, plants, and

---

4. Francis, *Laudato Si'*, 8–9, 27, 112, 150, 156, 166, 173. See also Wirzba, *Agrarian Spirit*, 93, 167.

5. McFague, *Super, Natural Christians*.

6. McFague, *Life Abundant*.

7. On noetic consequences of sin and the necessity of hermeneutical renewal, see also Wirzba, *Agrarian Spirit*, 63–76, 87–90, 94–97, 123–24, 165.

8. White, "Historical Roots," 36–37; Wirzba, *Paradise of God*, 10.

climate. Our modern money-economy places us at a distance from each other and nature. This way of life does not help us to foster a mindset of creation care. Instead, we have developed a blind spot for the soil, our communities, and our human position as part of the ecosystem of creation.[9]

This lifestyle determined by technology, capitalist and neoliberal economy, and consumerism is a fruit of modernity. Thinking about our practices, we cannot ignore the modern context where we live. To understand this context, we need to know something about its history. Bruno Latour has sketched the emergence of the modern attitude toward the world as secularization and immanentization of Christian eschatology. Latour follows Eric Voegelin, by pointing at Joachim van Fiore as a decisive figure. According to Fiore, we live now in the era of the Spirit. We have left the era of the Son with its eschatological judgment and can be certain about the arrival of God's kingdom on earth. Without any doubt, ascetic monks will realize the kingdom of God on earth, in the era of the Spirit. Increasingly, this eschatological vision is secularized. Eschatology has become a part of human historical activities. The promises of the afterlife are understood more and more in an immanent manner and become utopias. At the same time, the human actors who realize God's kingdom on earth are no longer ascetic monks. But what remains is the absolute certainty that we as humans will realize a perfect eschatological future on Earth. When religion and politics prove not to be able to do this, the result is frustration and frenzy. In this light, Latour understands the religious wars of the sixteenth and seventeenth centuries. Protestant and Catholic Reformation were becoming increasingly violent, and the religious conflict degenerated into wars. Due to these wars, religion started to lose its credibility. State (politics) and later the market (economy) remained as the actors in realizing the perfect future on earth. Progressively, Latour writes, heaven becomes an immanent reality, but paradoxically, the contact with the earth and its material reality is lost. In the meantime, Christian believers, living in a modernizing world, let go of the cosmos and focused on the eternal salvation of the soul. In a later and more liberal version, this narrowed soteriology was immanentized as well and transformed into a focus on ethics and moral formation.[10]

Belden Lane adds to this analysis, how the rise of capitalism and the colonization of America changed the attitude of the Puritans toward creation. In the seventeenth century, the early Puritans saw God's glory in his creation and even were willing to criticize anthropocentrism. They were

---

9. Cf. Wirzba, *Paradise of God*, 2–12; Wirzba, *Agrarian Spirit*, 13–20, 47, 120–24, 140–45, 158, 160.

10. Latour, *Facing Gaia*, 184–219.

active in gardening, which for them was a spiritual activity, and showed love for animals, actively opposing animal cruelty. However, their expectation of the millennium secularized and their gardening became a means to harvest fruit that could be sold for money on the market. Moreover, the colonization of the New World influenced their attitude toward creation. The Native Americans were compared to the Amalekites and Canaanites. Fighting these tribes that constituted a threat to the New Israel, they conquered the land. Instead of "honoring the indigenous people for their respect for their handiwork," the Puritan William Bradford saw the conquest of America "as a matter of God's chosen people overthrowing the insidious powers of darkness, exercising dominion in using fence and plow to master the world's wild, disordered state."[11] Their attitude toward the world changed: from a mirror of God's grandeur, creation became a territory open to submission and exploitation. Lane's conclusion is a sad one: "While inclined to celebrate an awesome God amidst the wonders of the natural world, its desire to possess can be cruelly twisted, leading to patriarchal, racist, and anthropocentric attitudes of dominion toward the 'other.'"[12] Lane thus shows a deep ambivalence in the Reformed tradition: an attitude of admiration for the Creator and his creation, together with a degeneration of this tradition due to colonialism and capitalism.[13]

Seen from a hermeneutical perspective, the ecological crisis calls Western Christians to confession, repentance, and conversion. Without conversion, we will remain enslaved as part of a system that we and our ancestors collectively created. Modernity and Western Christianity are twin sisters that together have shaped our modern world of urbanization, technology, capitalism, colonialism, and consumerism.[14] Our system causes ecological and social injustice. Enslavement to this system will make us reluctant, stubborn, deaf, and blind so that we are unable to see and understand. Moreover, as long as our guilt weighs on us like a burden, we will be stuck in mechanisms of self-justification, so that we will not be able to be honest about the consequences of our acts. Here, conversion and justification have hermeneutical significance. Forgiveness and justification will free us from our guilt and create new openness. Conversion has a hermeneutical impact, as our perspective is renewed. We need a new identity in Christ so that we do not live anymore as *homo incurvatus in se*, guilty sinners

11. Lane, *Ravished by Beauty*, 38.
12. Lane, *Ravished by Beauty*, 40.
13. Lane, *Ravished by Beauty*, 17–46.
14. On the rise of modernity, see also Wirzba, *Paradise of God*, 61–92; Wirzba, *Agrarian Spirit*, 93.

justifying themselves, and proudly or anxiously focused on their interests alone. To be open to God's creation, and our present and future neighbors, we need to participate in the death and resurrection of Jesus Christ. Only when we receive this new life, we will be able to discern between what is old and will be judged by God's "no" on the one hand, and what is justified by God's "yes" and has a future in God's reign on the other.[15]

It is a relief and a reason for hope that Scripture and creation both are part of the economy of the triune God. Living between pride and anxiety, between *hubris* and despair, we need God.[16] God is the Creator who did not leave his creation to our shortsightedness but gives the creation the future of his coming kingdom. God is the Son, who identified with us and our sins, and who makes us new. As the last Adam, he succeeded where Adam failed and reigns at the right hand of the Father. By participating in the last Adam, we can finally learn to live as God's image, within creation. In him, the entire creation is restored, and we are saved to live as creatures, as part of the ecosystem of creation. In him, we can lovingly share in the suffering of creation, hoping that we can contribute to its restoration. Now, Paul could write hopefully in Romans (Rom 8:19-21):

> For the creation waits in eager expectation for the children of God to be revealed. For the creation was subjected to frustration, not by its own choice, but by the will of the one who subjected it, in hope that the creation itself will be liberated from its bondage to decay and brought into the freedom and glory of the children of God.

Furthermore, God is the Spirit who unites us with Christ and who gives new life. When we are in despair, facing an ecological crisis, the Spirit is with us. Paul continues (Rom 8:26-27),

> The Spirit helps us in our weakness. We do not know what we ought to pray for, but the Spirit himself intercedes for us through wordless groans. And he who searches our hearts knows the mind of the Spirit because the Spirit intercedes for God's people in accordance with the will of God.[17]

---

15. Interestingly, according to Wirzba forgiveness is also a precondition for hope. See Wirzba, *Agrarian Spirit*, 181-87.

16. Wirzba mentions that according to Wendell Berry hubris and despair are "two of our culture's most damaging sins"; Wirzba, *Paradise of God*, 4.

17. On Romans 8 and ecological theology, see Burger, *Hoop voor een zuchtende schepping*.

We hear the voice of the triune God—the Father, Son, and Spirit—in Scripture. And God uses Scripture to restore us into his image, transforming us into Christlikeness, and renewing our understanding of God the creator, ourselves as creatures, our fellow creatures, and our world as God's creation. This is part of God's saving project, to realize his kingdom in his creation.

Our participation in Christ's death and resurrection—God's "no" and "yes" in his justifying judgment—calls us to discern between the old and new, lie and truth, and injustice and justice. This discernment will involve a critical reconsideration of our lifestyle and its practices as well as a critical deconstruction of our theological tradition. Our understanding is influenced by our practices but also by the theological tradition, which is the result of the *Wirkungsgeschichte* of Scripture in our communities. Scripture is canonical and has primacy here because Christ as the final Word of God is the fulfillment of the *Tanakh* and the center and climax of the history of salvation. Christ is "the firstborn over all creation," and "in him all things hold together" (Col 1:15–20).

However, the ecological crisis asks us urgent questions about the role of Scripture in theology and the Christian life. The ecological crisis manifests our ongoing capacity to be deaf and blind to what Scripture says. The noetic consequences of sin remain a problem for Christian believers, and apparently, we need an ecological crisis to awaken us. We were part of a tradition that read Scripture in an anthropocentric manner and did not offer enough resistance to a way of life that was destructive. It even contributed to the destructive modern practices of colonization. Neither the *sola scriptura* in Reformed theology nor the tradition of the church in Roman Catholic theology, nor the postliberal "theological interpretation," has protected us. What does this imply for Scripture? Kärkkäinen is right when he writes that we need eco-friendly hermeneutics, but that Scripture itself is not ecocentric.[18] Rereading Scripture with eco-friendly hermeneutics means that "green" elements of Scripture will be rediscovered and "green" implications of Scripture will be thought through. The ecological crisis makes clear the limitations of the *sola scriptura*: it cannot be the epistemological principle for the entire Christian life. Even if Scripture has the primacy, experience and empirical research can urge us to reread Scripture. Thus, we read Scripture also in the light of our experience, even if the interpretation of these experiences and empirical data in the light of Scripture is necessary. Scripture has the primacy for our knowledge of God and the way of salvation in Christ and the Spirit, even if it does not give us all knowledge of the content

---

18. Kärkkäinen, *Creation and Humanity*, 208.

of salvation. Happily, Scripture is part of the saving economy of the triune God, and it is God who saves us and this world, not Scripture.

A Christian believer will read the Scriptures over and again. As disciples of Christ, following him as our Lord, we have to read and reread them. We read the Scriptures because we believe in Jesus Christ. Here, we find our Lord. By reading Scripture, we can remain in Christ and we can be transformed in our thinking, feeling, and willing. We read Scripture in the light of Easter and are guided by the Spirit of Pentecost. It is the Spirit who breathes in the words of the Bible so that they do not remain dead letters but a Word of God that gives life. It is the living Word of God that transforms us into the likeness of Christ so that we receive the mind of Christ. And the more we participate in Christ, the more we will understand Scripture. We need this participation in Christ and inhabitation of the Spirit when facing the ecological crisis and its huge challenges.

To clarify what rereading the Scriptures in light of the ecological crisis involves, it is necessary to distinguish several aspects. First, regarding the craftsmanship of the exegete, the ecological crisis reminds biblical scholars of the fact that the biblical writers lived in a society that mainly consisted of small agrarian communities. Rereading could mean reading from an agrarian perspective. According to Ellen Davis, "Agrarianism is a way of thinking and ordering life in the community that is based on the health of the land and living creatures."[19] An agrarian reading takes seriously the mindset of the writers of the Bible, which often was an agrarian mindset. Reading through agrarian eyes means that the perspective of the historical-critical exegete is enriched and a blind spot has been removed.[20]

Second, taking seriously the non-urbanized but more agrarian world of the Scriptures may have an alienating effect. It might enlarge the strangeness of the biblical text. They had no tractors or other machines but used oxen and donkeys. To them, nature with its thorns and thistles, and the climate with its unpredictable weather, more often posed a threat than to us.[21] However, wrestling with this strangeness can have an enriching effect as well. And a text that remains strange in part still can be powerful and significant.

Third, apart from an agrarian reading, the ecological crisis can enlarge the reading interests of exegetes. Asking ecological questions about biblical passages can have a refreshing effect.[22]

19. Davis, *Scripture, Culture, and Agriculture*, 1.
20. Davis, *Scripture, Culture, and Agriculture*, 1–7.
21. Burger, "Theology without a Covenant of Works," 20–31.
22. An example of the effect of ecological question on readings of the Bible is

Fourth, the ecological crisis will stimulate us to develop "ecological literacy" (David Orr)[23] or an "agrarian mindset." According to Wirzba, "The definitive marker of an agrarian is not being a farmer, but being committed to the flourishing of people, fellow creatures, and the land altogether."[24] Such an agrarian mindset will open our eyes to new or forgotten themes: place and soil, beauty and wisdom, Sabbath and rest, ecological injustice, new creation, humanity as creation, the position of humanity within creation, the suffering of creation, and Christ as head of creation (cosmic Christology). This can result in new works in biblical theology or eco-theological books with parts on these themes.[25]

Fifth, the ecological crisis calls us to retell the story of the Christian faith. We need a new story full of forgiveness and hope about God's creation and humanity as part of it. This has to be a story where humanity is not isolated from the earth, soil, animals and plants, climate, and seas but is an integral part of the ecosystem of creation. Here, rereading Scripture and the work of eco-theology go hand in hand.[26] A wish for the future is that eco-theology will not develop into a distinct discipline, but is part of theology itself. Only in that case, the renewing of the mind has been successful.

Sixth, rereading the Scripture will affect our discernment. We discern the text of Scripture, and looking through the text, we discern God, creation, and ourselves in the light of Scripture. Here, Scripture influences us on different levels: who we are as creatures (identity), how we see creation (virtues), what we see (our selection), and how we understand what we see (seeing something as created). From Scripture, we learn to discern in faith as a recreated person, we learn as fellow creatures to see creation with love, to discern what is important, beautiful, just, and good, and to act in God's creation with hope for his coming reign.

Seven, this rereading of Scripture will only succeed when it is accompanied by spirituality. Wirzba has laid this out beautifully in several agrarian spiritual disciplines: learning to pray, learning to see, learning descent, learning humility, learning generosity, and learning to hope.[27]

In the end, this rereading of Scripture, the resulting transformation of the mind, and our way of living as a creature within God's creation has to

---

Horrell et al., *Ecological Hermeneutics*.

23. Via Bouma-Prediger, *For the Beauty of the Earth*; Hess, "Shifting Epistemologies, Shifting Our Stories."

24. Wirzba, *Agrarian Spirit*, xi.

25. See, e.g., Moo and Moo, *Creation Care*; Wirzba, *Paradise of God*.

26. See, e.g., Conradie, *Earth in God's Economy*.

27. Wirzba, *Agrarian Spirit*.

be understood as participation in Christ. Christ has identified with humanity, preached the arrival of the kingdom and embodied in his practice this reality, suffered as a result of sin and all its consequences, died for our sins, rose again for our justification, and was glorified to reign at the right hand of God. He has baptized us with his Spirit to make us share in who he is. He is the first human being who lives within God's creation as king and priest, so he makes creation flourish, reorders creation according to God's purposes, and dedicates creation as holy, giving it back to the Creator. His human life gives hope to the creation, suffering from an ecological crisis caused by fallen humanity.

Participation in Christ means that we can learn to understand our position within creation. We are creatures among other creatures. We are not above nature, but as embodied beings, we are part of nature ourselves and participate in larger ecosystems on which we are dependent for our survival. Christians have understood themselves as the crown of creation, but a rereading of Gen 1 and 2 demonstrates that not humanity but the sabbath is the crown of creation.[28] Reflections on the image of the "globe" are insightful as well. Bruno Latour has emphasized that this image represents a misleading ideal of knowledge: of divine, global knowledge, complete and transparent. We need to reconsider our image of the world. We are small creatures, living on planet Earth, under a celestial dome, and we do not have a God's eye point of view.[29] At the same time, it is significant that Christ only became human. He was incarnate and took the human flesh. He did not become a fish, a mammal, an insect, or a bird. His incarnation is crucial to the restoration of humanity, and the restoration of humanity is necessary for the restoration of creation (see Paul in Rom 8:19–21). A rereading of Scripture, together with the ecumenical dialogue with Eastern Orthodoxy can be a good reason to understand humanity's position within creation in priestly terms also, and not alone in kingly terms as dominion or stewardship.[30] This position within creation, furthermore, defines our epistemological and hermeneutical position within creation. Loving, seeing, knowing, naming, understanding, interpreting, and sanctifying by thankful prayer is an essential part of our participation in the reality of creation. The ecological crisis is a good occasion to reconsider our epistemic and hermeneutical attitude toward reality. Hopefully, this will contribute to our participation in Christ and the formation of the mind of Christ in us.

28. Boersema, *Thora en Stoa*, 82.
29. Latour, *Facing Gaia*.
30. See for an Eastern Orthodox perspective on the human position as priestly Theokritoff, *Living in God's Creation*, 64–79, 119–40, 186–92, 212–25; Zizioulas, "Priest of Creation." On anthropology, see further Conradie, *Ecological Christian Anthropology*.

Due to the global scale of the ecological crisis, we can no longer ignore that transformation and sanctification are a communal process, a process that needs a community, common action, and common practices. Only together we can reconstitute our practices and our way of life. It is a wonderful gift of grace that the body of Christ is not bound to national boundaries. The movement of the kingdom of Christ is universal. The practice where the heart of this movement beats is the liturgy of the church that is celebrated in all parts of the world. In the light of Scripture and the ecological crisis, we have to reform our practices. At the same time, renewed practices will contribute to the further renewal of our identity and our reading of Scripture. Still, it is important to note again that neither *sola scriptura* nor the church and her tradition have prevented the ecological crisis. We need the saving acts of the triune God to bring his kingdom and realize his new earth. Until Christ returns, the final salvation will remain hidden with Christ in God.

All these will not lead to a quick fix for all ecological problems. Sin has its effects on all humans and the history of sin and humanity is a history of many millennia. The ecological crisis in its present form is the result of a process of centuries. The history of the roots of this crisis shows that both believers and non-believers contributed to the present situation. In the Western world, Christians and non-Christians enjoy their consumerist lifestyle which causes ecological and social injustice. All creatures suffer from the crisis. Sometimes, Christians live with a worldview that is counterproductive and gives them a religious reason not to change their lifestyle. All human beings share in the problem. From all (non)religious directions people use their creativity to search for solutions. Although pneumatology needs a christological paradigm, the Spirit is present in all creation and works outside the church as well (common grace). Dealing with the ecological crisis, we face the eschatological tension between the already and not yet of the coming kingdom of God. At the same time, we do not know to which extent the solution to the present ecological crisis is identical to the final coming of the kingdom of God.

What the Spirit does using Scripture is to bring people to Christ and in Christ back to God. He teaches us to see the world *coram deo*, in the light of Scripture, and renews us to act accordingly. He aims to fulfill the prophecy of Isaiah (Isa 11:9):

> They will neither harm nor destroy
> on all my holy mountain,
> for the earth will be filled with the knowledge of the Lord
> as the waters cover the sea.

The largest resistance in human hearts is our resistance to God, through pride (I will build my own world and I will do it my way) or fear (I am afraid of God and hide myself from his face). Healing that resistance is only the beginning of the renewal of humanity. Yet, as the human heart is the major problem of this world, the healing of the human heart is the beginning of the healing of creation. And creation now waits hopefully, for humanity will be restored. This hope gives Christians the honesty to confess guilt, and the motivation to serve Creator and creation. This can be done together with others, each with their respective perspectives and motivations. Christians will do this in faith in Jesus Christ, in hope for God's kingdom, and in love for the Creator and his creatures.

Theological hermeneutics is the critical reflection on processes of understanding—firstly the understanding of Scripture, and secondly the understanding of God, the world, neighbors, and self in the light of Scripture. The ecological crisis confirms the complexity of these processes: our history, practices, guilt, and blind spots all hamper our understanding. Scripture alone will not change this. Up to the present day, a theology of "Scripture alone" has not been able to prevent Reformed Christians from contributing to the ecological crisis. Moreover, it has not led to the development of a theology that resisted effectively our ecological sins or our imperialist attitude toward creation. We can be thankful that Scripture never is alone. The best way to get access to the nature and function of Scripture is to see it as part of the economy of the triune God in the history of salvation.

Thus, the ecological crisis confirms the thesis of this book: we have to begin with Jesus Christ in whom God acts to save us and his creation; theological hermeneutics is part of the theological reflection on the renewal of the mind; and Scripture is the book that the triune God uses to bring us to Christ, to unite us with him, to fill us with his Spirit, and to make us participate in him, the last Adam.

Bibliography

Adam, Andrew K. M., et al. *Reading Scripture with the Church: Toward a Hermeneutic for Theological Interpretation*. Grand Rapids, MI: Baker Academic, 2006.

Augustijn, Cornelis. "Kuypers rede over 'De hedendaagsche schriftcritiek' in haar historische context." In *Abraham Kuyper: vast en veranderlijk: de ontwikkeling van zijn denken*, edited by Cornelis Augustijn and Jasper Vree, 109–48. Zoetermeer, The Neth.: Meinema, 1998.

Baker, Bruce D. "The Transformation of Persons and the Concept of Moral Order: A Study of the Evangelical Ethics of Oliver O'Donovan with Special Reference to the Barth-Brunner Debate." PhD diss., University of St. Andrews, 2010. https://research-repository.st-andrews.ac.uk/bitstream/handle/10023/975/Bruce%20D.%20Baker%20PhD%20thesis.PDF?sequence=6&isAllowed=y.

Barnhoorn, Floor, et al., eds. *De Bijbel in Nederland: de plaats van de Bijbel in kerk en samenleving*. Haarlem, The Neth.: NBG, 2018.

Barth, Karl. *Church Dogmatics*. Translated by Geoffrey William Bromiley and Thomas Forsyth Torrance. Edinburgh: T. & T. Clark, 1956.

———. *Die kirchliche Dogmatik*. 4 vols. Zürich, Switz.: Evangelischer Verlag A.G. Zollikon, 1932.

Bartholomew, Craig G. *Introducing Biblical Hermeneutics: A Comprehensive Framework for Hearing God in Scripture*. Grand Rapids, MI: Baker Academic, 2015.

———. "Introduction." In *A Royal Priesthood? The Use of the Bible Ethically and Politically: A Dialogue with Oliver O'Donovan*, edited by Craig G. Bartholomew, 1–45. Scripture and Hermeneutics 3. Carlisle, UK: Paternoster, 2002.

———. *A Royal Priesthood? The Use of the Bible Ethically and Politically: A Dialogue with Oliver O'Donovan*. Scripture and Hermeneutics 3. Carlisle, UK: Paternoster, 2002.

———. "A Time for War and a Time for Peace: Old Testament Wisdom, Creation, and O'Donovan's Theological Ethics." In *A Royal Priesthood? The Use of the Bible Ethically and Politically: A Dialogue with Oliver O'Donovan*, edited by Craig G. Bartholomew, 91–112. Scripture and Hermeneutics 3. Carlisle, UK: Paternoster, 2002.

Bartholomew, Craig G., and Michael W. Goheen. *The Drama of Scripture: Finding Our Place in the Biblical Story*. Grand Rapids, MI: Baker Academic, 2004.

Bauckham, Richard. *Bible and Mission: Christian Witness in a Postmodern World*. Grand Rapids, MI: Baker Academic, 2003.

Bavinck, Herman. *Gereformeerde dogmatiek.* 4 vols. 4th ed. Kampen, The Neth.: Kok, 1928.

———. *Reformed Dogmatics.* Vol. 1, *Prolegomena.* Edited by John Bolt. Translated by John Vriend. Grand Rapids, MI: Baker Academic, 2003.

———. *Reformed Dogmatics.* Vol. 2, *God and Creation.* Edited by John Bolt. Translated by John Vriend. Grand Rapids, MI: Baker Academic, 2004.

———. *Reformed Dogmatics.* Vol. 4, *Holy Spirit, Church and New Creation.* Edited by John Bolt. Translated by John Vriend. Grand Rapids, MI: Baker Academic, 2008.

Bavinck, J. H. *Religieus besef en christelijk geloof.* Kampen, The Neth.: Kok, 1949.

Bayer, Oswald. *Martin Luthers Theologie: eine Vergegenwärtigung.* Tübingen, Germ.: Mohr Siebeck, 2003.

———. *Theologie.* Handbuch systematischer Theologie 1. Gütersloh, Germ.: Gütersloher Verlagshaus, 1994.

Beek, A. van de. *De kring om de Messias: Israël als volk van de lijdende Heer: spreken over God 1,2.* Zoetermeer, The Neth.: Meinema, 2002.

———. *Lichaam en Geest van Christus: de theologie van de kerk en de Heilige Geest.* Zoetermeer, The Neth.: Meinema, 2012.

———. *Van Kant tot Kuitert en verder: de belangrijkste theologen sinds 1800.* 3e herz. ed. Kampen, The Neth.: Kok, 2009.

Beilby, James. "Contemporary Religious Epistemology: Some Key Aspects." In *The Enduring Authority of the Christian Scriptures,* edited by D. A. Carson, 795–830. Grand Rapids, MI: Eerdmans, 2016.

Bekkum, Koert van. "'Naar de klaarblijkelijke bedoeling zintuiglijk waarneembaar'. De kwestie-Geelkerken in theologie-historisch perspectief." In *De kwestie-Geelkerken: een terugblik na 75 jaar,* edited by George Harinck, 87–108. AD Chartas-Reeks 5. Barneveld, The Neth.: De Vuurbaak, 2001.

———. "Zekerheid en schriftgezag in Neo-Calvinistische visies op de historiciteit van de Bijbel." In *Geloven in zekerheid? gereformeerd geloven in een postmoderne tijd,* edited by Koert van Bekkum and Rien Rouw, 77–108. Barneveld, The Neth.: De Vuurbaak, 2000.

Bekkum, Koert van, and Gert Kwakkel. "De theologische boodschap van oudtestamentische teksten. Oorsprong en actualiteit van de Kamper aandacht voor de heilshistorie." In *Gereformeerde theologie stroomopwaarts. Terugkijken op 75 jaar vrijmaking,* edited by Erik de Boer et al., 79–94. TU-Bezinningsreeks 24. Amsterdam: Buijten & Schipperheijn, 2021.

Bell, Richard H. "'But We Have the Mind of Christ': Some Theological and Anthropological Reflections on 1 Corinthians 2:16." In *Horizons in Hermeneutics: A Festschrift in Honor of Anthony C. Thiselton,* edited by Anthony C. Thiselton et al., 175–97. Grand Rapids, MI: Eerdmans, 2013.

Belt, Henk van den. *The Authority of Scripture in Reformed Theology: Truth and Trust.* Studies in Reformed Theology 17. Leiden, The Neth.: Brill, 2008.

———. *"Kan een mens wel zeker zijn?": een moderne vraag in een disputatie van Herman Ravensperger (1586–1625).* Groningen, The Neth.: Faculteit Godgeleerdheid en Godsdienstwetenschap, Rijksuniversiteit Groningen, 2013.

———. "The Problematic Character of Sola Scriptura." In *Sola Scriptura: Biblical and Theological Perspectives on Scripture, Authority, and Hermeneutics,* edited by Hans Burger et al., 38–55. Studies in Reformed Theology 32. Leiden, The Neth.: Brill, 2018.

Bennema, Cornelis. "Christ, the Spirit and Knowledge of God: A Study in Johannine Epistemology." In *The Bible and Epistemology: Biblical Soundings on the Knowledge of God*, edited by Mary Healy and Robin A. Parry, 107–33. Milton Keynes, UK: Paternoster, 2007.

Berkhof, Hendrikus. "Neocalvinistische theologie van Kuyper tot Kuitert." In *Geloof dat te denken geeft: opstellen aangeboden aan prof. dr. H.M. Kuitert*, edited by K. U. Gäbler, 30–48. Baarn, The Neth.: Ten Have, 1989.

———. *200 Jahre Theologie: ein Reisebericht*. Neukirchen-Vluyn, Germ.: Neukirchener Verlag, 1985.

Berkouwer, Gerrit C. *De heilige Schrift II*. Dogmatische Studiën. Kampen, The Neth.: Kok, 1967.

———. *Holy Scripture*. Translated by Jack Rogers. Studies in Dogmatics. Grand Rapids, MI: Eerdmans, 1975.

Bernstein, Richard J. *Beyond Objectivism and Relativism: Science, Hermeneutics, and Praxis*. University of Pennsylvania Press, 2011.

Bernts, A. P. J., et al. *God in Nederland 1966–2015*. Utrecht, The Neth.: Ten Have, 2016.

Bielo, James S. *Words upon the Word: An Ethnography of Evangelical Group Bible Study*. Qualitative Studies in Religion. New York: New York University Press, 2009.

Billings, J. Todd. "Sacraments." In *Christian Dogmatics: Reformed Theology for the Church Catholic*, edited by R. Michael Allen and Scott R. Swain, 339–62. Grand Rapids, MI: Baker Academic, 2016.

———. *The Word of God for the People of God: An Entryway to the Theological Interpretation of Scripture*. Grand Rapids, MI: Eerdmans, 2010.

Black, Rufus. *Christian Moral Realism: Natural Law, Narrative, Virtue, and the Gospel*. Oxford Theological Monographs. Oxford: Oxford University Press, 2000.

Blomberg, Craig L. "Reflections on Jesus's View of the Old Testament." In *The Enduring Authority of the Christian Scriptures*, edited by D. A. Carson, 669–701. Grand Rapids, MI: Eerdmans, 2016.

Boersma, Hans. "All One in Christ: Why Christian Platonism Is Key to the Great Tradition." February 2020. https://www.hansboersma.org/articles-1/all-one-in-christ-why-christian-platonism-is-key-to-the-great-tradition.

———. *Heavenly Participation: The Weaving of a Sacramental Tapestry*. Grand Rapids, MI: Eerdmans, 2011.

———. *Nouvelle Théologie and Sacramental Ontology: A Return to Mystery*. Oxford: Oxford University Press, 2009.

———. *Sacramental Preaching: Sermons on the Hidden Presence of Christ*. Grand Rapids, MI: Baker Academic, 2016.

———. *Scripture as Real Presence: Sacramental Exegesis in the Early Church*. Grand Rapids, MI: Baker Academic, 2017.

Boersema, Jan J. *Thora en Stoa over mens en natuur: een bijdrage aan het milieudebat over duurzaamheid en kwaliteit*. Baarn, The Neth.: Callenbach, 1997.

Bonhoeffer, Dietrich. *Dietrich Bonhoeffer Works*. Vol. 6, *Ethics*. Edited by Clifford J. Green et al. Minneapolis, MN: Fortress, 2009.

———. *Letters and Papers from Prison*. Edited by John W. De Gruchy. Translated by Isabel Best et al. Dietrich Bonhoeffer Works 8. Minneapolis, MN: Fortress, 2010.

Borgman, Erik. "De ziel van het geloof en de theologie. De Bijbel lezen als belofte van genade." In *De Bijbel in Nederland: de plaats van de Bijbel in kerk en samenleving*, edited by Floor Barnhoorn et al., 46–58. Haarlem, The Neth.: NBG, 2018.

Bouma-Prediger, Steven. *For the Beauty of the Earth: A Christian Vision for Creation Care*. 2nd ed. Engaging Culture. Grand Rapids, MI: Baker Academic, 2010.

Bowald, Mark A. "The Character of Theological Interpretation of Scripture." *International Journal of Systematic Theology* 12 (2010) 162–83.

———. *Rendering the Word in Theological Hermeneutics: Mapping Divine and Human Agency*. Aldershot, UK: Ashgate, 2007.

Braaten, Carl E., and Robert W. Jenson. *Reclaiming the Bible for the Church*. Grand Rapids, MI: Eerdmans, 1995.

Bratt, James D. *Abraham Kuyper: Modern Calvinist, Christian Democrat*. Grand Rapids, MI: Eerdmans, 2013.

———. "Abraham Kuyper: Puritan, Victorian, Modern." In *Kuyper Reconsidered: Aspects of His Life and Work*, edited by Cornelis van der Kooi and Jan de Bruin, 69–81. Amsterdam: VU Uitgeverij, 1999.

Bremmer, R. H. *Herman Bavinck als dogmaticus*. Kampen, The Neth.: Kok, 1961.

Bretherton, Luke. *Hospitality as Holiness: Christian Witness amid Moral Diversity*. Aldershot, UK: Ashgate, 2006.

Brink, Gijsbert van den. *Almighty God: A Study of the Doctrine of Divine Omnipotence*. Kampen, The Neth.: Kok Pharos, 1993.

———. *Reformed Theology and Evolutionary Theory*. Grand Rapids, MI: Eerdmans, 2020.

———. "Social Trinitarianism: A Discussion of Some Recent Theological Criticisms." *International Journal of Systematic Theology* 16 (2014) 331–50.

Brinke, Henk ten. *Erfzonde? Onvermijdelijkheid en verantwoordelijkheid*. Utrecht, The Neth.: KokBoekencentrum Academic, 2018.

Brock, Brian. "Mercy, Compassion, and the Flesh: On the Inbreaking of Divine Mercy." In *Mercy: Theories, Concepts, Practices: Proceedings from the International Congress, TU Apeldoorn/Kampen, NL June 2014*, edited by J. H. F. Schaeffer et al., 31–49. Ethik im Theologischen Diskurs, Band 25. Zürich, Switz.: Lit, 2018.

Brock, Cory, and Nathaniel Gray Sutanto. "Herman Bavinck's Reformed Eclecticism: On Catholicity, Consciousness and Theological Epistemology." *Scottish Journal of Theology* 70 (2017) 310–32.

Brom, Luco van den. "Kuitert: een echt dolerend theoloog." In *Harry Kuitert: zijn God: schrijvers, theologen en filosofen over de God van Kuitert*, edited by Martien E. Brinkman and Henk Vijver, 42–51. Kampen, The Neth.: Ten Have, 2004.

Bruggen, J. van. *Het kompas van het christendom: ontstaan en betekenis van een omstreden bijbel*. Kampen, The Neth.: Kok, 2002.

———. *Paul: Pioneer for Israel's Messiah*. Phillipsburg, NJ: P & R, 2005.

Bruijne, Ad L. Th. de. "Christian Ethics and God's Use of the Bible." In *Correctly Handling the Word of Truth: Reformed Hermeneutics Today*, edited by Mees te Velde and Gerhard H. Visscher, 171–86. Lucerna CRTS. Eugene, OR: Wipf & Stock, 2014.

———. "Geworteld en dan opgebouwd wordend in Hem." In *Filosofie en theologie: een gesprek tussen christen-filosofen en theologen*, edited by K. van. Bekkum, 155–63. Amsterdam: Buijten & Schipperheijn in samenwerking met het Centrum voor Reformatorische Wijsbegeerte Amersfoort, 1997.

———. *Levend in Leviatan. Een onderzoek naar de theorie over 'christendom' in de politieke theologie van Oliver O'Donovan*. Kampen, The Neth.: Kok, 2007.

———. "Schilders vroege spiritualiteit en de latere vrijgemaakten." In *Wie is die man? Klaas Schilder in de eenentwintigste eeuw*, edited by Marius van Rijswijk, 49–80. AD Chartas-Reeks 22. Barneveld, The Neth.: De Vuurbaak, 2012.

Bruijne, Ad L. Th. de, and Hans Burger. *Gereformeerde hermeneutiek vandaag: theologische perspectieven*. Barneveld, The Neth.: De Vuurbaak, 2017.

Burger, Hans. *Being in Christ: A Biblical and Systematic Investigation in a Reformed Perspective*. Eugene, OR: Wipf & Stock, 2008.

———. "Het belang van een deelnemersperspectief voor de theologie." *Nederlands Theologisch Tijdschrift* 70 (2016) 321–37.

———. "Christologisch én pneumatologisch: Herman Bavinck en de relatie tussen schriftleer en christologie." In *Weergaloze kennis: opstellen over Jezus Christus, Openbaring en Schrift, Katholiciteit en Kerk aangeboden aan prof. dr. Barend Kamphuis*, edited by Ad de Bruijne et al., 126–35. Zoetermeer, The Neth.: Uitgeverij Boekencentrum, 2015.

———. "God's Character and the Plot of the Bible." In *Reading and Listening: Meeting One God in Many Texts: Festschrift for Eric Peels on the Occasion of His 25th Jubilee as Professor of Old Testament Studies*, edited by Jacob Dekker and Gert Kwakkel, 239–48. Amsterdamse cahiers voor exegese van de Bijbel en zijn tradities. Supplement Series 16. Bergambacht, The Neth.: Uitgeverij 2VM, 2018.

———. "God's Mercy and Practices of Mercy." In *Mercy: Theories, Concepts, Practices: Proceedings from the International Congress, TU Apeldoorn/Kampen, NL June 2014*, edited by J. H. F. Schaeffer et al., 99–114. Ethik Im Theologischen Diskurs, Band 25. Zürich, Switz.: Lit, 2018.

———. "'Het hart en wezen der christelijke religie zelve'. Over de praktische relevantie van de triniteitsleer." *Theologia Reformata* 55 (2012) 333–49.

———. "Hermeneutisch relevante triniteitsleer: De bijdrage van Ingolf U. Dalferth aan de trinitarische renaissance." *NTT Journal for Theology and the Study of Religion* 67 (2013) 101–16.

———. "Hoe moeten we vanuit evolutionair perspectief denken over cognitieve gevolgen van zonde en genade?" In *En God zag dat het goed was: Christelijk geloof en evolutie in 25 cruciale vragen*, edited by William den Boer et al., 305–18. Kampen, The Neth.: Summum Academic, 2019.

———. *Hoop voor een zuchtende schepping: reflecties over lijden en ecologie bij Romeinen 8*. Reformatorische stemmen 2020/1. Baarn, The Neth.: Willem de Zwijgerstichting, 2020.

———. *Life in Christ: The Significance of the Story of Jesus*. Edited by Jane deGlint-Sneep. Translated by Dick Moes. Eugene, OR: Cascade, 2023.

———. "The Story of God's Covenants: A Biblical-Theological Investigation with Systematic Consequences." *Calvin Theological Journal* 54 (2019) 267–99.

———. "'Theirs Are the Covenants': Israel and the 'Covenant of Grace.'" Forthcoming.

———. "Theology without a Covenant of Works: A Thought Experiment." In *Covenant: A Vital Element of Reformed Theology. Biblical, Historical and Systematic-Theological Perspectives*, edited by Hans Burger et al., 325–48. Studies in Reformed Theology 42. Leiden, The Neth.: Brill, 2021.

———. "Zelfverstaan en wereldverstaan tussen geslotenheid en openheid." In *Open voor God: Charles Taylor en christen-zijn in een seculiere tijd*, edited by Hans Burger and Geert Jan Spijker, 23–38. TU-Bezinningsreeks 14. Barneveld, The Neth.: De Vuurbaak, 2014.

Burger, Hans, et al. "Introduction." In *Sola Scriptura: Biblical and Theological Perspectives on Scripture, Authority, and Hermeneutics*, edited by Hans Burger et al., 1–16. Leiden, The Neth.: Brill, 2018.

Calvin, John. *Institutes of the Christian Religion: In Two Volumes*. Edited by John Thomas MacNeill. Translated by Ford Lewis Battles. The Library of Christian Classics 20. Philadelphia: Westminster, 1960.

Campbell, Constantine R. *Paul and Union with Christ: An Exegetical and Theological Study*. Grand Rapids, MI: Zondervan, 2012.

Carson, Don A. "Theological Interpretation of Scripture: Yes, But . . ." In *Theological Commentary: Evangelical Perspectives*, edited by R. Michael Allen, 187–207. 1st ed. London: T. & T. Clark, 2011.

Chandler, Daniel. *Semiotics: The Basics*. The Basics. London: Routledge, 2002.

Chaplin, Jonathan A. "Political Eschatology and Responsible Government: Oliver O'Donovan's 'Christian Liberalism.'" In *A Royal Priesthood? The Use of the Bible Ethically and Politically: A Dialogue with Oliver O'Donovan*, edited by Craig G. Bartholomew, 265–308. Scripture and Hermeneutics 3. Carlisle, UK: Paternoster, 2002.

Chen, Michael S. "Herman Bavinck and Augustine on Epistemology." *The Bavinck Review* 2 (2011) 96–106.

Clark, Tony. *Divine Revelation and Human Practice: Response and Imaginative Inspiration*. Cambridge: Clarke, 2010.

Cleveland, Christopher. *Thomism in John Owen*. Farnham, UK: Ashgate, 2013.

Clore, Gerald L. "Psychology and the Rationality of Emotion." In *Faith, Rationality, and the Passions*, edited by Sarah Coakley, 209–22. Malden, MA: Wiley, 2012.

Coakley, Sarah. "Dark Contemplation and Epistemic Transformation. The Analytic Theologian Re-meets Teresa of Avila." In *Analytic Theology: New Essays in the Philosophy of Theology*, edited by Oliver Crisp and Michael C. Rea, 280–312. Oxford: Oxford University Press, 2009.

———, ed. *Faith, Rationality, and the Passions*. Malden, MA: Wiley, 2012.

———. *God, Sexuality, and the Self: An Essay "on the Trinity."* Cambridge: Cambridge University Press, 2013.

Collicutt, Joanna. *The Psychology of Christian Character Formation*. London: SCM, 2015.

Colwell, John. *Living the Christian Story: The Distinctiveness of Christian Ethics*. Edinburgh: T. & T. Clark, 2001.

Conradie, E. M. *The Earth in God's Economy: Creation, Salvation and Consummation in Ecological Perspective*. Vienna, Aust.: Lit, 2015.

———. *An Ecological Christian Anthropology: At Home on Earth?* Aldershot, UK: Ashgate, 2005.

Dalferth, Ingolf U. *Der auferweckte Gekreuzigte: zur Grammatik der Christologie*. Tübingen, Germ.: Mohr Siebeck, 1994.

———. *Becoming Present: An Inquiry into the Christian Sense of the Presence of God*. Studies in Philosophical Theology 30. Leuven, Belg.: Peeters, 2006.

———. *Creatures of Possibility: The Theological Basis of Human Freedom*. Grand Rapids, MI: Baker Academic, 2016.

———. *Crucified and Resurrected: Restructuring the Grammar of Christology*. Grand Rapids, MI: Baker Academic, 2015.

———. *Evangelische Theologie als Interpretationspraxis: eine systematische Orientierung.* Forum Theologische Literaturzeitung 11/12. Leipzig, Germ.: Evangelische Verlagsanstalt, 2004.

———. *Existenz Gottes und christlicher Glaube: Skizzen zu einer eschatologischen Ontologie.* Beiträge zur Evangelischen Theologie 93. München, Germ.: Kaiser, 1984.

———. *Gedeutete Gegenwart: zur Wahrnehmung Gottes in den Erfahrungen der Zeit.* Tübingen, Germ.: Mohr Siebeck, 1997.

———. "Gott für uns. Die Bedeutung des christologischen Dogmas für die christliche Theologie." In *Denkwürdiges Geheimnis: Beiträge zur Gotteslehre: Festschrift für Eberhard Jüngel zum 70. Geburtstag*, edited by Johannes Fischer and Ingolf U. Dalferth, 51–75. Tübingen, Germ.: Mohr Siebeck, 2004.

———. *Gott: philosophisch-theologische Denkversuche.* Tübingen, Germ.: Mohr Siebeck, 1992.

———. "Hermeneutische Theologie—heute?" In *Hermeneutische Theologie—heute?*, edited by Ingolf U. Dalferth et al., 3–38. Hermeneutische Untersuchungen zur Theologie 60. Tübingen, Germ.: Mohr Siebeck, 2013.

———. *Jenseits von Mythos und Logos: Die christologische transformation der theologie.* Freiburg im Breisgau, Germ.: Herder, 1993.

———. *Kombinatorische Theologie: Probleme theologischer rationalität.* Quaestiones Disputatae 130. Freiburg im Breisgau, Germ.: Herder, 1991.

———. *Die Kunst des Verstehens: Grundzüge einer Hermeneutik der Kommunikation durch Texte.* Tübingen, Germ.: Mohr Siebeck, 2018.

———. *Malum: Theologische hermeneutik des bösen.* Tübingen, Germ.: Mohr Siebeck, 2008.

———. "Die Mitte ist aussen: Anmerkungen zur Wirklichkeitsbezug evangelischer Schriftauslegung." In *Jesus Christus als die Mitte der Schrift: Studien zur Hermeneutik des Evangeliums*, edited by Christoph Landmesser, 173–98. Berlin: de Gruyter, 1997.

———. *Radikale Theologie.* Forum Theologische Literaturzeitung 23. Leipzig, Germ.: Evangelische Verlagsanstalt, 2010.

———. *Religiöse Rede von Gott.* Beiträge zur Evangelischen Theologie 87. München, Germ.: Kaiser, 1981.

———. *Theology and Philosophy.* Eugene, OR: Wipf & Stock, 2001.

———. *Transzendenz und säkulare Welt: Lebensorientierung an letzter Gegenwart.* Tübingen, Germ.: Mohr Siebeck, 2015.

———. "Über Einheit und Vielfalt des christlichen Glaubens: Eine Problemskizze." In *Marburger Jahrbuch Theologie*, vol. 4, edited by Wilfried Härle and Reiner Preul, 99–137. Marburg, Germ.: N. G. Elwert Verlag, 1992.

———. *Umsonst: eine Erinnerung an die kreative Passivität des Menschen.* Tübingen, Germ.: Mohr Siebeck, 2011.

———. "Von der Vieldeutbarkeit der Schrift und die Eindeutigkeit des Wortes Gottes." In *Die Zukunft des Schriftprinzips*, edited by Richard K. Ziegert, 155–73. Bibel im Gespräch 2. Stuttgart, Germ.: Deutsche Bibelgesellschaft, 1994.

———. *Die Wirklichkeit des Möglichen: hermeneutische Religionsphilosophie.* Tübingen, Germ.: Mohr Siebeck, 2003.

———. *Wirkendes Wort: Bibel, Schrift und Evangelium im Leben der Kirche und im Denken der Theologie.* Leipzig, Germ.: Evangelische Verlagsanstalt, 2018.

Danielou, Jean. *From Shadows to Reality: Studies in Biblical Typology of the Fathers.* London: Burns & Oates, 1960.

Davis, Ellen F. *Scripture, Culture, and Agriculture: An Agrarian Reading of the Bible.* New York: Cambridge University Press, 2009.

De Cruz, Helen, and Johan de Smedt. "Reformed and Evolutionary Epistemology and the Noetic Effects of Sin." *International Journal for Philosophy of Religion* 74 (2013) 49–66.

Dee, J. J. C. *K. Schilder: zijn leven en werkk.* Goes, The Neth.: Oosterbaan & Le Cointre, 1990.

Dekker, Jaap. "Sacra Scriptura Sui Ipsius Interpres: Reinterpretation in the Book of Isaiah." In *Sola Scriptura: Biblical and Theological Perspectives on Scripture, Authority, and Hermeneutics,* edited by Hans Burger et al., 195–215. Studies in Reformed Theology 32. Leiden, The Neth.: Brill, 2018.

Douma, Jochem. *Grondslagen christelijke ethiek.* Christelijke Ethiek 1. Kampen, The Neth.: Kok, 1999.

Dülmen, Richard van, ed. *Entdeckung des Ich: die Geschichte der Individualisierung vom Mittelalter bis zur Gegenwart.* Köln, Germ.: Böhlau, 2001.

Dumbrell, William J. *Covenant and Creation: A Theology of the Old Testament Covenants.* Biblical and Theological Classics Library. Carlisle, UK: Paternoster, 1997.

Dussen, Ad van der. "De Bijbel als het Woord van God." Presented at the Theologische Studie Begeleiding, 2003, revised in 2015. https://ngk.nl/wp16/wp-content/uploads/2015/02/Dussen-BijbelWoordvanGod-20031126-20150619.pdf.

Dvorak, Rainer. *Gott ist Liebe: eine Studie zur Grundlegung der Trinitätslehre bei Eberhard Jüngel.* Bonner dogmatische Studien 31. Würzburg, Germ.: Echter, 1999.

Echeverria, Eduardo J. *Berkouwer and Catholicism: Disputed Questions.* Studies in Reformed Theology 24. Leiden, The Neth.: Brill, 2013.

———. "Divine Revelation and Foundationalism: Towards a Historically Conscious Foundationalism." *Josephinum Journal of Theology* 19 (2012) 283–321.

Eglinton, James. *Bavinck: A Critical Biography.* Grand Rapids, MI: Baker Academic, 2020.

Enns, Peter. *Inspiration and Incarnation: Evangelicals and the Problem of the Old Testament.* Grand Rapids, MI: Baker Academic, 2015.

Erickson, Millard J., et al. *Reclaiming the Center: Confronting Evangelical Accommodation in Postmodern Times.* Wheaton, IL: Crossway, 2004.

Eyghen, Hans van, et al. "Cognitive Science of Religion and the Cognitive Consequences of Sin." In *New Developments in the Cognitive Science of Religion: The Rationality of Religious Belief,* edited by Hans van Eyghen et al., 199–214. New Approaches to the Scientific Study of Religion 4. Cham, Switz.: Springer, 2018.

Ferguson, Sinclair B. *John Owen on the Christian Life.* Edinburgh: Banner of Truth Trust, 1987.

Fermer, Richard M. "The Limits of Trinitarian Theology as a Methodological Paradigm: 'Between the Trinity and Hell There Lies No Other Choice' (Vladimir Lossky)." *Neue Zeitschrift Für Systematische Theologie Und Religionsphilosophie* 41 (1999) 158–86.

Fickert, Valerie. *Erfahrung und Offenbarung: Ingolf U. Dalferths beitrag zur debatte.* Marburger Theologische Studien 124. Leipzig, Germ.: Evangelische Verlagsanstalt, 2016.

Foppen, Annemarie, et al. "The Most Significant Book of the Netherlands—And Its Ordinary Readers." *Journal of the Bible and Its Reception* 8 (2021) 107–33.
Ford, David F. *Self and Salvation: Being Transformed*. Cambridge Studies in Christian Doctrine 1. Cambridge: Cambridge University Press, 1999.
Fowl, Stephen E. *The Theological Interpretation of Scripture: Classic and Contemporary Readings*. Malden, MA: Blackwell, 1997.
Frame, John M. *The Doctrine of the Knowledge of God*. A Theology of Lordship. Phillipsburg, NJ: Presbyterian and Reformed, 1987.
Francis, Pope. *Laudato Si': On Care for Our Common Home. Encyclical Letter*. Vatican City: Vatican Press, 2015. https://www.vatican.va/content/dam/francesco/pdf/encyclicals/documents/papa-francesco_20150524_enciclica-laudato-si_en.pdf.
Fricker, Miranda. *Epistemic Injustice: Power and the Ethics of Knowing*. Oxford: Oxford University Press, 2007.
Fulks, Jeffery, et al. *State of the Bible: USA 2022*. N.p.: American Bible Society, 2022. https://1s712.americanbible.org/state-of-the-bible/stateofthebible/State_of_the_bible-2022.pdf.
Furnish, Victor Paul. "How Firm a Foundation? Some Questions about Scripture in the Desire of the Nations." *Studies in Christian Ethics* 11 (1998) 18–23.
Geertsema, H. G. *Het menselijk karakter van ons kennen*. Amsterdam: Buijten & Schipperheijn, 1992.
———. *Om de humaniteit: Christelijk geloof in gesprek met de moderne cultuur over wetenschap en filosofie*. Kampen, The Neth.: Kok, 1995.
Gentry, Peter John. *Kingdom through Covenant: A Biblical-Theological Understanding of the Covenants*. 2nd ed. Wheaton, IL: Crossway, 2018.
Gestrich, Christof. *Christentum und Stellvertretung: religionsphilosophische Untersuchungen zum Heilsverständnis und zur Grundlegung der Theologie*. Tübingen, Germ.: Mohr Siebeck, 2001.
Goldingay, John. *Old Testament Theology*. Vol. 1, *Israel's Gospel*. Downers Grove, IL: InterVarsity, 2003.
Goudriaan, Aza. *Reformed Orthodoxy and Philosophy, 1625–1750: Gisbertus Voetius, Petrus van Mastricht, and Anthonius Driessen*. Brill's Series in Church History 26. Leiden, The Neth.: Brill, 2006.
Graaf, Bas van der. "De Bijbel in het leven van jonge Amsterdammers." In *De Bijbel in Nederland: de Plaats van de Bijbel in Kerk en Samenleving*, edited by Floor Barnhoorn et al., 159–70. Haarlem, The Neth.: NBG, 2018.
Graaf, J. van der. "Hoe en waarom kwam de Gereformeerde Bond rond de eeuwwisseling op?" In *Beproefde trouw: vijfenzeventig jaar Gereformeerde Bond in de Nederlandse Hervormde kerk*, edited by J. van der Graaf, 13–95. Kampen, The Neth.: Kok, 1981.
Greijdanus, Seakle. *Schriftbeginselen ter schriftverklaring en historisch overzicht over theorieën en wijzen van schriftuitlegging*. Kampen, The Neth.: Kok, 1946.
Grenz, Stanley J., and Roger E. Olson. *Twentieth-Century Theology: God and the World in a Transitional Age*. Downers Grove, IL: InterVarsity, 1992.
Gunton, Colin. *The One, the Three, and the Many: God, Creation and the Culture of Modernity*. Cambridge: Cambridge University Press, 1993.
Hahn, Scott. *Kinship by Covenant: A Canonical Approach to the Fulfillment of God's Saving Promises*. Anchor Yale Bible Reference Library. New Haven: Yale University Press, 2009.

Hays, Richard B. *Echoes of Scripture in the Letters of Paul*. New Haven: Yale University Press, 1989.

———. *Reading Backwards: Figural Christology and the Fourfold Gospel Witness*. Waco, TX: Baylor University Press, 2014.

Healy, Mary. "Knowledge of the Mystery: A Study of Pauline Epistemology." In *The Bible and Epistemology: Biblical Soundings on the Knowledge of God*, edited by Mary Healy and Robin A. Parry, 134–58. Milton Keynes, UK: Paternoster, 2007.

Heidegger, Martin. *Sein und zeit*. 15., Durchges. Aufl. mit d. Randbemerkungen aus d. Handex. d. Autors im Anh. Tübingen, Germ.: Niemeyer, 1979.

Heideman, Eugene P. *The Relation of Revelation and Reason in E. Brunner and H. Bavinck*. Assen: Van Gorcum, 1959.

Hertog, Marchien den, and Froukje Holtrop, eds. *Hemelbestormers: geheimen van het gewelf in de Grote Kerk Naarden*. Zwolle, The Neth.: WBOOKS, 2021.

Hess, Mary E. "Shifting Epistemologies, Shifting Our Stories—Where Might We Find Hope for a World on the Brink of Climate Catastrophe?" *Religions* 13 (2022) 625.

Hettema, Theo L. "De viervoudige schriftzin: passage of slotzin? Lezing blokweek Noster godsdienstfilosofie Hoeven 16 juni 2004." http://home.kpn.nl/tlhettema/pdf/Viervoudig.pdf.

Hill, Charles E. "'The Truth above All Demonstration': Scripture in the Patristic Period to Augustine." In *The Enduring Authority of the Christian Scriptures*, edited by D. A. Carson, 43–88. Grand Rapids, MI: Eerdmans, 2016.

Hodge, Archibald Alexander, and Benjamin B. Warfield. *Inspiration*. Edited by Roger R. Nicole. Eugene, OR: Wipf & Stock, 2007.

Holmes, Stephen R. "Three versus One? Some Problems of Social Trinitarianism." *Journal of Reformed Theology* 3 (2009) 77–89.

Hoogland, Jan. "Orthodoxie, moderniteit en postmoderniteit." In *Filosofie en theologie: een gesprek tussen christen-filosofen en theologen*, edited by K. van. Bekkum, 132–54. Amsterdam: Buijten & Schipperheijn in cooperation with the Centrum voor Reformatorische Wijsbegeerte Amersfoort, 1997.

Horrell, David G., et al., eds. *Ecological Hermeneutics: Biblical, Historical and Theological Perspectives*. London: T. & T. Clark, 2010.

Horton, Michael S. *Covenant and Eschatology: The Divine Drama*. 1st ed. Louisville, KY: Westminster John Knox, 2002.

———. *Covenant and Salvation: Union with Christ*. 1st ed. Louisville, KY: Westminster John Knox, 2007.

———. *God of Promise: Introducing Covenant Theology*. Grand Rapids, MI: Baker, 2006.

Houtman, C. *De Schrift wordt geschreven: op zoek naar een christelijke hermeneutiek van het Oude Testament*. Zoetermeer, The Neth.: Meinema, 2006.

Houwelingen, P. H. R. van. *Timoteüs en Titus: pastorale instructiebrieven*. Commentaar op het Nieuwe Testament: Derde Serie. Afdeling Brieven van Paulus. Kampen, The Neth.: Kok, 2009.

Howson, Barry. "The Puritan Hermeneutics of John Owen: A Recommendation." *Westminster Theological Journal* 63 (2001) 351–75.

Huijgen, Arnold. *Lezen en laten lezen: gelovig omgaan met de Bijbel*. Utrecht, The Neth.: KokBoekencentrum Uitgevers, 2019.

Huijgen, Arnold, et al. "Biblical Exegesis and Systematic Theology: Toward Mutual Benefit." *Journal of Reformed Theology* 16 (2022) 173–93.

Huttinga, Wolter. *Participation and Communicability: Herman Bavinck and John Milbank on the Relation between God and the World*. Amsterdam: Buijten en Schipperheijn Motief, 2014.

Jackson, Bill. *The Biblical Metanarrative: One God—One Plan—One Story*. Corona, CA: Radical Middle, 2014.

Jamieson, R. B., and Tyler Wittman. *Biblical Reasoning: Christological and Trinitarian Rules for Exegesis*. Grand Rapids, MI: Baker Academic, 2022.

Jenson, Matt. *Gravity of Sin: Augustine, Luther, and Barth on Homo Incurvatus in Se*. London: T. & T. Clark, 2006.

Jenson, Robert W. *Canon and Creed*. Louisville, KY: Westminster John Knox, 2010.

———. *Systematic Theology*. Vol. 1, *The Triune God*. New York: Oxford University Press, 1997.

Johnson, Dru. *Biblical Knowing: A Scriptural Epistemology of Error*. Eugene, OR: Cascade, 2013.

Jong, Marinus de. "The Church Is the Means, the World Is the End: The Development of Klaas Schilder's Thought on the Relationship between the Church and the World." PhD diss., Theologische Universiteit van de Gereformeerde Kerken, 2019.

Jong-Van Campen, A. de. *Mystagogie in werking. Hoe menswording en gemeenschapsvorming gebeuren in christelijke inwijding*. Zoetermeer, The Neth.: Boekencentrum, 2009.

Jüngel, Eberhard. *Das Evangelium von der Rechtfertigung des Gottlosen als Zentrum des christlichen Glaubens: eine theologische Studie in ökumenischer Absicht*. 6 auflage. Tübingen, Germ.: Mohr Siebeck, 2011.

———. *Ganz werden*. Theologische Erörterungen 5. Tübingen, Germ.: Mohr Siebeck, 2003.

———. *God's Being Is in Becoming: The Trinitarian Being of God in the Theology of Karl Barth: A Paraphrase*. Translated by John Webster. Edinburgh: T. & T. Clark, 2001.

———. *Gottes Sein ist im Werden: verantwortliche Rede vom Sein Gottes bei Karl Barth: eine Paraphrase*. 2 auflage. Tübingen, Germ.: Mohr Siebeck, 1967.

———. *Wertlose Wahrheit: zur Identität und Relevanz des christlichen Glaubens: theologische Erörterungen III*. Beiträge zur evangelischen Theologie 107. München, Germ.: Kaiser, 1990.

Kaiser, Walter C., Jr., and Moisés Silva. *An Introduction to Biblical Hermeneutics: The Search for Meaning*. Grand Rapids, MI: Zondervan, 1994.

Kamphuis, J. *Signalen uit de kerkgeschiedenis: over de toekomst en de canon*. Groningen, The Neth.: De Vuurbaak, 1975.

Kapic, Kelly M. *The Ashgate Research Companion to John Owen's Theology*. Farnham, UK: Ashgate, 2012.

———. *Communion with God: The Divine and the Human in the Theology of John Owen*. Grand Rapids, MI: Baker Academic, 2007.

Kärkkäinen, Veli-Matti. *Christ and Reconciliation*. A Constructive Christian Theology for the Pluralistic World 1. Grand Rapids, MI: Eerdmans, 2013.

———. *Creation and Humanity*. A Constructive Christian Theology for the Pluralistic World 3. Grand Rapids, MI: Eerdmans, 2015.

———. "The Trajectories of the Contemporary 'Trinitarian Renaissance' in Different Contexts." *Journal of Reformed Theology* 3 (2009) 7–21.

———. *Trinity and Revelation*. A Constructive Christian Theology for the Pluralistic World 2. Grand Rapids, MI: Eerdmans, 2014.

Kasper, Walter. *Theologie und Kirche*. Mainz, Germ.: Matthias-Grünewald, 1987.
Keener, Craig S. *The Mind of the Spirit: Paul's Approach to Transformed Thinking*. Grand Rapids, MI: Baker Academic, 2016.
———. *Spirit Hermeneutics: Reading Scripture in Light of Pentecost*. Grand Rapids, MI: Eerdmans, 2016.
Kelsey, David H. *Proving Doctrine: The Uses of Scripture in Modern Theology*. Harrisburg, PA: Trinity International, 1999.
Kettler, Christian D. *The Vicarious Humanity of Christ and the Reality of Salvation*. Lanham, MD: University Press of America, 1991.
Keulen, Dirk van. *Bijbel en dogmatiek: schriftbeschouwing en schriftgebruik in het dogmatisch werk van A. Kuyper, H. Bavinck en G.C. Berkouwer*. Kampen, The Neth.: Kok, 2003.
———. "The Internal Tension in Kuyper's Doctrine of Organic Inspiration of Scripture." In *Kuyper Reconsidered: Aspects of His Life and Work*, edited by Cornelis van der Kooi and Jan de Bruin, 123–30. Amsterdam: VU Uitgeverij, 1999.
Keyes, Dick. *Beyond Identity: Finding Your Self in the Image and Character of God*. Eugene, OR: Wipf & Stock, 2003.
King, David M. "The Affective Spirituality of John Owen." *Evangelical Quarterly* 68 (1996) 223–33.
Klaassen, Maarten. *In Christus rechtvaardig: reformatorische perspectieven op rechtvaardiging en eenheid met Christus: een onderzoek naar rechtvaardiging en eenheid met Christus bij Maarten Luther, Philippus Melanchthon, Johannes Calvijn en John Owen*. [Apeldoorn, The Neth.]: Labarum Academic, 2013.
Kolb, Robert. "The Bible in Reformation and Protestant Orthodoxy." In *The Enduring Authority of the Christian Scriptures*, edited by D. A. Carson, 89–114. Grand Rapids, MI: Eerdmans, 2016.
Kooi, Cornelis van der. *Als in een Spiegel: God Kennen volgens Calvijn en Barth: Een Tweeluik*. Kampen, The Neth.: Kok, 2002.
———. *This Incredibly Benevolent Force: The Holy Spirit in Reformed Theology and Spirituality*. Annie Kinkead Warfield Lectures 2014. Grand Rapids, MI: Eerdmans, 2018.
Kooi, Cornelis van der, and Gijsbert van den Brink. *Christian Dogmatics: An Introduction*. Grand Rapids, MI: Eerdmans, 2017.
Kuitert, Harminus M. *Wat heet geloven? Structuur en herkomst van de christelijke geloofsuitspraken*. 2e dr. Baarn, The Neth.: Ten Have, 1977.
Kuyper, Abraham. "The Biblical Criticism of the Present Day." Translated by J. H. de Vries. *Bibliotheca Sacra and Theological Review* 241 (1904) 409–42, 666–88.
———. *Encyclopedia of Sacred Theology: Its Principles*. Translated by J. Hendrik de Vries. New York: Scribner, 1898.
———. "Geworteld en gegrond": *de kerk als organisme en instituut: intreêrede, uitgesproken in de Nieuwe Kerk te Amsterdam, 10 Augustus 1870*. 2e dr. Amsterdam: De Hoogh, 1870.
———. *On the Church*. Edited by John Halsey Wood and Andrew M. McGinnis. Abraham Kuyper Collected Works in Public Theology. Bellingham, WA: Lexham; 2016.
Lamont, John R. T. *Divine Faith*. Ashgate New Critical Thinking in Religion, Theology and Biblical Studies. Aldershot, UK: Ashgate, 2004.

Lane, Belden C. *Ravished by Beauty: The Surprising Legacy of Reformed Spirituality*. Oxford: Oxford University Press, 2011.

Latour, Bruno. *Facing Gaia: Eight Lectures on the New Climatic Regime*. Translated by Catherine Porter. Cambridge: Polity, 2017.

Laube, Martin. *Im Bann der Sprache: die analytische Religionsphilosophie im 20. Jahrhundert*. Theologische Bibliothek Töpelmann 85. Berlin: de Gruyter, 1999.

Lauster, Jörg. *Prinzip und Methode: die Transformation des protestantischen Schriftprinzips durch die historische Kritik von Schleiermacher bis zur Gegenwart*. Tübingen, Germ.: Mohr Siebeck, 2004.

Leder, Arie. "Divine Presence, Then the Covenants: An Essay on Narrative and Theological Precedence: Part One." *Nederduitse Gereformeerde Teologiese Tydskrif* 53 (2012) 179–93.

———. "Divine Presence, Then the Covenants. An Essay on Narrative and Theological Precedence (Part Three)." *Nederduitse Gereformeerde Teologiese Tydskrif* 55(2015) 685–99.

———. "Divine Presence, Then the Covenants: An Essay on Narrative and Theological Precedence (Part Two)." *Nederduitse Gereformeerde Teologiese Tydskrif* 54 (2013) 207–20.

Lehmkühler, Karsten. *Inhabitatio: die Einwohnung Gottes im Menschen*. Forschungen zur Systematischen und Ökumenischen Theologie 104. Göttingen: Vandenhoeck & Ruprecht, 2004.

Leslie, Andrew M. *The Light of Grace: John Owen on the Authority of Scripture and Christian Faith*. Göttingen: Vandenhoeck & Ruprecht, 2015.

Lindeboom, Lucas. *Blijf in het Woord van God: rede op den 33en gedenkdag van de Theol. School te Kampen door den aftredenden rector*. Heusden: A. Gezelle Meerburg, 1888.

Lubac, Henri de. *Exégèse médiévale: les quatre sens de l'Écriture*. Vol. 1. Paris: Aubier, 1959.

Macaskill, Grant. *The New Testament and Intellectual Humility*. 1st ed. Oxford: Oxford University Press, 2018.

Macchia, Frank D. *Jesus the Spirit Baptizer: Christology in Light of Pentecost*. Grand Rapids, MI: Eerdmans, 2018.

Manen, Gerben van. *Ontmoeting met God: een multiperspectivisch model in het spoor van Franz Rosenzweig en Kornelis Heiko Miskotte*. Zoetermeer, The Neth.: Boekencentrum Academic, 2017.

McConville, J. Gordon. "Law and Monarchy in the Old Testament." In *A Royal Priesthood? The Use of the Bible Ethically and Politically: A Dialogue with Oliver O'Donovan*, edited by Craig G. Bartholomew, 69–88. Scripture and Hermeneutics 3. Carlisle, UK: Paternoster, 2002.

McDougall, Joy Ann. "Lässt Sich die Praktische Bedeutung der Trinitätslehre Wiedergewinnen? Neue Horizonte in der Anglo-Amerikanischen Diskussion." *Evangelische Theologie* 58 (1998) 231–42.

McFague, Sallie. *Life Abundant: Rethinking Theology and Economy for a Planet in Peril*. Minneapolis, MN: Fortress, 2001.

———. *Super, Natural Christians: How We Should Love Nature*. London: SCM, 1997.

McGowan, A. T. B. *The Divine Spiration of Scripture: Challenging Evangelical Perspectives*. Nottingham, UK: Apollos, 2007.

McGrath, Alister E. *Christianity's Dangerous Idea: The Protestant Revolution—A History from the Sixteenth Century to the Twenty-First*. 1st ed. New York: HarperOne, 2007.

McIlroy, David H. *A Trinitarian Theology of Law: In Conversation with Jürgen Moltmann, Oliver O'Donovan, and Thomas Aquinas*. Paternoster Theological Monographs. Milton Keynes, UK: Paternoster, 2009.

McKim, Donald K. "John Owen's Doctrine of Scripture in Historical Perspective." *Evangelical Quarterly* 45 (1973) 195–207.

Meek, Esther Lightcap. *Loving to Know: Introducing Covenant Epistemology*. Eugene, OR: Cascade, 2011.

Meeuws, Hendrikus J. M. *Diaconie: van grondslagenonderzoek tot een pleidooi voor een diaconale mystagogie*. 2e dr. Gorinchem, The Neth.: Narratio, 2012.

Meijers, S. *Objectiviteit en existentialiteit: een onderzoek naar hun verhouding in de theologie van Herman Bavinck en in door hem beïnvloede concepties*. Kampen, The Neth.: Kok, 1979.

Merleau-Ponty, Maurice. *Phénoménologie de la perception*. 9me éd. Bibliothèque des idées. Paris: Gallimard, 1949.

Mietus, Leo. *Gunning en Kuyper in 1878: A. Kuypers polemiek tegen "Het leven van Jezus" van J. H. Gunning Jr.: een theologie-historische bijdrage*. Velp, The Neth.: Bond van Vrije Evangelische Gemeenten in Nederland, 2009.

Milbank, John. *Theology and Social Theory: Beyond Secular Reason*. Signposts in Theology. Oxford: Blackwell, 1993.

Moberly, R. W. L. "The Use of Scripture in *The Desire of the Nations*." In *A Royal Priesthood? The Use of the Bible Ethically and Politically: A Dialogue with Oliver O'Donovan*, edited by Craig G. Bartholomew, 46–64. Scripture and Hermeneutics 3. Carlisle, UK: Paternoster, 2002.

Moo, Douglas J., and Jonathan A. Moo. *Creation Care: A Biblical Theology of the Natural World*. Biblical Theology for Life. Grand Rapids, MI: Zondervan, 2018.

Moroney, Stephen K. *The Noetic Effects of Sin: A Historical and Contemporary Exploration of How Sin Affects Our Thinking*. Lanham, MD: Lexington, 2000.

Muller, Richard A. *Post-Reformation Reformed Dogmatics: The Rise and Development of Reformed Orthodoxy, ca. 1520 to ca. 1725*. 2nd ed. 4 vols. Grand Rapids, MI: Baker Academic, 2003.

Murphy, Nancey C. *Beyond Liberalism and Fundamentalism: How Modern and Postmodern Philosophy Set the Theological Agenda*. Rockwell Lecture Series. Valley Forge, PA: Trinity International, 1996.

"NBG-Onderzoek Bijbelgebruik in Nederland. Een Onderzoek van Het Nederlands Bijbelgenootschap in Samenwerking Met Onderzoeksbureau Blauw En Het Centrum Voor Contextuele Bijbelinterpretatie." https://bgs.detestomgeving.nl/wp-content/uploads/2017/09/NBG-rapport-onderzoek-V3_def.compressed.pdf.

Nieuwpoort, Ad van. "Omwille van de vrije Bijbel." In *De Bijbel in Nederland: de plaats van de Bijbel in kerk en samenleving*, edited by Floor Barnhoorn et al., 35–45. Haarlem, The Neth.: NBG, 2018.

Nullens, Patrick. *Leven volgens Gaia's normen? de verhouding tussen God, mens en aarde en de implicaties voor ecologische ethiek*. [N.p.: n.p.], 1995.

Oberman, Heiko A. *The Harvest of Medieval Theology: Gabriel Biel and Late Medieval Nominalism*. Cambridge, MA: Harvard University Press, 1963.

———. *Der Herbst der mittelalterlichen Theologie*. Translated by Martin Rumscheid and Hennig Kampen. Spätscholastik und Reformation 1. Zürich, Switz.: EVZ-Verlag, 1965.

O'Donovan, Oliver. "Christian Moral Reasoning." In *New Dictionary of Christian Ethics & Pastoral Theology*, edited by David John Atkinson and David Field, 122–27. Downers Grove, IL: InterVarsity, 1995.

———. *Church in Crisis: The Gay Controversy and the Anglican Communion*. Eugene, OR: Cascade, 2008.

———. *Common Objects of Love: Moral Reflection and the Shaping of Community: The 2001 Stob Lectures*. Grand Rapids, MI: Eerdmans, 2002.

———. "Deliberation, History and Reading: A Response to Schweiker and Wolterstorff." *Scottish Journal of Theology* 54 (2001) 127–44.

———. *The Desire of the Nations: Rediscovering the Roots of Political Theology*. Cambridge: Cambridge University Press, 1996.

———. *Entering into Rest*. Grand Rapids, MI: Eerdmans, 2017.

———. "Evangelicalism and the Foundations of Ethics." In *Evangelical Anglicans: Their Role and Influence in the Church Today*, edited by R. T. France and Alister E. McGrath, 96–107. London: SPCK, 1993.

———. *Finding and Seeking*. Ethics as Theology 2. Grand Rapids, MI: Eerdmans, 2014.

———. "The Moral Authority of Scripture." In *Scripture's Doctrine and Theology's Bible: How the New Testament Shapes Christian Dogmatics*, edited by Markus N. A. Bockmuehl and Alan J. Torrance, 165–76. Grand Rapids, MI: Baker Academic, 2008.

———. "The Natural Ethic." In *Essays in Evangelical Social Ethics*, edited by David F. Wright, 19–35. Exeter, UK: Paternoster, 1981.

———. *On the Thirty-Nine Articles: A Conversation with Tudor Christianity*. A Latimer Monograph. Exeter, UK: Paternoster, 1986.

———. "Prayer and Morality in the Sermon on the Mount." *Studies in Christian Ethics* 22 (2009) 21–33.

———. *The Problem of Self-Love in St. Augustine*. Eugene, OR: Wipf & Stock, 2006.

———. "Response to Respondents: Behold, the Lamb!" *Studies in Christian Ethics* 11 (1998) 91–110.

———. "Response to Walter Moberly." In *A Royal Priesthood? The Use of the Bible Ethically and Politically: A Dialogue with Oliver O'Donovan*, edited by Craig G. Bartholomew, 65–68. Scripture and Hermeneutics 3. Carlisle, UK: Paternoster, 2002.

———. *Resurrection and Moral Order: An Outline for Evangelical Ethics*. 2nd ed. Leicester, UK: Apollos, 1994.

———. "Scripture and Christian Ethics." *Theologia Reformata* 48 (2005) 121–29.

———. *Self, World, and Time*. Ethics as Theology 1. Grand Rapids, MI: Eerdmans, 2013.

———. *The Ways of Judgment: The Bampton Lectures, 2003*. Bampton Lectures in America. Grand Rapids, MI: Eerdmans, 2005.

O'Donovan, Oliver, and Michael Vasey. *Liturgy and Ethics*. Grove Ethical Studies 89. Bramcote, UK: Grove, 1993.

Oldhoff, Martine. "Hedendaagse theosis- en participatietaal overwogen met Paulus." *Kerk en Theologie* 68 (2017) 260–72.

———. "Soul Searching with Paul: A Theological Investigation of Cultural, Traditional, and Philosophical Concepts of the Soul." PhD diss., Protestantse Theologische Universiteit, 2021.

Oliphint, K. Scott. "Bonhoeffer, the Logos Principle, and Sola Scriptura." *Westminster Theological Journal* 72 (2010) 359–90.

Owen, John. *The Works of John Owen*. Edited by William H. Goold. Edinburgh: T. & T. Clark, 1862.

Paas, Stefan. "Post-Christian, Post-Christendom, and Post-Modern Europe: Towards the Interaction of Missiology and the Social Sciences." *Mission Studies* 28 (2011) 3–25.

Paddison, Angus. "The Authority of Scripture and the Triune God." *International Journal of Systematic Theology* 13 (2011) 448–62.

———. *Scripture: A Very Theological Proposal*. London: T. & T. Clark, 2009.

Pannenberg, Wolfhart. *Systematic Theology*. Vol. 3. London: Continuum, 2004. http://public.ebookcentral.proquest.com/choice/publicfullrecord.aspx?p=743047.

———. *Systematische Theologie*. Bd. III. Göttingen: Vandenhoeck & Ruprecht, 1993.

Pass, Bruce R. *The Heart of Dogmatics: Christology and Christocentrism in Herman Bavinck*. Forschungen Zur Systematischen Und Ökumenischen Theologie 169. Göttingen: Vandenhoeck & Ruprecht, 2020.

———. "Upholding Sola Scriptura Today: Some Unturned Stones in Herman Bavinck's Doctrine of Inspiration Herman Bavinck's Doctrine of Inspiration." *International Journal of Systematic Theology* 20 (2018) 517–36.

Pater, W. A. de, and Pierre Swiggers. Taal en teken: een historisch-systematische inleiding in de taalfilosofie. Wijsgerige Verkenningen 21. Leuven, Belg.: Universitaire Pers Leuven, 2000.

Paul, Herman. *De slag om het hart: over secularisatie van verlangen*. Utrecht, The Neth.: Uitgeverij Boekencentrum, 2017.

Peckham, John. *Canonical Theology: The Biblical Canon, Sola Scriptura, and Theological Method*. Grand Rapids, MI: Eerdmans, 2016.

Peels, Rik. "The Effects of Sin upon Human Moral Cognition." *Journal of Reformed Theology* 4 (2010) 42–69.

———. "Sin and Human Cognition of God." *Scottish Journal of Theology* 64 (2011) 390–409.

Perry, John. "Dissolving the Inerrancy Debate: How Modern Philosophy Shaped the Evangelical View of Scripture." *Journal for Christian Theological Research* 6 (2001) 1–8.

Phillips, D. Z. *Faith after Foundationalism*. London: Routledge, 1988.

Phillips, Jacob. *Human Subjectivity "in Christ" in Dietrich Bonhoeffer's Theology: Intergrating Simplicity and Wisdom*. T. & T. Clark Studies in Systematic Theology. London: Bloomsbury, 2019.

Piper, John, and Wayne A. Grudem. *Recovering Biblical Manhood and Womanhood: A Response to Evangelical Feminism*. Wheaton, IL: Crossway, 1991.

Plantinga, Alvin. *Warranted Christian Belief*. New York: Oxford University Press, 2000.

Porter, Stanley E. "What Exactly Is Theological Interpretation of Scripture, and Is It Hermeneutically Robust Enough for the Task to Which It Has Been Appointed?" In *Horizons in Hermeneutics: A Festschrift in Honor of Anthony C. Thiselton*, 234–67. Grand Rapids, MI: Eerdmans, 2013.

Putten, Bram van. "Stemmen met de voeten . . . Hoe wordt de Bijbel gelezen en wat doen mensen met wat ze leren?" In *De Bijbel in Nederland: de plaats van de Bijbel in kerk en samenleving*, edited by Floor Barnhoorn et al., 89–100. Haarlem, The Neth.: NBG, 2018.

Rauser, Randal D. *Theology in Search of Foundations*. Oxford: Oxford University Press, 2009.

Rehnman, Sebastian. *Divine Discourse: The Theological Methodology of John Owen*. Texts and Studies in Reformation and Post-Reformation Thought. Grand Rapids, MI: Baker Academic, 2002.

Renihan, Samuel D. *The Mystery of Christ: His Covenant and His Kingdom*. Cape Coral, FL: Founders, 2019.

Ricoeur, Paul. *Oneself as Another*. Translated by Kathleen Blamey. Chicago: University of Chicago Press, 1992.

Ridderbos, Herman N. *Heilsgeschiedenis en heilige schrift van het Nieuwe Testament: het gezag van het Nieuwe Testament*. Kampen, The Neth.: Kok, 1955.

Rieger, Hans-Martin. *Theologie als Funktion der Kirche: eine systematisch-theologische Untersuchung zum Verhältnis von Theologie und Kirche in der Moderne*. Theologische Bibliothek Töpelmann 139. Berlin: de Gruyter, 2007.

Rockström, Johan, et al. "Planetary Boundaries: Exploring the Safe Operating Space for Humanity." *Ecology and Society* 14 (2009) 1–32.

Rogers, Andrew P. *Congregational Hermeneutics: How Do We Read?* Explorations in Practical, Pastoral and Empirical Theology. Farnham, UK: Ashgate, 2015.

Rogers, Jack. *The Authority and Interpretation of the Bible: An Historical Approach*. San Francisco: Harper & Row, 1979.

Rose, Wolter H. "Messiaanse verwachtingen in het Oude Testament: Oorsprong en ontwikkelingen in de tijd na de ballingschap." In *Messianisme en eindtijdverwachting bij joden en christenen*, edited by Gerard C. den Hertog and Simon Schoon, 17–36. Zoetermeer, The Neth.: Boekencentrum, 2006.

Ryrie, Alec. *Unbelievers: An Emotional History of Doubt*. London: Collins, 2019.

Sarisky, Darren. *Reading the Bible Theologically*. Current Issues in Theology. Cambridge: Cambridge University Press, 2019.

———. *Scriptural Interpretation: A Theological Exploration*. Challenges in Contemporary Theology. Chichester, UK: Wiley, 2013.

———. "What Is Theological Interpretation? The Example of Robert W. Jenson." *International Journal of Systematic Theology* 12 (2010) 201–16.

Sarot, Marcel. "Christian Fundamentalism as a Reaction to the Enlightenment." In *Orthodoxy, Liberalism, and Adaptation: Essays on Ways of Worldmaking in Times of Change from Biblical, Historical and Systematic Perspectives*, edited by B. E. J. H. Becking, 249–67. Studies in Theology and Religion 15. Leiden, The Neth.: Brill, 2011.

Schaafsma, Petruschka, et al. "Vervreemding en Vertrouwen: Over Hermeneutiek En Theologie." *Nederlands Theologisch Tijdschrift* 67 (2013) 3–26.

Schaeffer, Jac. "Schilder mysticus." In *Wie is die man? Klaas Schilder in de eenentwintigste eeuw*, edited by Marius van Rijswijk, 205–60. AD Chartas-Reeks 22. Barneveld, The Neth.: De Vuurbaak, 2012.

Schee, Willem van der. "Kuyper's Archimedes' Point." In *Kuyper Reconsidered: Aspects of His Life and Work*, edited by Cornelis van der Kooi and Jan de Bruin, 102–10. Amsterdam: VU Uitgeverij, 1999.

Schilder, Klaas. *Christus in zijn lijden: overwegingen van het lijdensevangelie*. 2de herz. en verm. druk. Kampen, The Neth.: Kok, 1949.
Schleiermacher, Friedrich. *Der christliche Glaube nach den Grundsätzen der Evangelischen Kirche im Zusammenhange dargestellt (1830/31)*. Edited by Martin Redeker. Nachdr. der 7. Aufl. De-Gruyter-Studienbuch. 1960. Reprint, Berlin: de Gruyter, 1999.
Schol-Wetter, Anne-Mareike. "De Bijbel: verhaal en tegenverhaal." In *De Bijbel in Nederland: de plaats van de Bijbel in kerk en samenleving*, edited by Floor Barnhoorn et al., 23–34. Haarlem, The Neth.: NBG, 2018.
Schreiner, Susan E. *Are You Alone Wise? The Search for Certainty in the Early Modern Era*. Oxford Studies in Historical Theology. Oxford: Oxford University Press, 2011.
Schweiker, William. "Freedom and Authority in Political Theology: A Response to Oliver O'Donovan's *The Desire of the Nations*." *Scottish Journal of Theology* 54 (2001) 110–26.
Seeman, Bradley N. "The 'Old Princetonians' on Biblical Authority." In *The Enduring Authority of the Christian Scriptures*, edited by D. A. Carson, 195–237. Grand Rapids, MI: Eerdmans, 2016.
Short, T. L. "The Development of Peirce's Theory of Signs." In *The Cambridge Companion to Peirce*, edited by C. J. Misak, 214–40. Cambridge: Cambridge University Press, 2004.
Slenczka, Notger. "Die Kirche und das Alten Testament." https://www.theologie.hu-berlin.de/de/professuren/stellen/st/slenczka-die-kirche-und-das-alte-testament.pdf.
———. *Vom Alten Testament und vom Neuen: Beiträge zur Neuvermessung ihres Verhältnisses*. Leipzig, Germ.: Evangelische Verlagsanstalt, 2017.
Slot, Edward van 't. *Negativism of Revelation? Bonhoeffer and Barth on Faith and Actualism*. Tübingen, Germ.: Mohr Siebeck, 2015.
Smith, James K. A. *Desiring the Kingdom: Worship, Worldview, and Cultural Formation*. Grand Rapids, MI: Baker Academic, 2009.
———. *Imagining the Kingdom: How Worship Works*. Grand Rapids, MI: Baker Academic, 2013.
Smith, R. Scott. "Non-Foundational Epistemologies and the Truth of Scripture." In *The Enduring Authority of the Christian Scriptures*, edited by D. A. Carson, 831–71. Grand Rapids, MI: Eerdmans, 2016.
Smit, Peter-Ben. "Contextuele bijbelinterpretatie bestaat niet, en dat is maar goed ook." In *De Bijbel in Nederland: de plaats van de Bijbel in kerk en samenleving*, edited by Floor Barnhoorn et al., 72–85. Haarlem, The Neth.: NBG, 2018.
Spanje, Teunis E. van. *Inconsistency in Paul? A Critique of the Work of Heikki Räisänen*. Wissenschaftliche Untersuchungen Zum Neuen Testament 110. Tübingen, Germ.: Mohr Siebeck, 1999.
Spijker, W. van 't. "Enkele hoofdlijnen van de geschiedenis van de Christelijke Gereformeerde Kerken sinds 1892." In *Een eeuw christelijk-gereformeerd: aspecten van 100 jaar Christelijke Gereformeerde Kerken*, edited by W. van 't Spijker et al., 9–132. Kampen, The Neth.: Kok, 1992.
Staalduine-Sulman, Eveline van. "The Evangelical Movement and the Enlightenment." In *Evangelical Theology in Transition*, edited by Cornelis van der Kooi, 40–67. Amsterdam: VU University Press, 2012.

Steffen, W., et al. "Planetary Boundaries: Guiding Human Development on a Changing Planet." *Science* 347, January 15, 2015.
Stek, John H. "'Covenant' Overload in Reformed Theology." *Calvin Theological Journal* 29 (1994) 12–41.
Stewart, Columba. "Evagrius Pontus and the Eastern Monastic Tradition on the Intellect and the Passions." In *Faith, Rationality, and the Passions*, edited by Sarah Coakley, 67–79. Malden, MA: Wiley, 2012.
Sutanto, Nathaniel Gray. *God and Knowledge: Herman Bavinck's Theological Epistemology*. T. & T. Clark Studies in Systematic Theology 31. London: T. & T. Clark, 2020.
Talstra, Eep. "God. Biografie van een overlever." *Kerk en Theologie* 67 (2016) 97–112.
———. "The Spirit as Critical Biblical Scholar." In *The Spirit Is Moving: New Pathways in Pneumatology: Studies Presented to Professor Cornelis van der Kooi on the Occasion of His Retirement*, edited by Gijsbert van den Brink et al., 23–35. Leiden, The Neth.: Brill, 2019.
Tanner, Kathryn. *Christ the Key*. Current Issues in Theology. Cambridge: Cambridge University Press, 2010.
Taylor, Charles. *A Secular Age*. Gifford Lectures 1999. Cambridge: Belknap, 2007.
———. *Sources of the Self: The Making of the Modern Identity*. Cambridge, MA: Harvard University Press, 1989.
Thate, Michael J., et al. *"In Christ" in Paul: Explorations in Paul's Theology of Union and Participation*. Wissenschaftliche Untersuchungen Zum Neuen Testament 2. Reihe 384. Tübingen, Germ.: Mohr Siebeck, 2014.
Theokritoff, Elizabeth. *Living in God's Creation: Orthodox Perspectives on Ecology*. Foundations Series 4. Crestwood, NY: St. Vladimir's Seminary Press, 2009.
Thiselton, Anthony C. *Hermeneutics: An Introduction*. Grand Rapids, MI: Eerdmans, 2009.
Toren, Benno van den. *Breuk en brug: in gesprek met Karl Barth en postmoderne theologie over geloofsverantwoording*. Zoetermeer, The Neth.: Boekencentrum, 1995.
———. *Christian Apologetics as Cross-Cultural Dialogue*. London: T. & T. Clark, 2011.
Treier, Daniel J. *Introducing Theological Interpretation of Scripture: Recovering a Christian Practice*. Grand Rapids, MI: Baker Academic, 2008.
———. "What Is Theological Interpretation? An Ecclesiological Reduction." *International Journal of Systematic Theology* 12 (2010) 144–61.
Trimp, Cornelis. "Amerikaans fundamentalisme." In *Woord op schrift: theologische reflecties over het gezag van de bijbel*, edited by C. Trimp, 21–45. Kampen, The Neth.: Kok, 2002.
———. *Betwist schriftgezag. Een bundel opstellen over de autoriteit van de bijbel*. Groningen, The Neth.: De Vuurbaak, 1970.
———. "Heilige Geest en Heilige Schrift." In *Hoe Staan Wij Ervoor? Actualiteit van Het Gereformeerd Belijden*, edited by J. Kamphuis, 103–37. Barneveld, The Neth.: De Vuurbaak, 1992.
Tromp, Thijs. "Het verleden als uitdaging: een onderzoek naar de effecten van life review op de constructie van zin in levensverhalen van ouderen." Boekencentrum Academic, 2011.
Trueman, Carl R. *The Claims of Truth: John Owen's Trinitarian Theology*. Carlisle, UK: Paternoster, 1998.

Ulrich, Hans. "Mercy: The Messianic Practice." In *Mercy: Theories, Concepts, Practices: Proceedings from the International Congress, TU Apeldoorn/Kampen, NL June 2014*, edited by J. H. F. Schaeffer et al., 7–30. Ethik im Theologischen Diskurs 25. Zürich, Switz.: Lit, 2018.

Vanhoozer, Kevin J. "The Apostolic Discourse and Its Developments." In *Scripture's Doctrine and Theology's Bible: How the New Testament Shapes Christian Dogmatics*, edited by Markus N. A. Bockmuehl and Alan J. Torrance, 191–207. Grand Rapids, MI: Baker Academic, 2008.

———. *The Drama of Doctrine: A Canonical-Linguistic Approach to Christian Theology*. Louisville, KY: Westminster John Knox, 2005.

———. *First Theology: God, Scripture & Hermeneutics*. Downers Grove, IL: InterVarsity, 2002.

———. "Holy Scripture." In *Christian Dogmatics: Reformed Theology for the Church Catholic*, edited by Michael Allen and Scott R. Swain, 30–56. Grand Rapids, MI: Baker Academic, 2016.

———. *Is There a Meaning in This Text? The Bible, the Reader, and the Morality of Literary Knowledge*. Grand Rapids, MI: Zondervan, 1998.

Veenhof, Jan. "Honderd jaar theologie aan de Vrije Universiteit." In *Wetenschap en rekenschap, 1880–1980: een eeuw wetenschapsbeoefening en wetenschapsbeschouwing aan de Vrije Universiteit*, edited by W. J. Wieringa and M. van Os, 44–104. Kampen, The Neth.: Kok, 1980.

———. *De kracht die hemel en aarde verbindt: de identiteit van de Geest van God als relatiestichter*. Zoetermeer, The Neth.: Uitgeverij Boekencentrum, 2016.

———. "Openbaring. Geschiedenis. Bijbel. Drie kernmomenten van de theologie van Hoedemaker in hun onderlinge samenhang." In *Hoedemaker herdacht*, edited by G. Abma and J. de Bruijn, 135–54. Baarn, The Neth.: Ten Have, 1989.

———. *De Parakleet: enige beschouwingen over de parakleet-belofte in het evangelie van Johannes en haar theologische betekenis*. Kampen, The Neth.: Kok, 1974.

———. *Revelatie en inspiratie. De Openbarings- en Schriftbeschouwing van Herman Bavinck in vergelijking met die der ethische theologie*. Amsterdam: Buijten & Schipperheijn, 1968.

Veluw, A. H. van. *Waar komt het kwaad vandaan? Over God, schepping, evolutie en de oorsprong van het kwaad*. Heerenveen, The Neth.: Groen, 2010.

Venter, Rian. "Taking Stock of the Trinitarian Renaissance: What Have We Learnt?" *HTS Teologiese Studies / Theological Studies* 75 (2019) e1–e6.

Verkerk, Maarten J. *Sekse als antwoord*. Verantwoording 12. Amsterdam: Buijten & Schipperheijn, 1997.

Versluis, Arie. "'And Moses Wrote His Torah': Canon Formulas and the Theology of Writing in Deuteronomy." In *Sola Scriptura: Biblical and Theological Perspectives on Scripture, Authority, and Hermeneutics*, edited by Hans Burger et al., 137–58. Studies in Reformed Theology 32. Leiden, The Neth.: Brill, 2018.

Vetter, Martin. *Zeichen Deuten Auf Gott: Der Zeichentheoretische Beitrag von Charles S. Peirce Zur Theologie Der Sakramente*. Marburg, Germ.: Elwert, 1999.

Village, Andrew. *The Bible and Lay People: An Empirical Approach to Ordinary Hermeneutics*. Explorations in Practical, Pastoral, and Empirical Theology. Aldershot, UK: Ashgate, 2007.

Vissers, J. "Karl Barth's Appreciative Use of Herman Bavinck's Reformed Dogmatics." *Calvin Theological Journal* 45 (2010) 79–86.

Vlastuin, Willem van, and Kelly M. Kapic, eds. *John Owen between Orthodoxy and Modernity*. Studies in Reformed Theology 39. Leiden, The Neth.: Brill, 2019.

Volf, Miroslav. *Exclusion and Embrace: A Theological Exploration of Identity, Otherness, and Reconciliation*. Nashville: Abingdon, 1996.

———. *Free of Charge: Giving and Forgiving in a Culture Stripped of Grace*. Grand Rapids, MI: Zondervan, 2005.

Vries, Pieter de. *"Die mij heeft liefgehad": de betekenis van de gemeenschap met Christus in de theologie van John Owen (1616–1683)*. Heerenveen, The Neth.: Groen, 2000.

Vroom, H. M. "De gelezen schrift als principium theologiae." In *100 jaar theologie: aspecten van een eeuw theologie in de Gereformeerde Kerken in Nederland (1892–1992)*, edited by Martien E. Brinkman and A. J. van den Berg, 96–161. Kampen, The Neth.: Kok, 1992.

———. *De schrift alleen? Een vergelijkend onderzoek naar de toetsing van theologische uitspraken volgens de openbaringstheologische visie van Torrance en de hermeneutisch-theologische opvattingen van Van Buren, Ebeling, Moltmann en Pannenberg*. Kampen, The Neth.: Kok, 1978.

Watkins, Eric B. *The Drama of Preaching: Participating with God in the History of Redemption*. Eugene, OR: Wipf & Stock, 2016.

Watson, Francis. "Hermeneutics and the Doctrine of Scripture: Why They Need Each Other." *International Journal of Systematic Theology* 12 (2010) 118–43.

Webb, William J. *Slaves, Women & Homosexuals: Exploring the Hermeneutics of Cultural Analysis*. Downers Grove, IL: InterVarsity, 2001.

Webster, John B. *The Domain of the Word: Scripture and Theological Reason*. 1st ed. London: Bloomsbury, 2013.

———. *Holy Scripture: A Dogmatic Sketch*. Cambridge: Cambridge University Press, 2003.

———. *Word and Church: Essays in Christian Dogmatics*. Edinburgh: T. & T. Clark, 2001.

Weder, Hans. "Die Externität Der Mitte: Überlegungen Zum Hermeneutischen Problem Des Kriteriums Der Sachkritik Am Neuen Testament." In *Jesus Christus Als Die Mitte Der Schrift: Studien Zur Hermeneutik Des Evangeliums*, edited by Christoph Landmesser, 291–320. Berlin: de Gruyter, 1997.

Westphal, Merold. "Hermeneutics and Holiness." In *Analytic Theology: New Essays in the Philosophy of Theology*, edited by Oliver Crisp and Michael C. Rea, 265–79. Oxford: Oxford University Press, 2009.

———. "Hermeneutics as Epistemology." In *The Blackwell Guide to Epistemology*, edited by John Greco and Ernest Sosa, 415–35. Blackwell Philosophy Guides. Malden, MA: Blackwell, 1999.

———. "Taking St. Paul Seriously: Sin as an Epistemological Category." In *Christian Philosophy*, edited by Thomas P. Flint, 200–226. Notre Dame, IN: University of Notre Dame Press, 1990.

White, Lynn. "The Historical Roots of Our Ecological Crisis." In *The Care of Creation: Focusing Concern and Action*, edited by R. J. Berry, 31–42. Leicester, UK: InterVarsity, 2000.

Wierenga, L. *De macht van de taal, de taal van de macht: over literatuurwetenschap en Bijbelgebruik*. Kampen, The Neth.: Kok Voorhoeve, 1996.

Wijngaarden, Herman van, and Eline van Vreeswijk. "Een slag apart. 40% van de orthodox-protestantse jongeren leest elke dag in de Bijbel." In *De Bijbel in Nederland: de plaats van de Bijbel in kerk en samenleving*, edited by Floor Barnhoorn et al., 101–15. Haarlem, The Neth.: NBG, 2018.

Willard, Dallas. *Renovation of the Heart: Putting on the Character of Christ*. Colorado Springs: NavPress, 2002.

Wirzba, Norman. *Agrarian Spirit: Cultivating Faith, Community, and the Land*. Notre Dame, IN: University of Notre Dame Press, 2022.

———. *The Paradise of God: Renewing Religion in an Ecological Age*. Oxford: Oxford University Press, 2003.

Wisse, Maarten. "Contra et Pro Sola Scriptura." In *Sola Scriptura: Biblical and Theological Perspectives on Scripture, Authority, and Hermeneutics*, edited by Hans Burger et al., 19–37. Studies in Reformed Theology 32. Leiden, The Neth.: Brill, 2018.

———. *De Bijbel in het midden: het geloofsgesprek te midden van verschillen*. Utrecht, The Neth.: KokBoekencentrum Uitgevers, 2019.

———. *Scripture between Identity and Creativity: A Hermeneutical Theory Building upon Four Interpretations of Job*. Ars Disputandi Supplement Series 1. Utrecht, The Neth.: Ars Disputandi, 2003.

Wittgenstein, Ludwig. *On Certainty*. Edited by G. E. M. Anscombe and G. H. von Wright. Oxford: Blackwell, 1974.

———. *Philosophical Investigations*. Translated by G. E. M. Anscombe. 2nd ed. Reissued German-English ed. Reissued 2nd ed. Oxford: Blackwell, 1997.

Witzier, Arjan. *Lezen in het licht van de Geest: hermeneutische implicaties van het nieuwtestamentische spreken over het verlichtende werk van de Heilige Geest*. Utrecht, The Neth.: KokBoekencentrum, 2022.

Wolterstorff, Nicholas. *Divine Discourse: Philosophical Reflections on the Claim That God Speaks*. Cambridge: Cambridge University Press, 1995.

———. "Herman Bavinck—Proto Reformed Epistemologist." *Calvin Theological Journal*. 45 (2010) 133–46.

———. *Reason within the Bounds of Religion*. 2nd ed. Grand Rapids, MI: Eerdmans, 1984.

Woodbridge, John D. "German Pietism and Scriptural Authority: The Question of Biblical Inerrancy." In *The Enduring Authority of the Christian Scriptures*, edited by D. A. Carson, 137–70. Grand Rapids, MI: Eerdmans, 2016.

Woudenberg, René van. *The Epistemology of Reading and Interpretation*. Cambridge: Cambridge University Press, 2021.

———. "Filosofie en de verduistering van ons verstand." *Philosophia Reformata* 69 (2004) 140–50.

———. *Filosofie van taal en tekst*. Budel: Damon, 2002.

———. "Greijdanus' kentheologie." In *Leven en werk van prof. dr. Seakle Greijdanus*, edited by George Harinck, 165–74. Barneveld, The Neth.: De Vuurbaak, 1998.

———. "Over de noëtische gevolgen van de zonde: Een filosofische beschouwing." *Nederlands Theologisch Tijdschrift* 52 (1998) 224–40.

Wright, Christopher J. H. *The Mission of God: Unlocking the Bible's Grand Narrative*. Downers Grove, IL: IVP Academic, 2006.

Wright, N. T. *After You Believe: Why Christian Character Matters*. 1st ed. New York: HarperOne, 2010.

———. *The Climax of the Covenant: Christ and the Law in Pauline Theology*. Minneapolis, MN: Fortress, 1992.

———. *How God Became King: The Forgotten Story of the Gospels*. New York: HarperOne, 2012.
———. *Jesus and the Victory of God*. Christian Origins and the Question of God 2. Minneapolis, MN: Fortress, 1996.
———. *The New Testament and the People of God*. Christian Origins and the Question of God 1. London: SPCK, 1992.
———. *Paul and the Faithfulness of God*. Christian Origins and the Question of God 4. Minneapolis, MN: Fortress, 2013.
———. *The Resurrection of the Son of God*. Minneapolis, MN: Fortress, 2003.
Yarbrough, Robert W. "The Future of Cognitive Reverence for the Bible." *Journal of the Evangelical Theological Society* 57 (2014) 5–18.
Yong, Amos. *Spirit-Word-Community: Theological Hermeneutics in Trinitarian Perspective*. Ashgate New Critical Thinking in Religion, Theology, and Biblical Studies. Aldershot, UK: Ashgate, 2002.
Young, William. "Historic Calvinism and Neo-Calvinism." *Westminster Theological Journal* 36 (1974) 156–73.
Ypenga, Anko. "Sacramentum: Hugo van St.-Victor ([d.] 1141) en zijn invloed op de allegorische interpretatie van de liturgie en de sacramentele theologie vanaf 1140 tot aan Durandus van Mende ([d.] 1296)." PhD diss., University of Groningen, 2002.
Zimmermann, Jens. *Recovering Theological Hermeneutics: An Incarnational-Trinitarian Theory of Interpretation*. Grand Rapids, MI: Baker Academic, 2004.
Zizioulas, John. "Priest of Creation." In *Environmental Stewardship: Critical Perspectives, Past and Present*, edited by R. J. Berry, 273–90. ISSR Library. London: T. & T. Clark, 2006.
Zwiep, A. W. *Tussen tekst en lezer: een historische inleiding in de bijbelse hermeneutiek / Dl. I, De vroege kerk - Schleiermacher*. Amsterdam: VU University Press, 2009.
———. *Tussen tekst en lezer: een historische inleiding in de bijbelse hermeneutiek / Dl. II, Van moderniteit naar postmoderniteit*. Tweede druk. Amsterdam: VU University Press, 2014.

Name Index

A
Adam, A.K.M., 182n16
Aquinas, T., 24, 162, 185
Augustine, Saint, 35, 149, 160, 202, 219n143
Augustijn, C., 52n131, 57n158, 59n166, 60n169

B
Baker, B.D., 149n1, 155, 158n37, 175n125
Barnhoorn, F., 276n12
Barth, K., 69–70, 109–10, 120, 125, 146n145, 164n85, 181, 184n26, 207–8, 212, 292n84, 305n122
Bartholomew, C.G., 11n17, 47n107, 48nn110–11, 151n9, 166n97, 211, 234n24, 235, 239n37, 253, 267n113, 269n117
Backham, R., 234
Bavinck, H., 6, 16, 62, 70, 109, 173, 177–210, 212–13, 215, 219–23, 225–26, 228, 233, 236n31, 243, 271, 306n129, 315
Bavinck, J.H., 82n32, 88n52
Bayer, O., 47n109
Baylor, T.R., 5n6
Beek, A., van de, 5n7, 13n24, 23n15, 180, 195n80, 229n4, 233n21, 234n23, 241n46, 318n163
Beilby, J., 21n9
Bekkum, van, K. , 58n158, 58n162, 59n166, 60n169, 120n125, 261n95, 262n97, 270n118, 324n2
Bell, R.H., 89n53, 90n62

Belt, H., van den, 26n28, 28n33, 29n34, 31nn41–42, 41n94, 45n105, 183n19, 185, 186n34, 199n97, 202n108, 204n112, 205n115, 215n139, 220, 221n144
Bennema, C., 90n59
Berkhof, H., 49n115, 111
Berkouwer, G.C., 22, 70, 180n4, 194n79, 222n147
Bernstein, R.J., 23n16
Bernts, A.P.J., 276nn9–10
Berry, W., 328n16
Bielo, J.S., 278–80, 283–87
Billings, J.T., 6n8, 12n18, 40n92, 70n185, 266n109
Black, R., 158n37
Blomberg, C.L., 235n30, 237n34
Boersma, H., 15n31, 17, 19n3, 25n19, 25n21, 26n23, 47n107, 229, 249–56, 258, 261n95, 264nn101–3, 332n28
Bolsonaro, J., 81
Bonhoeffer, D., 161, 172n123, 181–82, 244
Borgman, E., 276
Bouma-Prediger, S., 331n23
Bowald, M.A., 12n18, 47, 59n165, 231n13–14, 269n117
Braaten, C.E., 182n16
Bradford, W., 327
Bratt, J.D., 49n113
Bremmer, R.H., 183n19
Bretherton, L., 150n4
Brink, G., van den, 21n7, 96nn90–91, 109n2, 180

NAME INDEX

Brinke, H., ten, 96n89
Brock, C., 179n3, 185n32
Brock, B., 287n65, 291n80
Brom, van den, L., 23n15
Bruijne, de, A.L.Th., 8n10, 21, 22n11, 29n35, 151n113, 154n25, 158n37, 170n119, 229n6, 246n59, 247
Bruggen, van, J., 65, 211, 246n62, 263n100
Bullinger, H., 30
Bultmann, R., 109–11
Burger, H., 5n7, 6n8, 8n10, 12n18, 33n49, 87n50, 88n52, 109n2, 112n17, 129n86, 134n105, 146n145, 154n21, 158n37, 165n91, 177n130, 221n145, 239n37, 240n42, 241nn44–45, 242n47, 243n49, 245n58, 256n88, 260n94, 292n81, 306n129, 311n152, 328n17, 330n21

C

Calvin, J., 26–27, 30, 31n42, 57, 79
Campbell, C.R., 242n47
Carson, D.A., 13n21, 13n22
Chandler, D., 294n87
Chaplin, J.A., 164n92
Chemnitz, M., 31
Chen, M.S., 202n108
Childs, B., 235
Clark, T., 86n49, 146n145, 292n83, 293n85, 295n88, 316n160
Clausnitzer, T., 87
Cleveland, C., 303n109, 304, 306n127
Clore, G.L., 93n80, 103
Coakley, S., 86nn47–48, 92n75, 94, 176n127, 270n120, 274, 284
Colenso, J., 49
Collicut, J., 320n168
Colwell, J., 175n125
Coster-van Urk, E., 277
Conradie, E.M., 331n26, 332n30
Cruz, de, H., 88

D

Dalferth, I.U., 6, 9n11, 9n12, 12, 13n24, 16, 20nn5–6, 21, 22n10, 27, 28n32, 31n40, 60n167, 65n178, 67n183, 70n185, 84n37, 95n87, 102n112, 102n114, 111–46, 148, 155n28, 171–72, 175, 178–80, 188, 204n113, 206–7, 209, 211–15, 222n148, 225, 228, 261, 273, 292
Danielou, J., 249n72, 253, 264n101
Davis, E.F., 330
Dekker, J., 211n124
Descartes, R., 29, 47, 75, 84
Dooyeweerd, H., 104
Douma, J., 246n60, 247n63, 247n65
Dülmen, R., van, 28n33
Dumbrell, W.J., 241n44
Dussen, van der, A., 180n8
Dvorak, R., 109n3

E

Ebeling, G., 122–23, 137, 141, 178
Echeverria, E.J., 21n9, 221nn145–46, 222n147, 222n149
Eglinton, J., 179
Enns, P., 261n95
Erickson, M.J., 21n9
Eygen, H., van, 88n52, 96n90

F

Ferguson, S.B., 303n109, 306n126
Fermer, R.M., 109n2
Fickert, V., 112nn16–17, 113n19, 119n44, 121nn52–53, 124n67, 142–45, 209
Fiore, J., van, 326
Foppen, A., 276nn10–11, 277
Ford, D.F., 297n91, 317nn161–62
Fowl, S.E., 12n18, 283
Foucalt, M., 79
Frame, J.M., 21n9
Francis, Pope, 325
Freud, S., 102
Fricker, M., 104n124
Fulks, J., 275n7, 276n8
Furnish, V.P., 165n91

G
Gadamer, H.G., 3
Geertsema, H.G., 23n15, 88n51
Gentry, P.J., 241n44
Gestrich, C., 95n88
Goheen, M.W., 239n37
Goldingay, J., 239n37
Goudriaan, A., 46n105
Graaf, B., van der, 276n14, 277n16
Graaf, J., van der, 62n170
Greijdanus, S., 236n30, 237n34
Grenz, S.J., 47n109, 48n111
Grotius, H., 29
Grudem, A., 248n70
Gunning, J.H., 59n166
Gunton, C., 19n3, 21, 22n11, 30n38

H
Hahn, S., 241n44
Haitjema, Th.L., 194n79
Hartmann, E., von, 185n30
Hauerwas, S., 158n37
Hays, R.B., 237n34, 238n35
Healy, M., 90n62
Hegel, G.W.F., 47n109, 48, 61
Heidegger, M., 3, 85, 292n82
Heideman, E.P., 183n19, 185n30, 188n48, 206n117
Hengstenberg, E.W., 49n112
Herrmann, J.W., 111
Hertog, M., den, 227n1
Hess, M.E., 331n23
Hettema, T.L., 265n108
Hill, C.E., 25n19
Hirsch. E.D., 264n106
Hodge, A.A., 62
Holmes, S.R., 109n2
Holtrop, F., 227n1
Hoogland, J., 21n9
Horrell, D.G., 331n22
Horton, M.S., 240, 241n44, 243, 262n97, 312n152
Houtman, D., 182n16, 224n151
Houwelingen, P.H.R., van, 260n93
Howson, B., 33n44
Huijgen, A., 12n19, 49n112, 62n172, 65n178, 231n12, 270n118
Hus, J., 25

Huttinga, W., 183n19, 251n78

I
Illyricus, M.F., 31

J
Jackson, B., 239n37
Jamieson, R.B., 230, 231n11, 234n25, 237n32, 244, 262n95
Jenson, M., 97n94
Jenson, R.W.. 12n20, 13n21, 15n30, 182n16, 212n133, 213n136, 225n155, 231nn16-17, 233n21, 234
Johnson, D., 89, 100, 316
Jong, M., de, 274n4, 296
Jong-van Campen, A., de, 101n108, 263n100, 284n54, 285, 287n64, 288-90, 292, 294, 296-97
Jüngel, E., 97, 98n95, 109-12, 120, 122-23, 141, 266, 319n167

K
Kaiser, W.C. Jr., 264n106
Kamphuis, J., 57n158
Kant, I., 29, 47, 61, 75, 111, 186
Kapic, K.M., 33n44, 33n49
Kärkkäinen, V.M., 14n29, 70n185, 109n2, 244, 329
Kasper, W., 266
Keener, C.S., 9n13, 14n27, 89n53, 90n60, 90n62, 91n65, 218n141, 224, 236nn30-31, 243n48, 244, 246n61, 250n76, 265n017, 312n153, 315n157
Kelsey, D.H., 2n1, 5n7, 6n7, 171, 206n116
Kettler, C.D., 146nn147-48, 147nn150-51
Keulen, D., van, 49n115, 53n133, 58n159, 183nn18-19, 184n28, 189, 196n85, 197n89, 198, 205n115
Keyes, D., 104n126
Kierkegaard, S., 154n25
King. D.M., 303n109
Klaassen, M., 33n49
Kolb, M., 26n26, 27n29, 27n31, 31n40

NAME INDEX

Kooi, C., van der, 14n29, 47n108, 180
Kuenen, A., 49
Kuitert, H., 22, 181–82,
Kuyper, A., 6, 15, 19, 48–62, 64, 67, 97n93, 100–2, 104–5, 185, 205, 213, 214n137
Kwakkel, G., 261n95, 262n97

L
Lacoste, J.Y., 150, 159, 168, 175
Lamont, J.R., 40n89
Lane, B.C., 326, 327nn11–13
Latour, B., 324, 326, 332
Lauster, J., 26n25, 27n28, 27n31, 31n40, 31n42
Leder, A., 96n88, 240, 241nn43–44
Lehmkühler, K., 311n152
Leslie, A.M., 29n34, 33–35, 36n63, 37n73, 40–44, 301n95, 303n109, 304–7, 311
Lessing, G.E., 181
Levinas, E., 85
Lindeboom, L., 213n135, 314
Lipsius, J., 47
Locke, J., 75
Loen, A.E., 185n30
Lubac, H., de, 235, 249n72, 253, 263, 2646n103
Luther, M., 26–28, 30–31, 65n178, 116–17, 120, 125

M
Macaskill, G. , 321
Macchia, F., 13, 14n25, 14n29, 244, 245n57, 265n107
MacIntyre, A., 3, 150n4
Manen, G., van, 208n121, 209, 210n123
Marx, K.M., 102
McConville, J.G., 166n97
McDougall, J.A., 109n2
McFague, S., 325
McGowan, A.T.B., 62n172
McGrath, A.E., 18n1, 28, 65–66,
McKim, D.K., 33n44
McIlroy, D.H., 157n35, 165n91, 175n125

Meek, E.L., 86n49, 100, 292n83, 295n88, 297n89, 316n160
Meeuws, H.J.M., 288, 289n68, 290, 296–97
Meijers, S., 180n4, 189n55
Merleau-Ponty, M., 3, 85,
Mietus, L., 59n166
Milbank, J., 19n3, 25n21
Moberly, R.W.L., 165n91, 166n97
Moltmann, J., 244
Moo, D.J., 94n84, 96n88, 331n25
Moo, J.A., 94n84, 96n88, 331n25
Moroney, S.K., 101–2, 103n118, 269n116
Muller, R.A., 24n18, 25n20, 25n22, 26n23, 27nn29–31, 30n39, 31n40, 31nn42–43, 41n94, 44, 47n107
Murphy, N.C., 21n9, 60n168

N
Nietzsche, F.W., 102
Nieuwpoort, A., van, 276n13
Noordtzij, M., 193n68
Nullens, P., 94n84

O
Oberman, H.A., 25, 26nn23–24
O'Donovan, O., 3n5, 6, 12, 13n24, 14, 16, 19n3, 20n4, 29n35, 93, 95nn85–86, 98–99, 101, 146–77, 179, 206, 216–17, 221n145, 226, 228, 244, 247, 255–57, 267n112, 273, 293, 302
Oliphint, K.S., 183n19, 185n32
Olson, R.E., 47n109, 48n111
Oldhoff, M., 89n53, 90nn60–61, 94, 312n153, 315
Oranje, B., van, 294
Owen, J., 14n29, 15, 19, 32–46, 61–62, 65, 67, 274, 300–12, 314–15

P
Paas, S., 19n2, 206n117
Paddison, A., 182n16
Pannenberg, W., 13, 25n21, 29n34, 29n36

NAME INDEX

Pass, B.R.. 180n4, 185n29, 182n31, 186nn35–36, 187n43, 188n48, 190n57, 191n58, 192n64, 194n74, 195n83, 196n85
Pater, W.A., de, 294n87
Paul, H., 83nn33–34, 94
Peckham, J., 21n9, 26n24, 182n16, 211, 222n148, 223n150, 225n156, 228n3
Peels, R., 89, 90n60, 90n63, 91n64, 91nn66–68, 92n73, 96n90, 97nn92–93, 101
Peirce, C.S., 120, 294n87
Perry, J., 29, 30n37, 49n112
Phillips, D.Z., 21n9
Phillips, J., 172n123, 207n120
Piper, J., 248n70
Plantinga, A., 22, 88, 92, 118n41
Plato, 35
Polanyi, M., 89n49, 100, 292n83, 295n88
Porter, S.E., 12n18, 13nn21–23
Putten, B., van, 276

R
Ramsey, R.P., 170n119
Ratzinger, J.A., 221n146
Rauser, R.D., 21n9, 29n36, 46n104
Rehnman, S., 303n109
Reniham, S.D., 241n44
Ricoeur, P., 3, 84–85, 234, 235n28, 246
Ridderbos, H.N., 193n70
Rieger, H.M., 146n146
Ritschl, A.B., 186
Robertson Smith, W., 49
Rockström, J., 323n1
Rogers, J., 33n44, 41n96, 46n105, 49n112, 62n172, 278–85, 321n171
Rose, W.H., 264n104
Rothe, R., 50
Ryrie, A., 26n23, 29n34

S
Sales, F., de, 162
Sarinsky, D., 1n1, 12n18, 67n182, 182n16, 210n124, 219n143, 228, 229n5, 234n26, 243n51, 262n97, 268, 270n119, 272n1, 273n2, 275n6
Sarot, M., 21n7, 21n9, 29, 30n37, 202n105
Schaafsma, P., 145n144
Schaeffer, J., 229n6, 230n9
Schee, W., van der, 53n132
Schilder, K., 6, 17, 229–32, 234, 241–42
Schleiermacher, F., 47–49, 61, 63, 186, 203
Schol-Wetter, A.M., 276n13, 277
Schopenhauer, A., 186
Schreiner, S., 29, 29n34
Schweiker, W., 165n91, 175n125
Seeman, B.N., 49n112, 62n172
Short, T.L., 294n87
Silva, M., 264n106
Slenczka, N., 233, 234n22
Slot, E., van 't, 181n14, 207n120
Smedt, J., de, 88
Smit, P.B., 277, 278n19
Smith, J.K.A., 83n34, 85n46, 86n46, 94, 297n91, 316
Smith, R.S., 21n9
Smith, W.R., 50
Spanje, van, T.E., 246n62
Spencer, H., 186
Spijker, W., van 't, 62n170
Spinoza, B., de, 47
Staalduine-Sulman, E., van, 49n112
Steffen, W., 323n1
Stek, J.H., 241n43
Stewart, O.S.B., 94n81
Sutanto, N.G., 179n3, 185n30, 185n32
Swiggers, P., 294n87
Swinburne, R., 118n41

T
Talstra, E., 262n96
Tanner, K., 146,
Taylor, C., 15, 19n3, 20n4, 25n21, 28n33, 47n107, 49n113, 73–86, 173n124, 176, 272
Thate, M.J., 242n47
Theokritoff, E., 332n30
Thiselton, A.C., 2n2
Torrance, T.F., 146, 293n85

363

NAME INDEX

Toren, B., van den, 21nn7–8
Treier, D.J., 12n18, 182n16
Trimp, C., 49n112, 62n172, 197n89, 214n138, 221n146
Tromp, T., 84n40
Trueman, C.R., 33n44, 34, 40–41, 301nn95–96, 303nn109–10, 310n150
Trump, D., 81

U
Ulrich, H., 287n65

V
Vanhoozer, K.J, 3n4, 6n8, 40n92, 66n180, 70n185, 89n53, 105n129, 166, 173n124, 175–76, 182n16, 211, 213n136, 231n15, 232, 232nn19–20, 236n31, 237n303, 240, 243, 264n106, 293n86, 295n88, 316n160, 320, 321n171
Veenhof, J., 14n29, 49n115, 52n130, 53n132, 60n169, 62n170, 179, 180n4, 196n85
Veluw, A.H., van, 96n89
Venter, R., 109n2
Verkerk, M.J., 104n126
Versluis, A., 211n131
Vetter, M., 294n87
Village, A., 278281, 283, 285–86, 287n63
Vissers, J., 184n26
Vlastuin, W., van, 33n44
Voegelin, E., 326
Volf, M., 93–94, 103–4, 297, 318–19
Vries, P., de, 33n49
Vreeswijk, E., van, 277n15
Vroom, H.M., 182, 185n33

W
Walton, B., 7n9
Warfield, B.B., 62, 180
Watkins, E.B., 239n37
Watson, F., 178n1
Webb, W.J., 247, 248n69
Webster, J., 5n6, 11, 40n92, 65n175, 70n185, 109n1, 144n138, 178, 179n2, 197, 206n117, 210–11, 222n148, 301n95, 305n122, 306n136, 313n154
Weder, H., 213n135
Westphal, M., 3n3, 10, 83n35, 92n75, 97n93, 102,
White, L., 325n8
Wieringa, L., 66n179, 181, 181, 192, 213–15
Wijngaarden, H., van, 277n15
Willard, D.M., 91n66, 104, 293n86, 297n90, 320n168
Winkworth, C., 87
Wirzba, N., 325n4, 325nn7–8, 326n9, 327n14, 328nn15–16, 331
Wisse, M., 66n180, 209, 228n3, 232n18, 265n106, 275
Wit, H., de, 275, 286
Wittgenstein, L., 3, 20n6, 63, 85
Wittman, T., 230, 234n25, 237, 244, 262n96
Witzier, A., 218nn142–43
Wolterstorff, N., 21n7, 21n9, 23n17, 60n168, 66n180, 211
Woodbridge, J.D., 47n107, 62n172
Woudenberg, R., van, 10, 66n180, 91n66, 91n68, 97n93, 104
Wright, C.J.H., 96n88, 234, 237n31, 239n37, 241n44
Wright, N.T., 13n21, 166, 173, 176, 236n30, 238, 239n37, 240, 246n62, 259n92, 262n97, 264n105, 293n86
Wycliff, J., 25

Y
Yarbrough, R.W., 45n103
Yong, A., 182n16
Ypenga, A., 253, 258n91, 263n99

Z
Zimmermann, J., 33n44, 33n50, 44, 301n95, 302n104, 306n125, 310n150
Zizioulas, J., 332n30
Zorreguieta, M., 294
Zwiep, A.W., 47n107, 48n110, 49n112, 102n116

Scripture Index

OLD TESTAMENT

Genesis

1–3	96
1–2	96, 332
1:26–30	94
2	89
2:19–20	88, 95
3	89, 97

Exodus

20	247

Psalms

8:6–9	94
22	252, 258–61
22:2	260
22:16	259, 264
63:2	94
104:30	256
110	259n92
119:18	305

Isaiah

7:14	264n105
11:9	333

Jeremiah

17:9	98

Daniel

7:13–14	259n92

Hosea

1:1	264n105
13:14	264n105

Zechariah

9:9–10	259n92
9:9	235

NEW TESTAMENT

Matthew

1:22	237n33
1:23	264n105
2:15	237n33, 264n105
2:17	237n33
4:14	237n33
5–7	170, 246
5:17	235
6:22–23	35n60
8:17	237n33
12:17	237n33
12:40	227
13:14	237n33
13:35	237n33
21:4	237n33
26:27–28	235
27:9	237n33

Mark

7:18–23	89
9:14–29	278
11:1–8	259n92
12:35–37	259n92
14:24–25	235
14:22–25	259n92
14:62	259n92

Luke

3:38	237
11:34–36	35n60
12:32–33	22n13
22:20	235
24	16–17, 235–36, 241, 268, 270, 312
24:19	235
24:21	235
24:25–26	268
24:25–27	42n98, 236
24:25	236
24:27	260
24:32	312
24:35	312
24:44	236, 260
24:45	236, 268, 312
24:46–49	236

John

1	90
1:1	42n98
1:14	42n98
1:17	268
2:22	237n33
3:3	319
3:7	319
3:14	227
4	275
6	313
7:38	14, 237n33
8:13	314
9	90
10	222, 313
10:35	237n33
12:38	237n33
13:15	288
13:18	237n33
14:17	312
14:26	312
15	222, 313
15:7	314
15:10	316
15:12–14	288
15:25	237n33
16:8	312
16:13	312
16:14	221
17:12	237n33
19:24	237n33
19:28	237n33
19:36–37	237n33
20:9	237n33
20:30–31	42n98

Acts

2:42	229
26:24	42n98

Romans

1:4	13
1:18–25	90
3:23	97
6	242
6:3–11	242
8	328
8:2	246
8:4	246
8:9–11	319
8:19–21	328, 332
8:20	2
8:23	217
8:26–27	328
8:29	313
10:17	42n98, 314
12:1–2	91n65
12:2	269, 302, 313, 319
13:14	246, 313, 319
15:20	22n13
16:25–26	42n98, 209

1 Corinthians

1–2	90, 90n62
1:30	318
2:7	252
2:9–16	145
2:10	58
2:16	7, 148
3:9	313
3:10–12	22n13
13:12	91, 320
15:55	264n105

2 Corinthians

2:10–16	14
3–4	40, 44, 62, 310
3	305
3:18	33
4	305
4:3–6	310
4:6	35
5:7	90
5:16–17	13, 90
5:16	7, 269
10	91
10:5	91, 319

Galatians

2:20	146
3	238
3:6–25	238
3:23–4:7	246
3:26–4:6	238
3:27	319

Ephesians

1:18	
2	242
2:12	242
2:13	242
2:15	242
2:15–16	243
2:19	243
2:20	22n13, 42n98, 242
2:21–22	242

3:3–12	209
4:17–19	90

Philippians

1:10	319
2:5	313
2:15	145
4:7	319
4:8	319

Colossians

1:15–20	329
1:26–27	209
2:7–8	148
2:9–10	147
3:1–4	208
3:3–4	157
3:4	146
3:10	91

1 Timothy

1:15	42n98
6:19	22n13
3:14	314
3:15	22n13
3:16	209, 266, 314

2 Timothy

2:19	22n13
3:15–17	42n98, 263
3:16	197
4:16–18	260

Hebrews

1:3	256
2:1–4	42, 42n97
2:4	42

1 Peter

2:6	22n13
3:15	314

2 Peter

1:16–21	42n98
3:2	42n98

1 John

1:1	42n98
2:11	90
3:2	223
3:16	288
4:7–8	316
4:12	298
12:16	316

www.ingramcontent.com/pod-product-compliance
Lightning Source LLC
Chambersburg PA
CBHW030431300426
44112CB00009B/948